# The EU Internal Market in Comparative Perspective

## Economic, Political and Legal Analyses

P.I.E. Peter Lang

Bruxelles · Bern · Berlin · Frankfurt am Main · New York · Oxford· Wien

Jacques PELKMANS, Dominik HANF
and Michele CHANG (eds.)

# The EU Internal Market in Comparative Perspective

## Economic, Political and Legal Analyses

"College of Europe Studies"
No. 9

Éditions scientifiques internationales
Brussels, 2008
1 avenue Maurice, B-1050 Brussels, Belgium
www.peterlang.com; info@peterlang.com

ISSN 1780-9665
ISBN 978-90-5201-424-1
D/2008/5678/35

Printed in Germany

Bibliographic information published by "Die Deutsche Bibliothek"
"Die Deutsche Bibliothek" lists this publication in the "Deutsche Nationalbibliografie"; detailed bibliographic data is available on the Internet at <http://dnb.ddb.de>.

# Contents

## Part III. The External Dimension of the Internal Market



## Part IV. The EU and Other Internal Markets

# Preface

The College of Europe participates in EU-Consent (http://www.eu-consent.net), a huge research network coordinated by Professor Wessels at the University of Cologne. In this framework, the editors carry out a project on the EU Internal Market which is co-funded by the European Commission (through EU-Consent) and the College of Europe.

The present book contains the results obtained after two years. Its concept and content were first discussed in a workshop (May 2006) and then more fully developed in a conference (April 2007), both organised in Bruges. The purpose and the structure of this publication are described in Chapter 1.

We would like to thank the contributors – but also those colleagues who discussed with us the preliminary papers during the preparatory workshop and conference. Editors and authors have greatly benefited from the observations and suggestions of Jacques Bourgeois, Juan Delgado, Eric de Souza, Uyen Do, Aylin Ege, Brigid Gavin, Laurence Gormley, Inge Govaere, Adrienne Héritier, Elise Muir, Rodolphe Muñoz, and Bastiaan van Apeldoorn. We also benefited from Jacqueline Minor's explanations of the Commission's Single Market policy.

The editors acknowledge gratefully the financial support of the European Commission and the College of Europe, and the invaluable assistance provided by Jana Fleschenberg and Funda Tekin (EU-Consent-Team, Cologne), Alessandro Marra, Matteo Negrinotti, Valérie Hauspie and Els De Brabander (College of Europe, Bruges). Jessie Moerman (College of Europe) edited carefully the manuscript – many thanks for her patience and her accuracy!

Bruges and Natolin (Warsaw), 28 January 2008

*Jacques Pelkmans, Dominik Hanf and Michele Chang*

CHAPTER 1

# Introduction, Purpose and Structure

Jacques PELKMANS, Michele CHANG
and Matteo NEGRINOTTI

## 1. The pre-dominance of the internal market

Few, if any, scholars of European integration would dispute the vital importance of the EU internal market. Despite Jacques Delors' confession that it was difficult to fall in love with the internal market, he swiftly grasped the fundamental significance of its deepening and widening for the pursuit of the major socio-economic objectives of the EC Treaty, as a robust basis for the position of the Community in the world economy and as a credible leverage for the testimony of European values in world politics. The Single European Act's 1992 programme constituted a major step in the advancement of the four freedoms mentioned in the Treaty of Rome (the free movement of goods, services, capital and labour). Moreover it ushered in an era of Euro-phoria that included not only the internal market but also allowed for important policy changes (such as the extension of the qualified majority vote). In addition, previously under-developed issue areas piggy-backed on the momentum behind the 1992 programme, giving environmental and social policy greater prominence than they had previously enjoyed. Given the significance of the Single European Act and the strides made towards completing the internal market, what often gets lost is the fact that, while the 1992 programme has been completed, the internal market has not. Despite the rhetoric, important exceptions prevent the four freedoms from being completely realised. For example, the vast services sector is a vital one to the EU economy yet it was only very selectively part of the 1992 programme. Indeed, much work needs to be done before the work of the internal market can be considered as finished.

Two decades later, and long after the EC-1992 programme had been completed, the EU internal market shows further deepening and widening. This has largely been accomplished by a series of seemingly unconnected or technical measures following the December 1993 White Paper on Growth and Competitiveness as well as several follow-up 'internal market strategies' between 1999 and 2006, sometimes blended with the Lisbon strategy (initiated in 2000). It also resulted from a continuous stream of new case law, in particular in sensitive markets or for predominantly national policies where the EU legislator appeared inapt, or simply failed, to address the question what the proper combination of free movement (or, establishment) and common regulation had to be while respecting national competences. Unlike the EC-1992 programme that was comprehensive in its goals as well as its rhetoric, subsequent measures to strengthen the internal market were piecemeal in nature. Nevertheless, the EC-1992 'completion' ranks high among the greatest of the EU's success stories and its accomplishments are significant despite the fact that the internal market is still work in progress.

The internal market and the prosperity it has helped EU citizens to reach, has served as a magnet to ever more European countries. From a Community of 10 Member States in the early 1980s, it has meanwhile grown to a Union of 27 Member States and 500 million people. Whilst the former communist countries eagerly sought an anchor to ensure human rights, democracy and other values the EU stands for, they opted for the EU as a presumably more effective route than merely the Council of Europe and the OSCE. For these countries this anchor function was and is inextricably linked with the benefits of the EU internal market. Given the values of the Union, Eastern enlargement is about prosperity. The internal market serves as a magnet because it greatly facilitates catch-up growth of Central European countries, given the institutions, the rules, their credibility and the very deep market integration with its endless opportunities. Lest it be forgotten, also Austria, Finland and Sweden switched from EFTA to the EU in 1995, motivated predominantly by the desire to be a full-blown participant in the internal market, rather than enjoying only partial benefits via the EEA without having much of a say in regulatory decisions.

## 2. A lack of interest?

In the light of the overwhelming significance of the internal market for what the EU has become today, one might perhaps expect the academic interest to be similarly massive. However, this is not the case, especially not once the formative years of the EEC were over. After a second wave of academic research inspired by EC-1992, relatively little systematic work has been published. In telling contrast to the multitude of centers or institutes studying EU domains such as competition policy, trade policy, transport policies, environmental policies, energy, agriculture or even social, the authors are not aware of the existence of a single institute for research on the internal market! Neither has there been much initiative with respect to the systematic collection of research, evidence, data and reporting on this vast terrain, even if it is next to impossible to grasp the overall dynamics and trends for scholars, policy-makers, national and EU legislators, business or consumers without such an information base. There are (or have been at one point in time) EU Observatories on Textiles & Clothing, on Media, on SMEs and on Social aspects but the far more complicated, extended and multi-faceted domain of the internal market – which nobody can really comprehend and follow properly without major investment in reporting and intelligence – has not been blessed with such a body. Recently, the European Economic & Social Committee has started an Observatory (http://www.eesc.europa.eu/smo/index_en.asp) with very limited resources and mainly for use of the Committee itself. Moreover, the Kangaroo Group, consisting of MEPs, independents and business executives, has tirelessly called attention to current policy issues and debates with respect to the internal market (http://www.kangaroogroup.org) Meritorious as these initiatives are, they are not (and cannot possibly be expected to) filling the gaping holes in information, in following trends and spotting relevant publications in the numerous, often highly specialised sub-domains of the internal market, let alone, in systematically bringing together academic work while stimulating more scholarly contributions.

## 3. Why so casual about the Union's main asset?

It is interesting to speculate what the reasons are for this lack of sustained interest in systematic and in-depth information as well as research on the internal market. A few difficulties are well-known to begin with. First, the internal market (=IM) is so incredibly comprehensive that, beyond the bare basics of the concept, one can expect a natural tendency on the part of scholars, policy-makers or observers to zoom in on one or a few sub-domains only. The upshot is an incentive structure leading almost everyone to favour a highly splintered approach to the IM, given one's own knowledge or specialisation or profession. Specialisation pays. In contrast, trying to master an overall IM approach seems daunting and the lack of systematic support via Observatories or centers adds to the discouragement. Second, the EU institutions tend to regard the IM as a cake to be cut up in many pieces. Thus, while at least 8 or 9 DGs in the Commission actively deal with the IM on a routine basis and some other ones now and then, there is only one IM Commissioner and numerous sub-domains are not easily recognisable as IM areas, labelled as they are in their own terms. The direct responsibilities of the IM Commissioner are the product of political and bureaucratic processes and have little or nothing to do with a sound conceptual approach to the IM, no matter how crucial the IM is for the Union. To some extent, this is replicated in the services of the Council and in the committee structure of the European Parliament. There are advantages for such a division of labour but the overall IM idea is merely paid lip service to, in this set-up. Indeed, there is a risk that the IM is felt to be a constraint in pursuing what are regarded as separate policies, rather than that the IM is automatically assumed as the hard core of the Union, with the specific sub-domain just being an instance of 'positive integration' necessitated by the overriding importance of the free movements.

Third, in terms of communication of EU achievements to the public, the IM has been presented more than once as being on the way towards 'completion' (the title of the EC-1992 White Paper of 1985). Little wonder that many citizens vaguely associate the IM with a 'done job', and that the current policy work, the new case law and ongoing research are regarded merely a kind of 'maintenance' of an inevitably technical, specialised nature. As a result, the inherent problems of communicating on such a broad area of EU activities have been amplified by the fact that EU citizens have been lulled into disinterest on the IM by the very successes of the past. Fourth, the EU itself is inconsistent as a creator, guardian and beneficiary of the internal market. In important sub-domains of the IM, the prominence of the internal market is ill-recognised and hence it suffers from undue fragmentation. We give two examples as illustrations. In network industries the EU has accomplished far-reaching liberalisation (and the accompanying regulation and competition policy refinement needed). However, these developments are more often than not connected to EU competition policies (which is to some extent correct once the liberalisation has gone ahead) whereas the first and foremost EU motive is and must be the IM! It is the IM which provides the EU with the legal basis to intervene in the first place – the Union is not competent to arrange national liberalisation, that is, without the IM. Once a potential for cross-border economic activities is restored by forms of liberalisation in a Member State, can EU competition policy begin to come into play. However, this logical sequence is not adhered to: even today the IM for network industries is profoundly fragmented (whether in broadcasting, telecoms, postal, electricity & gas, rail and even airlines) despite the progress in liberalisation, EU regulation and competition policy.

The other example concerns an even vaster area of economic activity: the truncated IM for services. In services, not only have blatant breaches of the IM rules and practices long been left unaddressed until, finally, a services strategy was adopted as a part of the Lisbon strategy in 2000, the hectic debates on the so-called Bolkestein draft directive of 2004 clarified that deep-seated misgivings about the IM persist in many quarters throughout the Union. In the Council and the European Parliament, the IM for services and the connected cross-border labour movements were frequently portrayed as a threat rather than the very foundation of the Union. It cannot be surprising in such a socio-political climate that a very broad category of derogations as well as restrictive interpretations of the IM rules in the directive were needed to have the directive finally adopted, although this largely prolongs the costly fragmentation of the IM which had to be overcome in the framework of the Lisbon strategy, if not the Treaty itself!

## 4. The role of internal market scholars

The four obstacles to sustained interest in systematic and in-depth information and research about the IM are probably not exhaustive. Nevertheless, the authors are of the view that these four reasons do explain the deep-seated inhibitions in the EU to be sufficiently transparent and well-informed about the internal market as a whole and more welcoming to sustained academic and other analysis. The upshot is counterproductive in the medium and long run: the IM as such is neither understood nor appreciated for what it is and what it signifies by a wider public throughout the EU, including large sections of the media and even national or sometimes European parliamentarians. This was exemplified by many debates during the 2002/03 Convention on a constitutional Treaty, the numerous misunderstandings and errors in the services discussions in the period 2004 – 2006 and the frequent caricatures of the IM in the French referendum debates in 2005 (and the fact that they were hardly withspoken), to mention only a few harmful instances. No communications strategy can ever even begin to substitute for such major shortcomings. The IM is the Union's most important asset and it should go without saying that it deserves permanent high-quality information and good asset management, to the benefit of its principal: the EU citizens.

The present book is written by internal market scholars. They might be capable of helping to offset to a modest degree the problematic consequences of the second, third and fourth reasons mentioned above. But this would hinge on the presence of a large, well-resourced and motivated network of reputable scholars permanently engaged with the IM. Unfortunately, however, the first disincentive mentioned above amounts to a powerful barrier to engage in sustained research and effective, durable networking on the internal market at large. The editors of this book seized on the opportunity offered by the huge CONSENT network to attempt to pursue a network approach for the three years that the funding provides. The idea behind the project is to revive a systematic academic analytical attention for the EU internal market. Of course, a single book cannot hope to accomplish such a revival alone. It is planned to produce additional products during this CONSENT project. More important still, the authors hope to ignite a renewed interest in the overall theme across the EU and beyond.

When setting out to prepare this venture, it rapidly turned out that there is no such 'thing' as an 'internal market scholar' in the literal sense of the word. Academic analysts working on the IM do exist (although their number would seem to be small due to the disincentives mentioned) but they are either IM lawyers, or economists interested in the IM or political scientists studying the politics connected to the IM. Thus, the question was raised whether it would be fruitful to bring no less than three disciplines together for a serious exchange on the nature and properties of the EU internal market. It is well-known that interdisciplinary studies are intrinsically difficult to conduct. The investment in one another's methods of analysis and thinking as well as the background literature is simply too large to pay off for most scholars. In addition, even if one succeeds in having a profound and truly mutual exchange in all openness, the published contributions are likely to rank low in the esteem of one's own discipline. In today's climate of almost permanent monitoring of publications in learned journals, interdisciplinary work is easily dismissed as a waste of time or an escape from the rigours of one's mono-disciplinary peer review. Nevertheless, our preliminary discussions clarified that the notion and meaning of the IM in each one of the three disciplines are far from identical. The common ground we expected to find in the same theme was less common than first taken for granted. The academic approaches would appear to differ, too – perhaps not surprising when working within three distinct disciplines but the point is that these distinct approaches entail distinct ways of looking at what we all conveniently call the internal market.

Examples of significant interaction between the three disciplines on IM topics abound. In the debates about the Bolkestein services draft directive, the legal need to do away with major violations of free movement and free establishment (also following ever firmer case law) while respecting certain derogations seemed obvious but (initially) few, if any, hard economic studies were available to support the claims (in itself, a curious omission after more than four decades of free services movement in principle); by the time these studies had become available and did indicate net welfare gains, the political legitimacy of the proposal had been seriously damaged, so much so that it inflicted more general damage on the Treaty discussions too. In the case of the proposed but never realised Community patent, the economic case is very powerful not only in terms of major costs prevented year after year but also in the dynamic sense of stimulating more innovation driven by the lure of a giant internal market, in particular for SMEs. This is one prominent example among several where legal and political obstacles have been thrown up for so long and on such flimsy grounds, even at the level of prime ministers in the European Council. A third example is ECJ case law in areas which are broadly spoken under national competences, but where the boundaries of the exercise of such national powers have to be defined so that the internal market is not fragmented more than is indispensable. Here, the economic meaning of boundary cases is usually trivial but the political sensitivities turn out to be great, in particular because ECJ case law may undermine national political compromises. Such illustrations may serve as reasons why the editors became convinced that the IM as a whole deserves to be analysed having all three perspectives in mind. This book is a first result of this conviction. The editors have attempted to resist the powerful tendency in every discipline to conveniently retreat into one's own jargon and traditions, and to reject the very low tolerance for exposure to ideas, emphases and approaches used in the other two disciplines.

## 5. Crossing disciplinary boundaries for the internal market

In stepping out of the 'protected' segmentation of European Integration studies, there is an immediate need to get some idea about the differences between the three disciplines as to the concept, place, meaning and importance or salience of the internal market. In the following, all we can do is to provide just a flavour of how distinct the approaches or perspectives of the internal market or significant parts of it are.

Between European law and economics, one stark contrast is undoubtedly the interest in precise interpretation (in case law and given a strong attachment to the treaties) versus the focus on broad means-end relationships, whether in economic theory or empirical economic analysis. These distinct approaches cause, perhaps unintentionally, the disciplines to develop appreciable barriers when communicating. We give three examples for the sake of illustration. First, whereas European law has had some difficulty in accepting that the 'internal market' and the 'common market' are materially the same, not least because the presence of both terms in the Treaty turns out to entail some institutional consequences, practically no economist would seem to be even aware of a possible distinction between the two, for the simple reason that it would not make any conceptual difference in economic analysis. Second, economics has long treated 'services' (except for two sectors, financial markets and transport) as the 'cinderella' of EU economic analysis – both theoretically and empirically[1] – whereas European law

[1] See Pelkmans, 1992, strongly encouraging fellow economists to invest in services research as a way to understand the potential of the IM better.

and especially the ECJ have been actively engaged for at least two decades in attempts to facilitate the deepening and widening of services market integration in considerable detail. Third, European law and the economics of European integration have developed sharply different, if not sometimes outright opposed, approaches and appreciation of a central principle of EU integration, namely, subsidiarity. Whilst EU lawyers regard subsidiarity as a procedural principle, often with misgivings about the 'fit' of the principle in the legal and institutional traditions of the EU, economists see and use it as a functional assignment principle for what ought and ought not be done at the EU level and why.[2] On the other hand, in an important subset of European law – especially competition law, EU regulation and network industries, all three of major importance for the internal market – economic analysis and EU law are no longer ignoring one another. Stronger, more and more attention is given to suitable combinations of the two disciplines when preparing EU regulation and regulatory impact assessment, in ECJ cases and in EU and national competition policy.

When it comes to political science, the contrast with the other two disciplines is first of all that the internal market has not figured as a prominent and well-researched subject in political science except to some extent in response to EC-1992 (see also Schmidt, in this volume). On a fairly high level of generality, the internal market does play a major role in the field. The ever lasting debate between (modern) neo-functionalists, and (as some denote them) neo-supranationalists, on the one hand, and (liberal) neo-intergovernmentalists, on the other, hinges in no small part on key moments, critical conduct of key actors as well as long-run processes (exposing functional linkages arising from pressures generated by 'integration deficits' in the *acquis* or unsolved issues) about the EU internal market. Nevertheless, political scientists seem more inspired by soft topics like 'new' forms of governance in Europe or relatively weak and very partial EU powers such as social policy than by the internal market. If and when political scientists show interest in the 'hard core' issues of the EU, apparently they seem drawn much more to common policies (trade, agriculture, environment, less so for transport and competition policy) and explicit regulation – with the visible political conflicts of interest or political bargaining in Council and the European Parliament – rather than the four free movements and the right of establishment, no matter how paramount these are for the internal market. One might see this as understandable since the several dozens of typical internal market directives every year prompt political

2 See Pelkmans, 2005, for a juxtaposition of how the two disciplines deal with subsidiarity.

and social lobbying of great variety, not to mention the colourful and continuously changing coalitions among Member States. Yet, there is a lot of social or political anxiety about, or support in favour of, as the case may be, cross-border liberalisation issues based on the four freedoms and establishment, not seldomly combined with competition concerns. This can even go so far as irritation about 'Brussels' becoming too powerful, even if the constraint on national regulation or (say) a regulatory tax is nothing else than the free movements themselves or mutual recognition. This so-called negative integration does not give rise to any rule or intervention from 'Brussels' and still it is sometimes perceived as 'centralising' because it may affect national 'institutions' or entitlements expected to be outside the realm of the EU level. In areas such as health, education and media – normally regarded as national or even regional competences – such perceptions can lead to politicisation of what the Treaty logic would treat as judicial.

With respect to free movement of persons, political scientists and lawyers tend to display a common interest in Justice & Home Affairs (with only incidental contributions from economics). At times, economists and political scientists find common ground in the political economy of specific internal market issues. Nonetheless, where the relatively smooth functioning and further development of the internal market does not ignite much political friction or (say) blocking minorities in Council, there is a suspicion that political science practices a kind of benign neglect. Political integration theory tells us that much of this 'a-political' work hinges on a 'permissive consensus' in EU countries leaving great discretion to the decision-making elites without endangering the political legitimacy of the EU project. But the permanent absence of explicit political debate because of the permissive consensus runs the risk of slowly eroding mechanisms of accountability and eventually the consensus itself. The eruptions of resistance and politicisation in the years 2004 to 2006 about the free movement of workers (but this time with a huge wage differential between origin and destination), the services directive (and indeed the labour market issues connected to it) and the perception (of some) that the internal market serves as (an unwanted) agent of globalisation, with the low-skilled blue collar workers in the West of the Union possibly being the losers in all three instances, have quite suddenly done away with the permissive consensus, impeding progress in the internal market. For economists attempting to show the economic rational of these steps forward as well as for European lawyers attempting to apply the Treaty and case law logic, the 'new' politicisation came rather unexpected. Unlike the typical political economy aspects of many directives, this politicisation is about the political legitimacy of (aspects of) the internal market and, by extension, about attempts to adopt a Treaty which would further facilitate what was now distrusted.

There might also be a *fundamental definition problem* for the internal market which plagues all three disciplines, but in distinct ways. The actual realisation of the internal market requires significant degrees of liberalisation of cross-border movements and considerable freedom to establish (oneself or a company) in other Member States. Such cross-border liberalisation is a necessary, not a sufficient condition for the EU internal market. Indeed, this basic requirement should *not* be confused with the *concept* of the internal market in the EU, neither in the Treaty nor in actual practice. The internal market is defined by what it takes to 'function properly' as the Treaty calls it. This can only mean, logically, that *both* liberalisation and regulation (whatever form this takes) are part and parcel of the internal market, *as well as* those common policies indispensable to pre-empt or avoid distortions or fragmentation of that internal market.

But this conceptual logic is not always applied in the three disciplines. More often than not, the IM is regarded as 'one of many common policies'. However, the very reason that these polices are common is derived directly from the idea that the internal market has to "function properly" for it to serve as the means to pursue effectively the aims in the Treaty. The point is of particular importance in political science where many studies are made of specific policies, without much of a (or, any) link with the IM. Common policies are hardly or not recognised as an inevitable result of a functional liberalisation logic. Rather, they are studied in terms of substance and this tends to be subject to political strategies, of interest to political scientists. This would suggest that political scientists tend to avoid the IM not only because it is technical but even more so because it tends to be functional and not so attractive from a political perspective, always interested in power relationships and their drivers.

Lawyers and economists may be more comfortable with the notion of a well functioning IM but it is only recently that more 'economic' (often, effect-based) approaches are beginning to be accepted in European law, including competition policy guidelines, and in regulation (e.g. in regulatory impact assessment). However, it is questionable whether and to what extent economics of European integration and European law are growing closer to and more familiar with each other. The resistance in both disciplines is profound and, it ought to be underlined, the legal and economic ways of reasoning remain quite distinct. Today's position might be summed up in the formation of an 'enclave' of economists and lawyers willing to invest deeply in order to be able to work together on the triptych 'competition policy, regulation and network industries (where the two are combined without exception)'. In the internal market the importance of the triptych is beyond any doubt, but the requirements for analysts to contribute effectively here are very demanding indeed. The enclave is therefore no more than a small elite and it seems to exert only a limited influence on the disciplines of European law and the economics of European integration at large.

Giving merely a flavour of how the three disciplines see and work with the IM is by definition partial and incomplete. It is worth exploring much more systematically and that is precisely an important reason to publish this book as an attempt to begin doing so.

## 6. The purpose and structure of the book

The purpose of this book is to enhance our understanding of the EU internal market by studying this vast area of European integration from the perspective of European law, EU political science and the economics of European integration together. The limitations or omissions of each discipline in comprehending the nature, logic and development (or, stagnation) of the internal market are clarified by direct exchange and complementarity, whilst a far richer perspective of the predicament of this foundation of the Union emerges. The cross-fertilisation is inspiring, indeed so much so that the editors plan to organise a follow-up.

Given the exploratory nature of this tri-disciplinary approach to the EU internal market, the editors opted for a simple and recognisable structure. The book focuses on four core subjects, dealt with by scholars from the three disciplines. These core subjects are: (1) the basic approaches to the internal market in the three disciplines, juxtaposed in part I; (2) a closer inspection of the EU internal market for services, conducted from an economic and from a legal analytical perspective in part II; (3) surveys of the external dimension of the IM in the three disciplines in part III; (4) and an attempt to learn lessons from the internal market approaches in Canada and the USA, with the two authors blending legal/institutional, economic and political aspects.

All chapters have gone through a process of discussion by scholars from the other two disciplines, in addition to the work of the editors, one from each discipline. It is hoped that the result is therefore more inter-disciplinary than multi-disciplinary. One cannot expect the former to be realised to the full extent, since the three disciplines have their own logic, traditions, proven value to serve relevant analysis and jargon. The ultimate value of the book lies in the interest of the readers: are readers only interested in an *à-la-carte* approach of the internal market, where everybody would 'pick & choose' selected chapters – typically the ones from one's own discipline – or does one seek the adventure of trying to grasp what other disciplines have to say about the very same internal market and thereby complement one's insight? The editors and indeed the authors have made an effort to keep all chapters as accessible as possible for experts in other disciplines. European market integration simply cannot lean solely on a mono-disciplinary perspective, even if such specialisation is fully justified when it comes to the technical deepening of analysis.

## 7. Introducing the substance of the book

Basing himself on the fundamental economic idea of a well-functioning internal market among otherwise independent countries, Jacques Pelkmans explores six concepts of the internal market which play or have played a role in the EU. The author also addresses the question how 'deep' in economic terms today's internal market integration is, insofar as the analytical economic literature allows us to establish that. While recognising the traditional view of the internal market as a means to achieve the EU aims, the author tries to flesh out this statement and to find its boundaries by addressing two provocative questions: do we need a more goal-oriented internal market and to which extent internal market can be used as a 'jack-of-all-trades'? He then outlines three alternative economic strategies for deepening and widening the internal market and, in the light of the proposed strategies, provides a first assessment of the November 2007 Commission proposal on a single market for 21st-century Europe.

Dominik Hanf depicts the legal concept of the internal market, firstly clarifying the legal meaning of the synthagms 'internal market', 'common market', and 'single market', whose correct comprehension is crucial for understanding and circumscribing EU and Member States regulatory powers respectively. The author then moves to the legal significance of the internal market within the EU institutional setting. In particular, assuming a constitutional perspective, Hanf explains the consequences for the regulatory and de-regulatory powers of the EU stemming from the qualification of the internal market as the economic constitution of the EU.

Political scientists have often preferred examining selected issues concerning the positive integration dimension of the internal market rather than focusing on the internal market as the combined result of negative and positive integration. In her contribution Susanne Schmidt, in contrast, tries to focus on the latter approach in looking at the institutional dynamics, the working and the consequences of the internal market. In particular, the combination of positive and negative integration as well as the role played by the new modes of governance (NMG), are carefully analysed. Furthermore, the author provides an enlightening analysis regarding the impact of the internal market for Member States, discussed not only in terms of Europeanisation, but also ]with reference to the suggestion that the internal market can be conceived as a neo-liberal project as well as in terms of political legitimacy.

Services are nowadays the cornerstone of European economy; however, the internal market for services is still fragmented: a patchwork in Arjan Lejour's words, because of the high degree of national regulation still existing in many sectors. The cost of regulatory heterogeneity is particularly evident in retail distribution and professional services sectors, where cross-border trade and FDI are almost inexistent.

*Eppur si muove!* (And yet it moves): the author shows, however, that cross-border trade and FDI in services are increasing, in particular in those sectors like networks industries touched by the liberalisation process. The economic impact on such a picture (or patchwork) of the services liberalisation as was proposed by the European Commission in the so-called Bolkestein proposal draft services directive is also analysed on the basis of a gravity model, with the innovative use of a heterogeneity index, which falls with increasing liberalisation. Furthermore, the author remarks how European service market integration could represent an advanced model in the framework of the WTO as far as the GATS is concerned.

The legal issues related to the internal market for services are explored in an authoritative contribution by Vassilis Hatzopoulos. The author firstly reviews the jurisprudence of the European Courts showing how the material scope of application of Art. 49 has been stretched by the case-law and how the justifications set forth in the Treaty have been applied, in particular with respect to public service obligations. On the basis of such case-law he highlights how the interpretation of the Treaty provisions on services has shifted from the mutual recognition paradigm to a near HCC (Home Country Control) principle in the field of services. The last part of Hatzopoulos' chapter is devoted to the analysis of the services directive (2006/123), assessing, on the one hand, whether this piece of legislation constitutes a retreat from case-law and, on the other, to which extent it could represent a step forward for the governance of the service economy in the IM.

To what extent and how the IM has been used to promote the common interest at a global scale: these are the queries Peter Holmes, Roland Klages and Sieglinde Gstöhl answer in their contributions, approaching the questions from the economic, legal and political point of view respectively.

Peter Holmes, in chapter 7, lucidly analyses the stages in the establishment of a common commercial policy and its impact on trade flows (from outside the Community), verifying whether it constitutes, as often blamed, the ditch of 'Fortress Europe'. In the second part of his contribution the author studies the internal effects of the external trade policy, focusing in particular on the repercussions from the EU membership of the WTO (in the beef hormones and the GMO cases) as well as from signing Regional Trade Agreements.

The contribution by Roland Klages sheds light on the legal framework underpinning the external commercial relations of the Community. He firstly reviews and pieces together the legal provisions enshrined in the Treaty itself, followed by the role played by the ECJ in the development of the external economic competences of the Community. He then turns to the legal consequences on the Community and national legal orders of the treaties concluded by the Community or to which the Community has adhered to. The analysis is carried out looking at the application to international agreements entered by the Community of two general constitutional principles of the EU legal order, namely: supremacy and direct effect.

The political dimension of externalising the internal market, in its three components: polity, policy and politics, is at the centre of the stimulating analysis by Sieglinde Gstöhl. After having examined the different combinations of these elements, the author applies this theoretical framework to study the agreements concluded by the Community with its many neighbours, showing not only how different they are, but foremost for explaining these differences on the basis of the different mixture of politics, polities and policies. The author also discusses the promotion of the internal market at a global level rather than regionally and draws some political implications of these processes in the conclusions.

In the last two chapters, European market integration is compared with the American and Canadian experiences, which are dealt with by Michelle Egan and François Vaillancourt respectively.

After having highlighted the similarities and differences between the American and the European political, economic and social histories, Michelle Egan carefully analyses the role of the institutional and constitutional framework in the establishment of the American internal market, pointing at the entrenchment between state building and market making as well as the role played in the US by the judiciary system in restricting the powers of state and municipalities in the area of intra-US trade. The author draws some lessons from the comparison of the US and the EU experience with the aim of providing insights for successful market integration in other regional markets.

The building of the Canadian market for goods, services, financial capital and labour is extensively set out by François Vaillancourt assuming a truly tri-disciplinary perspective. The author reviews these four markets showing firstly how the legal and institutional framework has contributed to the different levels of integration achieved in those markets. He then analyses the barriers to trade still in place and their impact on the Canadian economy. The role played by the political arena is also examined in considerable detail, on the one hand, in showing the impact of tensions in the Canadian federation, in particular with Québec, on the integration process at federal level; on the other, by singling out the importance of politics in the unilateral or multilateral initiatives undertaken by provinces in order to foster Canadian market integration.

## References

Pelkmans, J. (1992) EC92 as a Challenge to Economic Analysis, in Borner, S. & Grubel, H. (eds.) *The European Community After 1992, Perspectives From the Outside*, London, Macmillan Press.

Pelkmans, J. (2005) Subsidiarity between Law and Economics, *Research papers in Law* 2005/1, Bruges, College of Europe, Law dept. http://coleurop.be/template.asp?pagename=lawpapers.

# Part I

# The Concept and Meaning of the Internal Market

CHAPTER 2

# Economic Concept and Meaning of the Internal Market

Jacques PELKMANS

*Director and Jan Tinbergen Chair for European Economic Studies, College of Europe, Bruges & Chair on Business & Europe, Vlerick School of Management, Leuven/Gent*

## 1. Introduction[1]

What is 'the' internal market, as economists see it? Can economics formulate a single rigorous benchmark, against which Treaty design and the actual practice of building the internal market and making it work well can be assessed? How useful is it to dispose of a benchmark derived from economic theory, if the politics, the institutional complications of a two-level governance and legal aspects are merely considered as exogenous requirements or simply assumed to be appropriate? What are the benefits and costs of the various steps of the long and steep 'market integration ladder', whether in ex-ante economic analysis or in ex-post empirical verification? Once all of this would be known, why would the EU want an internal market (=IM) in the first place? Are such merits of the IM still the same today as 50 years ago, and, if not, what is or should be the value-added of a 'deeper' or 'wider' IM nowadays? Does economics have anything to tell about the political and/or legal prerequisites or complementarities which would render the IM more effective in serving EU goals?

The present paper is inspired by these questions, without claiming that all of them can be satisfactorily addressed, let alone, solved. It aims to facilitate an understanding of the economic approaches to 'the' IM idea(s) in the framework of this tri-disciplinary project. However, because 'the' IM is a massive undertaking and refers to an incredibly

---

[1] I am indebted to the conference participants for discussion and, in particular, to Michele Chang for very detailed further comments.

wide spectrum of markets and activities (with profound changes over time as well), it is inevitable to limit the exposition to a survey of the essentials.

The structure of the paper is as follows. Section 2 hopes to stimulate a conceptual discourse by distinguishing six different meanings of the IM, with the sixth one being the economic benchmark in an ideal setting. Section 3 looks at what the IM is meant for: the IM as a means, indeed as a means to what? This is done, first, by studying the EC Treaty design, followed by the quest for a more goal-oriented IM (presumably, instead of a legalistic or too instrumental approach). Thirdly, one can look at the IM as the 'workhorse' of the EU, serving many masters: a true 'jack-off-all trades'. Apart from some Treaty objectives, there is discussion about services (in a Lisbon context), innovation, social Europe and globalisation. Also a workhorse can be overtaxed.

Section 4 briefly considers the future of the IM: how can deepening and widening be pursued best, and is a functional, economic strategy feasible? Three stylised strategies are considered and the November 2007 Commission proposals are briefly assessed.

The final section sums up the conclusions.

## 2. Concepts of the internal market: an economic perspective

In economics, a market is an abstract notion of demand and supply coming together and determining price and non-price aspects of transactions. Linked to location and space, price and non-price aspects (e.g. quality, newness, etc.) are determined over the relevant geographical space. It is then a minor step to define market integration (Pelkmans, 2006: 6) "[…] as a behavioural notion indicating that activities of market participants in different regions or Member States are geared to supply-and-demand conditions in the entire Union". Later in this section, we shall explore a little further what the profound implications of this definition are. To some degree it can also be subjected to empirical measurement.

This 'classroom concept' was not in the minds of the founding fathers of the Community, the authors of the Spaak report (1956). Nevertheless, as shown by the routine application of economics to the definition of (relevant) markets in competition policy, there are ways to bridge the seemingly wide gulf between the theoretical notion and actual practice, also in the EU context. A possibly useful approach to narrow the gap in a stepwise fashion is to consider, in a stylised form, how the internal market notion in the EU was deepened and widened from a minimal initial idea to the much more ambitious IM of today.

Four stylised steps will be defined. For all four steps, one has to employ a practical, institutional notion of how to *establish* an IM and subsequently, how to make it *function properly* (i.e. not suffering from market failures). As is well-known, this requires a combination of negative and positive integration. The ideal IM can be defined as follows: "An IM attains the free movement of goods, services and factors of production, including the free establishment where relevant, accompanied by the necessary positive integration for the IM to function properly". Subsequently, the still more ambitious single market notion in economic federalism is touched upon before finally coming back to the purist economic benchmark of a single market.

## *2.1. The 'common market' at the outset*

The common market was not defined in the EEC Treaty. Prominent European lawyers all agreed that the four free movements and free establishment formed the basis (i.e. what Tinbergen (1954) called negative integration) but they disagreed about the extent of 'positive integration' complementing the freedoms. Thus, the common market had to include a common trade policy and a common competition policy (for its proper functioning, that is, preventing or correcting market power and other distortions of competition by market agents) but whether the CAP and/or a common transport policy were intrinsically part of 'the' common market, was disputed. However, whether this was of much practical importance is doubtful because the Treaty comprised many elements (including, of course, the CAP and a common transport policy) to complement the negative integration which seemed reasonably well specified. There were approximation and harmonisation articles (in some articles these words were used interchangeably, dependent on language) and there always was Art. 235, EEC, a catch-all article (under unanimity) permitting the Council to add new measures for the proper functioning of the common market. Economists mainly regarded the EEC as a customs union at first, thereby ignoring services and factor movements (which, at least formally, were clearly defined as part of the common market) but also neglecting what were then called 'non-tariff barriers'. In the early days, economists seemed to have little appreciation of the enormous potential significance of Art. 100, EEC (harmonisation) and the related Art.s 30, EEC and 36, EEC (forbidding, with derogations, such non-tariff barriers, now more correctly labeled as 'regulatory barriers').[2] Besides the customs union, economists were

2 This is likely to have been caused by the disinterest in regulation in economics at the time, but also by the arcane language of Art. 30, speaking of 'measures with an equivalent effect to quantitative restrictions'; until Dassonville, lawyers were also confused whether to assess this legalistically or functionally i.e. economically. One

interested in the common policies but (except for the common tariff) rarely in connection with the common market in some defined way. Towards the end of the transition period (say, 1969) the common market of the EEC consisted essentially of a common *goods* market, be it with a battery of regulatory barriers,[3] but including agri-food products (behind towering protection), free FDI inside the EEC, and the common policies for trade, competition and agriculture (not for transport). However, the common policies were not complete either: trade policy was undermined by national quotas *vis-à-vis* third countries (even interfering with the common market itself, via Art. 115, EEC) and competition policy (only for goods!) lacked a merger policy while state aids supervision remained weak. The much heralded accomplishment (in 1968) to agree to 'free movement of workers' was largely a phantom: the *acquis* was only agreed because it would render such migration *residual*, whilst imposing host-country control.

At the time, this common market *acquis* was viewed as a great achievement. There were two reasons for this praise: the EEC emerged out of a tariff-ridden world full of interventionism – which made the common market more attractive – and the Community appeared effective compared to other instances of regionalism in the world.[4] Yet, against the measuring rod of the Treaty, the common market was surely not in keeping with the implicit definition.

### 2.2. The common market after 25 years

Late March 1982 The Economist celebrated the 25th anniversary of the Community with a frontpage showing the leaders of the ten Member States on a graveyard, their faces turned to a headstone saying that the EEC was resting there "after 25 years of useless service". This cynical text was prompted more by Eurosclerosis (and poisonous budget quarrels, caused mainly by the CAP) than a well-defined idea of a deeper or wider IM but the frustration about the latter was evident as well. Why could the EEC not pull the Ten out of stagflation and return to the golden age of growth (1958-1973)?

should also not forget that economists, dealing with the EEC in the 1950s and 1960s, were mainly trade economists, normally focusing on tariffs and quotas. Until Baldwin's (1970) seminal work on 'non-tariff barriers', trade economists ignored regulatory and fiscal barriers, with only very few exceptions.

3 Most of which were not even 'mapped', see Pelkmans & Vollebergh, 1986, although the VAT breakthrough had been accomplished in 1967.

4 Other than EFTA, which was modest but worked well, regionalism in Latin America, Africa or the communist bloc (Comecon) was shallow and non-performing.

Based on detailed analysis (e.g. Pelkmans, 1985; 1986), the common market in 1982 can be proxied as follows. Added to the *acquis* of 2.1 above, were very partial attempts to harmonise (under vetoes), always in goods markets, the first beginnings of mutual recognition (all in the food sector), the start of European standardisation (only in electrical goods though), feeble attempts to tackle services (mainly, establishment in financial services, but in rudimentary ways), and the emergence of environmental regulation at EEC level. The economic meaning of much of these efforts was selective and modest. However, there were setbacks too. The agricultural market became more fragmented due to the discrepancies between 'green' and normal exchange rates; the so-called NICs (Japan, Hong Kong, Taiwan) caused trade protection to become 'national' via VERs and textile quotas, disrupting the customs union; exchange controls in countries such as France and Italy were tightened; state aids in steel went out of hand and the 'manifest crisis' of the ECSC did not immediately cause relief.

By 1982 a much better understanding had been developed of what it took to accomplish the common market (again, essentially in goods) but policy makers felt trapped in a Treaty which failed to provide the means and hard obligations needed.[5]

### 2.3. *The internal market in the Single Act*

The internal market idea in the Single Act has to be placed in context. In barely three years since 1982 the internal market had rapidly moved up the ladder of political priorities and the mapping of its many shortcomings had made great progress.

The Community was ready to consider the internal market in its entirety and improve it radically on the basis of the famous White paper. Conceptually, however, the White Paper was not a marvel and the exercise of 'completing' remained remarkably incomplete even when only paying attention to the rough contours of the proposals. Spending merely a few lines on an assertion that the proposals would boost growth in the Community, without analytical support or even a clue about how and why, is a curious foundation for a 'strategy'. The paper itself was very rich and no doubt radical at the time. Nevertheless, it

---

[5] In Pelkmans, 1985, it is argued at length that the Rome Treaty could never have accomplished 'the' common market it endeavoured to achieve, due to sequencing problems and conditionalities, the lack of a hard legal definition of the common market and vetoes. This would require Treaty revision on most of these points (which did happen late 1985). It would also require other working methods such as the establishment of an Internal Market Council (late 1982), focussed programmes, new views on standardisation and harmonisation inspired by mutual recognition (which emerged in 1985) etc.

was very weak (and selective) in services, silent on network industries, and contained only some unimpressive measures in factor markets or technology. Also, the inevitable links between common policies and the IM were not systematically pursued (see also e.g. the chapters by Holmes, Gstöhl, and Klages, in this volume).

The Single Act comprised two innovations, however, which would serve as powerful complements to the IM strategy. First, QMV was greatly extended to a host of IM topics. Second, the IM was (finally) defined as 'an area without frontiers' in which "the free movement of goods, persons, services and capital is ensured [...]" Just as in the White Paper, these frontiers were not just customs frontiers but also fiscal or regulatory frontiers. This concept of 'frontiers' pushed the idea of avoiding or overcoming fragmentation in the IM much closer to the notion of 'economic frontiers' which will be discussed in section 2.6. Observe that the word 'ensured' strongly suggests that sequencing problems can no longer be in the way of realising free movement. It is the combination of the Single Act and the 1985 White Paper which rendered the IM strategy so successful and enterprising, a sharp contrast with the pre-1985 years. True, it was helped at the outset by a few events which underlined forcefully that matters, first thought to be impossible, suddenly came within reach of a 'can-do Commission'.[6]

Summing up the IM concept in and around the Single Act might carry us too far for present purposes. Essentially, however, one ought to appreciate the definition of the IM in (what is now) Art. 14, EC; a series of horizontal initiatives (e.g. on competitive public procurement; on fostering mutual recognition); over 160 proposals of Old Approach type harmonisation (in industrial and agri-food products) which were expected to be feasible without vetoes; the New Approach (coupled to European standardisation) over a range of very broad sectors (construction products, machines, toys, etc.); a fairly liberal approach to four

---

6 In 1983 the so-called 'mutual information' Directive 83/189 had been adopted (meanwhile 98/34) which would develop into a low-key but formidable watchdog preventing thousands of new barriers from arising [see Pelkmans, Vos & di Mauro, 2000]; in May 1985, and entirely in the spirit of the White Paper (which advocated 'minimal harmonisation', based on reference to standards), which was then being drafted, a 'new approach to standardisation' was agreed (without this, the goods IM would have remained a dream); in December 1984 the leading customs officials of the Member States were forced by their ministers (!) to simplify and completely unify customs formalities into a single customs form (identical in all languages, too), replacing no less than 70 documents and laying the basis for a modern common customs at EU level and, later for eCustoms; also in May 1985 the ECJ sided with the EP and against the Council, since the latter had "failed to act" (Art. 175, EEC) in building the common transport policy, a shock which completely transformed the spirit of working in the Transport Council.

modes of transport (not rail and air, as network industries); an original approach to liberalisation of financial markets (based on mutual recognition and home country control) which avoided a harmonisation imbroglio, but also did not ensure sufficient market access (while failing to reform equity markets in the EU); the link between common policies and the IM was improved (e.g. a merger regulation and the removal of national quotas or VERs); and several technical customs measures as well as some minor initiatives in factor markets. If one accepts that the wider context matters as well – and in an economic perspective, it does – it is easy to find complementary initiatives building on the IM logic since 1985: (i) the new 'horizontal' approach to food products (feasible because of the profound impact of the ECJ mutual recognition doctrine) which transformed, sooner or later, all national food laws in the EU, and underpinned the (near-) removal of 'recipe-laws' in the IM *acquis*, an impressive instance of 'better regulation' having lowered the regulatory burden while increasing choice; (ii) the initially slow but gradually firm inclusion of all 7 network industries, which is still ongoing today because of its complexity and profound consequences; (iii) a much less restrictive approach to mutual recognition of diplomas, another instance where lead times are simply very long; and, not least, (iv) the ultimate consequence of the emerging 'common customs code', namely, the physical disappearance of customs at the inner frontiers, supported by a 'temporary' reliance on a reporting system keeping the destination principle in place for VAT. Also, (v) the complete elimination of exchange controls was accomplished by 1988 based on a convergence of macro-economic policy orientations of the Member States.

Altogether, the influential concept of the IM in the Single Act and the 'inner dynamics' prompted by it in various ways are impressive results. A simple comparison between the Dekker plan (Dekker, 1985), considered far too ambitious only 5 months before the White Paper, and the much greater accomplishments (than the White Paper had listed in its famous Annex of 300 measures) by the end of 1992, clarifies immediately how much IM ambitions had spiralled up since (see Pelkmans, 1994, for detail). From an analytical economic perspective, the deepening and widening was nevertheless grossly insufficient for it to be labelled as a 'single market'. The practical problems in goods markets remained numerous, a horizontal approach in services was absent and sectoral approaches were few (and seriously incomplete), migration of workers inside the Community was very cumbersome and there was no such thing as an IM for (codified) technology.

## *2.4. The IM concept after 50 years EU*

After EC-1992, the glamour of the IM quickly faded. EMU and the EURO took its place, closely followed by 'competitiveness' and a range of worthwhile but splintered actions over a very wide spectrum of EU activities. The one and a half decade since Maastricht have further deepened and widened the IM, however, despite the lacklustre backing at the highest political level. Towards the end of the 1990s, the neglect of IM strategies was partially overcome. Since 1999 two consecutive IM 'strategies' were pursued under Commissioner Bolkestein and a fundamental review was undertaken by the Commission in the autumn of 2006 and later, supported by the Spring 2007 European Council, which urged the Commission to come up with details of a 'vision'. The vision will be addressed in section 3.2. The Commission proposals of November 2007 are summarised and assessed in strategic terms in section 4.1. The Bolkestein strategies were in fact no more than splintered programmes of a highly technical nature, except perhaps for services. Appendix 1 provides an illustration of this point with respect to the 2003/2006 strategy. The inclusion of the IM in the Lisbon programme, although superficially fitting due to the 2010 objective, was not convincing because it has nothing to do with the *open method of coordination.*

**Figure 2.1. FDI outward and inward stocks in the EU-15 and EU-25 (FDI stocks in bn euro.)**

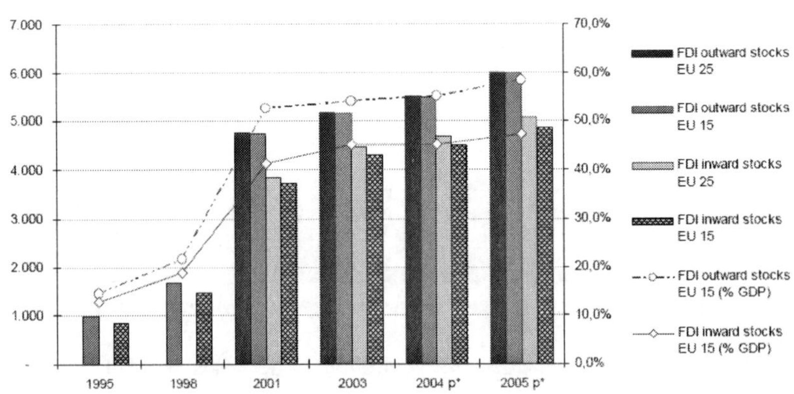


Source: Ilzkovitz *et al.*, 2007.

In terms of achievements since the early 1990s, one cannot fail to mention the great advance in the opening up of network industries[7] and the third wave of financial market integration prompted by the EURO and globalisation. But there is more, such as the almost forgotten repair of the IM for steel (since 1994, no longer distorted by state aids), the emergence of property rights legislation at the EU level (except the sad absence of a Community patent) and a series of EU Agencies dealing with safety questions (food, transport modes, medicines).

An encouraging aspect of recent IM activities is that the more sensitive gaps and restrictions are beginning to be addressed, a sign that the IM concept employed is becoming more encompassing (as it should, from an economic perspective). But the going is tough, as if one pushes a powerful spring ever further. Consider the following examples. First, in relying on Art. 86 for network industries, where should the lines be drawn for services of general (non-economic) interest, which are formally not part of the IM? Second, the Commission finally addressed services liberalisation (decades too late), but the upshot now is that neither a sectoral approach nor a horizontal approach seems promising (see 3.3.2). Third, intra-EU migration flows of workers are not only very low because of languages and 'social distance', but also because of a host of barriers allowing Member States to regard a migrant (let alone, a frontier worker) as a residual (see Pelkmans, 2006, Chapters 9 and 10, and Figure 2.2). Since 2004 this is temporarily obscured by a peak in East West flows. Only in 2001, in a low-key COM paper[8] a first attempt was made to start tackling these barriers one by one, a long and difficult route, no doubt. Fourth, (proper) regulation, liberalisation and competition issues in a future IM for professionals seems nothing less than a snake pit. But even here, there has been progress. Thus, in a three steps process, the mutual recognition of professional qualifications (hence, free movement of professionals) has been drastically simplified and somewhat improved.[9] Nevertheless, (domestic) self-regulation by associations of professionals tends to blend anti-competitive (and dispropor-

---

[7] But one hastens to add that a genuine IM in these sectors has not been accomplished due to political taboos in the Commission/Member States interface and the costly legal taboo of the Meroni doctrine, blocking the emergence of EU regulators.

[8] COM (2001) 116 of 1st March 2001, New European labour markets, open to all, with access for all.

[9] Following the 3rd General System of Mutual Recognition Dir. 1999/42 (OJ L 201 of 31 July 1999), consolidating no less than 35 transitional directives concerning crafts and trades professions, a simplification of the legal and procedural regime for professional recognition was accomplished with dir. 2001/19. This was followed by a further consolidation and simplification in dir. 2005/36/EC of 7 September 2005, replacing 12 directives on 7 professions (e.g. doctors, pharmacists, etc.) and 3 general Mutual Recognition directives.

tionate) with justified restrictive regulation, and this has the effect of inhibiting free movement and free establishment, too. After many years of neglect, the Commission finally began to address this complex issue, following its COM (2004) 83 of 9 February 2004, Report on Competition in Professional Services. However, the conservative Wouters ruling[10] in 2004, in which the ECJ said that a prohibition in Dutch law for lawyers and accountants to work together in the same company (other Members, rightly, allow this, so long as certain quality guarantees are ensured) could be justified, threw cold water on the efforts of the Commission. Selected progress in this problematic domain is now only found at Member State level and this is unlikely to help the IM much.

**Figure 2.2. Share of foreign nationals in percentage of resident working-age population, 2005**

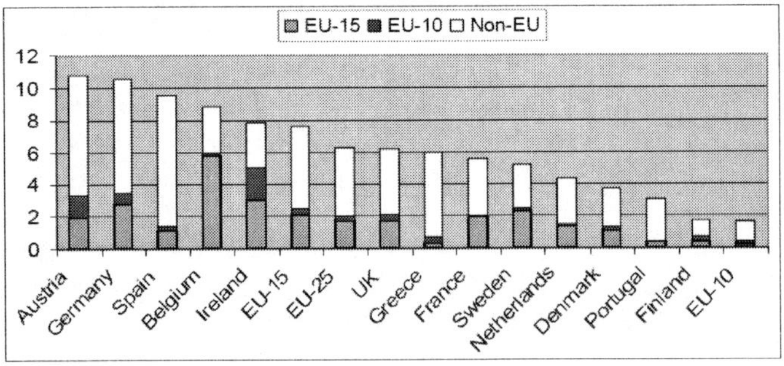

Source: Ilzkovitz *et al.*, 2007.

**Figure 2.3. Value of public procurement which is openly advertised as a per cent of total public procurement (EU-15)**

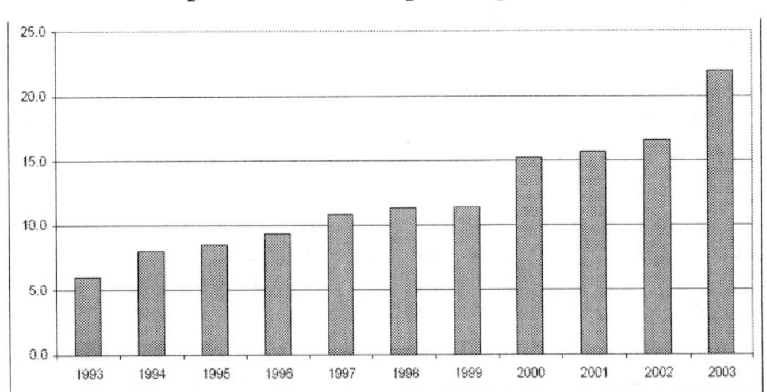


Source: DG Ecfin, Ilzkovitz *et al.*, 2007.

[10] ECJ, Case C-309/99 Wouters [2002] ECR 1-1577.

The IM after 50 years of EU can be stylised as reasonably working for goods (be it that the brilliant idea of mutual recognition turns out to be much more costly than long understood, and that public procurement is still not very EU-wide, see Figure 2.3), dramatically incomplete in services overall (and not functioning properly, even where it is formally open), advanced in capital markets and wholesale financial markets (but not retail), and truncated in codified technology.

Despite recent East-West migration, there is no prospect of an EU labour market at all. Within a few years, the East-West labour flows will dry up (given rapid convergence), and return migration is likely to occur, just like in the cases of Italy (later 1980s) and Spain (early 1990s). For regular migration, when wages are not so disparate anymore, the obstacles are still considerable.

Even stylising the IM in such a rough manner, it is still worthwhile noting that there are interdependencies amongst these points, e.g. a fragmented labour market raises the difficulties for opening up services markets (cf. Boeri, Nicoletti & Scarpetta, 2000), and obstacles in technology markets hinder intra-EU FDI as well as goods market integration.

## 2.5. The 'single market' notion in economic federalism

How much further can or should one go in pursuing an ideal concept of the IM? As a functional approach to subsidiarity[11] suggests, taking the IM as the proper conceptual framework for actual or potential cross-border flows (based on internalising the cross-border externalities as subsidiarity requires) or effects, can push the application of the IM idea very far indeed. The current range of restrictions, gaps and opt-outs which characterises the EU's IM can be considered as an indirect proof. Why? Well, lifting the restrictions and filling the gaps would entail very radical consequences, which have little to no socio-political support today. Thus, once the EU would seriously attempt to remove all barriers to cross-border migration (from diploma recognition, health insurance issues, tax problems, housing questions, social eligibility issues, non-portability of occupational pensions, etc.) as well as soften host country control, social policy competition would intensify, in turn leading, sooner or later,[12] to pressures to address some equity or welfare state

11 See e.g. Pelkmans, 2005a; Ederveen, Gelauff & Pelkmans, 2006.

12 Of course, since EU citizens have considerable 'stay-put' incentives due to languages, social habits and customs, this statement hinges on sufficient *actual* cross-border labour mobility taking place, even after Central Europe has narrowed the real income per capita gap to a small one. It is far from clear that actual cross-border migration in the Union will indeed be large enough to generate such pressures.

problems at least partially at the EU level. But equity-driven expenditures in the framework of an EU social 'union' are taboo; without political legitimacy for an EU social spending, restrictions have to protect the relative 'immunity' of the national welfare state! Similar 'neo-functionalist' incentives to engage in EU-level solutions might arise if services markets would genuinely become exposed to EU-wide competition. It is precisely their pre-emption which forms one key reason for fragmentation of the IM for services!

That is why it is interesting to study the logic of economic federalism and the place of the IM in it. Without going deep into the dynamics of market integration in federations such as Canada and the US (but see the chapters by Vaillancourt and Egan, in this volume), it is striking that economists interested in economic federalism (e.g. Oates, 1999 as a leading example; see also CEPR, 2003) pay almost no attention to the internal market. Their tradition emerges from public economics and the typical assumption is that, in a federation, the internal market simply *is* a single market. The actual practice in federations is a good deal more complex, however, whether one looks at company law, or services markets, the autonomy for local taxation, the mutual recognition of some professions or even network industries. One can find amazing (but rarely major) examples of fragmentation in mature federations such as Canada and the US. Still, the overall picture is that negative and positive federal solutions of market integration dominate, also in services, labour and technology (e.g. Pelkmans & Vanheukelen, 1988). A leaning towards federal solutions is rarely accepted easily in federal countries. Nevertheless, it is not nearly as problematic as in the Union because the federation is simply accepted as a 'given' in such countries, yet *itself* a major political issue in the Union. Hence, the federal level – unlike today's EU – can be assigned with regulatory and/or budgetary tasks which act as prerequisites for such a deep and wide market integration. The causality goes both ways: a federation has much more meaningful citizen rights, including the federal part of social security (including health and elderly care to some degree) and a commonness in parts of labour regulation, so that a 'right' for workers to move around freely is also underpinned by minimal means and less risks, leading to a better functioning of the common labour market; yet, having an IM for labour creates powerful incentives for a minimum of social rules and welfare state outlays at the federal level, since redistributive competition between the states of a federation would destroy itself. Unlike the EU, there is also no inhibition for federal taxation. In network industries, federations have federal regulators because these markets have to be federation-wide. It is probably also a reasonable inference (but hard to measure) that the diversity in the EU between 27 Member States is greater than the diversity in federations such as the US, Germany, Canada, Australia and even Switzerland.

For the future of the IM of the EU, what matters is that integration processes are 'bottom-up' and, as such, incomparable to federations where decentralisation and centralisation tendencies develop against the backdrop of a single country political system and constitution. Not only can many IM decisions of the EU in future be framed as 'centralisation' (whether negative or positive integration), and this might create opposition, but such decisions might also be regarded as eroding (precious) diversity.

Therefore, resistance to deeper and wider market integration is not always and automatically to be equated with 'protectionism' or vested interests, even if that will never go away. In federal systems, much of such opposition may have little chance, or might not arise in the first place (because there is less diversity) or, if very powerful, can be bought off. This insight has a profound significance for the application of subsidiarity to the IM. Whereas in federations a functional subsidiarity test will lead to relatively heavy and strict assignments to the federal level (both negative and positive), in the current predicament of the Union the roots of diversity in 'new' IM issues might be so strong that more centralisation would no longer satisfy (diverse) preferences. As a result, high (political) costs might be incurred. When preferences are strong and diverse, subsidiarity says that the costs of overriding them are likely to outweigh the benefits of doing things at the EU level, in other words, the costs of IM *fragmentation* might be consciously accepted in the light of the higher costs of *centralisation*. There are strong indications that, for services and labour, this explains the current status-quo to a large extent (Pelkmans, 2005a; 2007a; 2007b).

## *2.6. A single market in economic analysis*

A purely economic definition of market integration is based on the concept of 'economic frontiers' (Pelkmans, 2006). Markets are integrated if economic frontiers between them have been eliminated. An economic frontier is any demarcation over which actual or potential mobilities of goods, services, capital, labour, technology as well as communication flows are low or absent. On both sides of an economic frontier, the determination of prices, quality and quantity of goods, services and factors is influenced only marginally or not at all by the flows over the frontier. There is no a priori reason for assuming that economic frontiers coincide with territorial frontiers. There may be integration deficits inside countries and between them. Economic frontiers might have numerous reasons, ranging from spontaneous disinterest, conflicts (including bans, embargoes and war), or too high costs of information (given bad infrastructure and/or extreme poverty), to natural obstacles (mountains, swamps), languages and other cultural, ethnic or religious diversities, the conduct of market participants (whether via restrictive business practices or the exclusivity of network ties), regulations, protectionism, or a range of policies as well as equity eligibility and distinct currencies.

In the EU context of today, many of the former elements of economic frontiers hardly matter anymore because of smooth information flows, good infrastructure, the IM achievements thus far, the return of a lingua franca in Europe (be it English, this time), entrepreneurship and selective network effects (e.g. among migrants even when formal barriers would seem to be high). But many other barriers remain. The great advantage of the pure economic definition is that it provides a relatively simple benchmark, which can in principle be measured. The alternative of having no benchmark is daunting: how to deal systematically with a host of disparate barriers, formal or informal, behavioural or structural, regulatory, fiscal or budgetary, cultural and/or social, disparities in infrastructure, languages, network effects (e.g. engineers used to certain technical standards show selection biases), etc. The disadvantage is that the benchmark cannot distinguish desirable from undesirable integration: in using benchmarks, one inevitably suggests that moving closer to the benchmark is 'good'. This is likely to conflict with the justified aspects of 'diversity'.

**Figure 2.4. Price convergence between EU Member States**

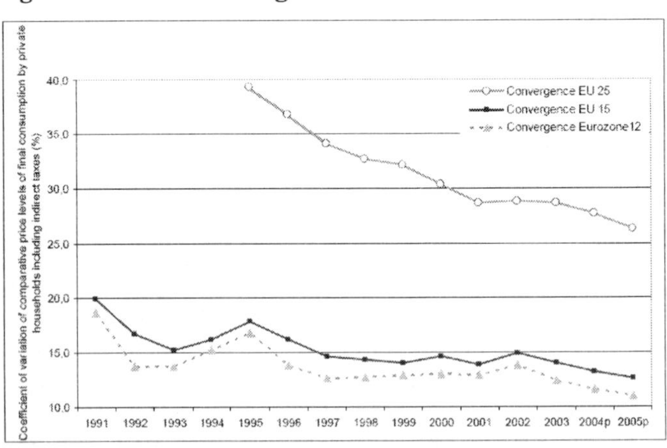


Source: Ilzkovitz *et al.*, 2007.

Thus, in combining the effects of increasing exposure to competition (EU-wide, one presumes) and diversity, price convergence trends inevitably run up to their natural limits. But nobody knows where such a limit might be. Moreover, price convergence in services – precisely because of subtle, yet far-reaching differentiation – is next to impossible to measure; yet, (tradable) services become more important and present a paramount issue for any future IM strategy.

In capital markets, interest rate convergence or proof of simultaneous movements (e.g. in equity markets) do not suffer from all these caveats. But in labour markets, wage convergence forms another complicated case. Wages converge both because of market integration *and* independent of it.

Singaporean wages have more or less converged with EU-15 wages without being 'integrated' with the Union. The reason is simply 'catch-up', of course. Indirectly, there is a powerful influence via the world economy, hence, also the EU. Inside the EU, intra-EU goods and services exchanges exercise strong convergent pressures on wages, despite the absence of an IM for labour. Similar orientations emerge from FDI with embodied technology in its wake or direct technological catch-up. Intra-EU migration might in theory be a faster route, if wage convergence were a goal in itself, but the residual character of migration in the Union causes it not to contribute much.

In recent years, the idea of economic frontiers has been endowed with a new empirical tool, that of '*home bias*'. Following Delgado (2006), greater market integration has to show up in the extent to which "[...] economic decisions have become less domestic and more European", in other words, a single market in the pure economic sense should have no 'home bias' at all.[13] Two indicators give an idea of what is measured. One is that the share of a country in any consumption basket is determined by the size (GNP) of its economy. So, if Germany amounts to (say) 18 per cent of the EU economy, German products should weight around 18 per cent in Germany's consumption of EU products; in fact, the figure might be closer to 80 or 85 per cent, leading to a 'home bias' of almost 70 percentage points. Another indicator (based on so-called gravity techniques) estimates that, when size and distance (which is costly in intra-EU trade) is accounted for, Germany would import (say) 15 per cent of its total consumption from a country of equal size and distance (in the EU). However, we know that the current share of German products in German consumption is 85 per cent, leading to a 'home bias' of no less than 70 per cent. The main

13 There is a swelling literature on EU home bias, e.g. Head & Mayer, 2000; Nitsch, 2000; Delgado, 2006; Portes & Rey, 2005; Mayer, & Zignago, 2005 and Combes, Lafourcade & Mayer, 2005. No justice can be done here to all the subtleties in these contributions.

point of this empirical work is that the EU is very far removed from any purist economic benchmark of a single market. But once again, the meaning of these (and other) home bias indicators is far from clear – even in Canada and the US there is serious home bias – there is no theory behind it, and the reliance on gravity techniques is less than ideal.

Nevertheless, it is crucial to appreciate that today's EU home bias is much more puzzling than that of three decades ago. A telling example can be found in the car industry. Dramatic restructuring over several decades have led 'national' car firms from the larger EU countries to evolve into truly European (if not global) car companies, with component suppliers having Europeanised (or globalised) as well. How French is a Peugeot still, how Italian an Fiat, how German a Volkswagen and how Czech a Skoda, even if there is still a significant degree of local preferences for what are somehow regarded as 'French' or 'Italian' (etc.) cars. Three decades ago, in the mid-1970s, 'national' car markets in the EC-9 had just opened up towards each other, after breaking down high tariffs. Hocking (1980) attempted to test the theory that a sector of differentiated, consumer durable goods will exhibit a very long adjustment period to full market integration, even when substantial economies of scale are a key drive for the 'Europanisation' of production. Inevitably, the initial export drive is based on production structures geared to domestic tastes and domestic income distribution. In other words, a testable proposition is that the share of imports will initially become high in those product types where a nation has relatively small sales, that is, fringe taste goods. Hocking indeed finds for the three car producing countries Italy, France, Germany a negative correlation between the share of imports (from the other two) and the relative size of that subsector. The home bias, in those days, was thus much stronger than today: car producers had not genuinely broken away from their home markets, components were mainly sourced in the home market or in-company and non-domestic FDI was exceptional (Fiat in communist countries) or absent. Figure 2.5 shows declining home bias for goods in the EU in the last 2 decades.

It is tempting to interpret this trend decline as a steady improvement of the degree of economic integration in the EU IM for goods. After all, it shows that EU-15 countries have gradually bought a higher share of their goods purchases in other EU countries rather than at home. At the present stage of empirical economic research on home bias it is however better to remain prudent about the exact meaning of these results. There are other estimates giving somewhat different results. In Head & Mayer (2000) the home bias is measured by first constructing the rate of purchases one would expect when buying without intra-EU border effects playing any role, and subsequently defining the bias as the 'excess' of purchases at home beyond this benchmark. The authors find a home bias of around 25 times: i.e. Europeans purchase 25 times more domestically than from equi-distant foreign (EU) suppliers in the mid-1970s, falling to around 13 in 1995. However, it is striking that the decline in the EC-1992 period (between 1987 and 1993) is insignificant (from 14 to 13). Head & Mayer decompose the border effect into a part caused by non-tariff barriers and a part explained by consumer preferences. The former cannot explain the cross-industry variation in the border effects before EC-1992, suggesting that EC-1992 did little to reduce home bias. In Figure 2.5 home bias (measured differently) also hardly declines in this period but falls considerably, later in the 1990s. Could that mean that the time-lags of the EC-1992 deepening of the IM should be thought of as being almost a decade? If not, why would home bias decline rather strongly recently? Nitsch (2000), employing yet another variant of what Head & Mayer propose, finds a home bias of around 12-13 in 1979 for the EU-10, falling to 7-8 in 1990, and a higher bias when including Spain and Portugal falling to around 10 in 1990. Again, the period 1985-1990 shows virtually no decline for the EU-10 (it does for the EU-12 but this is likely to be the enlargement effect and not so much the IM deepening). Of course, the present chapter is not the place to discuss the many technical problems of this kind of empirical economic research but it underscores that jumping to conclusions about the implied bolstering of actual market integration (by economic agents themselves) when home bias, as measured, declines, is anything but clear.

Indeed, as Balta and Delgado (2007) note, when considering this query with a view to the home bias literature, it is difficult to disentangle to what extent home bias is due to market imperfections that can be corrected by policies and due to non-policy related reasons such as consumer preferences or product characteristics. Moreover, foreign direct investment may well lead to an increase in home bias (other things equal) insofar as it replaces imports by production and this is not overcompensated by larger trade in intermediate inputs. To make matters even more complicated, autonomous trends of declining transport and communication costs have facilitated the spread of multi-stages supply chains over many countries (through off-shoring and outsourcing) and this may well tend to reduce home bias (other things equal). With respect to Figure 2.5, it is also important to note that the IM of services has been left out here – when taking goods and services together, the decline of home bias is bound to be much smaller given the strong home bias in services which is caused (apart from remaining barriers which seem to be much higher than in goods overall) by a greater inclination to serve clients in other EU countries via establishment rather than via free movement, and by the often decisive relationship of trust and proximity between supplier and client which tend to inhibit the search for alternatives even more than in goods.

**Figure 2.5. Declining home bias in the EU**

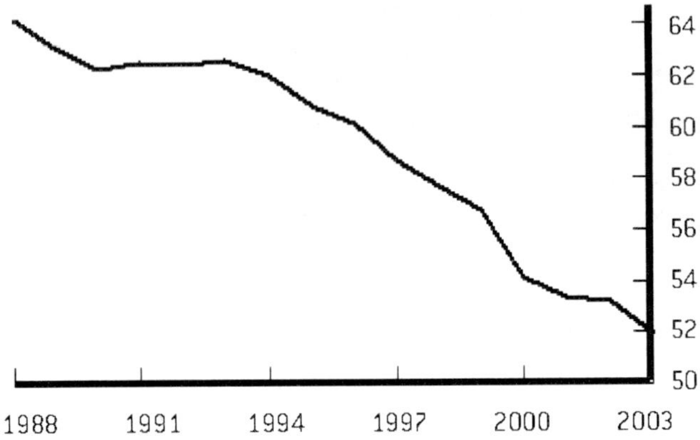

Source: Delgado, 2006.

In addition, it is good to realise what (goods) market integration means in actual practice in Europe. When discussing home bias, without further detail of what happens at the firm level in terms of structure and conduct of their economic operations, one has to rely on trade data only. But trade data may give a misleading perspective of how the IM (for goods here) actually functions. Empirical work by the EPIM research consortium and reported by Mayer and Ottaviano (2007) shows that most firms in the Union do *not participate* in the IM! Of course, this goes against an implicit notion of textbooks and typical IM policies that in principle very large segments of the total population of firms (say, all but the truly local shops) should and eventually would be lured by the Europeanisation of supply and demand and the removal of barriers as well as the more uniform regulatory setting (including standards) to seek opportunities in parts of the IM or throughout the EU at large. And one extra incentive to do so would consist in the arrival of competitive goods, traders and foreign companies in their home markets forcing price or quality changes or new modes of rivalry, as they exploit IM opportunities, too. Three key findings of Mayer and Ottaviano, 2007, include: (i) the exports of any EU country are driven by very few top exporters [f.i. the top 5 per cent of firms represents between 59 per cent and 88 per cent of all goods exports, dependent on the country] which means that most firms do not participate in the IM or only very marginally so; (ii) true Europeanisation in the sense that a firm exports a high share of its output to other EU countries only occurs in the case of a very small group of companies – if home bias is seen as the measuring rod, one would have to regard only these firms as 'integrated' in the IM, in turn implying that the relatively high home bias in the EU is caused by all these other firms not interested in or not capable of competing in the IM; (iii) these few top exporters also export EU-wide, i.e. to many locations, and do this for many distinct products.

Despite the criticism one might level at these attempts, their message is nevertheless not easy to dismiss: the myriad of measures and further deepening and widening notwithstanding, it is the *actual proper economic functioning* of the single market and with it the exposure to competition, which matters in economics. The ECJ has often employed language implying that the internal (goods) market should be no different from a domestic market. The interesting query is whether this statement of the ECJ ought to be interpreted in an economic sense, a legal sense (whatever that might mean) and/or in (political and wider legal) context.

The most interesting aspect of the purely economic interpretation of a single market is to be found in the two types of markets which have remained resistant to deepening: services and labour. Unlike for goods and financial capital, an ambitious interpretation of integration in these two markets may well be the source of profound frustration, if not a misunderstanding of what the drivers are of further progress.

## 3. The internal market as a means

The IM is a means to one or more ends. This is clear from the Treaty. It is also emphasised, *inter alia*, by the European Commission (2007) in its 'vision' paper of 21st February.[14] Nevertheless, it is exceedingly difficult to come to grips with the *means-ends* relationship(s) between the IM and the Union's aims. This section will touch on three aspects: Treaty design and the IM; the quest of a more goal-oriented IM (including the Commission's 'vision'); and the IM as a 'jack-of-all-trades' serving many masters.

### *3.1. Treaty design and the internal market*

The EC Treaty is designed around aims and means, supported by some core principles and an institutional framework. Ever since the Rome Treaty, the principal 'means' of the Community, supposed to

14 COM (2007) 60, A Single Market for Citizens, interim report to the 2007 Spring Council of 21st February.

foster the aims, is the 'common market'. But in an economic perspective, in fact a much wider internal market concept is required.[15]

The point is that, already in the Rome Treaty, the negative integration via the 'common market' and the positive integration via the means, then called, 'approximating economic policies' ought to be taken together. Without the common policies, some fiscal harmonisation (e.g. VAT) and regulation to overcome market failures (e.g. safety, health, environment & consumer protection, or, SHEC; presumably, intellectual and industrial property rights as well), negative (common) market integration would almost certainly not make much progress – in any event, such a common market would surely not function properly. In the Rome Treaty, these two (complementary) means are expected to serve four economic aims.[16] Three of these four aims amount to economic growth objectives, with slight specification. The language is quasi-constitutional that is, so general and vague that the sharp means-ends relationships needed for economic analysis, are lacking. Since Maastricht, the structure has not been altered radically, but the aims have been refined and modernised, and EMU is added as a third means.

One might object and insist that the EU budget should be included as a policy instrument, too. One could argue that structural funds & cohesion money are, in and by themselves, not part of the IM (which is correct), yet support the pursuit of some of the objectives. Similarly, one could maintain that the agricultural outlays have supported standard of living objectives of farmers, first via market mechanisms (be it in a very distorted way) and later via direct payments. In the following, the EU budget is largely ignored and the focus is on regulation, (cross-border) liberalisation and e.g. competition policies and other common policies where relevant.

For economists, the quasi-constitutional means-ends relationship between the IM and the Community's goals is ill-formulated. The economic generality significantly raises the analytical barriers to an understanding of the role and economic meaning of the internal market. Sound economic policy is usually seen as dependent on two requirements: a well-defined relationship between instruments and objectives (so that economic analysis can be fairly robust) and an adherence to the Tinbergen rule, that is, employ as many instruments as goals.[17] It is

---

15 The following discussion is easier to follow with the help of highly stylised 'flow-charts' on the economic structures of the Treaties of Rome, the Single Act, Maastricht and Amsterdam. See Pelkmans, 2006, Chapter 2.

16 And one political aim, left out here, the famous "ever closer union between the peoples of Europe".

17 One might add that the relative effectiveness of instruments should lead to specific assignments (sometimes called the Mundell rule).

obvious that 'the' IM cannot possibly satisfy these two requirements as this concept is far too general and encompassing. Therefore, one has to decompose 'the' IM in ways, such that meaningful relationships with the Treaty aims can be defined. However, that is not what is happening at the EU level. One reason is that the aims of the EC Treaty have changed. Rewriting of the aims occurred in Maastricht and again in Amsterdam. Neither the original four economic aims in Rome, and even less the six of Maastricht, nor the eight of Amsterdam, can easily serve the purpose of robust and well-defined *means-ends* relationships required for unambiguous economic policy. Hence, they are better regarded as purposefully wide and politically symbolic elements of the economic constitution of the Community. It is expected that they are made operational in more exact terms and variable over time, by the European Council and by the political entrepreneurialism of the Commission, and possibly the EP as well. Another reason is that the positive integration part of the IM (in current Treaty language, the 'common policies or activities') has far outgrown that specific role of overcoming (internal) market failures, in an impressive and long process of widening of scope of the application of EC powers. It is a problematic conceptual issue what exactly the 'economic' boundaries of the IM are, and therefore what positive integration (whether budgetary or regulatory intervention or other incentive-based policies) belongs to the IM and what are merely stand-alone political initiatives related to shared objectives. One can push this reasoning even further in the light of the multi-level-governance (MLG) structure of the Union: to what extent is the establishment and proper functioning of the IM hindered or fostered by what *Member States* do (or do not) within the range of competences they have maintained? Despite great progress in the IM and despite the considerable impact of actual or potential cross-border mobilities, hence, also competitive exposure, there can be little doubt that Member States still wield enormous influence with respect to economic structure and a range of social and economic variables (including their budgets and tax and expenditure structures) which matter in the short to medium run for economic agents. Yet another step further, on might query whether the optimal functioning of the IM does not depend as well on the design of multi-level-governance of the Union and the institutions which support or underlie (internal) market functioning. These issues bring us in the realm of subsidiarity. By far the most powerful application of the subsidiarity principle is found in the IM in the wide economic sense. This has been discussed elsewhere[18] and will be ignored here.

[18] E.g. Pelkmans, 2005a; 2005b; Ederveen, Gelauff & Pelkmans, 2006; several chapters in Gelauff, Grilo and Lejour (eds.), 2008.

### 3.2. Towards a more goal-oriented internal market?

The original Treaty design (based on the Spaak report) was clearly driven by an orientation on economic growth, be it under conditions. Catching up with the US, via market size (permitting scale and larger firm size), competitive exposure[19] and technological diffusion[20] were all viewed as being served by the emergence of the common market. During the 50 years of the Community, a combination of political strategy, penetrating case law development, the Commission's guardian role, Treaty amendments and autonomous market developments have resulted in the IM the EU enjoys today.

The paramount question has now become whether a meaningful IM strategy should continue to prioritise 'deepening' in the traditional sense of *overcoming market integration deficits* (negative and positive), or, whether the priorities should be *goal-driven.* If the latter, the IM aspects would then become a derivative of the pursuit of such goals, presumably in combination with means outside the strict IM realm. The first strategy can never be fully given up in the light of the Treaty design and the consequences for case law as well as the guardian role of the Commission. The *link* with the legal perspective is likely to be quite strong here (see the chapter by Hanf). The second strategy is based on a strong desire to improve the joint economic performance of the Union and the IM is regarded as one among several means. The latter strategy is bound to be driven much more by a *political* consensus at the European Council level, be it that the IM (and EMU) is 'hard law' based on the Community method, whereas much of the remainder is 'soft law', enjoys only minimal budget EU outlays and uses soft persuasion. This blend of hard and soft instruments would be up against domestic political systems and processes with their idio-syncratic logic. On the other hand, it is bound to be helped selectively by business coalitions and the social partners (and NGOs) at the EU level.

The contrast between the two Bolkestein strategies (in the period 1999 and 2006) and the new 'IM vision' paper by the Commission would seem to match the distinction between the two strategic orientations above. Consider Figure 2.6.[21]

---

19 Deeply influenced by the devastating account of the lack of competitive exposure in Western Europe, e.g. by Tibor Scitovsky (1958).

20 Stimulated by greater market opportunities, as emphasised time and again by the productivity centres of the OEEC at the time.

21 For the first Bolkestein strategy, see COM (1999) 464 of 5 October 1999, The Strategy for Europe's internal market; see Appendix 1 to the present chapter for the second strategy, based on COM (2003) 238 of 7 May 2003, Internal Market Strategy-priorities 2003-2006.

**Figure 2.6. Internal market vision of the Commission**

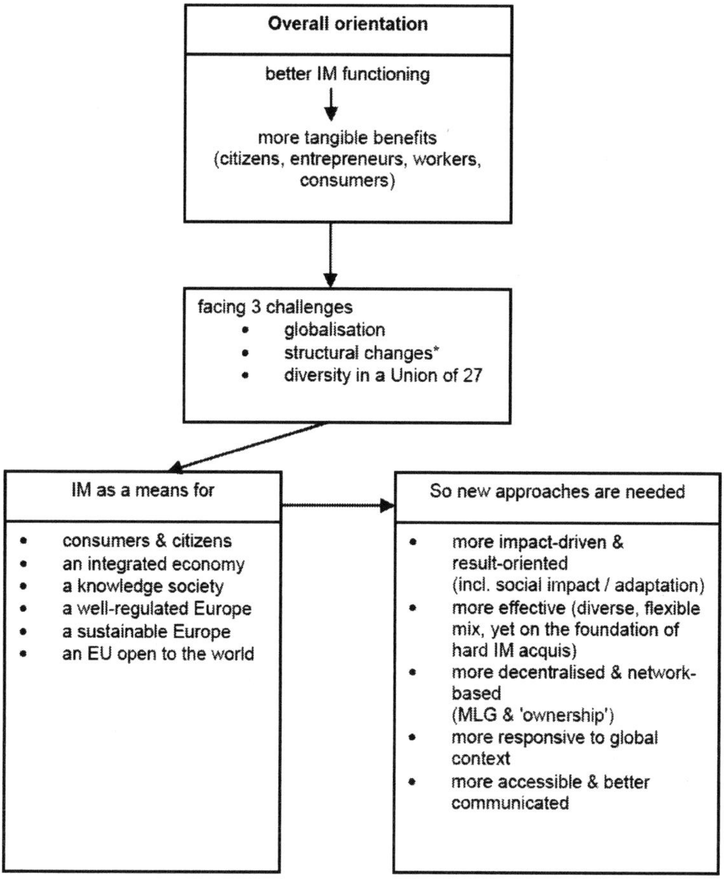

**Overall orientation**

better IM functioning

↓

more tangible benefits
(citizens, entrepreneurs, workers, consumers)

↓

facing 3 challenges
- globalisation
- structural changes*
- diversity in a Union of 27

↓

IM as a means for
- consumers & citizens
- an integrated economy
- a knowledge society
- a well-regulated Europe
- a sustainable Europe
- an EU open to the world

→

So new approaches are needed
- more impact-driven & result-oriented (incl. social impact / adaptation)
- more effective (diverse, flexible mix, yet on the foundation of hard IM acquis)
- more decentralised & network-based (MLG & 'ownership')
- more responsive to global context
- more accessible & better communicated

* rise of the knowledge economy, services, energy dependency, climate change, and ageing population

Source: COM (2007) 60 of 21 Feb. 2007 (cf. footnote 13).

The foundation of the new 'vision' is the better functioning of the IM, for the sake of 'more tangible benefits' and taking explicit account of three challenges: globalisation, structural changes and diversity in the Union. On the face of it, this is a very different approach than the classical view of (i) pursuing deepening and widening of the IM, (ii) based on overcoming integration deficits, and (iii) subsequently argue that all this supports the main aims of the Union. The new 'vision' appears to be more selective in first 'picking' fashionable issues such as

the knowledge society and a sustainable Europe, and then proposing to employ the IM as a 'means' to pursue these broad aims.

It would seem to blur the definition of the IM, in the beginning of section 2, by stretching the positive integration very far, without a rigorous link with (internal) market failures. 'The' knowledge society is not a sensible way of indicating a market failure if one were to rely solely on negative integration, hence justifying positive integration to overcome it. This does not mean that 'the' knowledge society idea is not rife with market failures but the links with the IM are not always clear and, moreover, very different, hence the compelling link with positive integration for the IM cannot be generalised.

An example: in Pelkmans & Casey (2004, a commentary on the Sapir report) we argued that the Sapir *et al.*, 2003 proposal to exercise quality control on *EU-funded* R & D done via European Research Council, though a good idea in itself, misses the point if we wish to raise the quality and effectiveness of publicly funded R & D in the EU.

Since 94 per cent of this R & D is at the Member State level and much is probably sheltered and 'duplicative', the better idea is to subject at least 50 per cent of this R & D to independent European quality control. Of course, nobody knows whether 50 or 80 per cent is the right figure, but the 6 per cent EU-funded is surely not an effective route. The example shows that the discretion in such approaches is so large that the link with the IM as such is entirely dependent on how ambitious one wishes to be in tightening the two levels of governance. Often, such tightening is politically sensitive, or, even outlawed in the Treaty.

Similar reasonings can be set up for a 'sustainable Europe'. Thus, climate strategy is a prominent part of sustainable Europe, but it is a world market failure, not (just) an EU one. Inside the EU the emissions trading system is constrained by the IM but major discretion remains with respect to the emission ceiling, the grandfathering (or not) of existing emissions by handing out permits, the differentiation amongst Member States and sectors, the period of the 'cap & trade', etc. Where the IM link is immediate, improvements can be made relatively easily. Thus, the too large discretion of Member States in the emissions trading systems' national allocation for the experimental period 2005-2007 led to arbitrary differences between national regimes of how a given emission of fully comparable types of output of e.g. two companies in two different Member States would be dealt with. These distortions will now disappear with the proposed harmonisation of national allocation rules. Without a direct IM link, discretion remains considerable.

However, upon a closer look, one can also argue that the new 'vision' amounts to the pursuit of an IM more 'integrated' with current EU policies – thus, an end to the autonomous IM driven by case law and 'required liberalisation' – and modernised in terms of institutions (especially in a MLG setting) and legitimation. The rationale behind that view would be that the classical approach to the IM has more or less exhausted its potential, even if major deficits have remained. Where deficits are significant, progress will depend critically upon a consensus with respect to positive integration.

In services, for example, regulatory consumer protection differs from Member State to Member State and the preparedness to go for a combination of minimum approximation and mutual recognition is, so far, hard to discern. Thus, retail markets are still fragmented in the IM. Indeed, consumer bodies sometimes advocate 'maximum harmonisation', a term going against the IM tradition since the Single Act and seemingly immune to a detached 'regulatory impact assessment' supporting 'better regulation'. Where service sectors are sensitive to (big) wage differentials, the 'origin principle' for services has been framed as the erosion of local wage and non-wage entitlements and/or a recipe for local job losses.[22] The Bolkestein experiment has heightened awareness in Europe that the IM for services has to be addressed much more seriously but a mere reliance on compelling free movement obligations will not do.

The predicament of the IM for labour is even worse. The Treaty is not supportive as Art. 3 does not mention the free movement of labour (only persons, and that is no coincidence), whereas Art. 39 (free movement of workers) has a *residual* character and is subjected to the host-country control principle, which eliminates the greatest incentive for migration, namely, a better remuneration. Europeans simply do not want an IM for labour. As Figure 2.2 shows, except for Ireland and Belgium, EU countries have few citizens from other EU countries (and, on average, only around one third are workers) and more non-EU immigrants and accepted asylum applicants. As mentioned, it took until 2001 before the Commission proposed to begin tackling the numerous barriers to intra-EU migration, barriers that would never be tolerated in the IM for goods. The many linkages between the national welfare states and labour market regulations usually override IM considerations. Given the deeply entrenched preferences in this regard, the subsidiarity principle will be of little help here (e.g. Pelkmans, 2005a).

---

[22] On the EU-15 side; remarkably few in the EU-15 have pointed out that the benefits of the origin principle would be appropriated by precisely the relatively *poor* workers from the new Member States (say, for a decade or so), while a rejection of the origin principle puts them at a *disadvantage*, given host country control and the Posted Workers Directive. See also Pelkmans, 2007a.

Therefore, the new Commission 'vision' gets around the hardest instances of non-deepening (so, less risk of losing legitimacy) while addressing well-recognised economic themes. Thus, it should appeal to citizens and consumers. Additional ways to enhance its socio-political legitimacy include that the social impact and adaptation ought to be taken much more into account, there should be better 'ownership' of the IM at the Member State level and it should be better communicated. None of this can be construed as a deviation of the classical IM, but it may raise the appeal of the IM. The vision is firm with respect to globalisation: the EU's IM should be open to the world and responsive to the global context. If the knowledge society is effectively promoted in the Union and, on the other hand, adaptation respected for its costs and difficulties, the IM does not have to be framed as an 'agent of globalisation' with the losers in Europe and the winners in e.g. Asia.

### *3.3. Is the internal market a 'jack-of-all-trades'?*

In the Amsterdam Treaty, in recent versions of the Lisbon strategy, or indeed in several Commission papers, the IM is apparently expected to serve many masters. It is a true jack-of-all-trades. If the IM would be literally regarded as a single 'means', this would be plainly impossible. The employment of 'the' IM for a range of aims or more specific objectives requires a suitable decomposition of both negative and positive integration.

#### *3.3.1. Treaty aims and the internal market*

There seems to be little point in discussing at length the (badly drafted) Amsterdam aims. But a few illustrative remarks may be useful. Take aim No. 6, on the environment.[23] This policy area is typically one where regulatory competition would lead to a 'race to the bottom', so that common minimum requirements are inevitable. Interpreting the wording 'high level' is of course up to the EU legislator. The IM has turned out to be the driver of practically all environmental legislation at EU level. This already occurred at a high speed when EU environmental powers were solely based on Art. 235, EEC (for a survey, see Rehbinder & Stewart, 1985), that is, *before* the Single Act.

But what about aim No. 2, a high level of employment and social protection, wording already inserted in the Treaty of Maastricht. The IM may be thought to have added extra jobs (but compared to what? a hard puzzle to solve convincingly) but how could it possibly be tasked with a high 'level', if that level depends on many variables which are *not* a

[23] This is aiming at a 'high level of protection' and 'improvement of the quality of the environment'.

function of the IM strictly spoken[24] and are often national, rather than EU. Neither is a high level of social protection the result of the IM. Such matters are firmly in the hands of Member States. The positive integration[25] is logical *for the migrants inside the IM* but otherwise refers to a decision in the Hannover European Council of 1988 not to engage in a 'race to the bottom', yet, *without* any major social harmonisation. To ensure that, a legal basis was created through this aim and two handfuls of directives (none of them, except the Worker Councils, deviating from the broad status quo amongst the Member States) about social protection were adopted. It amounts to a kind of standstill in the form of EC *acquis*.

Aims Nos. 1, 4, 5 and 7 of the Amsterdam EC Treaty all refer to economic growth or are closely related to it. This seems to be the key objective which the IM should be expected to promote. That was true in 1957 and it is true 50 years later. During the early years of the EEC, high economic growth (over 4 per cent real) was presumably mainly catch-up growth, a mixture of high rates of business and infrastructure investment, catching up with technology and productivity increases prompted by exposure to competition and intra-EEC economic openness. But it is hard to be sure since there were no Cecchini or Monti-type reports simulating EEC effects. In other words, in the 15 golden years of economic growth in the Community, which coincided with the first 15 years of the EEC's existence, it is tempting to attribute a good deal of the growth to the IM, but this is analytically hard to justify fully. The economic literature in those days considered the EEC as a mere customs union (including the CAP) and the range of static welfare effects calculated never exceeded a net of 1 per cent gain of GNP, often less. As late as 1972 an authoritative survey found no solid theory or empirical measurement of dynamic effects (labelled as 'nebulous'; see Krauss, 1972). Observe the contrast with today. The EU-15 finds itself in a period of much lower growth, although the new Member States enjoy healthy catch-up growth, with the IM as a significant handmaiden. The Cecchini report (1988) simulated a possible GNP increment of around 4.5-6.5 per cent over a number of years together as a result of the deepening of the IM under EC-1992, Baldwin & Venables (1995) report a mere 1.2 per cent, the Monti (1996) report (ex post) found that the Cecchini effect had materialised only to a modest extent, and the

---

24 For example relative and absolute wages and wage trends and their link with underlying productivity; non-wage mark-ups; the functioning of the national labour market; industrial structure (e.g. in line with comparative advantage); the local investment climate; etc.

25 E.g. on the portability of the years of social security entitlements in another Member State, ever since 1971, currently based on Regulation (EC) 883/2004.

recent DG EcFin paper by Ilzkovitz *et al.*, 2007 finds a moderate 0.6 per cent after 10 years.[26] If extended to the EU-25, Ilzkovitz *et al.* report a simulated GNP increment of 2.18 per cent by 2006. Note that GNP increments can be regarded as serving the growth aims of the Treaty, but in economic terms they are not defined as economic growth (which is a path of annual increments over a long period of time); they are *one-off*. Baldwin (1989) once suggested that EC-1992 would have a medium-term growth bonus since the marginal productivity of capital would be pushed up and the medium-term adjustment would result in a higher growth path for a while. I am not aware that this has been empirically verified after 1992 or recently. The conclusion is that the level of sophistication in economic modelling about the growth effects of the IM has improved enormously, only to find that what can be simulated (even if that is far from the full IM effect) yields low GNP increments over a fairly long period of time. Extra GNP might be welcomed as a value-added compared to the scenario in which the IM would not exist.[27] Alternatively, it can be regarded as a risk because the deepening and widening of the IM is usually justified by the EU growth imperative, and, yet, the EU-15 impact, demonstrated so far in empirical economic research (even if very incomplete), turns out to be small. Were one to study the growth paths of selected EU-15 countries (even leaving out the special case of Ireland), one is likely to find that the differential of real economic growth between Member States after ten years is going to be much bigger than the yield from the IM. That might be interpreted as follows: sound domestic growth policies are what matters and, for slow growth countries which typically tend to be reform-resistant, the IM is only going to be of marginal help.

Alternatively, one might consider the incomplete coverage of empirical studies as a sign that the factual economic growth impulse from deepening and widening the IM is far greater than such studies suggest.

---

26 It is based on a 0.9 percentage point decline of price-cost mark-ups and a modest increase in total factor productivity (a proxy for dynamic effects) of only 0.5 per cent; as to network industries, only electricity and telecoms were included. Most of this work is related to the kind of modelling in Allen, Gasiorek & Smith, 1998, which links restructuring in sectors directly with competition pressures resulting from the IM. However, exposure to competition due to the IM is bound to have powerful positive effects on cost minimisation and a search for best technology (so-called X-efficiencies); there are numerous informal accounts of drastic X-efficiency improvements in previously sheltered services and network industries. These effects are not included. From Ilzkovitz *et al*, it is also not clear whether services sectors have been included in the QUEST simulations, or, for that matter, (wholesale) financial markets.

27 But, presumably, the status-quo of market access under the WTO would, however, have to be assumed as given! This implies that the status-quo of the WTO would have emerged without the EU, a doubtful proposition.

Some illustrations of what is *not* measured or even proxied may help the reader to appreciate the argument: (i) the enormous progress in the IM for codified technology (based on IPRs); (ii) the deepening of the EU financial capital markets (Cecchini merely proxied some financial services in a highly stylised form; see Gianetti *et al.*, 2002, for a much richer approach, suggesting up to 1 per cent of GNP extra); (iii) network industries such as gas, postal, airlines, broadcasting and freight rail; (iv) sectors with low level of regulation, which can and do exploit the services IM such as testing and certification, industrial cleaning, etc.; (v) despite distortions and budget costs, the IM for agro-food product under common health and safety rules has drastically improved but tends to be ignored; (vi) the gains from intra-EU labour migration (modest but not trivial, certainly not for new Member States); etc. As noted before, X-efficiency improvements (probably far more important than static allocative gains) are not directly measured. Also, the gains from competitive public procurement in the IM are not always in, even if very hard to verify in a reliable fashion.

### *3.3.2. Other deliverables of the internal market*

Given the nature and size of the present chapter, only four other 'deliverables' will be touched upon briefly: the IM in 'Lisbon' as a label for a range of socio-economic performance indicators; innovation; Social Europe and employment; globalisation.

#### 3.3.2.1. The IM in Lisbon

Wrapping the Lisbon blanket around the IM efforts is an ambiguous strategy. It is possibly useful to generate greater commitment at the highest political level for exceptionally sensitive agenda's or dossiers, such as the support for a horizontal services liberalisation programme and (in the 2002 Barcelona European Council) the consistent drive to open up all the network industries. But it creates confusion amongst politicians who fail to understand that the IM is not 'negotiable' and not a voluntary cooperative exercise like the other items of Lisbon. The IM has little or nothing to do with the social indicators or those on e.g. education. And the IM risks being discredited along with the Lisbon process, even though it is driven by a different logic and far more stringent commitments. It is probably best to focus on the dossier par excellence which connects Lisbon with the IM: services!

The EU inaugurated a services strategy at the outset of the Lisbon process, but, in fact, three decades too late! The experiment of the

Bolkestein directive, eventually adopted in amended form late 2006,[28] was nevertheless a stimulating one. First, it showed the deep resistance against exposure to competition in many subsectors, be it via requests (to the EP) for more derogations from the origin principle, or plain opposition fuelled by the labour aspects (and uncertainty, it should be added) or based on fears that the borderlines between the services IM and genuinely social services were blurred. Second, it made clear that economists have neglected solid research on the IM for services for decades, reflected in the soft RIA of the Bolkestein draft Directive.

Kox & Rubalcaba (2007) demonstrate that, in particular, business services contribute directly (by strong structural growth, far higher than manufacturing or agri-food) to EU growth for decades, as well as indirectly via spill-overs (such as innovations, knowledge diffusion and the reduction of human capital indivisibilities at the firm level).

**Figure 2.7. Services and manufactured goods trade in 2004 (as a per cent of GDP)**

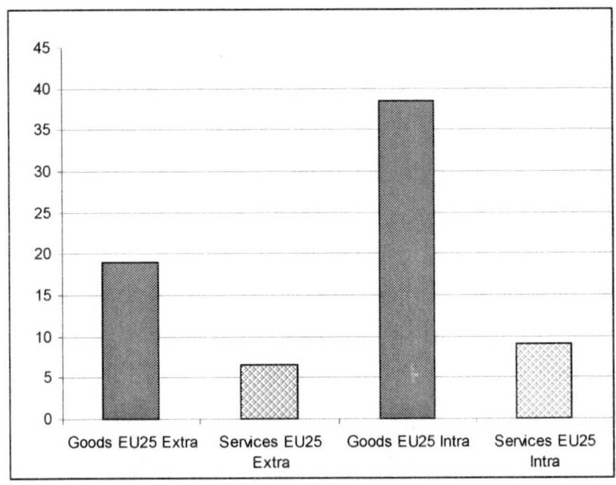


Source: Ilzkovitz *et al.*, 2007.

Second, how can one distinguish rigorously between the retreat to 'core business' in many manufacturing companies, which causes business services (at first being inside companies) to shift from manufactur-

[28] The Bolkestein draft Directive is found in COM (2004) 2 of 13 January 2004; the adopted Directive on 'Services in the Internal Market' is Dir. 2006/123 of 27 December 2006 (OJ EUL 376/36 of 27 December 2006). See Hatzopoulos, in this volume, for an authoritative legal survey of all the issues and the links with case-law. See Lejour in this volume for an economic analysis of the IM for services; see Pelkmans, 2007b for an economic discussion of the Directive.

ing to 'the' business services sector and hence boost its (statistical) growth, from a growth effect driven by the IM, weak as it still is due to barriers?[29]

**Figure 2.8. Exposure of domestic business services markets in the EU to international competition**

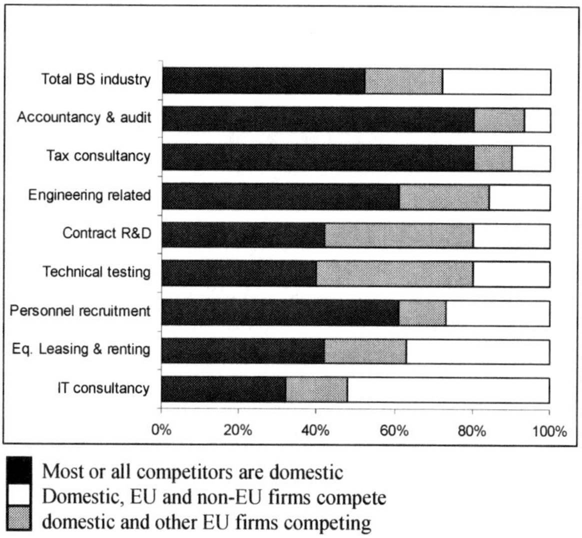

Total BS industry
Accountancy & audit
Tax consultancy
Engineering related
Contract R&D
Technical testing
Personnel recruitment
Eq. Leasing & renting
IT consultancy

0% 20% 40% 60% 80% 100%

Most or all competitors are domestic
Domestic, EU and non-EU firms compete
domestic and other EU firms competing

Source: Kox & Rubalcaba, 2007.

### 3.3.2.2. Innovation and the internal market

The European Innovation Scoreboard 2006 is the 6th attempt to measure the Union's performance in comparison with major world competitors. It does that by composing an index of 25 input and output indicators.

29 An extra difficulty here is the importance of establishment as a mode of market access for business services. Much establishment in business services is not caught by Eurostat statistics (as it is too small) and that renders even a 'guesstimate' of the IM effect next to impossible. See also Lejour, in this volume.

**Figure 2.9. EU-25 innovation gap towards US and Japan**

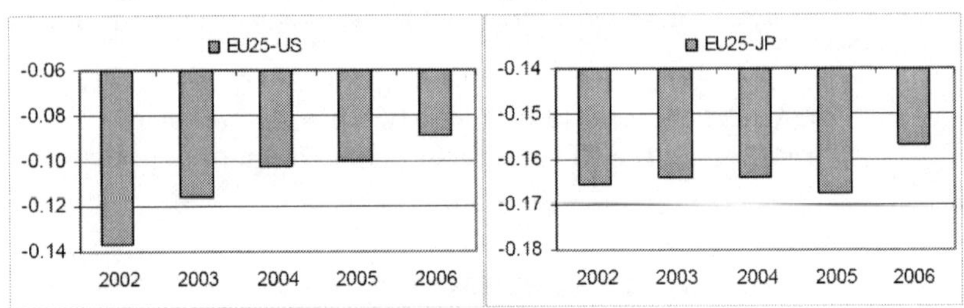


Note: The vertical axis represents the difference between SII scores of EU-25 and US & Japan respectively.
Source: Innovation Scoreboard, 2006.

The main conclusion is that the EU-25 is still behind the US and Japan but catches up slowly with the US, and even more slowly with Japan. What the actual or potential contribution of the IM represents, is not discussed. However, that would be an important question to answer, whether from a business point of view or for public policies at both levels of government. The debates typically concentrate on the costly failure of political leaders (since 1962!) to create a Community patent and one at low cost (e.g. translations and later litigation costs). Perhaps it is possible to stylise the contribution of the IM in 'innovation systems' and consider the impact of IM deepening on innovation. After all, everything else equal, market size has a positive impact on innovation.

3.3.2.3. Social Europe, employment and the internal market

Opening up and exposure to competition is one of the keys for obtaining a higher standard of living (aim 7 in the Amsterdam Treaty) or economic growth in general. Yet, it inevitably raises fears about winners and losers. This was true 50 years ago when France, by signing the Rome Treaty, gave up its indicative planning and considerable trade protection (as far as the EEC-Six were concerned). It was also the case under EC-1992 but did not lead to more than occasional or (sparse) sectoral protests. The Cecchini simulation showed a net gain of 1.8 million jobs, but only after a temporary adjustment which first went through net job losses. Nowadays, many less skilled workers in the EU-15 regard the Eastern enlargement of the IM as a threat to their jobs, whether due to 'delocalisation', direct competition in goods or services markets or direct competition in the local job market. Some labour unions even go so far as mistrusting the IM as 'an agent of globalisation' (see below). These fears were of course most prominent in the year of enlargement. And precisely then, in 2004, the Commission proposed to open up services, based on the widely misunderstood origin principle. For workers in those segments of the labour market, also pressed to engage in domestic reforms of their long-fought entitlements as 'insiders', while made nervous about their pensions in the long run, Europe (read, the IM) was believed to have become indifferent to adverse social impact. If one adds the occasional sentiments about the opening up (and labour shedding) of network industries, justified or not, and the nervousness about the 'safe havens' (against EC competition law or state aids) of numerous social services at the municipal level and in 'health' more generally, it becomes clear that all these aspects of Social Europe had not been approached in a 'strategic' fashion. The weak growth performance and relatively high unemployment levels in a number of Member States in that period did not help either.

This chapter is not the place to discuss that[30] but these fears and queries cannot be dismissed by references about the benign effects of the IM in general. Ilzkovitz *et al.* (*op. cit.*) report an EU-25 job gain induced by the IM of 2,75 million by 2006. If the prospective losers would not fear to be jobless more than very briefly and not incur major wage losses, there would hardly be a problem. But Social Europe is a MLG construction, with the emphasis on the *national* level. Both the (in)flexibilities in labour markets and the social security entitlements are national, not EU, and the overall level of unemployment is only very partially, if at all, a function of the IM. This brings us back to Lisbon, an attempt to come to grips with a MLG Social Europe but with the ever-so-soft open method of coordination. However, from the point of view of the IM, the success of Lisbon does seem to matter: the more successful the national reforms in labour markets and modern social protection, the less resistance to certain sensitive aspects of the IM, which in turn could ignite some extra dynamism in the Union's economy. These sensitive elements would include the free movement of workers from the new Member States and a more ambitious approach to the free movement of services (than in the newly adopted directive). Its additional virtue would be that the workers in the Union, East and West, would not be opposed to each other. After all, a detached perspective of the debate on the IM makes one wonder how the use of free movement rights by *poor* (Central European) workers, in the search for a better standard of living, can possibly be *anti*-social? As various migration studies show, the gains for the mobile workers are massive and the loss to local workers in the EU-15 countries tiny, be it that there is a sectoral concentration. It is precisely in these few sectors that two negative effects cumulate: a lot of illegal labour (causing downward pressure of

30 See Pelkmans, 2007a, for the 'social' nature of European integration.

total labour costs and the twisted use of a loophole in Community law about the 'independent-without-personal', who – in accepting negotiated services contracts – can evade host-country control (i.e. compulsory local wages), come on top of all the other concerns. In late 2007, with growth having returned to all of EU-15 and with falling jobless rates everywhere, these sensitivities have (temporarily) faded away. Moreover, convergence with the new Member States turns out to be faster than expected. Indeed, in countries such as Poland and Romania, rapid wage increases can be observed in sectors having seen strong out-migration. This might open the eyes of many to the benefits of an IM for workers.

#### 3.3.2.4. The internal market and globalisation

The IM is open except for (selected temperate zone) agricultural goods. It would be good for the EU itself if Doha would succeed, so that tariff barriers in agro-food would drastically decrease, such that imports exercise a disciplinary effect. In services, the IM is, for all its defects, much more open than anything contemplated in Doha. In FDI the EU has always been very liberal indeed (national treatment, already in the Rome Treaty). In capital the EU has no restrictions. In labour the Member States are restrictive but one can discern an increasing preparedness to devise immigration policies for skilled workers and researchers, and to coordinate at least in such a way that wasteful competition for such immigrants is avoided.

The IM can be deepened, especially in services and labour as well as in codified technology. This will raise productivity and reduce vulnerabilities for world competition. Highly specific improvements are harder, yet good to keep on the programme (e.g. the defence equipment market although with few illusions about its speed). But for the remainder, the IM as such is not capable of offering special answers for globalisation. It is no coincidence that Ilzkovitz *et al.* (*op. cit.*) do not offer convincing answers either. The EU is already quite globalised itself, with massive two-way FDI over the North Atlantic and frantic activities in China and indeed Asia at large. For many others in the world, Globalisation means that they want to export to the EU! Fears about off-shoring and sub-contracting are understandable but it has little if any connection to the IM as such.

To portray the IM as the 'agent of globalisation' is apparently meant as an accusation. Even if some multinationals might exhibit objectionable conduct in some poor countries, there is no such issue in the IM: in the large and deep IM, the combination of scale, relatively easy entry or rivalry and a credible competition regime disciplines virtually all such companies. Globalisation also implies low or no tariff and quota protection and even regulatory trade policy under the aegis of the WTO SPS and TBT codes as well as the case law of the Appelate Body. This creates opportunities for all in the world (including EU consumers and traders) and forces EU companies to remain on their toes if they find themselves in import competition. If comparative advantages have turned against a Union of high wages and another skill composition, globalisation benefits both (poor) export countries and the rich EU. It is difficult to see why the Union should not globalise and why the IM would have to be changed for that purpose.

**Figure 2.10. Ratio of intra and extra-EU manufacturing trade to GDP (per cent)**

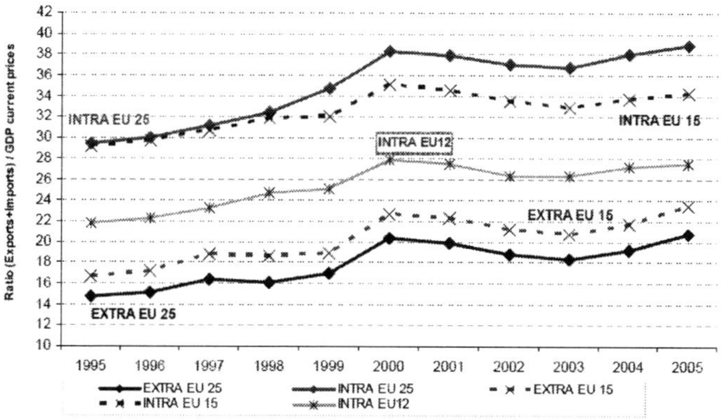

Source: Ilzkovitz *et al.*, 2007.

Given the manifest case in favour of globalisation, with due attention to losers at both levels of government, the strategy is for business to learn to think and act global and for economic agents in the Union to adjust. In an open IM, these processes are to some extent 'EU domestic' as the lines between intra-EU and extra-EU are more and more blurred. Thus, the IM has at best a modest additional policy role, unless one counts external market access strategy as part of the IM. Ilzkovitz *et al.* (pp. 79-80) suggest that the EU and trading partners should agree on 'common standards', in particular with respect to consumer and environmental regulation. The argument to pursue this is based on the competitive disadvantage of high 'quality of life' standards or regulations. This is a vexed issue, however, also from an economic perspective. Against the drawback of competitive disadvantage, there is the risk of 'raising rivals' costs', a regulatory strategy to throttle the competitive exposure of European business against low-cost rivals.[31] Presumably, a superior approach and not a priori considered 'protectionist' by trading partners, is to organise private intercontinental value-chain management with full and independent certification as well as public reporting, complemented at home in the IM by EU-wide quality marks for recognition by consumers and actively supported by consumer organisations and NGOs. Extreme-low-cost free riders in business would then remain isolated. In environmental regulation, the scope for enforcing EU rules is much greater.

## 4. More internal market: three economic strategies

Three economic strategies to accomplish 'more IM' will be set out. Their logic may be distinct, the underlying economic justifications largely overlap: incremental strategies (in section 4.1); the IM as the core of an Economic Union serving the 'proper functioning of monetary union'; and deepening and widening of the IM as rationalised by the functional Subsidiarity test (in section 4.3).

### *4.1. Incremental 'strategies' for the internal market*

Should the two internal market strategies under Commissioner Bolkestein now be succeeded by another one under McCreevy? The consultation of mid-2006 on the internal market gave the impression of 'more of the same'; it did not look 'strategic' at all. However, in September 2006 the Commission suddenly changed course and announced a more fundamental review for the Spring European Council in March 2007. Figure 2.6 illustrates the 'vision' of an emerging IM strategy proposed by the Commission in February 2007.

The Commission suggestions and the responses in the consultation yielded two conclusions: (i) a follow-up strategy should fill *specific* 'gaps' currently found in services, retail financial services, insurance, transport, energy, taxation, free movement of workers and intellectual property (most, if not all, of this is 'more of the same' but helpful); (ii) the choice of priorities ought to be more *horizontal*, that is, in fostering market dynamism and innovation (one might query how the EU level can do this?, see 3.3.2.2.), better regulation, better implementation and enforcement taking more account of the global context and more effective communication to citizens and SMEs. Both incremental approaches are up against severe limits. Practically all these areas have

[31] In the WTO, the GATT rules impose non-discrimination between all 'like products', irrespective of differences (in 'quality-of-life' standards) in their production process, e.g. labour conditions, animal welfare or (say) less or more $CO_2$-intensive. This legal constraint should also be taken into account.

been tested more than once and progress is likely to be selective and slow. In by far the most important area – services – no initiative will be possible before 2011 (the *rendez-vous* clause of Dir. 2006/123), unless the ECJ would declare the adopted directive null and void, which is not impossible. In all other fields the constraints are largely known and the increments when making headway will be modest.

There is indeed a tricky communication problem on the internal market. That was also the case in 1984/85. To the experts in those days, accustomed to work in relative obscurity on IM issues, the emergence of business coalitions (such as the European Round Table of Industrialists forging detailed IM plans), business confidence expressed via spectacular cross-border mergers in 1987 and an outright 'europhoria' following the Cecchini report in 1988, came as a total surprise. One should not entertain any hope of this surprise happening again. The EC-1992 episode was unique, it will never come back. Yet, this communication 'trap' creates a very serious obstacle for getting the political attention the IM requires and the publicity it needs for wide support. Dashing any hope that history will repeat itself should not be read as resignation. It means that tackling specific 'IM deficits' will not be facilitated by an overall consensual drive to 'complete' the IM. Thus, each time, the economic case has to be made in a convincing way and socio-political insistence should not be too concentrated so that a 'blocking minority' can be maintained. It also means that a horizontal approach (e.g. justifying a 'deeper' IM as a boost to innovation, or, improving the economic functioning of the IM via 'better regulation') has to be much more than just a cloak. The analytical economic case for a more complete or better functioning IM supporting well-accepted economic aims of the Union will have to be compelling.

The Commission's 'new approach' of the IM, as finally proposed in November 2007, echoes some of these points.[32] One may categorise the proposals as 'new' in some respect, as will be briefly outlined below, and more driven by economic analysis than legal 'IM deficits', but as a strategy it is nevertheless an 'incremental' one for the IM.

The proposals closely follow the vision paper of February 2007 (see figure 2.6, infra, in section 3.2). They have four aspects:

i. Deliver more results for citizens, consumers and SMEs.

---

32 European Commission, A single market for 21st century Europe, COM (2007) 724 of 20 November 2007. See also SEC (2007) 1518 of 20 November 2007 on 'Instruments for a modernised single market policy'; and SEC (2007) 1519 on the External Dimension of the Single Market Review. Two other papers deal with a quick-scan of the IM *acquis* (SEC (2007) 152) and the methodology for product market and sector monitoring (SEC (2007) 1517).

This is essentially 'more of the same' but the way it is approached should express that the IM policies are "responsive to the expectations and concerns of citizens", and "foster the right conditions for small and medium-sized business". It includes a 'global approach to consumer rights across the EU' (so far an area with still considerable and resistant fragmentation), tackling more effectively the retail financial services, a new initiative on pharmaceuticals, a Small Business Act for Europe in 2008 as well as a proposal for a European Private Company to facilitate cross-border activities of SMEs.

ii. Take better advantage of globalization.

The Commission firmly agrees with our points made in section 3.3.2.4, noting that the "[...] single market is Europe's best asset in reaping the benefits of globalisation". Apart from a solid but customary plea for multilateral and bilateral (FTA-based) deepening of trade with EU partners and ensuring "that the benefits of openness reach European citizens" (something which critically hinges on sufficient competitive rivalry in wholesale and retail markets but is not new at all), the strategic elements worth paying attention to is for the EU "to take the lead in setting benchmarks", act as a "global standard-setter"[33] and, through regulatory cooperation, convergence of standards and equivalence of rules, to foster "convergence to the top" rather than a "race-to-the-bottom".[34] Somewhat risky, the Commission calls this "expanding the regulatory space of the single market, [...] ensuring that European norms are a reference for global standards". Again, nothing new here, except that the EU approach is suggested to change from an ad-hoc case-by-case approach (which indeed has been successful) to a strategic one.

iii. Open new frontiers of knowledge and innovation.

Again the proposals agree with the main point of section 3.3.2.2, noting that the "Single market can be a platform to stimulate innovation in Europe". The 'single market for knowledge and innovation' is to be stimulated by a new strategy for industrial property rights, a standardisation strategy (with an emphasis on the R&D/standards link) and a series of e-activities.[35]

---

33 In areas mentioned "such as product safety, food safety, environmental protection, public procurement, financial regulation and accounting".

34 As David Vogel (1995) first demonstrated eloquently with respect to food safety and environmental regulation between the US and the EU.

35 Such as e-invoicing, e-authentication & signatures (mutually recognised) and e-Customs.

iv. Encompass a strong social and environmental dimension.

This appeal responds to 'legitimate concerns' of workers and citizens about social rights and about compensation of losses. However, though the spirit is clear and the concern about socio-political legitimacy of the IM well expressed, no significant further actions are proposed.

Moreover, the proposals deal extensively with what is denoted as 'delivering results': much more drive to render IM policies 'impact-driven' (e.g. with a consumer scoreboard); better enforcement and still more resources for and use of SOLVIT (the non-judicial consultative, rapid-action approach to remove obstacles in cross-border transactions); rendering the IM more accessible and, above all, better communicated, all elements which are hopefully instrumental to raise awareness and foster 'political and citizens' ownership of the IM.

The present chapter is not the place for a detailed assessment of these proposals. But, as this overview clarifies, the 'newness' of the approach is not its decisive characteristic at all. Anyway, what matters is whether it improves the functioning of the IM and/or accomplishes widening and/or deepening. It also matters strategically that political ownership and socio-political legitimacy is not dealt with lightly. Therefore, given the constraints in today's IM and European integration at large, the proposals can broadly be welcomed.

### 4.2. Economic union, serving the proper functioning of Euroland

The IM is the core of the Economic Union, which in turn forms the backbone of the monetary union.[36] A stylised summary of prevailing economic thought is reproduced below as Table 2.1.[37] The table focuses on the macro-economic stabilisation function, in addition to the efficiency function of the EU level of government.

An economic union needed for the monetary union to 'function properly' would have to live up to two requirements: (i) an appropriate adjustment capacity of the union's economy, thereby augmenting the net benefits of the common currency; (ii) fiscal policy coordination, such that the price stability aim of Euroland cannot be endangered. For the purpose of the present paper, we are interested in (i).

36 The Economic Union is not defined in the Treaty or in any authoritative document endorsed by EU leaders. The economic literature on economic union before Maastricht was undisciplined and unhelpful for Treaty design (Pelkmans, 1991).

37 Table 2.1 is taken from Pelkmans, 2006, p. 381.

It is striking that much of what ought to be achieved can only result from joint strategies with the Member States (allowing structural change, fostering mobilities, regulatory reform, and stabilisers with the right incentives) and to some extent with the social partners at national level (industrial relations; flexicurity).

**Table 2.1: Economic union serving monetary union**

| | | |
|---|---|---|
| **monetary union** | | |
| → irrevocable exchange rates // euro | | |
| → price stability | | |
| → European Central Bank | | |
| → entry conditions | | |
| → policy obligations / Growth & Stability Pact | | |
| **EMU** | → | fiscal conditionalities |
| **economic union** | | |
| IM, plus cohesion + Lisbon/OMC, with appropriate adjustment capacity, | | |
| → Member States' level (structural change / mobilities) | | |
| → social partners / flexibilities / flexicurity | | |
| → (possible) stabilisers (MS/EU levels) | | |
| → regulatory reform at EU and MS levels | | |

The bottom panel of Table 2.1. assumes that smooth adjustment can be accomplished this way, without any form of 'political union', which would incorporate what Tietmeyer (1994) calls an irrevocable 'solidarity community'.[38] Again, this would be unique when comparing EMU with any other modern monetary union, say, in federations.

Knowing that the IM is vital for the 'economic union' supporting 'monetary union', the EU cannot avoid a fundamental strategic choice between a kind of *federal economic model* and a soft, consensual approach of economic coordination. The former requires that the IM would have to be deepened in e.g. services and labour as a logical foundation for a significant equity and spending role of the EU level. The latter implies reducing rigidities at the national level, and thereby improving the functioning of the IM without any change in EU powers and without having to opt for a much more ambitious IM in the short-to-

[38] In a recent review of the economic fundamentals of the EU's monetary union, de Grauwe (2006) concludes that, in the longer run, the euro will only be sustainable with a 'political union'. However, this 'political union' remains completely undefined, let alone, any recommendation of how to get there.

medium run. Note how critical this strategic choice is for the future of the IM: either, joint strategies with the Member States work effectively in altering the EU into a flexible economy at all levels (a daring supposition, but one that would reduce the pressure on the IM to be 'complete'), or, substantial progress towards an IM for services and labour is thwarted by the very lack of a convincing 'solidarity mechanism' at the EU level which is irrevocable (i.e. constitutional). Since an EU solidarity community is out of the question for a long time to come, the only option is the former, but the institutional architecture for effective joint strategies with the Member States is weak, at best. Such strategies are bound to be intergovernmental, voluntary, and very 'softly' coordinated. One might interpret the Lisbon approaches (I and II) in this vein. Apart from the obvious problem that Euroland does not coincide with the IM or Lisbon, the 'governance failure' of Lisbon cannot be expected to be overcome. In such a weak setting, and without significant redistribution functions at the EU level, the subsidiarity case for EU coordination (that is, what is the value added to move beyond the Member State level?) is quite limited (see also Pisani-Ferry & Sapir, 2006). In that event, there is little hope that a much more ambitious IM incorporated in the economic union will come into being and/or that joint strategies will yield a major and lasting contribution to the adjustment capacity underlying the monetary union.

### *4.3. IM and subsidiarity*

The functional application of a subsidiarity test is inspired by the economics of federalism. It can be helpful in avoiding unjustified centralisation whilst exposing false arguments by unwilling Member States frustrating solid improvements of the IM where a good subsidiarity case can be made.[39] It would be illusionary, however, to suggest that this will carry us very far in actual EU practice. The political sensitivities in areas where subsidiarity would call for considerable change do not go away simply because a rational, analytical case is provided. Thus, the income support in the CAP could better be pursued at the Member State level (in a tight EU framework, to be sure) and EU subsidies to (relatively) poor regions in rich EU Member States would seem to be pointless and roundabout, but politics is decisive here, not a functional test. More narrowly about the IM, there can be little doubt that a genuine IM for network industries requires regulators at the EU level, but the Meroni doctrine[40] will first have to be circumvented.[41]

39 Pelkmans, 2005a; Pelkmans, 2005b; Ederveen, Gelauff & Pelkmans, 2006.

40 The Meroni doctrine originates from a 1958 ruling of the ECJ. It pre-empts EU-level independent regulators from coming into being on constitutional grounds. However, the functional logic to have EU regulators for the IM of network industries is so

Despite these political and institutional realities, the systematic employment of functional (not: political) subsidiarity tests is likely to contribute to a less politicised debate about gradual improvements of the IM architecture and substance. The fact that subsidiarity tests are now included routinely in RIAs at the EU level and begin to be practiced by national parliaments (inspired by the new Treaty of Lisbon) might well set in motion a trend of assessing in a more detached fashion what it takes to have a better functioning IM for Europe. Still, many politicians regard subsidiarity as a 'political' tool, expressing in some vague sense sentiments about (too much) centralisation, without realising that the principle ought to be seen as working *both ways*: protecting Member States' powers, where there is no value-added at the EU level, but just as well, shifting (the application of) powers to the EU level when the functional case can be made, so that the IM works better for the economic performance of the EU.

## 5. Conclusions

In economics, there are theoretical approaches to the IM (with a significant increase in sophistication during the last two decades), empirical approaches inspired by such theory, simulations inspired by such theory, empirical approaches verifying the actual degree of market integration (such as 'home bias') and finally there is a great deal of applied economic work which may be inspired by analytical economic traditions but has to cope with the day-to-day practice of the development of specific proposals to deepen and widen it. An unconstrained definition of the IM has never really changed for economists, however: it implies the full liberalisation and proper regulation (combined with common policies where appropriate) of goods and services market as well as those of mobile factors of production. The EU has minor difficulties in goods markets still, but huge obstacles in services and still bigger ones in labour markets. For codified technology, progress has been impressive except for patents, and in financial capital markets there are no formal barriers but different standards and high

powerful that EU networks of national regulators in combination with the Commissions' role in competition policy (and the economic freedoms) become more and more important. In electricity, gas and telecoms, one observes the emergence of EU 'regulatory networks' as an ever closer substitute for a single EU regulator.

41 Note that, in SEC (2007) 1518 of 20 Nov. 2007, p. 27, the Commission once again pleas for strong cooperation between (national) regulators. Examples in financial services, electronic communications and electricity & gas are provided. This is as far as the Commission can go under Meroni. Of course, there is also the query whether the Commission would be all that keen to see fully-independent European regulators emerge!

trade costs in equity. The economists' concept of 'the' IM is therefore still far away.

Economists have difficulty in coping with the phenomenal differentiation in IM issues, not only with respect to highly differentiated and technical regulation, but also for numerous barriers to market integration. Thus, it may perhaps come as a surprise to political scientists and lawyers that aggregate studies on IM effects are relatively few, but once one realises the magnitude and complexity of the task, the paradox may be appreciated.[42] Aggregated studies on the IM cannot easily be cumulated from the sixties to today, yet, in principle, the economic gains from the IM should be calculated from the beginning. The more recent empirical studies do not report impressive gains, although, in fairness, they do not cover the years before (say) 1990. Nevertheless, until a decade ago, the idea was that the EU's IM had become quite integrated, at least for goods. The 'home bias' literature has presented a new puzzle to economists as it shows that Europeans may not be so integrated after all.

The IM paradox is that it is (too) often regarded as a boring and uninspiring subject in European integration and at the same time, it is used as the EU's workhorse par excellence to pursue an incredible range of objectives. The Treaty design of the EC is even such that the IM (and EMU) are the only significant means, selectively supported by the EU budget, for (in Amsterdam) no less than 8 socio-economic aims. Consultations and the 2007 Commission 'vision' exacerbate this 'workhorse' function. An IM driven mainly by the goals to be pursued is likely to be a more fruitful approach than the classical extrapolation of the legal 'completion' route, which is close to being exhausted for political reasons. The economic case for deeper services market integration is only beginning to be built up by economists now; if it comes to the largest segment outside tourism (business services) the contribution to EU economic growth is already disproportionably high and deeper market integration might accentuate that. The link between the IM and innovation is also critical for Europe's growth but current scoreboards fail to indicate *how the IM* can stimulate (except for a true EU patent). The debate about the 'social dimension' of the IM is most curious from an analytical perspective because the anxiety seems to be very much an EU-15 phenomenon (in contrast to the new Member States) and the construction of the IM itself provides few arguments for arguing an 'a-social' outlook (see Pelkmans, 2007a). Anyway, most of the social

42 Moreover, the 'aggregated' studies are, in fact, based on sweeping generalisations of e.g. regulatory impact, and invariably leave out a number of details or specific manifestations of the IM (see 3.3.1).

framework is profoundly national. The EU is itself one of the leading 'globalisers' and the IM supports such moves forcefully. It is very hard to understand how the IM with a huge market and such diversity could not be a useful preparatory ground for globalisation. The issue which deserves attention is to appreciate the problem of identifiable losers. A balancing act might be necessary when advocating 'standards' (in fact, what is meant is mainly regulations) at world level for reasons of preserving competitiveness: the 'level-playing field' versus 'raising rivals' costs'.

The political legitimacy of deepening and widening the IM is a paramount issue which has to be taken serious by economists (and the EU institutions). Between the three routes to 'more IM', the incremental strategy is bound to be selective and cumbersome (as indeed it was under the two strategies pushed by Commissioner Bolkestein), but possibly fruitful in the longer run. The November 2007 Commission proposals on a 'new approach' to the IM clearly belong to the class of incremental strategies. Feasible, presumably, but working only gradually and with a piecemeal structure of initiatives. The 'economic union' approach is heavily dependent on MLG aspects (which cause complexity without effectiveness, yet, remain inevitable in the Union) and some measure of common equity (or, 'solidarity' in Tietmeyer's famous wording when still Bundesbank president), which is unlikely to come about in the foreseeable future. The functional subsidiarity approach is still insufficiently recognised by the current generation of politicians. Setting consensual aims and firmly backed strategies might work for the IM, if and only if the question of political legitimacy (which, in and by itself, is helped by a goal-driven IM, as long as voters can associate with such goals) is convincingly addressed in the MLG framework at both levels of government.

# Appendix

Conditions for business (patent; other IPR; I. Acc. Stand; Corporate governance/take-over; SE for SMEs
Conditions for business (patent; other IPR; I. Acc. Stand; Corporate governance/take-over; SE for SMEs
Free movement of goods (MR, standards, eco-design; unsafe goods)
Slimming Regulation (see Better Regulation)
IM STRATEGY 2003-2006
Free movement services (Fin. Services; Action Plan; Services Dir (!); ext. Of 98/34
Enforcement acquis (more/swifter sanctions; decentralising; consumer prot.; administrative cooperation)
Network Industries (all + state aids: PPPs)
Better info (various) (new MS)
Procurement (SOLVIT for PROC; national supervisors; e-proc.; defense
Reducing tax obstacles (parent/subsidiarity Dir. revision; mergers; corporate tax base harm.; car registr. tax out)

## References

Allen, C., Gasirorek M. & Smith A. (1998) The Competition Effects of the Single Market in Europe, *Economic Policy* 27, October.

Baldwin, R. (1970) *Non-tariff Distortions of International Trade*, Washington D.C., Brookings Institution.

Baldwin, R. (1989) The Growth Effects of 1992, *Economic Policy* 9.

Baldwin, R. & Venables, A. (1995) Regional Economic Integration, in Grossman, G. & Rogoff, K. (eds.), *Handbook of International Economics*, Vol. 3, North Holland, Amsterdam/New York.

Balta. N. & Delgado, J. (2006), Home Bias and European Market Integration, *Bruegel Working Paper*, December.

Boeri, T., Nicoletti G. & S. Scarpetti (2000) Deregulation and Labour Market Performance, in Galli, G. & Pelkmans, J. (eds.) *Regulatory Reform and Competitiveness in Europe*, Vol. 1, Cheltenham, Edward Elgar.

Cecchini, P. *et al.* (1988) *The European Challenge 1992*, Wildwood House, Aldershot (also published in all other EC languages under different titles), 1988.

CEPR (2003) Built to last: a political architecture for Europe, CEPR, London.

Combes, P.P., Lafourcade, M. & Mayer, T. (2005) The Trade-creating Effects of Business and Social Networks: Evidence from France, *Journal of International Economics*, Vol. 66, pp. 1-29.

Dekker, W. (1985) *Europe – 1990*, Brussels-Eindhoven (Philips).

Delgado, J. (2006) Single Market Trails Home Bias, *Bruegel policy brief* 5, October.

Ederveen, J., Gelauff, G. & Pelkmans, J. (2006) Assessing Subsidiarity, *CPB Document* 133, November, www.cpb.nl.

Engel, Ch. & Rogers J. (2004) European Product Market Integration after the Euro, *Economic Policy* 19, July.

Grauwe, P. de (2006) What Have We Learnt about Monetary Integration Since the Maastricht Treaty?, *Journal of Common Market Studies*, Vol. 44, 4, pp. 711 – 730.

Hatzopoulos, V. (2007) Legal Aspects of the Internal Market for Services, in Pelkmans, J., Chang, M. & Hanf, D. (eds.) *The EU Internal Market in Comparative Perspective: Economic, Political and Legal Analyses*, Brussels, PIE Peter Lang, Chapter 6.

Hatzopoulos, V., & Do, U.T. (2006) *The Case Law of the ECJ Concerning the Free Provision of Services: 2000-2005.*

Head, R. & Mayer, T. (2000) Non-Europe: the magnitude and causes of market fragmentation in the EU, *Weltwirtschaftliches Archiv*, Vol. 126, 2.

Ilzkovitz *et al.* (2007) Steps towards a Deeper Economic Integration: The Internal Market in the 21[st] Century. A Contribution to the Single Market Review, DG. Ecfin, *Economic Papers* 271, January.

Kox, H. & Rubalcaba, L. (2007) Analysing the Contribution of Business Services to European Economic Growth, BEEP research paper 9, College of Europe, Bruges, February. http://www.coleurop/eco/publications.htm.

Krauss, M., (1972) Recent Developments in Customs Union Theory, an Interpretive Survey, *Journal of Economic Literature*, Vol. 10, 2.

Mayer, T. & Ottaviano, G. (2007), The Happy Few: The Internationalisation of European Firms, Brussels, *Bruegel Blueprint Series.*

Mayer, T. & Zignago, S. (2005) Le marché unique et l'intégration commerciale en Europe, in *Politiques macroéconomiques et politiques structurelles en Europe*, Report for the French Council of Economic Analysis. (http://www.cae.gouv.fr/).

Monti, M. (1996) *The Single Market and Tomorrow's Europe*, Office of Official Publications of the EC, Luxembourg and Kogan Page, London.

Nitsch, V. (2000) National Borders and International Trade: Evidence from the EU, *Canadian Journal of Economics*, Vol. 33, pp. 1091-1105.

Oates W. (1999) An Essay in Fiscal Federalism, *Journal of Economic literature*, Vol. 37, 3, pp. 1120-1149.

Pelkmans, J. (1985) The Institutional Economics of European Integration, in Cappeletti, M., Weiler J. & Secombe, M. (eds.) *Integration through Law – Europe and the American Federal Experience*, Vol. I, Book I, Walther de Gruyter, New York/Berlin.

Pelkmans, J. (1986) *Completing the Internal Market of Industrial Products*, Office for Official Publications of the EC, Luxembourg/Brussels, Document Series.

Pelkmans, J. (1991) Towards Economic Union, in Ludlow P. (ed.), in *Setting EC Priorities, 1991-1992*, London, Brasseys, 1991.

Pelkmans, J. (1994) The Significance of EC-1992, *The Annals*, American Academy of Political and Social Sciences, No. 531, January.

Pelkmans, J. (1995) Comment in Sykes, A. *Product Standards in Internationally integrated Goods Market*, Washington D.C., Brookings Institution.

Pelkmans, J. (2001), Making EU Network Industries Competitive, *Oxford Review of Economic Policy*, autumn, Vol. 17, 3.

Pelkmans, J. (2005a) *Testing for Subsidiarity*, Bruges, College of Europe, BEEP briefings 13, (www.coleurop.be/eco/publications.htm).

Pelkmans, J. (2005b) Subsidiarity between Law and Economics, Bruges, College of Europe, *Research Papers in Law*, (www.coleurop.be/template.-asp?pagename:lawpapers).

Pelkmans, J. (2006) *European Integration, Methods and Economic Analysis*, Pearson Education, wholly revised and restructured 3rd edition (pp. 447).

Pelkmans, J. (2007a) How Social is European Integration?, Bruges, College of Europe, *BEEP briefing 18*, October. (www.coleurop.be/eco/publications.htm)

Pelkmans, J. (2007b) Deepening Services Market Integration, A Critical Assessment, *Romanian Journal of European Affairs*, December, Vol. 6, 4.

Pelkmans, J. & Casey, J.P. (2004) Can Europe Deliver Growth?, *BEEP briefing* n° 6, January 2004; also as *CEPS Policy Briefing* 45, (in Italian) in Europa da Vicino, January.

Pelkmans, J. & Vanheukelen, M. (1988) The Internal Markets of North America, Fragmentation and Integration in the US and Canada, *Research on the 'Cost of Non-Europe', Basic Findings*, Vol. 16, Office for Official Publications of the EC, Luxembourg.

Pelkmans, J. & Vollebergh, A. (1986) The Traditional Approach to Technical Harmonisation: Accomplishments and Deficiencies, in Pelkmans J. & Vanheukelen M. (eds.) *Coming to Grips with the Internal Market*, Maastricht, EIPA, Working Document.

Pelkmans, J., Vos E. & di Mauro L. (2000) Reforming Product Regulation in the EU: a Painstaking, Iterative Two-level Game, in Galli, G. & Pelkmans, J. (eds.) *Regulatory Reform and Competitiveness in Europe*, Vol. 1, Cheltenham, E. Elgar.

Pisani-Ferry, J. & Sapir A. (2006) Last Exit to Lisbon, a Report to the EU Finance Ministers, abridged version as *Bruegel Policy Brief* 2, March.

Rehbinder, E. & Stewart, R. (1985) Environmental Policy Protection, in *Integration Through Law*, Vol. 2, New York/Berlin, de Gruyter, W.

Scitovsky, T. (1985) *Economic Theory and Western European Integration*, London, Allen and Unwin.

SER (2005) The Directive on Services in the Internal Market, The Hague, Socio-Economic Council, Report 2005/7, 2005.

Sharpf, F. (1999) *Governing in Europe. Effective and Democratic?*, Oxford, OUP.

Sykes, A. (1995) *Product Standards for Internationally Integrated Goods Markets*, Washington D.C., Brookings Institution.

Spaak, P.H. *et al.* (1956) Spaak Report, Report of the Heads of Delegation of the Foreign Ministries, in French, Brussels, mimeo.

Tinbergen, J. (1954) *International Economic Integration*, North-Holland, Amsterdam.

Vogel, D (1995) *Trading up: Consumer and Environmental Regulation in a Global Economy*, Cambridge, MA, Harvard Harvard University Press, Cambridge (US).

Wasmer, E. & von Weizsäcker, J. (2007) A Better Globalisation Fund, *Bruegel Policy Brief*, 2007/1 (www.bruegel.org).

CHAPTER 3

# Legal Concept and Meaning of the Internal Market

Dominik HANF

*Professor of European Law and Director of the European Interdisciplinary Studies Programme, College of Europe (Bruges and Natolin/Warsaw)*

## 1. Introduction

The establishment of a common market, the integration of the Member States' economies, was the Community's first economic and political objective.[1] Although conceived as a substitute for more far-reaching projects of a political union, it laid down an ambitious plan: to free the movement of products and production factors while securing fair competition across the Community.

The common market was to be implemented using a set of still unique supranational institutions and procedures to provide for more efficient decision-making and enforcement mechanisms than those available under more traditional forms of intergovernmental cooperation. The founding fathers of the Communities hoped that the process of economic integration would progressively lead to a form of a political union among the participating Member States.[2]

Today it is safe to state that the founding fathers' expectations have been partially met – but yet not fully achieved. This holds also true for the objective of establishing a common market – which, since the

1 Strictly speaking, the Common Market is a *means* to achieve the far-reaching objectives of the Community such as balanced economic growth (see Article 2 and 3 EC Treaty). Given the considerable economic and political implications of a project to establish a transnational Internal Market, this "means" is commonly considered as an *objective of its own* (or what economists would name an "instrumental objective").

2 It is still worthwhile to read the text of the Declaration made by Robert Schuman on 9 May 1950. The text is available on the European Union's Internet site at http://europa.eu/abc/symbols/9-may/decl_en.htm.

signing of the Single European Act (SEA) in 1986, is commonly labelled 'internal market'.[3] Whatever precise concept of the internal market one adopts, it arguably remains the European Union's main and most wide-ranging objective while forming its political, economic and legal backbone.

Although removing obstacles to trade had already served as a powerful tool for creating and enhancing the powers of a (federal) state,[4] in particular in the US,[5] the concepts of common or internal market had no commonly recognised specific legal meaning. One can thus inquire about the legal definition of the internal market (section 2). More fundamental is, however, its legal significance as the basic constitutional framework of the European Union (section 3) – in particular in its function of allocating powers to the Union (section 4). Finally the two main problems concerning the use of these powers are worth to be pointed out (section 5).

## 2. A legal definition of the internal market

As already noted, the concept of an 'internal market' has been introduced into the Founding Treaties of the European Union in 1986. It did not substitute but was added to the older 'common market' concept used in the original version of the Treaty of Rome. However, neither of these terms – nor the 'single market'[6] term used sometimes as well – is an established 'self-explanatory' legal notion. Its meaning can therefore only be derived from the substantive Treaty provisions.

---

3 On the possible differences which might exist between these denominations see infra in section 2.

4 For a critical assessment of this correlation see Paul Kapteyn, The Stateless Market. The European Dilemma of Integration and Civilization (Routledge, New York, 1996).

5 See the contribution of Michelle Egan to this volume.

6 Although being very much used in the political arena, most notably in the Communications of the Commission (see most recently "A Single Market for the 21st century Europe", 20.11.2007 COM(2007)725 final), the term "Single Market" has not a very prominent standing in legal texts. This stems probably from the fact that the Treaties do not use it – a rule that is confirmed by a very minor exception to be found in an annex of the Act of Accession 2005 (section I.A.1.a. of Annex VIII to Article 38 AA 2006 concerning measures for farmers experiencing the competitive pressure of the single market). The term "Single Market" is not used in the titles of secondary acts – except in the case of a non binding Council Resolution ("on making the Single Market work", OJ C 334/1-3). Within the legal texts produced by the institutions (leaving apart the market definition sections in competition cases), the term "Single Market" is used as synonym to "common" or "internal" market" in the context of state aids, taxation, or in relation to concrete goods or services.

As to the original common market, a definition could mainly be derived from three sets of Treaty provisions: first, those relating to the free movement of products and production factors – i.e. the 'four freedoms'[7] and the related articles enabling the Community to harmonise national laws;[8] second, those aiming at establishing a system of undistorted competition;[9] third, on the external side, the provision enabling the Community to establish a common commercial policy.[10]

This, read together with the 'principles' of the EC Treaty,[11] led the European Court of Justice[12] to consider that "trade between Member States [should] take place in the conditions [which are] as close as possible to those prevalent on a domestic market".[13] In a judgment issued in 1982 – before the elaboration and entry into force of the SEA – the Luxembourg judges stated: "The concept of a *common market* as defined by the Court in a consistent line of decisions involves the elimination of all obstacles to intra-Community trade in order to merge the national markets into a *single market* bringing about conditions as close as possible to those of a genuine *internal market.*"[14]

The three notions were thus understood as being synonymous – as describing the objective of the Community to replace the various national markets by one which should benefit "not only commerce as such but also private persons who happen to be conducting an economic transaction across national frontiers".[15]

This comprehensive 'global' concept was questioned when the Member States agreed on the SEA in 1986 – (as we know today) a quite successful attempt to revive the original common market project, which had stalled after initial successes. Beside substantive improvements, in

---

7 They can be found today in Articles 39 (workers), 43 (self-employed and companies), 49 (services), 56 (capital) EC Treaty.

8 These are to be found in many sector-specific articles and in particular two (since the SEA three) general clauses one finds today in Articles 94, 95 and 308 EC Treaty.

9 Articles 81 to 89 EC Treaty. According to a more traditional reading the general harmonisation powers of the Community mentioned in the previous note belong to this category, too.

10 Articles 133, 310 and 308 EC Treaty – see on this Roland Klages' contribution in this volume.

11 See the current Articles 2 and 3 (lit. a, b, c, g, h) EC.

12 The ECJ has a monopoly to interpret the provisions of the Treaty and of the secondary acts adopted by the institutions (see Article 220 and Articles 226 to 244 EC Treaty).

13 Case 159/78 Commission/Italy [1979] ECR 3247 at 7.

14 Case 15/81 Schul I [1982] ECR 140 at 33 (emphasis added).

15 ECJ, Case 15/81 [1982] Schul I ECR 140 at 33.

particular concerning decision-making,[16] it included a re-branding of the old concept under the label 'internal market'. As the new terminology could not be consistently replaced throughout the EC Treaty,[17] this political marketing exercise caused in fact some legal headaches.

The Treaty defines the 'internal market' as "an area without internal frontiers in which the free movement of goods, persons, services and capital is ensured".[18] In emphasising the removal of internal borders, this definition is somewhat broader than the older concept of a common market.[19] However, it is also considerably narrower than the common market as it does neither include its external aspects nor the system of undistorted competition. This difference raises some complex questions, in particular about the precise scope of the Community's general harmonisation powers,[20] which were a subject of a heated debate between legal scholars.[21]

Legal practice preferred to avoid such discussions.[22] This is understandable if one considers that the parallel use of different terms in the

---

16 On the SEA see e.g. Jean De Ruyt, L'acte unique européen (Presses de l'ULB, 1987).

17 It is not unusual that various 'generations' of Treaty provisions co-exist, which are not always easy to reconcile. Member States have been traditionally reluctant in proceeding to linguistic "updating" of Treaty texts. Since the latter would also be subject to the cumbersome Treaty amendment procedure (see Article 48 EU), entailing a considerable risk of failure and, hence, of "de-legitimising" decisions which were already approved. The French and Dutch refusal of the 'Constitutional Treaty' demonstrates that such fears are not unfounded.

18 Article 14.2 EC Treaty.

19 See on this point Claus Dieter Ehlermann, "The Internal Market Following the Single European Act", 24 [1987] *Common Market Law Review* 364.

20 If the Treaty concept of an 'internal market' were to be understood as being more limited in scope than the older concept of a 'Common Market', this could have an impact on the scope of Article 95 EC – the main innovation introduced by the SEA allowing the Community legislate without a need for unanimity within the Council. In such a reading, Community measures eliminating distortions of competition would have to be based on the old provision of Article 94 EC (requiring unanimity) while Article 95 EC would be restricted to measures aiming at realising or facilitating the 'four freedoms' as mentioned in Article 14 EC. See on this L. W. Gormley, 'Competition and Free Movement: Is the Internal Market the Same as the Common Market?', [2002] European Business Law Review 517.

21 Other questions related to the '1992' deadline mentioned in Article 14 EC and its implications. See for a fulminating assessment of that time – which was rebutted by subsequent interpretation and practice – see P. Pescatore, 'Some Critical Remarks on the Single European Act', 24 [1987] *Common Market Law Review* 9. In fact, the deadline was neither meant to institute a new transitional period nor to produce any legal effect (in contrast to Article 8 para. 7 of the original EEC Treaty).

22 See Case C-300/89 Commission/Council (titanium dioxide) [1991] ECR I-2867 and Case C-376/98 Germany/EP and Council (tobacco advertising) [2000] ECR I-8419.

Treaty was the result of two coinciding political considerations – to re-brand the common market project without taking the risk of a thorough linguistic revision of the Treaty. Furthermore the SEA aimed at confirming the original objective of European integration and at improving the Community's capacities to realise it. It made therefore sense not to abandon the 'global' approach outlined by the European Court of Justice and to treat the 'common', the 'internal' and the 'single' market as interchangeable concepts.

## 3. The legal significance of the internal market: an economic constitution?

What appears to be more important than the legal definition of the Internal Market is its legal significance within the particular institutional setting of the European Union. Although various amendments have considerably enlarged the list of Community tasks and activities, the provisions related to the establishment and functioning of an Internal Market – four freedoms, competition rules, harmonisation powers, external trade policy – are still figuring prominently in the EC Treaty. Since the SEA, a particular emphasis is laid on the removal of frontiers.

Some legal scholars, inspired by the German *Ordoliberalismus*, have vigorously advocated a reading of the EC Treaty as an economic constitution based on the principles of free market access and free competition.[23] In their view, the Treaty endorses only Community action contributing directly to the achievement of these principles through the removal of obstacles – excluding from its scope any further measure in policy fields such as consumer, social or environmental policy. This interpretation, which already squared hardly with the text of the original EEC Treaty,[24] cannot any more be seriously upheld in the light of the Treaty revisions enacted since 1986 which codified to a large extent the legislative activities undertaken by the Community in various policy fields.[25]

---

23 See A. Müller-Armack, "Die Wirtschaftsordnung des Gemeinsamen Marktes" (1964), in *idem*, Wirtschaftsordnung und Wirtschaftspolitik (Rombach, Freiburg 1966), 401 *et seq.*

24 The genesis of the EEC Treaty and many of its provisions dismiss the theory that establishing a Common Market is only about removing national obstacles to trade (de-regulation at national level) while excluding – or severely limiting – the possibility to enact (re-)regulation at Community level to address market failures. The real question was (and remains) how to identify market failures and how to remedy them.

25 As Ordoliberals had to admit not later than with the adoption of the Treaty of Maastricht, see E.-J. Mestmäcker, "On the Legitimacy of European Law" (1993), in *idem*, *Wirtschaft und Verfassung in der Europäischen Union. Beiträge zu Recht, Theorie und Politik der europäischen Integration* (Nomos, Baden-Baden 2003), 133

Although this approach proved to be too narrow, it had the merit of highlighting already in the early 1960s the particular legal character of the Treaty provisions on the Internal Market: they are the basic – i.e. constitutional – institutional and substantive rules governing cross-border economic activities.[26] They consist of two main sets of substantive provisions: on the one hand, the prohibitions directed to Member States and private undertakings to restrict the free movement or free competition; on the other hand, the rules enabling the Community to promote or to flank the use of these economic freedoms.[27] It is against this background that the ECJ had defined the common market as a (transnational) market operating under conditions similar to an internal – i.e. national – market.[28] As already observed, that ambitious understanding has been confirmed by the positive definition of the internal market inserted into the Treaty by the SEA.

These Treaty provisions forming the Community's economic constitution do not, however, command a 'simple' cross-border liberalisation[29]: the principles of economic freedom go along with exceptions[30] and the powers of the Union are not limited to removing national obsta-

---

*et seq*. For an account in the light of the more recent "constitutional debate" see C. Joerges, "What is left of the European Economic Constitution?" (EUI Working Paper Law 2004/13 available at http://www.iue.it/PUB/law04-13.pdf) with extensive references.

26 This explains why scholars have always been tempted to compare content and effect of these provisions with those of the US-American constitution, see for a more recent comparison G.G. Howells, "Federalism in USA and EC – The Scope for Harmonised Legislative Activity Compared", 5 (2002) *European Review of Private Law* 601 *et seq*.

27 As noted above, these powers include commercial policy. Particular rules (and, hence, markets) were established for agriculture (including fisheries) and transport.

28 See supra footnote 13. This definition endorsed by the ECJ raises of course the question how integrated national markets, in particular of large federal states, are (and have to be) in practice. See on this the contributions of Michelle Egan and François Vaillencourt in this volume.

29 For economists, it is a truism that (cross-border) liberalisation embodies the removal of existing barriers to trade and the establishment of regulation to tackle market failures. In the political, but also much of the legal discourse, the term 'liberalisation' is mostly used to describe the removal of *national* regulations embodying Member States' policy choices (de-regulation), while (re-)regulation characterises the setting up of new regulation at federal or *supranational* level.

30 Established by the Treaty itself or recognised by the ECJ as being 'reasonable'. See on this jurisprudential technique C.W.A. Timmermans, 'Rule of Reason, Rethinking another Classic of EC Legal Doctrine', in A Schrauwen (ed.), *Rule of Reason. Rethinking another Classic of EC Legal Doctrine* (Europa Law Publishing, Groningen 2005), vi. *et seq*.

cles to trade but entail also the possibility of setting its own rules in order to safeguard public interests.[31]

The legal perspective on the internal market focuses therefore on the way in which these broad constitutional rules – which do leave a considerable margin to determine speed, extent and regulatory density of deregulation at national level and re-regulation at Community level – are applied. In the particular institutional setting of the Union, the degree of re-regulation (positive integration) is determined by the political institutions of the Community (Commission, Council and Parliament), the degree of deregulation (negative integration) mainly by the ECJ acting in concert with market actors and/or the Commission. In constitutional terms, this perspective implies a careful analysis of the not always easy relationship between the Community judiciary, on the one hand, the (Community and national) legislator, on the other hand.

## 4. The function of the internal market in allocating regulatory powers to the Union

It is the field of the internal market that the Union has the most extensive powers to delimit national competences, be it by means of prohibitions or by setting its own rules. The internal market fulfils hence an important function: to allocate powers to the Union. Consequently, it attracts most of the inquiries relating to a possible overstretch of Community competences at the expense of those of the Member States.

Two sets of questions are normally analysed in this context. The first, are there limits to the Community powers to re-regulate the internal market and, if so, how should they be determined? Second, where are the limits of the ECJ's power to delimit national measures through the interpretation of the prohibitions established by the Treaty?

### *4.1. Regulatory powers of the Union*

An 'evergreen' in the legal debate is the question of the precise scope of the powers enabling the Community to enact legislation aiming at establishing or regulating the Internal Market. As long as harmonisation required unanimity and no co-decision, this has been a rather academic debate.[32] This changed since the SEA as it deprived increasingly the single Member States to veto legislative proposals.

---

31 Safeguarding such interest might also entail (in principle temporary) limitations on free movement, see e.g. Case C-233/94 Germany/Parliament and Council [1997] ECR I-2405.

32 See for an early assessment U. Everling, I.E. Schwartz, C. Tomuschat, Die Rechtsetzungsbefugnisse der EWG in Generalermächtigungen, insbesondere in Art. 235 EWGV, Europarecht 1976, 1 *et seq*.

A functional understanding of the internal market would indicate that the general provisions to legislate[33] could be used for adopting any measure related to any policy field as long as it effectively contributes to the establishment or a better functioning of that transnational market. This classical – and in my view appropriate – understanding of the Community's general harmonisation powers implies that they could be considered as 'unlimited' as long as they were used to improve the conditions for the free movement of products and production factors.[34] Following this line of reasoning, the Community could have adopted measures in the field of immigration prior to the inclusion of the policies related to the 'Area of Freedom, Security and Justice' by the Treaty of Amsterdam into the EC Treaty: most of them are in fact inextricably linked to the free movement of persons within the Internal Market.

This example illustrates, as do also the cases of social, environmental and consumer protection, that the Member States were not ready to accept such a functional conception. Instead of following the logic of the Internal Market, they have progressively added a range of specific provisions for many policy fields – often combined with a limitation of the scope of possible measures[35] – in order to limit the substantive scope of the general provisions.

This attempt to delimit the potential reach of Community competences was to a considerable extent successful because the Court of Justice accepts giving preference to these new specific provisions unless the harmonisation measure pursues *primarily* the objective of free trade.[36] This obligation imposed on the legislator to establish a 'centre of gravity' in order to use its internal market competences obviously reduces the scope of Union powers to re-regulate the market at a common level.

---

33 Articles 94, 95 and 308 EC Treaty (and Article 133 EC Treaty for the external field).

34 See René Barents, "The Internal Market Unlimited: Some Observations on the Legal Basis of Community Legislation", 30 [1993] *Common Market Law Review* 85.

35 Such limitations include the prescription of Directives to be transposed by the Member States at the expense of directly applicable regulations, the imposition of minimum harmonisation, and also the exclusion of the very possibility to adopt harmonisation measures.

36 According to the Court, specific powers are to be used for measures aiming primarily at realising (environmental, social etc.) policy objectives while those dealing primarily with freeing trade (and incidentally with specific policy issues) have to be based on the general powers. The difficulty to establish that distinction is mirrored by the considerable number legal basis disputes brought to the ECJ – without providing for much clarification beyond the case actually settled. On the use and abuse of the "legal bases disputes" see H. Cullen & A. Charlesworth, 'Diplomacy by other means: the use of legal basis litigation as a political strategy by the European Parliament and Member States', 36 (1999) *Common Market Law Review* 1243 *et seq.*

At the same time, pressure mounted to define more narrowly the potential scope of the general regulative power of the Community contained in Art. 95 EC, which served as the main tool for realising the 1992 programme and was thus quickly vilified as agent for the creeping expansion of Community competences.[37] Again, the Court sought to address these concerns: while confirming the general character of Art. 95 EC, the Court stressed that its use could only be justified for adopting measures improving *effectively* the functioning of the Internal Market.[38]

One logical consequence – which is however rarely drawn and likely to be rejected by most observers – of this interpretation is that Art. 95 EC empowers the Community to harmonise national rules which the Court has found to be restricting the free movement. As long as such measures address primarily and effectively these restrictions and improve substantively the free movement, they could, hence, also concern policy fields in which the Community has no explicit powers to act.[39]

### *4.2. Deregulatory powers of the Union*

This sub-section concentrates on the considerable deregulatory effects of decisions taken by the Court of Justice acting upon request of market operators or the Commission.

The important role played by the ECJ – 'activated' by market operators interested in striking down obstacles to cross-border activities (and 'cooperating' with the Commission and national courts)[40] – in develop-

---

37 It has become fashionable to quote and to argue on the basis of the Laeken Declaration of the European Council (2001, available at http://www.ena.lu/) which in fact raised the question of "how to ensure that a redefined division of competence does not lead to a creeping expansion of the competence of the Union" and of a possible revision of Articles 95 and 308 EC. Unfortunately, the subsequent works on Treaty revision – reflected in the Treaty of Lisbon signed in December 2007 – consider much less the equally important issue mentioned in the same paragraph of that Declaration: "How are we to ensure at the same time that the European dynamic does not come to a halt? In the future as well, the Union must continue to be able to react to fresh challenges and developments, and must be able to explore new policy areas."

38 See supra at footnote 222.

39 This consideration makes clear that both the scope of the four freedoms (see infra section 4.2.) and of the Community's harmonisation powers are closely interrelated and that a wide understanding of the former entails also a larger scope of application for the latter. Otherwise, one submits implicitly that the "negative" aspect of the Internal Market has a wider scope than its 'positive' (on this see e.g. G. Davies, "Can Selling Arrangements be Harmonised?" 30 (2005) *European Law Review* 370 *et seq.*). Please note that a similar – equally contested – reasoning applies also to the relationship between the internal and the external dimension of the Internal Market.

40 The Court recognised very early (Case 26/62 Van Gend en Loos [1963] ECR 1 on customs duties) the direct effect (and primacy) of the fundamental freedoms as laid

ing economic integration by invalidating protectionist national measures is today widely recognised.[41] Has the ECJ interpreted the four freedoms in a consistent way? This is an important practical question for market operators and national regulators but also in a broader political perspective: coherence and predictability of the case law is rightly seen as the necessary corollary to the considerable – and not fully democratically legitimised – power conferred to judges.

For historical reasons, the case law of the Court was shaped in the field of the free movement of goods, followed by the free movement of workers and self-employed. The free provision of services, the freedom of establishment for companies and the free movement of capital developed only quite recently. This, together with the different wording of the treaty provisions relating to the four freedoms, explain that market restrictions are dealt with differently according to the freedom concerned – involving sometimes, but not generally, a different substantive result.

The method used by the Court is – despite some variations over time and according to the fields concerned – quite consistent.[42] Any national measure affecting the four freedoms – be it openly or covertly, intended or accidentally[43] – has normally to be justified by overriding non-

---

down in the Treaty, except for the movement of capital which was made first made effective by the secondary legislator in 1988 before being "constitutionalised" with the Treaty of Maastricht (see on this Cases C-163, 165 and 250/94, Sanz de Lera [1995] ECR I-4830).

41 Although many lawyers tend perhaps to overstate – and non-lawyers sometimes to underestimate – the role of the judiciary in championing negative integration. See, however, F.W. Scharpf, "Negative and Positive Integration in the Political Economy of European Welfare States" in G. Marks *et al.* (eds.), *Governance in the European Union* (Sage, London 1996, 15 *et seq.*).

42 A good overview with extensive references to the case law is given by P. Oliver and W.-H. Roth, "The Internal Market and the Four Freedoms", 41 (2004) *Common Market Law Review* 407 *et seq.*

43 Restrictions to the free movement of persons (workers and self-employed) and companies, to the supply of services in all variants and to capital movements are tested and have to be justified. This is also true for the free movement of goods, despite a rather unfortunate attempt of the ECJ in the Keck judgment (C-267-8/91, [1993] ECR I-6097) to limit the tendency of market operators to challenge all sort of national economic regulation by recourse to Article 28 EC. Although this judgment has caused some confusion in the Court's subsequent case law (but see C-405/98 Gourmet, [2001] ECR I-1795) and in the debate among legal commentators, it deals only with the excesses of the ECJ's case law and confirms in fact the successful approach taken by the Court in this area following the Cassis de Dijon judgment (Case 120/78, [1979] ECR 649). This has neither been substantively affected by the fact that the Court reserves a particular interpretation to restrictions of product exports (Case 15/79 Groenveld, [1979] ECR 3409).

economic public policy reasons[44]. The justification test is, in principle, applied more strictly in cases involving national measures affecting market access than for rules concerning the way operators have to behave on a national market.[45] As possible exceptions are delimited narrowly, this entails far-reaching obligations for the Member States such as the recognition of other Member States' standards, qualifications or controls. This makes it very difficult for national authorities to justify regulations, including, in particular, sensitive fields,[46] which hamper, be it openly or only in fact, a cross-border economic operation. The Court has thus invalidated – or severely limited the substantive scope of application of – numerous national provisions in fields like company law, consumer protection, taxation, media law, social policy including healthcare, environmental policy or cultural and linguistic policy.

The field in which the ECJ has gone particularly far is the free movement of citizens. In assimilating the Treaty provisions to fundamental rights and reading them in conjunction with such rights, the judges managed to stretch considerably the scope of the free movement provisions. As a result, the rights originally granted to workers and self-employed allowing and facilitating to migrate and to integrate into the host Member State (rights to move, to reside, to stay and to receive equal treatment, the latter extending to taxation and social benefits), apply today potentially to all citizens of the Union – be they economically active or not. Although these developments were partly endorsed by the Community legislator and the Member States, the case law gives

---

44 They can either be recognised by the Treaty itself or, in a rather generous way, by the ECJ. The expansion of the reasons serves as corollary to the Court's expansive reading of the prohibitions and acknowledges the fact that the list of legitimate public policy considerations contained in the Treaty were formulated back in the 1950s.

45 If the latter can, however, also amount in fact to a restriction of market access – a question which the ECJ considers on the basis of an economic analysis (not just of the formal rules). See e.g. Case C-442/02, CaixaBank France [2004] ECR I-8961.

46 This becomes clear from the recent case law dealing with the two 'latecomers' of the four freedoms, the establishment of companies and the movement of capital. In line with earlier case law developed in the field of goods, workers and self-employed, the ECJ has dealt with various 'hot' issues. It has e.g. allowed companies to use these freedoms as an instrument to choose a particular national corporate governance regime (C-212/97 Centros, [1999] ECR I-1459), to challenge special rights by which Member States try to retain control over formally public owned companies in 'strategic' sectors ('golden shares', see e.g. Case C-367/98, Commission/Portugal [2002] ECR I-4731), to write off (within certain limits) losses made by subsidies in other Member States (C-446/03 Marks & Spencer [2005] ECR I-10837) and imposes also limitations on the application of national taxation rules designed to prevent companies to establish branches in low-tax Member States (Case C-196/04, Cadbury Schweppes [2005] ECR, I-11779).

regular preference to the interest of individuals at the expense of Member State interests to avoid different forms of 'welfare tourism'. In this field, one detects therefore not only the judges' sympathy with the individual citizens concerned but also a firm will to go beyond a 'mere' economic integration.[47]

It is also possible to find cases, in which the Court shows respect for national sensitivities and departs from its tendency to invalidate national measures imposing or simply leading to a higher burden on cross-border operators. One striking example was until recently the gaming industry,[48] other include national restrictions which are rooted in fundamental values or human rights considerations.[49] Also in the question of labour standards the Court has traditionally been more cautious and always upheld that the host Member State is entitled to apply its domestic labour regulation (minimum wages, working time etc.) to posted workers.[50] More recently, the Court has however begun to check more closely to which extent such measures are effectively justified.[51]

In the light of the rather impressive list of policy fields affected by the case law one could conclude that negative integration championed by the ECJ contributes greatly to a limitation of Member State regulatory powers and, hence, to the infamous phenomenon of 'competence-creeping'. This conclusion is not always correct, as the necessary adjustments at national level remain often limited. However, when the removal of national requirements enhances regulatory competition (as currently in the field of company law or in some service sectors), it sometimes facilitates harmonisation at Community level.

---

47 This refers in particular the case law related to job-seekers (Case C-292/89) Antonissen [1991] ECR I-745), students and other economically inactive citizens (see Case C-184/99, Grzelczyk [2001] ECR I-6192, C-209/03 Bidar [2005] ECR I-2119, C-456/02 Trojani [2004] ECR I-7573). – The temptation to grant citizens the benefits of Community law appears also to motivate in the Court's case law on the right to extend the national social security coverage to healthcare services received abroad (see e.g. Case C-157/99 Smits and Peerbooms [2001] ECR I-5473). The ECJ itself admits incidentally that this extension might be problematic: it allows Member States to invoke the financial stability of their social security systems – an economic justification which is otherwise never admitted. For an overview see K. Lenaerts and T. Heremans, "Contours of a European Social Union in the Case-Law of the European Court of Justice", 2 (2006) *European Constitutional Law Review* 101 *et seq*.

48 See the line of cases starting with C-275/92 Schindler, ECR [1994] I-1039, but see now the judgment of 6 March 2007 C-338/04, Placanica [2007] nyr in the ECR.

49 Case C-36/02 Omega [2004] ECR I-9609.

50 Case C-113/89, Rush Portuguesa [1990] ECR I-1417.

51 Cases C-49/98, C-50/98, C-52/98 to C-54/98 and C-68/98 to C-71/98, Finalarte, [2001]. ECR I-7831 and most recently in Case C-341/05 Laval (judgment of 18 December 2007, nyr in the ECR).

## 5. Conclusion

As could be observed, the internal market is not only an important political and economic objective of the European Union but also constitutes a fundamental legal concept. It embraces most of the substantive powers of the Union, serves as its economic constitution and fulfils therefore also the function of allocating powers to the Community.

Two main intertwined problems can be observed: the predominance of judge-driven negative integration and the still considerable difficulties of the Community to effectively make use of its regulatory powers.

For a constitutional lawyer it is not uncommon to observe an active role of those judges whose task is to interpret the 'supreme law of the land'.[52] It is also true that the judges do not normally 'produce' their cases but are confronted with questions posed by other institutions and – in particular – by individuals. Finally, it is correct that judges can feel obliged to reply on the basis of the constitutional rules at hand – and be they incomplete – in cases in which the political decision-making institutions failed to produce comprehensive rules to implement the principles of economic freedom.[53] At some point, one might nevertheless wonder whether that failure of the legislator is sufficient a reason to legitimise an extensive use of power by non-elected judges – in particular when decisions, entailing complex assessments of conflicting interests, imply the removal of a national measure which might not be easily compensated by positive integration measures. Some of the citizenship-cases, but also decisions in the field of health-care and direct taxation, illustrate this problem.[54]

---

52 For a comparison between Europe and the US, it is still worth to consult M. Capelletti, M. Secombe and J. Weiler (eds.), *Integration Through Law. Europe and the American Federal Experience* (de Gruyter, Berlin/New York 1986-1988).

53 This refers to famous formula of "La carence du législateur communautaire et le devoir du juge" used by the former Judge Pescatore to justify the ECJ's 'activism' (in G. Lüke *et al.* (eds.), *Rechtsvergleichung, Europarecht und Staatenintegration. Gedächtnisschrift für Léontin-Jean Constantinesco* (Heymann, Köln 1983), 559 *et seq.*).

54 Granting non-discriminatory access to higher education (see Case 293/83 Gravier [1985] ECR 593, following Case 152/82 Forcheri [1983] ECR 2323) can have a serious impact on – and in fact threaten the model of – a public-funded educational system in a member state, while the Community has no recognised competences to remedy such imbalances by setting its own rules. This problem explains the concerns of smaller countries or regions such as Austria and Wallonia sharing their border – and language – with far bigger neighbors (see Cases C-47/93, Commission v Belgium [1994] ECR I-1593 and C-133/05, Commission v Austria.[2006] I-36). – Similar problems could arise in the field of public health-care or, due to the difficulty to make use of existing regulatory powers requiring unanimous decision-making in the Council, of taxation.

Less fundamental considerations point to the limits of judge-driven negative integration, too. It entails in fact three major disadvantages: first, even the most extensive reading of the prohibitions cannot eliminate national provisions hampering free movement but being justified by overriding public interests; second, as judgments apply to one case and tackle isolated problems, it is difficult to apply them generally;[55] third, even when a multitude of judgments merge finally into a coherent legal framework, it acquires only slowly, if ever, an effect which could be compared to a codified 'positive' piece of legislation.[56]

This explains that important developments of the case law – such as the judge-made principle of mutual recognition[57] – might only have a quite limited immediate effect for the market operators. Most of them benefited only indirectly – since it helped the Commission to 'convince' the Member States to agree on harmonisation measures. Another example will probably be offered by the recent 'service-directive': although doing little more than codifying the Court's case law, its practical effect might perhaps be greater than a decade of law-'making' by judicial means.[58] In other words, a rather modest harmonisation measure is more likely to entail positive (at least medium term) effects on market integration than many landmark decisions of the ECJ.

This implies that the internal market should ideally be realised by the political institutions – Commission, Council and Parliament. These appear, however, to be less prepared to take up its responsibilities than one could expect. In the name of subsidiarity and flexibility, and based on a timid reading of the Treaty provisions governing its decision-making powers in the field of the Internal Market, they tend to produce

---

55 The Commission tries to tackle this problem by publishing 'interpretative communications'.

56 Another disadvantage is that the ECJ still admits, at least in principle, the idea of 'reverse discrimination': unless not excluded by a harmonisation measure or banned by national law, Member States can apply internally measures which would not be admissible in cross-border situations. Although formally respecting the division of powers established by the Treaty, this does not fit easily into a fuller concept of the Internal Market. The Court provides thus often an answer for the – 'hypothetical' – case that a cross-border element might appear at closer inspection of the facts by the national judge (see e.g. Case C-448/98 Guimont, [2000] ECR I-10663). This has the useful "side-effect" that the latter will, in practice, tend to apply that solution also to the purely internal situation because 'reverse discrimination' is in many cases not compatible with the equality principle established in domestic (constitutional) law.

57 See on the many faces of this principle the contributions recently published in 14 (2007) 5 *European Public Policy* 667 *et seq*. Including the interesting closing remarks made by M. Poiares Maduro, "So close and yet so far: the paradoxes of mutual recognition" at 814 *et seq*.

58 See Vassilis Hatzopoulos' contribution to this volume.

predominantly soft measures, minimum and optional harmonisation,[59] or useful but not very ambitious codifications of case law. Although producing comprehensive sets of regulation at supranational level is certainly a considerable challenge in many respects, it seems that such half-hearted 'measures' are suspicious from a legal point of view: they are unlikely to produce comprehensive legal frameworks for economic operators – and likely to produce just a new push towards judge-driven integration.[60]

59 A striking example in this respect is the approach to defensive measures adopted by the Takeover Bids Directive 2004/25/EC (OJ 2004 L 142/12).

60 For a contrasting view see S. Weatherill, Why Harmonise?, in T. Tridimas and P. Nebbia (eds.), *European Union Law for the Twenty-First Century. Rethinking the New Legal Order* (Volume 2: Internal Market and Free Movement Community Policies, Hart, Oxford 2004) 11 *et seq*.

CHAPTER 4

# The Internal Market Seen from a Political Science Perspective

Susanne K. SCHMIDT[1]

*Professor of Political Science at the University of Bremen*

## 1. Introduction

European integration research has become an important subfield of political science. The relaunching of the internal or single market, previously known as common market, in the late 1980s must certainly be seen as one or even the major incident for the European Union. From its success followed the introduction of the Euro, the Northern enlargement of the mid-1990s, and it was a basis to shoulder the ongoing challenge of Eastern enlargement. Likewise, it is probably fair to say that cooperation in the second and third pillar, in the Common Foreign and Security Policy as well as in Justice and Home Affairs, could not have happed in the same way, had there not been the successful first pillar with the internal market. Moreover, the success of the internal market has had implications beyond Europe in fostering other regional trade areas, none of which has gotten yet to such a depth and importance.

Yet, the internal market has been at once in the focus and out of focus of political science research on Europe, this article argues. It has been in the focus, because being a cornerstone of European integration it is important in almost all its political science research. Thus, it has figured prominently in theoretical discussions as well as in empirical research, as different regulatory policies, monetary union, or the enlargement rounds were broadly researched. Recently, new modes of governance receive much attention, mainly in the form of the open

[1] I would like to thank the editors of the volume and the participants of the internal market workshop in Bruges, in particular Jacques Pelkmans, Elise Muir and Michele Chang.

method of coordination, which is used for instance in employment policy and also pensions. Again, the reference to the internal market is clear, given the imbalance between the unified monetary policy and the lack of macroeconomic coordination such as for wages. Because of this centrality, the present article can only give an approximate account of political-science research into the internal market.

Thus, the internal market, being the cornerstone of the integration process, rightly presents itself as the anchor of much political-science research. And yet, *it does not*. Because if we take the four freedoms of the Treaty, being in the centre of the internal market, there has been little political-science interest in them, which is also true for mutual recognition as a central mechanism on which the internal market builds. In the context of much political-science research, the internal market is thus taken to refer to a specific period – before Maastricht, to a specific kind of policies – regulatory, or to the first pillar of the EU's structure. However, the single market does not so much refer to a policy field, even if, by granting the four freedoms (goods, services, capital and persons), it has a great impact on what happens in the European Union, including other specific policy fields. Michelle Everson makes a similar argument in the context of the debate on the EU's democratic deficit.

> Somewhat paradoxically, the growing emphasis upon the need for effective 'political' direction or governance within Europe may thus be argued to have distracted attention from what is, at one and the same time, the root cause of Europe's putative 'democracy deficit' and the primary arena of continuing European integration: i.e. the Internal Market (Everson, 2002: 155).

The article presents the political-science perspective on the internal market as follows. It starts with the way the internal market has been reflected in the theoretical discussion on European integration. It then takes three steps, looking at the institutional dynamics, the working of the internal market, and at its consequences. A major political-science insight into the institutional dynamics of the internal market is the possible friction between negative and positive integration. In the European Union, it is easier to liberalise than to re-regulate markets. The text then turns to new modes of governance which have been increasingly discussed during the last years, given the shortcomings of traditional legislation to cope with governance challenges. As will be seen, the workings of the internal market have not received much attention. Regarding the consequences of the internal market, the Europeanisation literature focuses at the Member state level. Despite the broad influence of the distinction between positive and negative integration, there is a positive-integration bias in Europeanisation research due to its focus on the compliance of Member States with European secondary law. Thus, the 'negative' side of integration, the impact of the Treaty and its market freedoms on the Member States has been relatively ignored. So far as a 'neoliberal' bias in the internal market has been discussed, it was again rather with view to legislative initiatives, like the take-over or the services directives, which were then regarded as a triumph of liberal, Anglo-Saxon capitalism. Again, the focus has been more on legislation, on positive integration, than on courts, and negative integration (such as the rulings on the freedom of establishment). Also the discussion on the legitimacy deficit of the European Union hardly focuses on the Court, but rather on the question of whether such a deficit exists, and how the Parliament can ameliorate it. The article closes with an assessment of where the main future challenge lies.

## 2. The internal market as a focus of theory: whose primacy?

In political science, European integration is traditionally studied by the sub-discipline of 'international relations'. That is important to know because it is relevant for the kind of questions being asked. International relations are a subfield being particularly theory-driven, and these theories focus on the relevance of sovereignty interests of governments vis-à-vis the impact of international institutions. From this perspective, European integration has been analysed predominantly with a view to the question whether governments remain fully in control of the integration process, as the strand of intergovernmentalism holds, or whether supranational institutions such as the Commission or the Court imply that governments partially loose control over the way integration proceeds, as the strands of neofunctionalism and supranationalism respectively argue.

For this central theoretical dispute structuring much political-science research on European integration, the internal market has been instrumental. In a widely cited article Sandholtz and Zysman argued that the Commission under President Delors with the support of the European Round Table of Industrialists had been decisive for the internal market programme to come off (Sandholtz and Zysman, 1989). As a political entrepreneur, the Commission managed to convince the Member States' governments of the advantages of completing the internal market with the 1992 programme, given the international economic conditions of competition with the USA and Japan. Sandholtz and Zysman thus stressed the importance of the *supranational* actor Commission. *Neo-functionalism* would go beyond this supranationalist explanation in emphasising the functional interdependence between different policy fields, leading to a 'spill over' into other areas. Similar to the approach of Sandholtz and Zysman, neofunctionalism sees that European and national elites are responsible for pushing forward this process.

A few years after Sandholtz and Zysman, Moravcsik gave an equally convincing account of the Single European Act being the result of the interests of the largest Member States, notably France, Germany and the UK, thereby refuting the importance of the Commission (Moravcsik, 1991). The question of the extent of government control over the integration process, which lies at the heart of this debate, has been relevant for much political-science research on European integration following the debate between Sandholtz/Zysman and Moravcsik (Schmidt, 1996). At the same time, the conflicting analyses of Sandholtz/Zysman and Moravcsik are better reconcilable than they seem at first sight, since they focus on the 1992 programme and the Single European Act respectively; that governments were more at the forefront in the latter and the Commission and large enterprises in the former therefore does not need to be contradictory.

The deep institutionalisation of the EU with the internal market and the transition to qualified-majority voting as well as the increasing role of the EP has reduced the importance of international-relations analyses to European integration research. No longer does it seem as relevant to argue about the extent of sovereignty transfer as it is to understand how the political system of the European Union functions, and how its institutions play out to influence policy-making. This has raised the importance of comparative politics, as another part of political science, in the analysis of the European Union (Hix, 1994; 2005).

Rather than debating either-or-distinctions characterising the EU, institutional analyses can show under which conditions governments loose control over the integration process and supranational actors acquire the ability to independently influence the course of integration (Pollack, 1997). It is from this interest in the institutional dynamics of European integration that a major finding on the characteristics of the internal market stems, the distinction between positive and negative integration.

## 3. The institutional dynamics of integrating the internal market

As a political system, the European Union has particular strengths and weaknesses. As a result, some decisions are more easily taken than others. This is captured by the distinction between positive and negative integration that is central for understanding the development of the internal market. Related to this distinction is the discussion on new modes of governance, needed to supplement the governance of the internal market in those cases where the classic Community method, consisting of the legislative process between the Commission, the Council, and the European Parliament, does not suffice.

### *3.1. Positive and negative integration*

When building the internal market, national differences have to be overcome. In order to achieve this, two options exist – differences can be simply abolished, which is negative integration, or they can be overcome by joint action, which is positive integration. The distinction between positive and negative integration is important because the two ways of creating a market have very different preconditions (Scharpf, 1999). Positive decisions in the Council and Parliament, for instance regarding the regulation of markets, face high agreement costs of qualified majority or unanimous voting in the Council, along with varying degrees of involving the European Parliament. Measures of negative integration, in contrast, are supported by the market freedoms and competition law laid down in the Treaty. They can be realised by the Commission and the Court, given the direct effect and supremacy of EC law, and, in their pure sense, do not require further decisions of the Council or Parliament. Negative integration, moreover, is not restricted to facilitating cross-border exchange but may threaten domestic institutions:

> But, as was true of dental care abroad, retail price maintenance for books, public transport, or publicly owned banks, the only thing that stands between the Scandinavian welfare state and the market is not a vote in the Council of Ministers or in the European Parliament, but merely the initiation of infringement proceedings by the Commission or legal action by potential private competitors before a national court that is then referred to the European Court of Justice for a preliminary opinion. In other words, it may happen any day. Once the issue reaches the ECJ, the outcome is at best uncertain (Scharpf, 2002: 657).

When discussing positive and negative integration, it is important to keep in mind that this distinction is ambiguous because of its double reference. Primarily, it refers to the thrust of policies (whether they are market-shaping or market-making). In addition, it also refers to their institutional background, either in the legislative process or in the decisions and case law of the Commission and the ECJ. Secondary law, doubtlessly, may include market-shaping and -making. Actions of the Commission and the ECJ may similarly realise both. However, primary law is much stronger on market-making (that is, liberalising markets) than on market-shaping (that is, regulated markets), due to the far-reaching provisions on market freedoms (of goods, services, capital and persons) and competition law, which are not matched by 'positive' rights of the same importance.

Although the distinction between positive and negative integration has been well recognised almost everywhere, it is striking that political-science research focused disproportionately on the legislative process and positive decision-making, rather than on the impact of negative integration. Following the observation of Scharpf of a joint-decision trap inhibiting Council decision-making (Scharpf, 1988), many researchers set out to show that there are in fact many European laws offering a high level of protection (Eichener, 1993; Héritier, 1999). This can be explained by several aspects of the EU's political system: the sector-specific Councils which make it easier to agree for instance on environmental policies since only environmental ministers are involved; the duty of the Commission to propose policies exhibiting a high level of protection; and the veto possibilities of the European Parliament, to name but a few important explanations (Kohler/Koch, Conzelmann and Knodt, 2004: 164-166).

To argue that there is a bias of attention towards Council decision making is not to say that the impact of the ECJ has been forgotten – the ECJ is well-researched in political science, but as an actor and an extraordinary international court, not so much as a relevant policy-maker (Alter, 2001; Conant, 2002). Possibly an exception are the analyses of general (economic) interest services (Héritier and Soriano, 2003), as the liberalisation processes of the utilities are well-researched and the remaining scope of national policies is directly dependent on the Court. But in general, articles such as by Martinsen on the impact of the market freedoms on the health policies of Denmark and Germany (Martinsen, 2005) are few – compared to the very many analyses of different directives or regulations covering social policy, environment, and the like. We will get back to this point.

### *3.2. New modes of governance*

With the deepening of integration, due to the internal market, and encountering the problem of agreeing on the further communitisation of related policy fields (such as employment policy), the so called new modes of governance (NMG) have become an important topic of research. As the integration of additional policy fields into the normal legislative process of the EU seems neither feasible nor desirable, attention shifted to alternative modes of how to secure coordination. While it is primarily hoped to achieve social coordination, in addition, NMG are also seen as an answer to the increased legitimacy crisis facing the Union.

New modes of governance are those that allow for the provision of governance functions in an innovative, but not yet established, way. Authors who attempt to positively characterise NMG generally emphasise that these new modes achieve governance functions more voluntarily, drawing in a wide range of relevant actors. In so doing, the legitimacy and effectiveness of political decisions is thought to be enhanced (Héritier, 2003: 106). Topics studied in the context of the debate on NMG include the Open Method of Coordination (OMC), comitology, and independent regulatory authorities.

'New' seems to relate as much to the context in which a particular mode of governance is brought to bear as to the mode itself and its true novelty, because some forms of NMG in the EU are well-established elsewhere, like the independent regulatory authorities in the USA. Rather than attempting a positive definition of NMG aiming to delineate its features, several authors therefore prefer a negative definition, defining NMG in the EU as all forms of governance deviating from the classic Community method (i.e. the adoption of directives and regulations by the Council and the Parliament based on proposals from the Commission) (Eberlein and Kerwer, 2004: 122; Scott and Trubek, 2002: 1, 5). This definition makes it possible to take into account all 'new' forms in the EU context, without limiting the analysis because of previous alternative definitions (e.g. no legal measure or the necessary inclusion of private actors).

Again, there is a curious absence of the internal market in the discussion of new modes of governance. As Joerges and Godt argue: "The most important of Europe's institutional innovations is hardly mentioned any longer in the debates on the so-called 'new modes of governance'" (Joerges and Godt, 2005: 95). They here refer to mutual recognition, that was 'invented' by the Court in the Cassis judgement and subsequently instrumentalised by the Commission to build up the internal market.

With mutual recognition, markets can be integrated by simply recognising each other's regulations, rather than attempting to formulate a common position to regulation through harmonisation. Compared to harmonisation, negotiation costs and implementation costs of new regulation can be evaded. At the same time, markets can be entered, without having to adapt to the regulation of the importing state, as is the case with national treatment (i.e. non-discrimination). Mutual recognition thus seems to square the circle, and as such it is of significant appeal, shown for instance by its more recent use in the context of justice and home affairs (Schmidt, 2007). Nevertheless, there has not been much attention to it,[2] especially when compared to the well-researched Open Method of Coordination. This is despite the fact that most probably many political scientists would agree that OMC has had less impact on integration than mutual recognition. But the latter has only raised some interests at the beginning, when fears were still dominant on an expected race to the bottom (Sun and Pelkmans 1995). When matters evolved in a less clear-cut fashion, since mutual recognition is normally coupled with minimum harmonisation for instance, interest waned, and, as a result, there are hardly any empirical studies on how it functions. How do national administrations cooperate in the internal market to enable mutual recognition? How is it decided, whether to mutually recognise products regulated according to the product specifications of different Member States or whether to seek an exemption from the general interest? What are the preconditions for making mutual recognition a successful form of governance? Trust is normally mentioned, but how does it build up, and who needs to trust whom for the internal market to be built on this principle? To all these are questions we largely lack the answers.

## 4. A closer look at the internal market

For the 1992 programme the judgment of the ECJ in the case Cassis-de-Dijon 'inventing' mutual recognition was crucial.[3] That this case turned out to be important for the internal market programme attracted the interest of political scientists who analysed the way the Commission assumed leadership over the internal market project and the extent to which ideas – as opposed to interests – can be seen to matter in the launch of the internal market (Alter and Meunier-Aitsahalia, 1994; Garrett and Weingast, 1993). Following the 1992 programme, including the new approach to technical standards and minimum harmonisation, some political scientists have analysed its – rather complicated – workings, where minimum harmonisation sets down essential requirements which are then filled in by standards bodies (Egan, 2001).

However, interest in the four freedoms and the way they manage to achieve integration has been low or absent from political science. In 2005, Fabio Franchino published a review of the themes of articles in three leading political science journals on European Integration (*Jour-*

2 I have recently edited a special issue of the Journal of European Public Policy on the topic of 'mutual recognition as a new mode of governance' (August 2007, Vol. 14 (5), assembling different papers on the topic, and redressing the neglect to some extent.

3 Interestingly, as Genschel shows, the Commission had already spoken about mutual recognition in the 1960s (Genschel, 2007).

*nal of Common Market Studies; Journal of European Public Policy*, and *European Union Politics*), from 1994 onwards.[4] While he counted 34 articles on environmental policies, he found six on the movement of persons, four on the movement of services, three on mutual recognition, two on movement of goods, and one on movement of capital in all these years.

> There are some worrying signs that we are spending too much time and resources on some clearly secondary policies and ignoring core ones. Some undeniably important areas, such as agriculture, competition, and free movement, deserve at least as much attention as does social policy (Franchino, 2005: 246).

Thus, there is not much to be reported on the core of the internal market, the free movement provisions, from a political-science perspective. Political science, it appears, is often too preoccupied with the most recent developments and fashions. It is to be hoped that this will change after the attention and contention raised by the services directive.

A look in the recent Handbook of European Union Politics, which summarises the state of the art, and its article on the internal market confirms this view (Young, 2007). Political science research on the single market has predominantly consisted of research interested in the analysis of regulatory policy making, with a heavy emphasis on the legislative process. There has been much more interest in the positive integration of markets, in re-regulation in environment, social policy, or food safety, and the like, than on market-making. However, as Young also shows in a table summarising (some) research on the single market, there is one major exception: the liberalisation of the utilities or network sectors, which were previously largely monopolised or at least heavily regulated, has attracted significant attention (Young, 2007: 380).

Of these sectors, telecommunications is probably the one having been analysed the most, justified by the significant liberalisation moves agreed at the European level. Air transport, road haulage, and electricity are not covered as much, but probably there has been sufficient attention. Postal services in contrast, in line with the relative slowness of the liberalisation process, as well as railways, have been less present in research. All these instances of market-making are also ones where the legislative process in the European Union was important and this has been analysed predominantly. These sectors were not liberalised by somehow subsuming them under the free movement but with regard to the initiative of the Commission, submitting legislative proposals to the Council and Parliament. However, as I have also attempted to show in

4 European Union Politics only started to appear in 2000.

previous work (Schmidt, 1998; 2000), the instruments that the Commission finds in competition law have been highly relevant for the successful European integration of these sectors.

## 5. Consequences of the internal market

What are the consequences of the internal market for the Member States? Three major ones will be dealt with. In political science the implications of European integration are being discussed under the heading of Europeanisation. This literature is discussed first, turning then more specifically to claims about the internal market as a neoliberal project. The last consequence to be discussed is the legitimacy crisis of the European Union.

### *5.1. Europeanisation*

The relative neglect of central characteristics of the internal market can also be observed if we look at some newer strands of political-science research related to the internal market, namely the research on Europeanisation. There are several definitions of Europeanisation. While early definitions included the perspective of European integration, that is "the creation of authoritative European rules" (Risse, Green, Cowles and Caporaso, 2001: 3), in the meantime, a consensus emerged to restrict Europeanisation to "the impact that European policies in particular and European integration in general have on national polities, politics and policies" (Töller, 2004: 1; also Eising, 2003; Kohler-Koch, 2000). Thus, after analysing the working of the European political system in terms of the structure of its polity, the character of its politics, and the nature of its output (the policies), political scientists have taken a step back and started to look at the multi-level system as a whole, including the national level. Europeanisation research thus asks, "What difference does it make" and looks at the impact of European integration at the national level. Again, it is striking that researchers often equate the consequences of membership with the implementation of secondary law (Töller, 2004a: 2). Thus, Europeanisation research has brought up a literature on Member States' compliance with EU secondary law (Börzel, 2001; Falkner *et al.*, 2004) but tended to neglect other kinds of impacts which are related to the general obligations of being a Member state, namely through the primary law of the Treaty.

What would be an example of such Europeanisation effects, moving beyond positive integration? Currently, Germany faces a heated political debate on the introduction of a minimum wage, which most Member States already have. This debate can be related directly to the internal market. Under the services freedom, self-employed persons and companies can take up temporary work throughout the Union, notwithstanding the exemption period agreed for the free movement of labour after the Eastern enlargement. But workers have to be paid at or more than the national minimum wage, if there is one, also under the free movement of services. For wages, the European Court of Justice diverted from the common principle of home-country regulation in favour of host-country regulation when interpreting the services freedom in the judgement Rush Portuguesa (C-113/89). But since Germany does not have a minimum wage but collective wage agreements, which the ECJ does not treat as a functional equivalent, East Europeans can work in Germany for only a couple of Euros an hour. Thus, after Eastern enlargement, Germany was surprised to find its labour market under pressure, given that it had negotiated an exemption from the freedom of movement. Ever since this annoying realisation, minimum wages have been debated in Germany, though they imply a considerable institutional rupture, given that a neutral role of the state in wage politics is deeply enshrined. This hesitant stance towards minimum wages is fostered by the competitive advantage the missing minimum wage is giving German companies. Thus, for instance, Danish slaughterhouses re-located to Northern Germany in order to profit from cheap East European labour (Schmidt, Blauberger and Van den Nouland, 2007).

This is just one example of how negative integration impacts on Member States; many more could be found (Töller, 2004). Yet, Europeanisation research pays little attention to these effects. Maybe this is due to the fact that they are less easily monitored from above. While directives need to be implemented and whether this happens can then be followed tracking down the laws transposing different directives in the Member States, the impact of negative integration makes itself felt at the national level, and the relationship of national reforms to European processes is often held to be opaque. Politically, it is difficult to attribute domestic reforms to European integration as politicians fear to undermine the 'permissive consensus' of European integration (Schäfer, 2006).

### *5.2. The internal market as a neoliberal project*

Negative integration is a liberal principle. It would indeed be surprising to argue that political scientists do not recognise the neoliberal character of the integration process, which favours liberalisation processes rather than a further involvement of the state. They do, as the discussion on positive and negative integration already showed. Building on it, one strand of the debate on the internal market is closely linked to the varieties of capitalism literature (Hall and Soskice, 2001). Thus, Höpner and Schäfer (2007) argue that the way the internal market has been pushed forward in the last years, including the takeover directive, the services directive and the judgements of the ECJ on the right of establishment is forcing Rhenish capitalism to adapt to the liberal Anglo-Saxon variant. By undermining the constitutional basis of economic orders, European integration impacts now on the fundamental societal consensus of Member States. Again, there is much more emphasis on analysing the legislative process than on following the development of the Court's reasoning.

That the internal market is becoming more controversial could be observed recently with the contention surrounding the directive on port services, but most of all the horizontal services directive. In January 2004, the Commission first published the latter proposal. It aimed at a horizontal approach to realising the services market, spanning almost all services sectors, after the attempts with sector-specific directives, for instance for financial services, had proven cumbersome and lengthy, and met with limited success. Thus, this one directive was to liberalise about half of all economic activity of the Member States. The directive, aiming at better realising the freedom of services and of establishment, followed largely the principle of home-country control, seeking to minimise the possibilities of Member States to enforce host-country rules. Accordingly, the reactions to the draft directive were vivid. The Bolkestein directive, as it became known after the (at the time) responsible Commissioner for the internal market, was the first example of an internal market directive arousing significant political debate – albeit in a mostly negative and critical sense. In the course of the discussion, the EU constitutional Treaty was voted down in the Netherlands and France, owing much to the neo-liberal impression of European integration, the services directive was offering (Howarth, 2007: 94). As Commissioner Frits Bolkestein said when presenting his proposal: "Some of the national restrictions are archaic, overly burdensome and break EU law. Those have simply got to go. A much longer list of differing national rules needs sweeping regulatory reform".[5]

After ample debate, a revised services directive was adopted in late 2006. The legislative process of the services directive was instructive in several ways (Nicolaïdis and Schmidt, 2007). While European integration before could often proceed as a rather 'neutral' process, beyond the left-right dimension characterising domestic politics (Genschel, 1998), the services directive showed that these times are gone. Depending on the way markets are regulated, distributive issues are raised, and the

5 Services: Commission proposes directive to cut red tape that stifles Europe's competitiveness. Reference: Press release IP/04/37, 13.01/2004 of the European Commission.

way these are decided needs legitimation. Next to emphasising the increased need for legitimating the internal market project – no longer just seen as a question of Pareto-efficiency, legitimating itself through the surplus being generated (Majone, 1998) – the conflict on the services directive showed something else: the existing split between old Western and new Eastern Member States. With different levels of economic development among the Member States, distributional issues are bound to be evaluated differently. Due to their lower wage-levels, the new Member States could profit from services liberalisation. Even though a compromise was found, the services directive clearly showed that the Union is now faced with a much more difficult situation for decision-making.

### *5.3. Legitimacy*

Legitimacy issues of European integration came to the fore alongside the internal market. As long as *de facto* unanimity voting in the Council had assured each Member state a veto right on all decisions, the legitimacy of European integration could be assured via the national level. As governments are accountable to their parliament, the delegation of competences to the European level could be legitimised. But as the Single European Act furthered qualified-majority voting, in particular to be able to realise the internal market, the legitimacy of European integration had to be bolstered at the European level as such. Following the consultation procedure introduced with the SEA, the European Parliament has entered a road of unparalleled institutional success, increasingly acquiring veto rights over the different policy fields, turning the EU into a bicameral system (Farrell and Héritier, 2003).

Yet, parlamentarisation of the EU as an answer to the perceived legitimacy deficit is contentious. As solidarity among the peoples of the different Member States is low, given that there is no European Demos, the EU lacks the necessary basis for majority decisions (Kielmansegg, 1996). European elections are normally second-order national elections, limiting the legitimacy that can be generated this way. Recently, Føllesdal and Hix have argued that a politicisation of European decisions is desirable, which could strengthen the democratic process from below, contributing to a political European-wide debate (Føllesdal and Hix, 2006). Bartolini, against this, has warned that politicisation could not easily be contained but would put the Union as a whole at risk, given among other things very weak European party structures (Bartolini, 2006). The way the discussion of the services directive led to the failure of the Constitutional Treaty in France shows that such a fear is well-founded. How the Union can assure its legitimacy is therefore difficult territory, which explains why the emergence of new modes of governance has been welcomed also from this angle. New modes of governance promise innovative avenues of legitimation given that the established route of parlamentarisation shows such limits in the context of the EU.

Another strand of the discussion of legitimacy is even more closely related to the internal market. In important contributions to the debate, Majone (Majone, 1998) and Moravcsik (Moravcsik, 2002) have argued that the whole debate on the democratic deficit rests on false premises. Given that European policy-making is predominantly regulatory, and not redistributive, the need for input-legitimation is low.[6] Regulatory policy-making is Pareto-efficient, i.e. it improves the general welfare without lessening the individual welfare of anyone. As everyone profits from Pareto-efficient regulatory policy-making, it is legitimated by its output. In addition, much regulatory policy-making is also delegated to independent regulators at the national level – monetary policy and cartel control being prime examples. This has the rationale that the benefits of regulatory policies often can only be achieved if it is removed precisely from direct political input, i.e. if it relies solely on output-legitimation and not on input-legitimation. The policy fields, which require input-legitimation, on the other hand, are still the domain of the Member States, namely all welfare policies and taxes.

While this argument has much intellectual force, the discussion so far has already pointed to its limits. Regulatory policy-making in the EU simply cannot be seen as being restricted to cases of Pareto-optimality. Rather, regulatory decisions, such as the services directive, have significant re-distributive consequences. As European integration reaches deeper and deeper into the institutional economic set-up of the Member States, affecting the national tax base (Genschel, 2002) as well as capitalist and welfare institutions, output legitimation is insufficient.

Again, also in the discussion of the legitimation of European integration, there has been a relative bias in favour of policy-making by the Council and the European Parliament. The question in how far the case law of the ECJ is legitimated, given its pivotal role in the internal market, exemplified most clearly by the Cassis-de-Dijon judgement, is rarely asked. This is amazing since very early in the academic discussion of the European integration process, Weiler pointed to the 'dual character' of the political system, where, in times of Council indecision and weakness, the Court was delivering major rulings (Weiler, 1981; 1991). Case law is often an alternative to legislative decisions in the

---

6 The distinction between input-legitimation (government by the people) and output-legitimation (government for the people) has been forwarded by Scharpf (1999: Chapter 1).

Council and Parliament. While individual decisions of the Court may be debated as to their implications, in political science there has not been a broader discussion on the problems arising from strong supranational courts, whose judgements can hardly be overturned in the legislative process, given the unanimity or qualified majority requirements necessary for changing the underlying secondary law or the Treaty. Instead, the Court has been seen more prominently as a means to lessen the legitimatory deficit, in granting individual rights (Conant, 2002; Kelemen, 2006).

## 6. Conclusion

Political scientists look at politics. Thus, the comparative disregard for the ECJ as against the focus on the legislative process leading to directives or regulations agreed by the European Parliament and the Council, is understandable. After much enthusiasm also for 'softer' modes of governance, attention could however shift again, given the upcoming challenges. What is going to happen? Beyond the realm of 'high' politics in the 2nd and 3rd pillar, in a Union of (at least) 27 and a regulatory state at that, the reform of existing regulatory policies is likely to pose a significant challenge. With the increased heterogeneity of Member States' interests, compromises are all but easy. At the same time, Member States cannot switch back to national policy-making once a Community regulatory policy is in place so that the status quo will be a serous constraint, given that regulatory policies outdate quickly. A large *acquis communautaire* in need of relatively constant reform and a group of Member States not being able to agree, is a significant future challenge. In this situation, either flexible agreements of a subset of Member States are a solution, or the Court may step in. As Weiler argued, times of political disagreement are a time of a powerful court (Weiler, 1981). And Tsebelis and Garrett have given an explanation for this argument based on the problems that principals face, when they want to rein in an agent, if they themselves have conflicting interests what it should do (Tsebelis and Garrett, 2001).

A strengthened Court can deliver rulings where Member States are not able to agree. But with Member States being divided over integration as they are, the Court is likely to be seen as lacking the legitimation for these decisions. This will in particular be true, given the depth that integration has reached, when principles of the internal market challenge Member States' welfare states and economic systems. How the deeply institutionalised internal market, having been shaped by 12 to 15 Member States, will function in a heterogeneous EU of 27+, and as such being perceived as a legitimate political order, is one of the great challenges.

## References

Alter, K. J. (2001) *Establishing the Supremacy of European Law – The Making of an International Rule of Law in Europe*, Oxford, Oxford University Press.

Alter, K. J. & Meunier-Aitsahalia, S. (1994) Judicial Politics in the European Community. European Integration and the Pathbreaking Cassis de Dijon Decision, *Comparative Political Studies* 26, pp. 535-561.

Bartolini, S. (2006) Mass Politics in Brussels: How Benign Could It Be?, *Zeitschrift für Staats- und Europawissenschaften* 4, pp. 28-56.

Börzel, T. A. (2001) Non-compliance in the European Union: Pathology or Statistical Artefact?, *Journal of European Public Policy* 8, pp. 803-824.

Conant, L. (2002) *Justice Contained. Law and Politics in the European Union*, Ithaka/London, Cornell University Press.

Eberlein, B. & Dieter Kerwer, 2004: New Governance in the European Union, *Journal of Common Market Studies* 42, pp. 121-142.

Egan, M. P. (2001) *Constructing a European Market. Standards, Regulation, and Governance*, Oxford, Oxford University Press.

Eichener, V. (1993) Entscheidungsprozesse bei der Harmonisierung der Technik in der Europäischen Gemeinschaft: Soziales Dumping oder innovativer Arbeitsschutz?, in Süß, W. & Becher, G. (eds.) *Politik und Technologieentwicklung in Europa: Analysen ökonomisch-technischer und politischer Vermittlung im Prozeß der Europäischen Integration*, Berlin, Duncker & Humblot, pp. 207-236.

Eising, R. (2003) Europäisierung und Integration. Konzepte in der EU-Forschung, in Jachtenfuchs, M. & Kohler-Koch, B. (eds.) *Europäische Integration*, Opladen, Leske und Budrich, 2nd edition, pp. 387-416.

Everson, M. (2002) Adjudicating the Market, *European Law Journal* 8, pp. 152-171.

Falkner, G. *et al.* (2004) Non-Compliance with EU Directives in the Member States: Opposition through the Backdoor?, *West European Politics* 27, pp. 452-473.

Farrell, H. & Héritier, A. (2003) Formal and Informal Institutions Under Codecision: Continuous Constitution-Building in Europe. *Governance: An International Journal of Policy and Administration* 16, pp. 577-600.

Føllesdal, A. & Hix, S. (2006) Why there is a Democratic Deficit in the EU: A Response to Majone and Moravcsik, *Journal of Common Market Studies* 40, pp. 603-624.

Franchino, F. (2005) The Study of EU Public Policy: Results of a Survey, *European Union Politics* 6, pp. 243-252.

Garrett, G. & Weingast, B.R. (1993) Ideas, Interests, and Institutions: Constructing the European Community's Internal Market, in Goldstein J. & Keohane O. R. (eds.) *Ideas and Foreign Policy. Beliefs, Institutions and Political Change*, Ithaca, NY, Cornell University Press, pp. 173-206.

Genschel, P. (1998) Markt und Staat in Europa, *Politische Vierteljahresschrift* 39, pp. 55-79.

Genschel, P. (2002) *Steuerwettbewerb und Steuerharmonisierung in der Europäischen Union*, Frankfurt/Main, Campus.

Genschel, P. (2007) Why no mutual recognition of VAT? Regulation, taxation and the integration of the EU's internal market for goods, *Journal of European Public Policy* 14, pp. 743-761.

Hall, P. A. & Soskice, D. (eds.) (2001) *Varieties of Capitalism. The Institutional Foundations of Comparative Advantage*, Oxford, Oxford University Press.

Héritier, A. (1999) *Policy-Making and Diversity in Europe*, Cambridge, Cambridge University Press.

Héritier, A. (2003) New Modes of Governance in Europe: Increasing Political Capacity and Policy Effectiveness?, in Börzel, T.A. & Cichowski, R.A. (eds.) *The State of the European Union*, New York, Oxford University Press, pp. 105-126.

Héritier, A. & Moral Soriano, L. (2003) Politics and Adjudication: Problem Definition and Conflict Solution in European Electricity Policy, in Engel, C. & Héritier, A. (eds.) *Linking Politics and Law*, Baden-Baden, Nomos, pp. 151-167.

Hix, S. (1994) The Study of the European Community: The Challenge to Comparative Politics, *West European Politics* 17, pp. 1-30.

Hix, S. (2005) *The Political System of the European Union*, 2nd edition, New York, NY, St. Martin's Press.

Höpner, M. & Schäfer, A. (2007) A New Phase of European Integration: Organized Capitalisms in Post-Ricardian Europe, *MPIfG Discussion Paper* 07/4, Cologne, Max-Planck-Institute for the Study of Societies.

Howarth, D. (2007) Internal Policies: Reinforcing the New Lisbon Message of Competitiveness and Innovation, *Journal of Common Market Studies* 45, pp. 89-106.

Joerges, C. & Godt, C. (2005) Free trade: the Erosion of National, and the Birth of Transnational Governance, *European Review* 13, pp. 93-117.

Kelemen, R. D. (2006) Suing for Europe. Adversarial Legalism and European Governance, *Comparative Political Studies* 39, pp. 101-127.

Kielmansegg, P. (1996) Integration und Demokratie, in Jachtenfuchs, M. & Kohler-Koch, B. (eds.) *Europäische Integration*, Opladen, Leske und Budrich, pp. 47-72.

Kohler-Koch, B. (2000) Europäisierung: Plädoyer für eine Horizonterweiterung, in Knodt M. & Kohler-Koch, B. (eds.) *Deutschland zwischen Europäisierung und Selbstbehauptung*. Frankfurt/Main, Campus, pp. 11-31.

Kohler-Koch, B., Conzelmann, T. & Knodt, M. (2004) Europäische Integration – Europäisches Regieren, in Kohler-Koch, B., Conzelmann, T. & Knodt, M. (eds.) *Grundwissen Politik*, Wiesbaden, VS Verlag für Sozialwissenschaften.

Majone, G. (1998) Europe's 'Democratic Deficit': The Question of Standards, *European Law Journal* 4, pp. 5-28.

Martinsen, D. (2005) The Europeanization of Welfare – The Domestic Impact of Intra-European Social Security, in *Journal of Market Studies* 43, pp. 1027-1054.

Moravcsik, A. (1991) Negotiating the Single European Act: National Interests and Conventional Statecraft in the European Community, *International Organization* 45, pp. 19-56.

Moravcsik, A. (2002) In Defence of the 'Democratic Deficit': Reassessing Legitimacy in the European Union, *Journal of Common Market Studies* 40, pp. 603-624.

Nicolaïdis, K. & Schmidt, S.K. (2007) Mutual recognition 'on Trial': the Long Road to Services Liberalization, *Journal of European Public Policy* 14, pp. 717-734.

Pollack, M. A. (1997) Delegation, Agency, and Agenda Setting in the European Community, *International Organization* 51, pp. 99-134.

Risse, T., Green-Cowles, M. & Caporaso, A. (2001) Europeanization and Domestic Change: Introduction, in Green-Cowles, M., Caporaso, A. & Risse T. (eds.) *Transforming Europe*, London, Cornell University Press, pp. 1-20.

Sandholtz, W. & Zysman, J. (1989) 1992: Recasting the European Bargain, *World Politics* 42, pp. 95-128.

Schäfer, A. (2006) Nach dem permissiven Konsens. Das Demokratiedefizit der Europäischen Union, *Leviathan* 34, pp. 350-376.

Scharpf, F. W. (1988) The Joint-Decision Trap: Lessons from German Federalism and European Integration, *Public Administratio*n 66, pp. 239-278.

Scharpf, F. W. (1999) *Governing in Europe: Effective and Democratic?* Oxford, Oxford University Press.

Scharpf, F. W. (2002) The European Social Model: Coping with the Challenges of Diversity, *Journal of Common Market Studies* 40, pp. 645-670.

Schmidt, S. K. (1996) Sterile Debates and Dubious Generalisations: European Integration Theory Tested by Telecommunications and Electricity, *Journal of Public Policy* 16, pp. 233-271.

Schmidt, S. K. (1998) Commission Activism: Subsuming Telecommunications and Electricity under European Competition Law, *Journal of European Public Policy* 5, pp. 169-184.

Schmidt, S. K. (2000) Only an Agenda Setter? The European Commission's Power over the Council of Ministers, *European Union Politics* 1, pp. 37-61.

Schmidt, S. K. (2007) Mutual Recognition as a New Mode of Governance, *Journal of European Public Policy* 14, pp. 667-681.

Schmidt, S. K., Blauberger, M. & Van den Nouland, W. (2007) Jenseits von Implementierung und Compliance – Die Europäisierung der Mitgliedstaaten, in Tömmel, I. (ed.): Die Europäische Union: Governance und Policy-Making, *Politische Vierteljahresschrift, Sonderheft*, pp. 275-296.

Scott, J. & Trubek, M.D (2002) Mind the Gap: Law and New Approaches to Governance in the European Union, *European Law Journal* 8, pp. 1-18.

Sun, J.M. & Pelkmans, J. (1995) Regulatory Competition in the Single Market, *Journal of Common Market Studies* 33, pp. 67-89.

Töller, A. E. (2004) The Europeanization of Public Politics – Understanding Idiosyncratic Mechanisms and Contingent Results, *European Integration online Papers* 8.

Tsebelis, G. & Garrett, G. (2001) The Institutional Foundations of Intergovernementalism and Supranationalism in the European Union, *International Organization* 55, pp. 357-390.

Weiler, J. H. H. (1981) The Community System: The Dual Character of Supranationalism, *Yearbook of European Law* 1, pp. 267-306.

Weiler, Joseph H. H., 1991: The Transformation of Europe, *The Yale Law Journal* 100, pp. 2402-2483.

Young, A. R. (2007) The Politics of Regulation and the Internal Market, in Jørgensen, K.E., Pollack, M.A. & Rosamond, B. (eds.) *Handbook of European Union Politics*, London, Sage Publications, pp. 373-394.

# PART II

# ESTABLISHING THE INTERNAL MARKET FOR SERVICES

CHAPTER 5

# Economic Aspects of the Internal Market for Services

Arjan LEJOUR

*CPB Netherlands Bureau for Economic Policy Analysis*

## 1. Introduction

Since January 2007, 27 countries form the European Union (EU), covering most of Europe. This constitutes a market of about 500 million consumers, if national markets are integrated at least. For goods the 500 million consumer market seems to be reality, but for services it is still utopia at least seen from an economic perspective.[1] 27 Member States have implemented their own systems of regulating services; such as market entry, competition, quality and sometimes even prices. For some services, the degree of regulation isolates these markets from the internal market. In these services sectors cross-border trade and foreign direct investment are hardly possible. These are extremes, most notably the case for network services. For most sectors national regulatory systems do not isolate markets, but fragment them in 27 different markets per services sector.

If there is an internal market for services it resembles patchwork and Europeans have to work hard to sew them together. The EC Treaty aims at the free movement of services, but this statement still expresses more ambition than realism. The basic idea of this paper is to underpin the metaphor of the patchwork, and to discuss (recent) developments in integrating services markets. Although the European market for services is patchwork, the quilts are much more uniform than for the global market for services. In that respect Europe's efforts to integrate national services markets can be applauded as an experiment from which others

1 See the contribution of Pelkmans (2007) on the progress of the internal market for goods, capital and labour.

could learn such as the WTO with regard to the General Agreement on Trade in Services (GATS) and the EU and US with respect to a transatlantic services market.

The fragmentation of European services industries is no status quo. Cross-border trade and foreign direct investment in services are increasing. Section 2 presents the recent trends. Some of the underlying causes for the increased interwovenness of services markets is deregulation of services industries and increased competition in many European countries. Section 3 presents the recent patterns on product market regulation in services using OECD indicators. These patterns clearly reflect deregulation policies.

Although less regulation promotes competition and even foreign competition, differences in country-specific regulation also hamper trade in services. Section 4 motivates the importance of reducing these differences in regulation. Section 5 describes some of the recent initiatives by the European Commission to integrate national services markets. The focus is on the services directive, but also some other initiatives for financial services, retail distribution and energy markets are discussed briefly. Section 6 considers the prospects of further integrating national services markets in order to make the quilts more uniform.

## 2. Trends in services trade

Only a small fraction of services products, like standard software packages, can be stored and shipped in boxes like traditional merchandise exports. In most other cases – think of holiday or hairdressers – it is difficult to separate production and consumption of the service in time and space. As a consequence, either the producer or the consumer must go abroad for an international transaction takes place. The producer can set up a production unit abroad or can be represented by an employee sent abroad on a temporary basis. While exporting and production abroad are optional supply forms for manufacturing firms, in some services industries the only feasible way to supply a foreign market is establishing a local subsidiary (Sampson and Snape, 1985). The GATS Treaty therefore identifies four modes of international services supply, as shown in Figure 5.1. The figure shows that international services deliveries through commercial presence abroad is the dominant supply form (57 per cent). This differs per services sector. Kirkegaard (2007) argues that foreign commercial presence is 8 to 9 times as important as cross-border trade in computer and IT related services for the US. Also in financial services foreign commercial presence as much more important than cross-border trade.

**Figure 5.1. Shares of types of international transactions in world services trade**

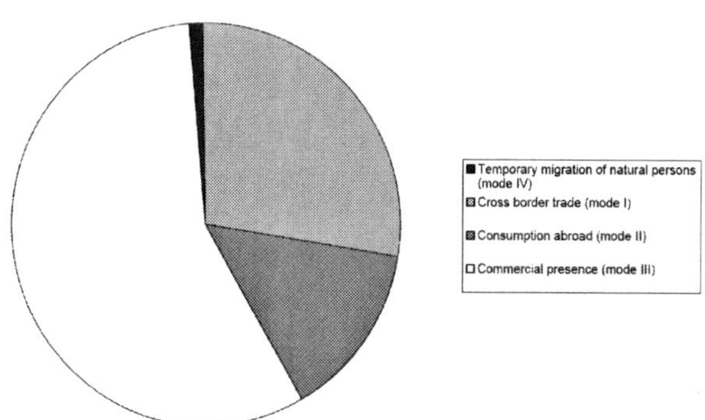


## *2.1. Cross-border trade (and consumption abroad)*

In the period 1985 to 2001, EU cross-border trade in goods and services has increased on average by about 8.4 per cent per year. In 1985, the EU-15 countries exported services for about 173 billion US dollar which was a quarter of EU goods exports. In 2001 the value of services trade has increased to 633 billion dollar, but still this was only 28 per cent of EU goods exports. Traditionally the services sectors transport and travel are responsible for the largest share in international services trade. In 2004, both sub-sectors accounted for half of total EU-25 exports in services. This held despite the fact that exports in transport grew less than for total services exports in the EU,[2] as is shown in Table 5.1. External EU-25 services exports were about 450 billion $ in 2004.

In recent decades, trade in business services has rocketed. Its annual growth has been 15 per cent since 1985.[3] Exports also surged for computer and information services, royalties, other business services, financial services, insurance, and communication services (OECD 2003a). The main subcategories with other business services are merchanting services, legal, accountancy and management services, Architect and engineering services, R&D and intra-firm services. Trade in government services and personal services are relatively unimportant.

---

2 This was in particular due to the modest growth in 'other transport' (mainly road transport).

3 Note that this growth rate is biased by a net increase in trade of about 80 per cent in 1992 due to a change in the statistical classification system. Without this break in the data, the growth rates would be about 5 percentage points lower.

**Table 5.1: EU exports in services, 2004**

| | Value in billion US dollar | % share in total exports | % of intra-EU exports to world exports | % value growth intra-EU exports 1985-2001 |
|---|---|---|---|---|
| Total services | 1064.0 | 100.0 | 57.7 | 10.5 |
| Transport | 230.1 | 21.6 | 50.2 | 8.2 |
| – Sea transport | 101.6 | 9.6 | 39.6 | 10.3 |
| – Air transport | 77.9 | 7.3 | 48.9 | 13.8 |
| – Other transport | 50.6 | 4.8 | 73.5 | 3.5 |
| Travel | 276.2 | 26.0 | 69.8 | 11.1 |
| Communicat. services | 25.2 | 2.4 | 69.1 | 14.8 |
| Construction | 22.4 | 2.1 | 47.3 | 11.2 |
| Insurance | 35.7 | 3.4 | 56.0 | 15.3 |
| Financial intermediation | 71.3 | 6.7 | 55.7 | 16.9 |
| Computer & info | 56.4 | 5.3 | 61.2 | NA |
| Royalties & licence fees | 41.9 | 4.0 | 42.5 | 14.6 |
| Other business services | 258.8 | 24.3 | 54.2 | 15.2 |
| Personal services | 13.5 | 1.3 | 54.1 | 10.8 |
| Government services | 21.7 | 2.0 | 48.4 | 6.4 |

Source: OECD, 2006 and own calculations.

Of all EU-25 services exports, on average 58 per cent is destined for the other EU countries. For travel, communication services, computer and information services and other transport is it higher. It is low for sectors as construction, air transport, sea transport, government services, and royalties and licence fees.[4] A large part of government services relates to receipts from foreign governments and international organisations amongst others for renting military equipment or buying second-hand equipment.

## *2.2. Trade orientedness*

To what extent are EU services sectors oriented towards foreign trade? In some services sectors cross-border trade is more important than in others. The differences in their openness to cross-border trade can be due to the nature of the service or to regulatory barriers.

For a trade-orientedness indicator we use the value of exports by a services sector divided by value added in that sector.[5] This trade-orientedness indicator shows the 'tradability' of services products in specific sectors. Table 5.2 presents the results. In business services, the

---

4 Royalties and license fees is not really a sub-sector; it consists of transactions related to patents, and copyrights.

5 Note that this indicator only indicates the degree of internationalisation with respect to exports. In principle the home market could be closed for imports, although this situation is hardly realistic. If home markets are closed for foreign competition, firms are often not very competitive which restrains their export possibilities.

picture is mixed. The Netherlands, the UK and to a smaller extent Spain have a strong trade orientation in this sector, whereas markets in France, Germany and Italy appear to be rather inward-oriented.

**Table 5.2: Trade orientedness for various EU countries, 2001**

| | France | Germany | Italy | Netherl | Spain | UK |
|---|---|---|---|---|---|---|
| Transport and communication | 20.4 | 17.7 | 9.2 | 70.8 | 13.1 | 20.2 |
| Financial intermedia-tion and insurance | 3.2 | 7.8 | 2.2 | 4.0 | 6.4 | 52.6 |
| Other business services | 5.8 | 5.3 | 7.4 | 20.8 | 10.7 | 15.8 |
| Personal services | 3.1 | 0.4 | 1.3 | 4.1 | 2.4 | 3.4 |
| Government services | 0.5 | 3.7 | 0.9 | 3.2 | 1.0 | 5.2 |
| Total services | 5.3 | 6.1 | 5.2 | 13.1 | 7.5 | 7.7 |
| Total goods | 21.8 | 27.5 | 21.2 | 48.3 | 22.1 | 21.0 |

Source: OECD, 2003a, 2003b and own calculations. Trade orientedness is defined as value of exports divided by value added times 100. Data in the last two rows are from Eurostat, 2006a and reflect the average of exports and imports divided by GDP.

Table 5.2 also shows that exports in transport and communication are relatively high in all EU countries. Only in the UK openness in finance is higher than in transport and communication. That reflects the special position of the UK as financial centre. Its trade orientedness is higher than the financial services sectors in other EU countries. However except for transport services, the tradability of goods is much higher than for commercial services.

## *2.3. The role of FDI in services*

Services trade only reflects the internationalisation of cross-border trade and consumers crossing the border (modes I and II) according to the balance of payment data. It misses the degree of internationalisation by foreign establishments in services markets (mode III). Data on sales of foreign establishments in services are rather scarce and incomplete. An indicator for foreign presence in a country is the foreign capital stock. Figure 5.2 presents the average annual growth of the FDI stocks in the EU-15 between 1995 and 2003 for various economic sectors.[6]

[6] For transport the data are between 1995 and 2002.

**Figure 5.2. FDI stocks in EU-15: average annual growth between 1995 and 2003**

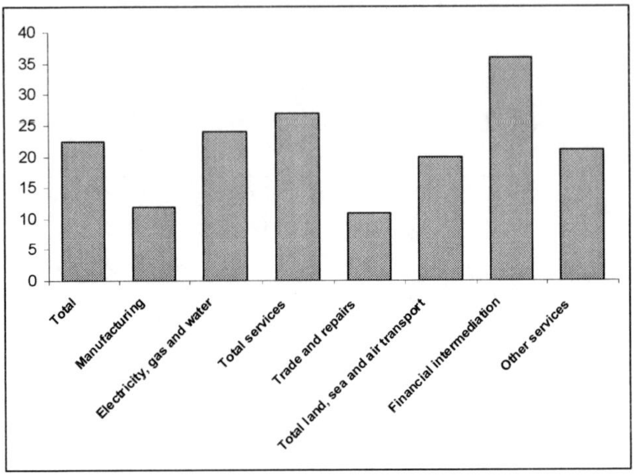

Source: Eurostat, 2006b.

The figure shows that the FDI stock in services grows much faster than in manufacturing, in particular due to growth in financial intermediation. FDI grows also faster in sectors as transport, other services (mainly other business services) and network industries like electricity, gas and water than in manufacturing.

About two thirds of the FDI stocks in the EU is directed to services sectors (UNCTAD, 2006).[7] Given the differences in FDI growth rates, the contribution of services will increase. UNCTAD (2004) mentions the rising share of services in value added, the externalisation of services of independent providers, the growing services intensity in the production of goods, the deregulation of services markets and the liberalisation of FDI policies as underlying reasons for increased FDI in services sectors. Moreover, greater competitive forces in services markets have led to market-seeking behaviour abroad. Section 3 focuses on one of these arguments: the role of deregulation in services markets.

---

7 The relatively small difference in FDI stock growth rates between total services and total already reflects the importance of FDI in services in the total economy. The growth rate in manufacturing is much lower. It has a sizable but no large impact on the total growth rate, reflecting the shrinking importance of manufacturing.

**Table 5.3: FDI inflow intensity: sectoral share in total service-FDI inflows divided by the sector's share in total domestic services production, selected countries, 1998-2000[a)]**

| | Germany | France | UK | Spain[c)] | Netherlands | USA[b)] |
|---|---|---|---|---|---|---|
| Retail & wholesale trade | 0.1 | -0.4[e)] | 0.5 | 0.3 | 0.5 | 1.3 |
| Other business services | 1.9 | 1.5 | 0.4 | 1.9 | 0.2[d)] | 0.4 |
| Travel | 0.0 | 0.1 | 0.2 | 0.1 | 0.2 | 1.0 |
| Communication | 1.2 | 0.8 | 6.4 | 4.3 | 3.0 | -1.3 |
| Transport services | 0.0 | 0.2 | 0.0 | 0.1 | 0.1 | 0.6 |
| Financial intermediation | 1.1 | 4.5 | 2.6 | 0.7 | 7.9 | 4.1 |
| Insurance (incl. auxiliary services) | -0.1 | 0.5 | 1.0 | 0.0 | 1.2 | 3.0 |
| Unweighted average | 0.6 | 1.0 | 1.6 | 1.1 | 1.9 | 1.3 |

a) Services sector shares in total domestic services production are for the year 1999, except for Germany (1998).

b) USA FDI inflow data refer to 1998.

c) For Spain, production data for real estate and business services, and for tourism and other services refer to 1998, while data on communication, financial intermediation, and insurance refer to 1997.

d) This does not count the FDI inflows in financial holding companies.

e) The negative value reflects a net FDI outflow (disinvestment).

Data source: Kox *et al.*, 2004.

The activities by foreign services multinationals tend to be spread quite unevenly over domestic services industries in the EU. Kox *et al.* (2004) illustrate this using the concept of 'FDI inflow intensities', i.e. the share of a particular sector in total services FDI inflows to the sector's share in domestic services production. This indicator would be one if a services sector attracts a share of FDI inflows that corresponds with its share in domestic production.

Table 5.3 indicates that services sectors like retail and wholesale trade, tourism and transport account for much less FDI inflows than corresponds with their share in domestic services production. In the UK, the Netherlands and Spain, 'other business services' attracts a relatively low share of direct investment compared to the sector's size; the opposite holds for France and Germany. Communication gets relatively strong attention from foreign investors, which may well be due to deregulation that took place in the late 1990s, combined with the auctions for mobile phone licenses. Except in the Netherlands, financial intermediation attracts relatively much FDI.

## 3. Regulation of services markets

Regulation is important in services markets. One reason is the need to provide universal services in energy and telecom sectors and to regulate the role of monopolies. A second reason consists of the asymmetries in information and the necessity to ensure quality for users. Quite often these regulations hamper competition because they deter market entry of domestic and foreign firms, restrict the behaviour of firms and sometimes regulate prices. Faini *et al.* (2005) stress the need for more reform to increase competition and consequently productivity and innovation. However, most European countries have liberalised many services sectors since the 1980s, albeit at a different speed. This section presents some recent trends in regulating services markets.

### 3.1. Regulatory reform in energy, transport and communication

Conway and Nicoletti (2006) have recently updated regulatory indices for many services markets.[8] Telecom and energy cover some of the industries in which anti-competitive regulation has traditionally been relatively strong in OECD countries, because these sectors were long (and partly still are) characterised by natural monopoly segments and network externalities. Moreover, firms have typically been burdened with non-economic objectives (such as universal services obligations).

**Figure 5.3. Regulatory reform in energy, transport and communications (1975-2003), breakdown by regulatory area**

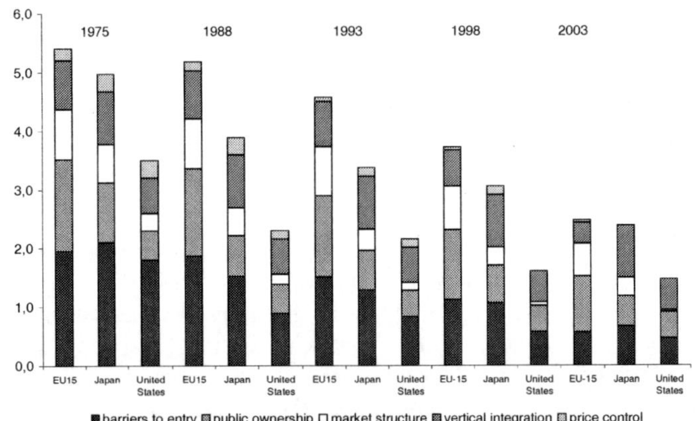


Source: Conway and Nicoletti, 2006. Simple averages of the regulatory indicators for seven industries: electricity, gas, road freight, railways, air transport, post and telecommunications. Europe is defined as EU-15.

---

8 Although the quality of the OECD indicators is very high, these type of indicators are by definition imperfect, in particular if these are used to indicate their impact on the economy. Moreover, also enforcement of regulation is important for the impact on competition. This is not measured by these indicators.

Legal restrictions to entry, widespread public ownership, and extensive cross-subsidies are common in these markets. Over time, technological advances, the evolution of governance and regulatory techniques, as well as increasing international exposure have made liberalisation and privatisation increasingly possible. According to these indicators, product market policies have become more market friendly recent decades as is shown by Figure 5.3.

The indicators suggest that regulation in these sectors was restrictive in all OECD countries in the 1970s, though more so in Europe and Japan. Since 1975, regulation has changed in most of the regulatory areas covered by the indicator, but were most pronounced in reducing entry barriers and, to a lesser extent, public ownership.

Price controls have been eliminated almost completely. However, market and industry structures remain largely unchanged. Eurostat data (structural indicators) on telecommunication prices show a substantial downward trend. For some EU Member States prices are even halved. This could be due to more competitive market forces, made possible by less restrictive regulation.

**Figure 5.4. The timing of reforms in energy, transport and communication**

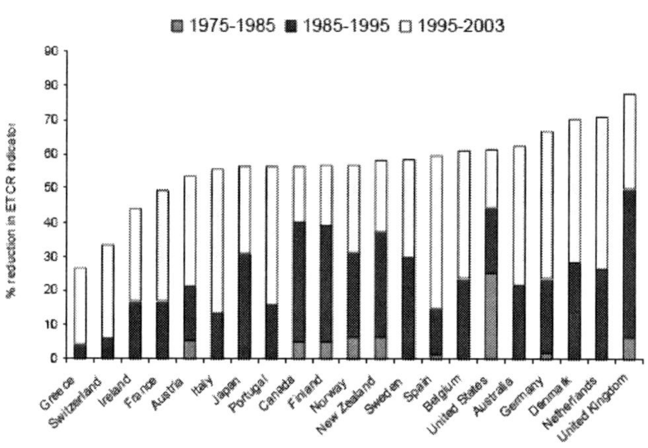


Source: OECD international regulation database.

Figure 5.4 shows that the United States was the first country to begin reforming product market regulation in the early 1980s. Other countries, like the United Kingdom, the Nordic European countries and Japan started reforms a little later. In most other European countries product market reforms accelerated in the mid-1990s.

The cross-country dispersion of product market regulation increased in relative terms until the late 1990s. In the EU countries this policy divergence appears to have been more pronounced, despite efforts to harmonise through the Single Market Programme. From the beginning of this century, however, regulation in the EU has converged more rapidly than in the past.

As a result of these trends in product market reform, the aggregate product market indicator suggests that English-speaking countries, some small European countries and Germany have energy, transport and communication markets more open to competition than the rest of Europe. In particular in France, Ireland and Greece these services markets are less open to competition.

Conway and Nicoletti (2006) also conclude that there is considerable variation in the stringency of regulation across industries. In some industries, such as road freight, air transport, and telecommunications, regulation appears to have been completely overhauled. In other industries, such as gas, postal services, and rail transport, regulatory reforms appear to have been minor. The timing of reform has also varied widely across industries, with road freight and airlines being liberalised (and privatised) earlier than other industries and electricity and telecoms being reformed over the past decade.

## 3.2. Regulation in retail distribution and professional services

In retail distribution and professional services, markets are composed of many competing private firms. Hence, competition issues are inherently different than in energy, transport and communications, where public legal monopolies were not uncommon. The regulatory policies in retail distribution and professional services are based either on consumer protection or urban planning motivations or both. Being essentially country-specific, they have led to a wide dispersion of regulatory approaches, each being insulated by the low tradability of professional and retail trade services. Trade, technological developments and other global factors have less impact in these sectors. Reform trends have been less pronounced than in energy, transport and communication.

### 3.2.1. Retail distribution

The retail sector is often subject to numerous regulations that weaken competition. Conway and Nicoletti (2006) observe large differences in the indicator of retail regulation across OECD countries, suggesting very different policy approaches (Figure 5.5). In addition, the levels in regulation have changed little between 1998 and 2003, implying little evidence of recent policy convergence in this sector. Operational restrictions and barriers to entry are the most common forms of regulation in retail distribution. Barriers to entry definitively hamper market access of foreign providers, and operational restrictions are often also discriminatory, because the regulations usually require another conduct than in the home country.

### *3.2.2. Professional services*

Conway and Nicoletti (2006) argue that regulation in the professional services often limits competition by restricting entry, allowing for price fixing, granting exclusive rights to perform particular services, and restricting advertising and business structures. These regulations are claimed to be in the interest of consumers because they improve quality of services and overcome information asymmetries.

**Figure 5.5. Regulation in retail distribution**

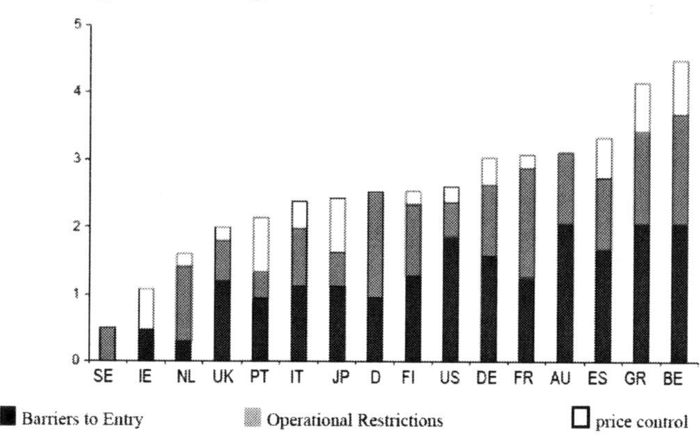


Source: Conway and Nicoletti, 2006.

In practice, however, there is little empirical evidence that indicates a positive impact on consumer welfare, as is also concluded by Faini *et al.* (2005).

The indicators of regulation in professional services (Figure 5.6) suggest that in Denmark, Sweden, Finland, UK, Ireland, and the Netherlands barriers to entry into professional services are less strict compared to other EU countries and Japan, while differences among restrictive countries mostly reflect differences in conduct regulation – that is restrictions on price setting, advertising, form of business, and inter-professional cooperation.

**Figure 5.6. Regulation in professional services in 2003**

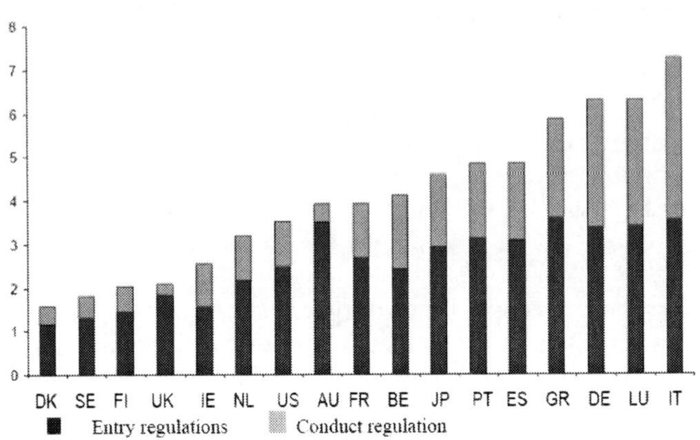


Source: Conway and Nicoletti, 2006.

On average entry regulation is more prominent than conduct regulation. In some countries conduct regulation is nearly absent. If the lack of conduct regulation does not affect the quality of the services in these countries, other Member States have less reason to stick to conduct regulation.

The analysis of regulation in the sectors energy, transport, communication, retail and professional services show that overall regulation has decreased the last decades in most EU countries. This is helpful for integrating national services markets because regulatory systems are fragmenting the services markets. However, many barriers are still in place, in particular on market entry in retail distribution and professional services and public ownership in energy, telecommunication and transport markets. These barriers also hamper expansion of foreign services providers. Although the analysis above does not cover all services sectors and not all EU countries (we miss many business services and the new EU Member States), we have no indication that this analysis is not representative for Europe's other services markets.

## 4. National regulatory obstacles for the internal market

Section 3 concluded that market-reform policies reduced the degree of regulation at many services markets in Europe, but regulation did not disappear. We will not discuss the need for regulation, but focus here on the consequences of national regulation for integrating services markets.

Many of such (market-entry) regulations for services providers affect fixed costs of services firms, see Box 4.1.

**Box 4.1: Examples of national regulations for services providers that affect fixed costs**

- Firms start-up licenses and associated authorisation requirements.
- Service-providing personnel must have locally recognised professional qualifications (may necessitate re-qualification).
- Obligatory membership of local professional association.
- Owners or managers of service-providing firm must have local residence or nationality.
- Firms must have a specific legal form.
- Requirement that services providers have nationally recognised liability insurance or professional indemnity insurance.
- All services activities in destination country fully subject to administrative and tax procedures (i.e. host country country control).
- Limitations on inter-professional co-operation or on the variety of services provided by one firm (may require unbundling).
- Temporary services personnel from origin country subject to rules of the social security system of the destination country.
- Impediments for material inputs, suppliers and personnel from origin country (necessitates search for new local suppliers).

The fact that national services markets are regulated is not in itself an important barrier to international services trade. Kox and Lejour (2005) illustrate this by a thought experiment. Suppose that all countries have the same type of regulation, for instance, a qualification requirement for providers producing a particular service product. Since qualification costs are mainly fixed costs, it would cost an exporting firm a one-off effort in its home country to comply with the qualification criteria. Once having incurred these fixed costs, it could allow the firm to reap economies of scale by expanding its market into additional EU Member States.

However, such a uniform system of regulation does not exist in Europe. Countries developed their own systems of regulation rooted in their own culture and institutions.

They have often have little confidence in the quality of each other's legal regimes and are reluctant to adapt their own regimes where necessary to facilitate cross-border activities. The result is that each national authority uses its own system of quality safeguards to protect services buyers. This is a great nuisance for international trade. Services exporters are confronted with different regulations and requirements, leading to additional costs when firms want to do business in other EU Member

States. These costs can be a prohibitive barrier for entering export markets.

Kox and Lejour (2005) argue further that the fact that these fixed qualification costs are specific for that national market implies that the costs cannot be spread out over production destined for other EU markets. The consequence is that the regulatory heterogeneity limits intra-European economies of scale.

**Figure 5.7. Cost effect of regulatory heterogeneity in EU internal market**

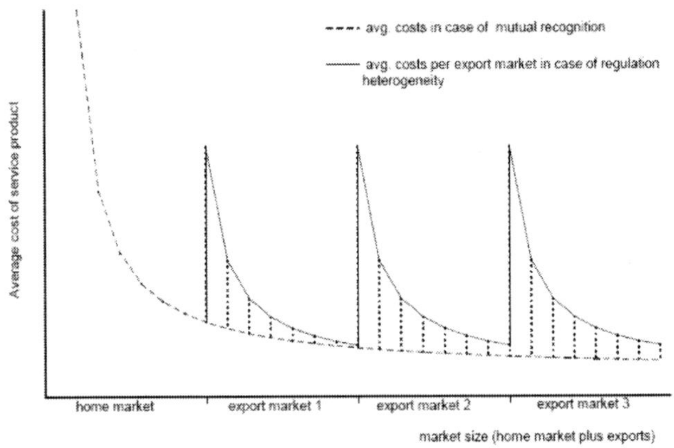

Note: The cost effect is shown in the perspective of the exporting firm.

Figure 5.7 pictures these effects for a services provider who subsequently enters a number of national export markets in the EU. The presence of national qualification requirements gives rise to country-specific fixed transaction costs for the services exporter. Implicitly, the shaded area in Figure 5.7 shows the firm-level cost and efficiency gains that can be attained by a system that allows firms to achieve more economies of scale in dealing with regulation requirements.

Qualification requirements and associated costs for legal and other assistance are mostly independent of firm size. Hence, the market-entry deterring effect will be strongest for small and medium-sized firms. They form the large majority of services providers. In a survey among a large number of business services firms in the EU, 44 per cent of the firms mentioned costs as a 'very important' barrier to setting up a local operation in other countries (CSES 2001: 43).

Those firms that were able to estimate the size of the setup costs estimated the latter to be of the order of 6 months sales proceeds (*ibid.*: 191).

Not only services providers are hampered by the heterogeneity in regulatory regimes. Regulation heterogeneity suppresses foreign competition and the entry of foreign services providers with new products and innovative working methods. It implicitly restricts the choice possibilities for domestic firms that want to purchase business services. The domestic price of business services will be higher than necessary (compared to the open-borders case).

## 5. Current initiatives to integrate services markets

Section 4 argues that differences in national regulation affect the internationalisation of services providers negatively and thereby contributes to fragmenting European services markets. However, recent developments indicate that the future could at least be a little bit different. Most European countries try to reform services markets by reducing entry barriers, barriers to competition and eliminating price controls (see section 3). At the same time FDI increases abundantly. Moreover, the European Commission takes initiatives to integrate services markets and a common services market is also a key element of the Lisbon reform programme. These initiatives are of a much more recent date than the *single market programme*.

The 'single market programme' focussed mainly on the integration of goods markets (for details, see Pelkmans in this volume). Services markets were not totally neglected, but for many commercial services single market policies were lagging behind. Hatzopoulus (2007) discusses the history of legal initiatives (including ECJ case law) to improve services market integration; except for the services directive. Section 2 argues that cross-border trade in services grew at about the same speed as trade in goods, but given the rising share of services in GDP, international markets for services opened, though not as fast as for goods. In identifying the role of the single market for various sectors, Nahuis (2004) found that for many services the internal market did not increase cross-border trade substantially. For most goods sectors he did identify such a trade effect of the internal market. The questionnaire of CSES (2001) among services providers on the barriers to internationalisation gives convincing anecdotic evidence of the statistical evidence mentioned. Lejour and de Paivra Verheijden (2007) show that services trade between the provinces of Canada is about twice as large as between the EU Member States (measured as share of services value added), but even in Canada the internal market for services has its hiccups. However, Vaillancourt (2007) concludes that these hiccups do not restrict trade in goods and services significantly.

This section discusses some of the recent Commission initiatives to integrate services markets. We concentrate on the highly-debated services directive, integration of financial markets, retail and wholesale markets and network industries.

## *5.1. Services directive*

In 2004 the European Commission proposed the services directive in order to slash the regulatory barriers between national services markets. Several studies indicate that bilateral trade and foreign direct investment in services could be boosted substantially. Kox and Lejour (2006a) approach the issue by quantifying the market-entry costs of country-specific regulations, accounting for differences in product-market regulations between each EU country pair.[9] The degree of bilateral policy heterogeneity between countries is used as a proxy for sunk export costs; it may differ between each pair of countries. Applied in gravity equations for bilateral services trade in the EU, regulatory heterogeneity in policy areas like competition and trade regulation appears to have a robustly negative trade impact. At detailed level Kox and Lejour subsequently estimate to what extent the draft Directive would affect bilateral policy heterogeneity.

Intra-EU FDI in services could increase by 18 to 36 per cent. In particular less heterogeneity in barriers to competition and a lower level of FDI restrictions contribute to more foreign direct investment. The services directive does not eliminate all heterogeneity in barriers to competition. Also some FDI restrictions in destination countries will remain in place. If all this heterogeneity in regulation would be eliminated, services FDI could increase by about 130 per cent in Europe on average.

With respect to cross border trade, the heterogeneity in barriers to competition and explicit barriers to trade and investment hamper further market integration. The draft services directive would increase bilateral services trade within the EU by 30 to 62 per cent, which is 2 to 5 per cent of total EU trade. A complete elimination of heterogeneity of would nearly triple intra-EU commercial services trade.

These numbers are stunning and are out-of-sample predictions. However, these numbers underpin the relevance of regulation and differences in regulation as barriers for intra-EU transactions in services.

---

9 Using country-wise data on about 200 different items in product-market regulations from the OECD International Regulation database. The indicator is decomposed into five different areas of product-market regulation.

In order to estimate the macro-economic importance of the services directive, De Bruijn *et al.* (2007) have fed the estimated trade impacts (not the FDI effects) into an applied general equilibrium model called WorldScan. They conclude that European consumption could increase on average by 0.5 to 1.2 per cent. If also the effects of more FDI are added (derived from Lejour *et al.*, 2007) consumption could increase by 0.5 to 1.5 per cent. The limited openness of commercial services for trade and foreign investment explains why these macro-economic effects are relatively modest. However, expressed in terms of the 2004 European GDP, the measures would add 35 to 95 billion Euros. This still ignores the productivity and innovation impacts of more trade and FDI.

Copenhagen Economics (2005) also analyses the EU proposals with an applied general-equilibrium model. Their model also accounts for FDI effects. According to their simulation results, overall consumption in the European Union would increase by 0.6 per cent. This is somewhat smaller than the results reported by Kox and Lejour (various; *op. cit.*).

### 5.2. Financial services

Financial integration in Europe has proceeded quickly since the late 1980s. The introduction of the euro was an important landmark. It underpinned and stimulated integration of euro-derivative markets, equity and bond markets. However, in banking, integration proceeded less well. Some banks from different countries merged, but the efforts by ABN/AMRO to acquire a bank in Italy were seriously hampered in 2006 (though ultimately succeeded). Further more, ECB (2006) stresses that dispersion of national retail interest rates is also caused by differences in consumer protection rules, differing tax treatment, structural differences in the banking sector and the level of technology and competition in the national financial sectors. The Commission formulated proposals to address some of these issues. Ilzkovitz *et al.* (2007) point out that further efforts might be necessary in order to reduce the costs of cross-border clearing and settlement transactions, the costs being far higher than for domestic transactions.

It is hard to assess the costs and benefits of financial integration. The London School of Economics (2002) estimated that GDP might increase by 1.1 per cent in the long run caused by higher investment and private consumption as well as higher employment by integrating equity and bonds markets. The costs of capital are reduced by 0.5 per cent points. This and other studies do, however, not deal explicitly with the integration of the banking sector.

## *5.3. Retail and wholesale services*

The average contribution of wholesale and retail trade to total productivity growth was 27 and 26 per cent respectively in the US between 1994 and 2003 while it was only 10 and 7 per cent respectively in Europe. Moreover, productivity growth in US was on average much higher than in the EU. McGuckin *et al.* (2005) explain the difference in performance by the early start of using ICT in the US and the remaining regulatory obstacles within and between European countries. The major obstacles to productivity growth are store opening hours, land usage restrictions (in particular on large stores) and labour laws. Land usage rules hamper entry and exit of firms and reducing the possibilities to economies of scale by larger firms. Dhyne *et al.* (2006) argue that the competitive pressure of larger retailers, like Wal-Mart, also stimulated other stores to improve technological and organisational structures. These results suggest that regulatory reforms on land usage and opening hours could increase productivity growth in Europe. It has to be noted however that land usage laws are more relevant in Europe. Land is much scarcer because of the higher population density in Europe. Differences in taste could also hinder the development of standardised large retailers all over Europe.

## *5.4. Network industries*

Section 3 shows that many countries have reformed their network industries, and have tried to open up these industries to more competition. Initiatives of the European Commission have been helpful to proceed on the reform path. However, the level of regulation within Europe is very uneven. The unbundling of vertically-integrated monopolies (often state-owned) sometimes meets fierce resistance because of vested interests and the fear that public interests are not taken sufficiently into account in liberalised network industries. It is however necessary to introduce competition which could finally lead to higher productivity and lower prices. The expansion of interconnections between national networks could reduce the physical barriers for foreign competition. Within network industries regulation is a critical issue. The question is whether national regulatory practises have to be harmonised, or the principle of mutual recognition should be introduced or host country rules. Gual (2008) analyses the various integration strategies with respect to regulation for the telecom, electricity and banking sector. The optimal form of regulation is sector or even sub sector dependent. He concludes that there is no single path towards deregulation and integration, and that integration should never be an aim in itself.

### *5.5. Dynamic effects*

Most of the estimates on the effects of integration European services markets only mention trade and investment effects or the static efficiency effects. Assessments of the dynamic effects are lacking because economists do not fully understand the mechanisms to measure them and data are nearly not available. However, Faini *et al.* (2005), Ilzkovitz *et al.* (2007) and Kox and Lejour (2006b) conclude that the primary economic gains come from more market entry. Improved market access will subsequently stimulate competitive selection and productivity growth. Competitive selection will lift average productivity, bolster the role of SME firms in exports, intensify knowledge spillovers, and strengthen innovation by incumbent firms. Moreover, increased FDI in liberalised services markets will also increase average productivity. This can be expected to be beneficial for the number of available services varieties, for services quality, and for the price of services.

The literature on the relation between trade openness and income growth may provide a clue on the size of the dynamic effects. The empirical relationship between openness and income is subject to debate. Some influential papers estimate that 1 percentage point more trade openness causes income to grow by 0.6 per cent in the short term, and 1.1 per cent when also long-term effects are counted (Frankel and Rose, 2002). Applying the latter estimate, the 2004 draft services directive could increase European GDP by 2 to 5 per cent. These long-run effects incorporate the effects of extra competition, productivity spillovers, extra innovation and productivity growth. Nicoletti and Scarpetta (2003) estimate that entry liberalisation in services towards the OECD average could boost productivity growth by 0.1 to 0.2 per cent in some European countries.

## 6. Prospects for further integration of Europe's services markets

In 2007 the European Union reviews its single market policies. Ilzkovitz *et al.* (2007) state that the single market opened up perspectives for restoring confidence of European business and for improving the performance of European companies through the formation of a better integrated, more competitive and innovative market place. The removal of barriers was intended to create an integrated market in which producers and consumers could reap the benefits of economies of scale. Moreover, fiercer competition is expected to result in efficiency gains and to stimulate innovation and the dynamic efficiency of the EU economy.

It is clear that the markets for goods are well integrated, but the path towards a more dynamic and innovative economy is not convincingly taken. Comparisons with the United States show substantial gaps in growth rates in several services sectors. A higher level of regulation in Europe and the fragmented services markets do explain a substantial part of these differences. The higher level of regulation in Europe and the differences in regulation which also hamper internationalisation ask for renewed single market policies for services markets if we want to harvest the benefits of integrated services markets. After the laborious battle on the services directive this proposal will probably not meet much enthusiasm.

Moreover, the horizontal approach of the services directive has probably to be abandoned in formulating new directives, because much more tailor-made proposals for market integration of specific services sectors are needed. These proposals need much capacity, and efforts and sector specific knowledge.

It is probably exaggerating to rename DG Internal Market and Services to DG Internal Market for Services but there are many opportunities to integrate specific services markets further and reap the benefits from market integration if Member States want to do so. Examples are retail and wholesale, network industries, financial services, and many business services. The 2006 services directive is a good start for business services, in particular the one-shop idea to fulfil all administrative inquires for foreign firms. From the OECD indicators we know that many entry barriers remain. Eliminating these barriers would stimulate foreign entry and introduce extra competition. The fierce debate on the services directive also showed that the acceptance of foreign regulation on imported services without domestic control is in many cases not acceptable at this moment. The alternative could be more detailed proposals on specific regulatory burdens to integrate national markets for each services market. This requires much more effort and time. Egan (2007) points out that market integration can not be seen in isolation. In the US it was part of a larger project of institutional development. Also regulatory and political evolution is necessary to underpin market integration. Evolution takes time and this is true in particular for services where regulation and the institutional environment is even more important than for goods.

We have to accept that low-hanging (EU) fruit is already harvested. By their nature services markets are harder to regulate properly, but it could be the only way to a more dynamic and innovative services economy. The size of the market and less regulatory barriers are important causes for faster growing markets in the US. It seems worthwhile to pursue further integration in order to try to grasp the large welfare effects possible by extra competition and effects on productivity and innovation. If not all Member States are interested, enhanced cooperation between some Member States could set the stage, although large scale markets are needed to generate larger economic effects.

## References


Bruijn, de R., Kox, H. & Lejour, A. (2007) Economic Benefits of an Integrated European Market for Services, *Journal of Policy Modelling*.

CSES (2001) *Barriers to International Trade in Business Services – Final Report*, Study commissioned by the European Commission, CSES/European Commission, Brussels.

Conway, P. & Nicoletti, G. (2006) Product Market Regulation in the Non-manufacturing Sectors of the OECD Countries: Measurement and highlights, *OECD Economics Department Working Papers* 530, Paris.

Copenhagen Economics (2005) *Economic Assessment of the Barriers to the Internal Market in Services*, Study commissioned by the European Commission. (www.copenhageneconomics.com).

Dhyne, E. *et al.* (2006) Price Changes In The Euro-Area and the US: Some Facts from Individual Consumer Price Data, *Journal of Economic Perspectives*, 2006, Vol. 20, pp. 171-192.

ECB (2006) *Differences in MFI Interest Rates across Euro Area Countries*, Statistics Publication, Frankfurt, September.

Egan, M. (2008) The Emergence of the US Internal Market, in Pelkmans, J., Chang, M. & Hanf, D. (eds.), *The EU Internal Market in Comparative Perspective: Economic, Political and Legal Analyses*, Brussels, PIE Peter Lang, Chapter 10.

European Commission (2004) Proposal for a Directive of the European Parliament & of the Council on Services in the Internal Market, SEC (2004) 21, Brussels, 13 January.

Eurostat (2006a) Structural Indicators; Economic Reform; Trade integration of Goods and Service.

Eurostat (2006b) Economy and Finance, Balance of Payments – International Transactions, EU Direct Investment Positions, Breakdown by Country and Economic Activity, Luxembourg.

Faini R. *et al.* (2005) Contrasting Europe's Decline: Do Product Market Reforms Help?, Paper presented at Breugel seminar.

Frankel, J. & Rose A (2002) An Estimate of the Effect of Common Currencies on Trade and Income, *Quarterly Journal of Economics*, 117, 2, pp. 437-466.

Gual, J. (2008) Integrating Regulated Network Markets in Europe, Chapter 10 in Gelauff, G., Grilo, I. & Lejour, A. (eds.), *Subsidiarity and Economic Reform in Europe*, Springer.

Hatzopoulos, V. (2008) Legal Aspects of the Internal Market for Services, in Pelkmans, J., Chang, M. & Hanf, D. (eds.), *The EU Internal Market in Com-*

*parative Perspective: Economic, Political and Legal Analyses*, Brussels, PIE Peter Lang, Chapter 6.

Ilzkovitz, F. *et al.* (2007) Steps towards a Deeper Economic Integration: the Internal Market in the 21st century. A contribution to the Single Market Review, *DG EcFin Economic Papers*, 271, Brussels.

Karsenty, G. (2000) Just How Big Are the Stakes? An Assessment of Trade in Services by Mode of Supply, in Sauvé, P. & Stern, R.M. (eds.) *Services 2000: New Directions in Services Trade Liberalisation*, Washington D.C., Brookings Institution.

Kirkegaard, J.F. (2007) Offshoring, Outsourcing and Production Relocations – Labor Market Effects in the OECD and Developing Asia, *Singapore Economic Review*.

Kox, H.L.M., Lejour, A.M. & Montizaan, R. (2004) The Free Movement of Services within Europe, *CPB Document* 69, The Hague, CPB.

Kox, H.L.M. & Lejour, A.M. (2005) Regulatory Heterogeneity as Obstacle for International Services Trade, *CPB Discussion Paper* 49, The Hague, CPB. (www.cpb.nl)

Kox, H.L.M. & Lejour, A.M. (2006a), The Effect of the Services Directive on intra-EU trade and FDI, *Revue Économique*, Vol. 57 (4), pp. 747-769.

Kox, H.L.M. & Lejour, A.M. (2006b) Dynamic Effects of European Services Liberalisation: More to Be Gained, in *Global Challenges for Europe*, Report by the Secretariat of the Economic council, Part 1, Prime Minister's Office Publications 18, pp. 313-142. (http://www.vnk.fi/hankkeet/talousneuvosto/tyo-kokoukset/globalisaatioselvitys-9-2006/en.jsp)

Lejour, A.M., & de Paiva Verheijden, J.-W. (2007) The Tradability of Services within Canada and the European Union, *Service Industries Journal*, Vol. 27, pp. 389-410.

Lejour, A.M., Rojas-Romagosa, H. &. Verweij, G. (2007) Opening up Services Markets within Europe: Modelling Foreign Establishments, *CPB Discussion Paper* 80, The Hague, CPB. (www.cpb.nl)

London School of Economics (2002) Quantification of the Macroeconomic Impact of Integration of EU Financial Markets. (http://europa.eu.int/comm/internal_market/en/finances/mobil/overview/summary-londonecon_en.pdf)

McGuckin, R., Spiegelman, H. van Ark, B. (2005) Can Europe match US Productivity Performance? Perspectives on a Global Economy, conference Board Research report R-1358-05-RR, Washington D.C.

Nahuis, R. (2004) One Size Fits All? Accession to the Internal Market, an Industry-level Assessment of EU Enlargement, *Journal of Policy Modelling*, 26, pp. 571-586.

Nicoletti, G. & Scarpetta, S (2003) Regulation, Productivity and Growth: OECD evidence, *OECD Economic Department Working paper*, 347, Paris.

OECD (2003a), OECD Statistics on International Trade in Services; Partner Country Data & Summary Analysis, Paris.

OECD (2003b) Structural Analytical database, Paris.

OECD (2006) OECD Statistics on International Trade in Services; Detailed tables by service category, Paris.

Pelkmans, J. (2008) Economic Concept and Meaning of the Internal Market, in Pelkmans, J., Chang, M. & Hanf, D. (eds.) *The EU Internal Market in Comparative Perspective: Economic, Political and Legal Analyses*, Brussels, PIE Peter Lang, Chapter 2.

Sampson, G. & Snape, R. (1985) Identifying the Issues in Trade in Services, *The World Economy*, Vol. 8, pp. 171-181.

UNCTAD (2004) World Investment Report 2004, Geneva.

UNCTAD (2006) World Investment Report 2006, Geneva.

Vaillancourt, F. (2008) Canada's Internal Markets: Legal, Economic and Political Aspects, in Pelkmans, J., Chang, M. & Hanf, D. (eds.) *The EU Internal Market in Comparative Perspective: Economic, Political and Legal Analyses*, Brussels, PIE Peter Lang, Chapter 11.

CHAPTER 6

# Legal Aspects of the Internal Market for Services

Vassilis HATZOPOULOS

*Professor at the Democritus University of Thrace and in the Legal Studies Department of the College of Europe in Bruges*

## 1. Introduction

The internal market for services is one of the objectives set by the founding fathers of the EC back in 1957. It is only in the last ten-fifteen years, however, that this aspect of the internal market has seriously attracted the attention of the EC legislature and judiciary.[1] With the exception of some sector-specific directives dating back in the late 1980s, it is only with the deregulation of network industries, the development of electronic communications and the spread of financial services, in the 1990s that substantial bits of legislation got adopted in the field of services. Similarly, the European Court of Justice (ECJ, the Court) left the principles established in *Van Binsbergen* back in 1973, hibernate for a long time before fully applying them in *Säger* and constantly thereafter.[2] Ever since, the Court's case law in this field has grown so important that it has become the compulsory starting point for any study concerning the (horizontal) regulation of the internal market in services. The limits inherent to negative integration and to the casuistic approach pursued by judiciary decisions have prompted the need for a general legislative text to be adopted for services in the internal market. This text, however, hotly debated both at the political and at the legal level, has ended up in *little more* than a complex restatement of the

---

1 It is telling, in this respect, that the first ever edited volume on services in the internal market only appeared in 2001, see M. Andenas and W.-H. Roth (eds.), *Services and Free Movement in EU Law* (2001) OUP, Oxford.

2 Case C-76/90 *Säger* [1991] ECR I-4221.

Court's case law. It may be, however, that this 'little more' is not that little.

In view of the ever expanding application of the Treaty rules on services, promoted by the ECJ (para. 1),[3] the Directive certainly appears to be a limited regulatory attempt (para. 2). This, however, does not mean that the Directive is a toothless, or useless regulatory instrument (conclusion: para. 3).

## 2. An ever expanding application of the Treaty rules: the case law of the ECJ

### *2.1. A large definition of the concept*

In the EC Treaty (Article 50) services are defined in a negative manner, as being all "services [...] where they are normally provided for remuneration, in so far as they are not governed by the provisions relating to freedom of movement for goods, capital and persons." This is an empirical definition given at a time when services only played a residual economic role. However, the subsequent development of the service economy, the diversification of existing services and, most importantly, the creation of new ones – enhanced by new technologies –, have radically changed the economic reality from the one prevailing in 1957.

This 'service revolution' needed be reflected in the way the Treaty rules are applied. This task has been taken up by the Court which, in its recent case law, has revolutionised all three elements of the definition given in Article 50 of the EC Treaty: the concept of services itself (1), the existence of remuneration (2) and the 'residual' relationship with the other Treaty freedoms (3).

#### *2.1.1. The concept of services: a conceptual stretch*

The Court has considerably stretched the concept of services, in three ways: it has recognised that future or even virtual services may benefit from the Treaty rules (2.1.1.1), it has increasingly applied the Treaty rules to services which have hereto been excluded from their scope (2.1.1.2) and it has extended the application of the Treaty rules in cases where there is no clear extraterritorial element (2.1.1.3).

---

3 For a more extensive and systematic presentation of the same case law see V. Hatzopoulos and U. Do, 'The Case Law of the ECJ Concerning the Free Provision of Services: 2000-2005' (2006) *CMLRev* 923-991; the analysis here follows to some extent the structure of this earlier article, but is far more condensed.

2.1.1.1. Virtual – future services

When the Court decided, in *Alpine Investments*,[4] that the mere existence of *virtual* cross border recipients of services, was enough for Article 49 EC to apply, many writers were dismayed.[5] However, seven years later, in the *Carpenter* case,[6] the Court took a much bolder step in this respect. It held that Mr. Carpenter, whose profession entailed 'selling advertising space in medical and scientific journals and offering various administrative and publishing services to the editors of those journals' was a service provider in the Article 50 EC sense of the term, since many of his clients were established in other Member States. The Court was satisfied that this was so a) despite the fact that the bulk of Mr. Carpenter's services were provided to his overseas clients without him having to move there and b) without the Court identifying any specific cross-border service actually provided by Mr. Carpenter. This preliminary finding of the Court seems to confirm that the existence of virtual service recipients in other Member States is enough for Article 49 EC to come into play.

This point was taken further in *Omega*.[7] The referring Court acknowledged that the prohibition of the 'play to kill' game could frustrate the leasing contracts for machinery, that Omega had concluded with an undertaking established in the UK, thus limiting its freedom to receive services (and possibly goods). The Court was not impressed by the fact that, at the date of the adoption of the contested measure, no contract had been concluded between the parties, since the contested 'order is capable of restricting the *future development* of contractual relations between the two parties'.[8] Therefore, not only *virtual* but also *future* services fall into the ambit of Article 49 EC, provided that, in view of the specific facts of each case, they are likely to materialise.

2.1.1.2. Bringing 'excluded' services under Article 49 EC

a. Transport services

Transport services are subject to the specific Treaty rules (Articles 70-80 EC) and to secondary legislation adopted for their application.

---

4 Case C-384/93, *Alpine Investments* [1995] ECR I-1141, annotated by Hatzopoulos in CML Rev. (1995), 1427-1445.

5 Coppenhole and Devroe [1995] *JTDC*, 13; also Devroe and Wouters (1996) JTDC, 60. See however our annotation in this Review for a refutation of the critical position expressed by these authors.

6 Case C-60/00, *Carpenter* [2002] ECR I-6279.

7 Case C-36/02, *Omega* [2004] ECR I-9609. See also the annotation by Ackermann, CML Rev. (2005), 1107-1120.

8 *Omega* rec. 21, emphasis added.

Hence, they evade the application of Article 49 EC. The ensuing Regulations 4055/86[9] and 2408/92[10] have been held by the Court to fully transpose the free movement principles to maritime and air-transport services, respectively.[11] It is, therefore, striking that in the last five years only the Court had to deal with no less than six cases, involving four Member States, where it applied Article 49 EC next to the sector specific rules. Hence, in Commission v. Italy, embarkation tax[12] the Italian republic was condemned, under both Regulation 4055/86 and Article 49, for applying differential taxes to passengers travelling between domestic ports, and those travelling to a non Italian destination. In *Sea Land*,[13] the Court accepted that, in a similar vein to Article 49 EC, the Regulation provisions could be invoked by an undertaking against its own State of origin.[14] In *Geha*,[15] concerning vessels voyaging to Turkey, the Court combined the material rule of Article 49 EC (prohibition of any measure rendering more difficult the provision of services between Member States) with the territorial scope of the Regulation (covering traffic between Member States and third countries) with the effect of applying Article 49 to a situation where no trade between Member States was at stake.

Similarly, the Court has condemned discriminatory national taxes on air transport, on the basis of both the sector specific secondary legislation and of Article 49.[16]

b. Procurement – concession contracts

More striking is the case-law of the Court concerning public procurement. In this field we can distinguish two parallel trends. First, the Court simultaneously applies Article 49 EC and the sector specific

---

9 Council Regulation (EEC) No 4055/86 of 22 December 1986, applying the principle of freedom to provide services to maritime transport between Member States and between Member States and third countries, (1986) OJ L 378, p. 1.

10 Council Regulation (EEC) No 2408/92 of 23 July 1992 on access for Community air carriers to intra-Community air routes, (1992) OJ L 15, p. 33.

11 For Regulation 4055/86 on maritime services, see Case C-381/93 *Commission v. France, transport services* [1994] ECR I-5145; for Regulation 2408/92 on air-transport, see Case C-70/99, *Commission v. Portugal, Airport Taxes* [2001] ECR I-4845.

12 Case 295/00, *Commission v. Italy*, Embarkation Tax [2002] ECR I-1737.

13 Case C-430/99, *Sea-Land* [2002] ECR I-5235.

14 The same conclusion had already been reached in *Commission v. France*, [1994] ECR I-5145.

15 Case C-435/00, *Geha Naftiliaki*, [2002] ECR I-10615.

16 Case C-70/99, *Commission v. Portugal, Airport Taxes* [2001] ECR I-4845; Case C-447/99, *Commission v. Italy, Air Departure Tax* [2001] ECR I-5203; Case C-92/01, Stylianakis, [2003] ECR I-1291.

Directives in order to complete possible lacunae contained in the latter. This tendency is illustrated by reference to case *Commission v. France, Nord Pas de Calais*,[17] where the Court held that, on top of the technical rules contained in the Works Directive 93/37/EC, a general requirement of non-discrimination also applied. This judgment paved the way for the second and most important trend in the Court's case-law, namely the application of Article 49 EC (and the public procurement Directives) to concession contracts, which are not covered by any text of secondary legislation. In a series of judgments starting with *Telaustria*,[18] a case concerning a concession in the field of telecommunications, the Court held that the principle of non-discrimination also applies to concession contracts (and presumably any other type of contract which involves public funding and is not covered by the Procurement Directives). *Coname*[19] concerned the direct award, in Italy, of a contract for the service covering the maintenance, operation and monitoring of the methane gas network. In its judgment the Court further explained that the above requirement of non-discrimination carries with it a further requirement of transparency, satisfied by adequate publicity. This trend was further pursued some months later in *Parking Brixen*,[20] another Italian case concerning the construction and management of a public swimming-pool. The Court found that "a complete lack of any call for competition in the case of the award of a public service concession does not comply with the requirements of Articles 43 EC and 49 EC any more than with the principles of equal treatment, non-discrimination and transparency".[21] The same was confirmed some days later in *Contse*,[22] concerning the award of a contract for the supply of home oxygen equipment in Spain.

c. Health and social security

Even more important than the application of Article 49 EC to transport, public procurement and concession contracts is the extension of the scope of that same provision to embrace social security and health services.

---

17 Case C-225/98, *Commission v. France, Nord Pas de Calais* [2000] ECR I-7445.

18 Case C-324/98 *Telaustria* [2000] ECR I-745.

19 Case C-231/03, *Coname* [2005] ECR I-7287.

20 Case C-458/03, *Parking Brixen* [2005] ECR I-8612.

21 Id. para 48.

22 Case 234/03, *Contse*, [2005] ECR I-9315.

*Social security*

In *Duphar*[23] in the field of goods, *Poucet and Pistre*[24] in the field of services and constantly thereafter, the Court has held that "Community law does not detract from the powers of the Member States to organise their social security systems". However, the Court has subsequently qualified this general statement. In a series of judgments concerning the applicability of the competition rules, the Court has gradually drawn a dividing line between funds (and other entities involved in social security and health care) which operate within the market and those which are outside (the market) and are governed by solidarity. The former should fully abide by all the competition rules, subject to Article 86(2), while the latter are exempted altogether from the application of the said rules.[25] There is no hard and fast rule for the above distinction, rather the Court refers to a set of criteria. Elements which would point to a non-market entity, include: a) the social objective pursued, b) the compulsory nature of the scheme, c) contributions paid being related to the income of the insured person, not to the nature of the risk covered, d) benefits accruing to insured persons not being directly linked to contributions paid by them, e) benefits and contributions being determined under the control or the supervision of the state, f) strong overall state control, g) the fact that funds collected are not capitalised and/or invested, but merely redistributed among participants in the scheme, i) cross-subsidisation between different schemes and j) the nonexistence of competitive schemes offered by private operators.[26]

It would be reasonable to assume that the same criteria also help determine the scope of application of Article 49 EC. Indeed, this was confirmed, in *Freskot*,[27] concerning a public body set up by the Greek legislation for the prevention of, and compensation for, damage caused to agricultural holdings by natural disasters. Therefore, it should come as no surprise that in recent cases concerning the taxation of contribu-

---

23 Case 238/82, *Duphar and Others v. Netherlands State*, [1984] ECR 523, para 16.

24 Joined Cases C-159/91 and C-160/91, *Poucet and Pistre*, [1993] ECR I-637, para 6.

25 See Case C-238/94, *FFSA*, [1995] ECR I-4013; Case C-70/905, *Sodemare*, [1997] ECR I-3395; Case C-67/96, *Albany*, [1999] ECR I-5751; Joint Cases C-155/97 and C-157/97, *Brentjens*, [1999] ECR I-6025; and Case C-219/97, *Drijvende*, [1999] ECR I-6121, respectively. On these three cases, see Idot, "Droit Social et droit de la concurrence: confrontation ou cohabitation (A propos de quelques développements récents)", (1999) *Europe*, chron. 11; Case C-218/00, *Batistello*, [2002] ECR I-691; Case T-319/99, *FENIN v. Commission*, [2003] ECR II-357; Joined Cases C-264/01, C-306/01, C-354/01 and C-355/01, *AOK Bundesverband*, [2004] I-2493.

26 For a more detailed analysis of those criteria, see Hatzopoulos, 'Health law and policy the impact of the EU' in De Burca (ed.), *EU Law and the Welfare State: In Search of Solidarity*, EUI/OUP (2005), pp. 123-160.

27 Case C-355/00, *Freskot v. Elliniko Dimosio*, [2003] ECR I-5263.

tions paid to, and the benefits received from, insurance funds established in other Member States, the Court engaged into a fully fledged application of Article 49 EC. *Danner*[28] and *Skandia*[29] concerned tax arrangements regarding a voluntary (third pillar) and an occupational (second pillar) pension schemes, respectively. It remains that first pillar compulsory pension schemes do not qualify as services under the Treaty.[30]

*Health*

Even more spectacular has been the development of the Court's case law in relation to health services. The importance of the relevant judgments may be appreciated by the fact that all the (old) Member States have occasionally intervened in the proceedings before the Court in this field, essentially with positions opposed to the ones finally adopted by the Court. This case law, lengthy, highly technical and politically controversial, has been presented in detail by several authors and does not find its place here.[31] It is reminded, however, that a patient from any Member State moving abroad, may, next to urgent treatment provided by virtue of the European Insurance Card (ex document E 111):

- receive outpatient treatment[32] in any other Member State and obtain refund from their home State, at the tariffs applicable in this latter State; no prior authorisation is necessary for such a refund to be obtained, since the relevant right stems directly from Article 49 EC;

---

28 Case C-136/00, *Danner*, [2002] ECR I-8147.

29 Case C-422/01, *Skandia*, [2003] ECR I-6817. Further for this case see 2.2.2. below. A similar factual situation was present in the earlier case C-302/98, *Sehrer*, [2000] ECR I-4585, concerning sickness insurance contributions, but it was dealt with under the rules on establishment.

30 See *Freskot*. n° 27 above, Duphar and Poucet & Pistre cited above.

31 See V. Hatzopoulos, 'Killing national health and insurance systems but healing patients? The European market for health care services after the judgments of the ECJ in *Vanbraekel* and *Peerbooms*', CML Rev. (2002), 683-729, and more recently 'Health law and policy, the impact of the EU', n. 26 above. See also G. Davies, 'Welfare as a service', (2002) *LIEI* 27-40; P. Cabral, 'The internal market and the right to cross-border medical care', (2004) *ELRev*, 673-685, and A.-P. van der Mei, 'Cross-border access to health care within the EU: Some reflections on *Geraets-Smits and Peerbooms* and *Vanbraekel'*, (2002) *ML*, 289-215 and 'Cross-border access to medical care: Non-hospital care and waiting lists', (2004) *LIEI*, 57-67. More recently see A. Dawes, 'Bonjour Herr Doctor: national healthcare systems, the internal market and cross-border medical care within the EU', (2006) *LIEI*, 167-182. For a full account of the relationships between EU and Health Law see T. Hervey and J. McHale, *Health Law and the European Union*, CUP (Cambridge, 2004).

32 Inpatient treatment has been restrictively defined, see Case C-8/02 *Leichtle* [2004] ECR I-2641.

- receive any kind of treatment in other Member States in the same conditions (tariffs, refund, indemnity etc. – but for the duration) as patients of the host State, provided they have obtained prior authorisation (document E 112) by their home institution, according to Article 22 of Regulation 1408/71;
- force the delivery of the above authorisation (for receiving treatment abroad) whenever the treatment objectively necessary for their medical condition[33] is not available in their home State or is not available within a reasonable waiting time, taking into consideration the specific needs of each particular patient;[34] this is also a right directly stemming from Article 49 EC.

These rights benefit all people insured with the competent institution of one Member State, irrespectively of whether the home State[35] a) operates a refund system, like the one followed (principally) in France, Germany and Luxembourg,[36] b) operates a benefits-in-kind system by contracted in physicians and hospitals, as is the case in the Netherlands,[37] or c) offers benefits-in-kind by essentially public institutions, as it is the case in the UK and Italy.[38]

#### 2.1.1.3. Application of the Treaty rules when there is no extraterritorial element

##### a. General case law

The general rule according to which the Treaty provisions on free movement only apply to interstate situations has been under fire for over ten years now.[39] In the field of goods, the judgments in cases *Lancry* and

33 For the objective assesment of the necessity of the treatment, independently from national preferences, see Case C-368/98, *Vanbraekel*, [2001] ECR I-5363.

34 Case C-385/99, *Müller-Fauré*, [2003] ECR I-4509 and Case C-372/04, *Watts*, [2006] ECR I-4325.

35 The threefold classification which follows is simplistic, for the needs of demonstration, and does not account for the special characteristics of each one of the national systems.

36 See Case C-158/96, *Kohll*, [1998] ECR I-1931; Case C-56/01, *Inizan*, [2003] ECR I-12403; Case C-193/03, *Bosch*, [2004] ECR I-9911.

37 Case C-157/99, *Smits & Peerbooms*, [2001] ECR I-5473; *Vanbraekel* and *Müller-Fauré*, all cited above.

38 *Watts*, above.

39 See amongst others: D. Simon and F. Lagondet, 'Libre circulation des marchandises et situations purement internes: chronique d'une mort annoncée', (1997) *Europe* chron. 9; Tagaras, 'Règles communautaires de libre circulation, discriminations à rebours et situations dites « purement internes »' in *Mélanges en hommage à Michel Waelbroeck*, Vol. II (Bruylant 1999), 1499; R. Papadopoulou, 'Situations purement internes et droit communautaire: un instrument jurisprudentiel à double fonction ou

*Simitzi v. Kos,*[40] *Pistre* and *Guimont*[41] stand for the idea that 'Article [28] cannot be considered inapplicable simply because all the facts of the specific case before the national Court are confined to a single Member State'.[42] This same idea was transposed in *Reisch,*[43] a case concerning the free movement of capitals. Finally, in relation to workers, the Court, indirectly in *Surinder Singh*[44] and then, in a more direct way in *Angonese,*[45] has been ready to apply Articles 43 and 39 EC, respectively, to situations which only remotely presented some trans-national element.

However, it is in the field of free movement of services, with its judgment in *Carpenter*, that the Court took the boldest step away from the need to establish a trans-border element as a precondition to the application of the Treaty rules. The Court focused on the fact that Mr. Carpenter's activity consisted in the provision of advertising services and that some of these services were offered to recipients in other Member States. Thus, the Court identified the two elements upon which the application of Article 49 EC lies, that is a) some service activity b) provided temporarily over borders. However, the Court avoided examining whether the two elements merged, in other words, whether any specific trans-border service provision was at stake and how this was affected by the contested measure – if at all. Consequently, Article 49 EC was found to apply.

b. Extra-territorial by nature?

Further to the Court's broad approach to the existence of some trans-national element illustrated in *Carpenter*, some recent judgments seem to suggest that certain categories of services are by definition trans-national. Hence, the Court applies Article 49 EC without ever identify any specific trans-border service movement.

The *first* category of services in which this seems to hold true is transport. In all the cases discussed above (*b*), the Court took for granted that Article 49 EC applied, and only at a subsequent stage did it exam-

---

une arme à double tranchant?', (2001) *CDE*, 96-129; Shuibhne, 'Free movement of persons and the wholly internal rule: time to move on?', *CML Rev.* (2002), 731.

40 Case C-363/93, *Lancry*, [1994] ECR I-3957 and Joined Cases C-485/93 and C-486/93, *Simitzi v. Kos*, [1995] ECR I-2665.

41 Case C-448/98, *Guimont*, [2000] ECR I-10663.

42 *Pistre*, n. 24 above.

43 Joined Cases C-515/99, C-519/99 to C-524/99 and C-526/99 to C-540/99, *Reisch e.a. v. Salzburg*, [2002] ECR I-2157; compare paras 24-27 of this judgment with paras 21-24 of *Guimont.* See also Case C-300/01, *Salzmann*, [2003] ECR I-4899.

44 Case C-370/90, *Surinder Singh*, [1992] ECR I-4265.

45 Case C-281/98, *Agnonese*, [2000] ECR I-4139.

ine whether in fact services to and from other Member States were more severely affected. Therefore, the existence of some trans-border element did not constitute a prerequisite to the application of Article 49 EC, but one of the appreciations inherent in its application.

A *second* category of services in which the Court applies Article 49 EC without insisting upon the existence of some trans-border element are advertising services. This may be illustrated by reference to the very judgment in *Carpenter*.[46] In a more explicit way, in *Gourmet*,[47] a case in which a Swedish undertaking was opposing the total ban imposed by Swedish law on the advertising of alcoholic beverages, the Court held that "even if [the prohibition] is non-discriminatory, [it] has a particular effect on the cross-border supply of advertising space, *given the international nature of the advertising market* in the category of products to which the prohibition relates, and thereby constitutes a restriction on the freedom to provide services within the meaning of Article 59 [now 49]".[48]

The *third* category of services deemed to be transnational are TV broadcasting and telecommunications services. Hence, in *De Coster*,[49] which concerned a municipal tax imposed on parabolic antennae, the Court dealt dismissively with the lack of extra-territoriality, simply recalling that "it is settled case-law that the transmission, and broadcasting, of television signals comes within the rules of the Treaty relating to the provision of services". In *Mobistar*,[50] which concerned a municipal tax imposed on GSM retransmission pylons, the Court took for granted that Article 49 EC applied to telecommunications services, but then found no violation of the aforementioned provision as there was no affectation of trans-border services.[51] This is yet another striking example of the Court 'internalising' the existence of a trans-frontier element: it is no longer used as a precondition to the applicability of the free movement of services rules, but rather, as an appreciation 'internal' to

46 *Carpenter*, n. 6 above, para 29. It is true that in Case C-134/03, *Viacom Outdoor*, [2005] ECR I-1167, concerning a municipal tax imposed on billboard advertising, the Court declined the application of Art. 49, but that was more because of the lack of any substantially restrictive effect the contested measure, rather than because of the lack of any trans-border element.

47 Case C-405/98, *Gourmet*, [2001] ECR I-1795.

48 *Ibid.*, para 39, emphasis added.

49 See also the note by Wenneras, 'The *De Coster* Case: Reflections on Tax and Proportionality', (2002) *LIEI*, 219-230.

50 Joined Cases C-544/03 and 545/03, *Mobistar & Belgacom*, judgment of 8 September 2005, nyr.

51 Id., paras 32 and 33.

the said rules, leading the Court's assessment as to the existence of a violation.[52]

c. No need for extraterritoriality when EU legislation in the field?

It has been shown above that the Court applies the Treaty rules together with, or instead of, the public procurement Directives.[53] Long before that, the Court had already decided that the procurement directives apply to wholly internal situations.[54] Henceforth, after the judgments in *Coname* and *Parking Brixen*, it is clear that in the field of public procurement and/or concession contracts, Article 49 EC shall apply without there being a need to establish a trans-border element. The reason given for this is that the detailed secondary legislation in this field is not merely aimed at the abolition of all discriminations based on nationality, but also – and essentially – at the creation of a level playing field for all European companies to compete unfettered by national regulatory regimes.[55] The fact that principles enshrined in secondary legislation apply irrespective of the presence of a trans-national element has been clearly confirmed, more recently, in relation to the Data Protection Directive,[56] in *Österreichischer Rundfunk*.[57] This finding could lead to a greater number of services being governed by Article 49 EC without any transnational element being necessary; in any case, it could offer a plausible explanation for some of the judgments presented above.[58] In fact, all transport, telecommunications and TV broadcasting, and to a lesser extent advertising, have been regulated at EU level by secondary legislation texts.

### *2.1.2. Remuneration*

The existence of remuneration is, according to Article 50 EC, the feature which gives any activity its economic nature, thus bringing it within the scope of the Treaty freedoms. According to the Court 'the essential characteristic of remuneration lies in the fact that it constitutes

52 This seems to constitute a shift from previous case-law, in particular Case C-108/96, *Mac Quen*, [2001] ECR I-837.

53 See 2.1.1.2 above.

54 Case C-243/89, Commission v. Danemark, Storbaelt, [1993] ECR I-3353.

55 *Ibid.*, para 33.

56 Directive 95/46/EC of the Council of 24 October 1995 (1995) OJ L281/31.

57 Joined Cases C-465/00, C-138/01 and C-139/01, *Österreichischer Rundfunk*, [2003] ECR I-4989, para 42. See also Keppenne and Van Raepenbusch, 'Les principaux développements de la jurisprudence de la Cour de Justice et du Tribunal de Première Instance, Année 2003', (2004) *CDE*, 439-513, who also make out this point.

58 See 1.1.1.3 b above.

consideration for the service in question and is normally agreed upon between the provider and the recipient of the service'.[59] This definition, however, has been considerably widened in recent cases. In *Deliège* the Court accepted that non-professional athletes could nonetheless receive remuneration for their 'services' in an indirect way, through TV broadcasting, sponsorships, participation in publicity campaigns etc. In the healthcare cases discussed above (3.1.1.2), the Court accepted that "the payments made by the sickness insurance funds [for treatment delivered to insured patients], *albeit set at a flat rate*, are indeed the consideration for the hospital services and unquestionably represent remuneration for the hospital which receives them".[60] Thus, consideration was found to exist not only in triangular situations,[61] but, more importantly, in situations where the correlation between services received and moneys paid is only indirect if economically nonexistent. Further, in *Danner* and *Skandia*[62] the Court accepted that remuneration can be paid well in advance for a service which is to be delivered over 30 years later, i.e. the payment of an old-age pension. The above judgments leave us with a concept of remuneration which is extremely flexible, if not ever expandable – a serious challenge for legal certainty.

### *2.1.3. Abandoning the 'subsidiary' character of the rules on services in relation to the other fundamental freedoms*

According to the black letter of Articles 49 and 50 EC, the rules on services are supposed to apply to situations where no other Treaty freedom applies; they have a subordinate character. In this respect, services (Article 49) were traditionally distinguished from establishment (Article 43) by virtue of their temporary nature. Hence, in the *German insurance* case,[63] the Court held that as soon as the service provider acquired some stable infrastructure in the host State, the Treaty provisions on establishment became applicable. This position was later reviewed in *Gebhard*,[64] where the Court recognised that a provider of services within the meaning of Article 49 EC could make use of some permanent infrastructure in the host State. Nevertheless, the Court insisted on the temporal character of the provision of services. It stated that "not only the duration of the provision of the service, but also its

59 Case 263/86, *Belgian State v. Humbel*, [1988] ECR 5365, para 17.

60 *Smits & Peerbooms*, n. 37 above, para 58, emphasis added.

61 Which has already been accepted since Case 352/85, *Bond van Adverteerders and Others*, [1988] ECR 2085, para 16.

62 Both cited above n. 28 and 29.

63 Case 205/84, *Commission v. Germany, Insurance*, [1986] ECR 3755.

64 Case C-55/94, *Gebhard*, [1995] ECR I-4165.

regularity, periodicity or continuity"[65] may bring it under the rules on establishment. This made commentators conclude that service provision must be of an 'episodic' or 'irregular' nature.[66]

In its most recent case low, however, the Court seems to be abandoning the temporal criterion in favour of a more economic one. Indeed, the Court seems ready to treat economic activities which qualify as services under Article 49 EC, irrespective of their duration. Hence, in *Schnitzer*[67] the Court held that a Portuguese construction company which had been on a construction site in Germany for over three years could, nevertheless, invoke the rules on services, in order to evade the full application of the German legislation. The Court acknowledged that the nature of the activity is readily ascertainable and can safely lead to legal qualifications, while its duration, periodicity, etc., are not.[68]

Some months later, the Court judged of the compatibility with Article 49 EC of a Portuguese law which concerned undertakings offering private security services. The fact that this piece of legislation only applied to undertakings operating on the Portuguese territory for periods exceeding a calendar year, had no incidence.[69]

These judgments further confirm and justify earlier cases a) where the long duration of an activity had not precluded the application of the rules on services[70] and b) concerning 'naturally' trans-border services,[71] such as TV broadcasting, telecommunications or transport,[72] where the Court applied Article 49 EC without taking into account any temporal consideration.

Not only does this recent case law make clear that it is the economic nature – and not the duration – of the activity that constitutes the main criterion for its legal classification, but also, it creates a presumption in favour of the application of Article 49 EC in all service situations. At

65 Gebhard para 21.

66 See V. Hatzopoulos, Recent developments of the case law of the ECJ in the field of free of services 1994-1999", CML Rev. (2000), p. 43-82, 45, where this restrictive approach of the Court was also criticised as being inappropriate in view of the current development and sophistication of services.

67 Case C-215/01, *Schnitzer*, [2003] ECR I-14847.

68 *Schnitzer*, para 39.

69 Case C-171/02, Commission v. Portugal, Private Security Firms, [2004] I-5645.

70 See e.g. Joined Cases C-369/96 and C-376/96, *Arblade and Leloup*, [1999] ECR I-8453.

71 For which see 1.1.1.3, above.

72 Case C-17/00, *De Coster*, [2001] ECR I-9445; Joined Cases C-544/03 and C-545/03, *Mobistar and Belgacom*, judgment of 8 September 2005, nyr.; and Case C-92/01, *Stylianakis*, [2003] ECR I-1291, respectively.

the same time, it does away, once and for all, with the myth of services being a subsidiary category.

### *2.1.4. Outer limits: non-economic services (of general interest)*

The rules on services apply to a great many activities, but leave intact services of general interest with no economic character. From an economic viewpoint, services with no economic character are those from which it makes no sense to exclude 'free-riders', who are not ready to pay for them. More precisely, three conditions should be met for a service linked to the general interest to qualify as non economic: a) an objective necessity for such a service to be provided, b) important fixed but nearly non-existent variable costs, linked to the number of beneficiaries and c) (some) people unwilling to pay for such a service, if they had to. Hence, services like police, the army, garbage collection, funeral services do not, in principle, fall within the ambit of Article 49 EC. Such services may be classified into two broad categories: a) 'social' services which are essentially unmarketable, precisely because they do not embody market values and b) 'strategic' services which the State would hardly trust any other entity to pursue.[73] In the former category the Court has held i.a. that the organisation of primary pension schemes,[74] the setting up of a mandatory indemnity system for farmers,[75] the running of old-age houses,[76] all fall outside the scope of Article 49 EC. In the latter category, the Court has held i.a. the coordination of air-traffic control,[77] the operation of a body entrusted with preventive anti-pollution surveillance[78] and the organisation of communal funeral services[79] not to come within the Treaty rules.

However, despite their social character, complementary and voluntary (second and third pillar) pension schemes come within the Treaty rules,[80] just like healthcare services.[81] Likewise, public security and public order are not fields exclusively reserved to the State police, but may be partly secured by market forces, i.e. private security compa-

---

73 See C. Scott, 'Services of General Interest in EC Law: Matching Values to Regulatory Technique in the Public and Private Sectors' (2000) ELJ 310-325, 313.

74 Joined Cases C-159 & 160/91 *Poucet & Pistre* [1993] ECR I-637.

75 Case C-355/00 *Freskot v. Elliniko Dimosio* [2003] ECR I-5263.

76 Case C-70/95 *Sodemare* [1997] ECR I-3395. In the meantime some uncertainty had been created by the judgment of the Court in Case C-238/94 *FFSA* [1995] ECR I-4013.

77 Case C-364/92 *Eurocontrol* [1994] ECR I-43.

78 Case C-343/95 *Cali e Figli* [1997] ECR I-1547.

79 Case 30/87 *Bodson* [1988] ECR 2479.

80 See *Danner* and *Skandia*, above n. 28 and 29.

81 See above 2.1.1.2.

nies.[82] The distinction between services which do and those which do not have an economic nature is not an easy one to draw, at the first place, as it depends on basic political and social choices concerning the role of the State. It is dynamic too, depending both on the way the State accomplishes its missions and on market forces and private entrepreneurship. One thing is beyond doubt, however: whenever remuneration may be shown to exist for any given service, this service will be treated as having a commercial nature. Therefore, the extremely flexible and ever expanding concept of remuneration used by the Court,[83] may only lead to the correlative restriction of the number and scope of services excluded from the Treaty rules.

### 2.2. A set of rules (violation/exceptions) closely comparable with that on the other freedoms

Concerning the material scope of Article 49 EC, three remarks need to be made. First, concerning the way the rules on services are held to be violated (2.2.1); second, concerning justifications to such violations (2.2.2); and, third, concerning the provision of services of general interest (2.2.3).

#### 2.2.1. Violation of Article 49 EC

The case law of the Court in the field of services during these last years has increased exponentially.[84] The substantive analysis of the relevant judgments does not find its place here. If we were to sum up the bulk of the Court's case law, the concept of convergence between the fundamental Treaty freedoms would emerge.[85] This general statement should, nevertheless, be qualified by two further remarks.

---

82 See above n° 69.

83 Discussed above at 2.1.2.

84 The ECJ has gone from deciding 40 cases in the five year period between 1995-1999 to deciding over 140 cases based on Art 49 EC between 2000-2005; see V. Hatzopoulos and U. Do, 'The Case Law of the ECJ Concerning the Free Provision of Services: 2000-2005' (2006) *CMLRev* 923-991.

85 For the 'bringing together' of the four freedoms see, among many: P. Oliver and W. Roth, 'The internal market and the four freedoms' *CML Rev.* (2004), 407-441, 430 *et seq.*, and V. Hatzopoulos, 'Trente ans après les arrêts fondamentaux de 1974, les quatre libertés: quatre?' in Demaret, Govaere, Hanf (eds.), *30 Years of European Legal Studies at the College of Europe – 30 ans d'études juridiques européennes au Collège d'Europe: Liber Professorum 1973/74-2003/04*, P.I.E.-Peter Lang (Bruxelles, 2005), pp. 185-201. See also Caputi, Jambrenghi & Pullen, 'The use of Articles 30 and 52 to attack barriers to market access: an overview of the ECJ's case law', (1996) *ECLR*, 388; Bernard, 'La libre circulation des marchandises, des personnes et des services dans le traité CE sous l'angle de la compétence', (1998) *CDE*, 11-45; Oliver, 'Goods and services: two freedoms compared', in *Mélanges en hommage à*

*First*, the Court has consistently refused to transpose on services the *Keck* dichotomy, between selling arrangements, on the one hand, and product characteristics, on the other.[86] Nevertheless, *second*, after a period of seemingly limitless expansion of the material ambit of Article 49 EC,[87] the Court in its recent case law has introduced some kind of a 'rule of law' to its application. The most striking illustration is offered by the judgment of the Court in *Mobistar*,[88] where the Court after repeating the mantra that every measure "which is liable to prohibit or further impede the activities of a provider of services established in another Member State" is contrary to Article 49 EC, made the following remarkable statement: "measures, the only effect of which is to create additional costs in respect of the service in question and which affect in the same way the provision of services between Member States and that within one Member State, do not fall within the scope of Article 59 [now 49] of the Treaty."[89] In this way it introduced in the field of services, a dichotomy between expenses/other hindrances whereby the scope of Article 49 EC is to be limited. It is submitted that this distinction is the transformation of the *Keck* dichotomy in the field of services and, indeed, the real rationale of the *Keck* dichotomy itself.[90] The practical result is that Member States are free to maintain regulations of a purely economic nature, to the extent that they are non-discriminatory, but are under strict scrutiny concerning the administrative and other requirements imposed on service providers.

---

*Michel Waelboreck*, Vol. II (Bruylant 1999), pp. 1377-1405; O'Leary, 'The free movement of persons and services' in Craig and de Bùrca, *The Evolution of EU Law* (Oxford 1999), pp. 377-416; see also in Andenas and Roth (eds.), *Services and Free Movement in EU Law* (Oxford 2001) the extremely interesting contributions by Poiares Maduro, pp. 41-68, Snell and Andenas, pp. 69-140, Jarass, pp. 141-163, and Hansen, pp. 197-210.

86 See, among many cases, Case C-384/93, *Alpine Investments*, [1995] ECR I-1141, annotated by V. Hatzopoulos in *CML Rev*. (1995), 1427-1445; and Case C-405/98, *Gourmet*, [2001] ECR I-1795 and among the many commentators, A. Biondi, 'Advertising alcohol and the free movement principle: the *Gourmet* decision', (2001) *ELRev*, 616-622; Kaczorowska, 'Gourmet can have his Keck and eat it!', (2004) *ELJ*, 479-494; and J. Stuyck, 'Gourmet: une nouvelle brèche dans la jurisprudence « Keck »?', (2001) *CDE*, 683-706.

87 See e.g. Case C-17/00, *De Coster*, [2001] ECR I-9445 and Wenneras, "The *De Coster* Case: Reflections on Tax and Proportionality", (2002) *LIEI*, 219-230.

88 Joined Cases C-544/03 and C-545/03, *Mobistar and Belgacom*, judgment of 8 September 2005, nyr.

89 *Mobitel*, para 31.

90 For a brief comment of this distinction see our comment on *Alpine Investments* in (1995) *CMLRev* 1427-1445.

### *2.2.2. Justifications to restrictions*

Convergence is also the first word to describe the case law of the Court concerning justifications admitted to restrictions of Article 49 EC. Convergence, in this respect is to be observed at two levels. First, it is observed between the various fundamental freedoms.[91] Second, and more interestingly for the purposes of the present study, convergence is also increasingly observed between express and judge-made justifications. Hence in *Gambelli* the Court indistinctively considered whether such restrictions *are acceptable* as exceptional measures expressly provided for in Articles 45 and 46 EC, or *justified*, in accordance with the case-law of the Court, for reasons of overriding general interest; it answered this question based only on a classical 'mandatory requirements' analysis.[92] More strikingly still, in *Commission v France, Loi Evin* the Court openly held that "the freedom to provide services may [...] be limited by national rules justified by the reasons mentioned in Article 56(1) of the EC Treaty, read together with Article 66, or for overriding requirements of the general interest".[93] The *second* main characteristic of the Court's case law on justifications, is the use of a stringent necessity/proportionality test of the contested national measures. Examples may be drawn i.a. from the judgments in *Gambelli*[94] and *Placanica*, in the field gambling.[95] The Court recognised that the protection of consumers and other reasons of general interest could justify restrictions to betting ativities. However, such restrictions would only be admissible if the invoked objectives are pursued by the State in "a consistent and systematic manner"; this cannot hold true where the Member State in question also adopts/maintains measures which favour gambling. A similar logic prevailed in *Finalarte*, concerning posted workers. The Court found that the host Member State could extend its restrictive legislation to posted workers, provided that "those rules confer a genuine benefit on the workers concerned, which significantly adds to their social protection".[96] The national Court was left to verify

---

91 See already V. Hatzopoulos, n. 66 above, p. 72. See also Hatzopoulos, 'Exigences essentielles, impératives ou impérieuses: une théorie, des théories ou pas de théorie du tout?', (1998) *RTDE* 2, 191-236; O'Leary and Fernandez-Martin, 'Judicially created exceptions to the free provision of services', Andenas and Roth (eds.), pp. 163-196.

92 Case C-243/01, *Gambelli*, [2003] ECR I-13031, para 60, emphasis added.

93 Case C-262/02, *Commission v. France, Loi Evin*, [2004] ECR I-6569, para 23.

94 Cited above n. 92.

95 Joined Cases C-338/04, 359/04 et 360/04, *Placanica*, judgment of March 6, 2007, nyr.

96 Joined Cases C-49/98, C-50/98, C-52/98 to C-54/98 and C-68/98 to C-71/98, *Finalarte*, [2001] ECR I-7831, para 42.

whether this condition was met, according to the grid of analysis provided by the Luxembourg Court itself.[97]

### *2.2.3. Respect for public service: financial setup is free but no extra administrative burdens*

In the cases in which the free movement of services could be held to enter directly into conflict with the provision of some service of general economic interest, the Court gave clear prevalence to the latter over the former. In the early *Corbeau* and *Almelo* judgments the Court had developed the concept of 'severability', whereby profitable activities should remain subject to the Treaty rules, while non-profitable ones would evade them.[98] In the most recent case law, however, this idea is being severely limited, if not altogether abandoned. In *Deutsche Post* the Court was really fast in admitting that Article 86(2) EC could justify exceptions to the Treaty rules, to the extent that such exceptions were indispensable for the pursuit of activities of general economic interest.[99] More importantly, in *Glöckner*[100] which concerned emergency and other ambulance services, the Court held the two to be inseparable and altogether outside the scope of the competition rules: monies generated by the latter services could enable the operators concerned to discharge their general-interest task in conditions of 'economic equilibrium'. For one thing, the test of 'economic equilibrium' is different from the previous logic of 'severability', based on the criterion of mere viability of services of general interest. Moreover, the readiness with which the Court accepted in *Deutsche Post* that the fees charged by the monopolist were necessary for the discharge of its general interest obligations, without examining in any detail the accuracy of such a statement, takes *Glöckner* a step further, as it shows the Court's increasingly hands-off approach towards the financing of activities of general interest. Further, the Court has undertaken to set the conditions under which public funds given to an entity entrusted with the provision of some service of general interest, do not qualify as state aids.[101]

---

97 More on this case and in general on the topic of posted workers see below, at 2.2.2.3.

98 Case C-320/91, *Corbeau*, [1993] ECR I-2562 and Case C-393/92, *Almelo*, [1994] ECR I-1477. See for these judgments Wachsmann and Berrod, 'Les critères de justification des monopoles: un premier bilan après l'affaire *Corbeau*', (1994) *RTDE*, 39. See also Baquero Cruz, 'Beyond competition: services of general economic interest and EC law' in De Burca (ed.), n. 26 above, pp. 169-212.

99 Case C-147/97, *Deutsche Post*, [2000] ECR I-825.

100 Case C-475/99, *Glöckner*, [2001] ECR I-8089.

101 Case 280/00 *Altmark Trans* [2003] ECR I-7747; see also O. Dupéron 'Le régime des services publics en droit communautaire: des précisions apportées par la Cour de justice des Communautés européennes', (2003) *Petites affiches* n° 229 p. 6-12;

However, if *financing* the services of general interest is increasingly left to the discretion of the States, the same is not true with other, *administrative restrictions*, such a prior authorisation requirement.[102]

## *2.3. From mutual recognition to a near home country control (HCC) principle*

Since the judgment in *Säger* the Court invariably holds that 'a Member State may not make the provision of services in its territory subject to compliance with all the conditions required for establishment'.[103] Moreover, the principle of mutual recognition has occupied an ever increasing role in the Court's case law in relation to services. Through a series of judgments, the Court transforms this functional general principle of EC law,[104] into two more specific but far-fetched principles, the furtherance of which should only be achieved through legislative means. First the Court pushes mutual recognition towards some kind of 'home state' control (2.3.1) which, in turn, creates the need for close cooperation between Member States' authorities (2.3.2).

### *2.3.1. Towards a general application of an imperfect home state control?*

On many occasions the legislation of Member States has been condemned for failing to take into account conditions fulfilled or guarantees offered by service providers in their home State. Hence, in *Commission v. Italy, transport consultants*[105] the Italian legislation required

---

J.-L. Clergérie, 'La légalité d'une contrepartie d'obligation de service public' (2003) *Dalloz* Jur. p. 2814-2817; M. Merola & C. Medina, 'De l'arrêt *Ferring* à l'arrêt *Altmark*: continuité ou revirement dans l'approche du financement des services publics' (2003) CDE, p. 639-694. On the basis of this judgment the Commission has issued the so called 'Altmark Package', also known as the 'Monti-Kroes Package', consisting of three texts: Directive 2005/81/EC modifying Directive 80/723/EEC on the transparency of financial relations between Member States and public undertakings OJ [2005] L 312/47; Decision 2005/842/EC, on the application of Article 86(2) of the EC Treaty to State aid in the form of public service compensation granted to certain undertakings entrusted with the operation of services of general economic interest, OJ [2005] L 312/67; and the 'Community Framework for State aid in the form of public service compensation' 2005/C OJ [2005] C 297/4.

102 Case C-205/99, *Analir*, [2001] ECR I-1271. See Slot, CML Rev. (2003), 159-168.

103 Above fn. 2, para 13.

104 See Hatzopoulos, *Le principe communautaire d'équivalence et de reconnaissance mutuelle dans la libre prestation de services*, Sakkoulas/Bruylant (1999), pp. 73-100. For a different account see "Mutual Recognition" in Barnard and Scott (eds.), *The Law of the Single European Market, Unpacking the Premisses*, Hart (Oxford, 2002), pp. 225-267.

105 Case C-263/99, Commission v. Italy, Transport Consultants, [2001] ECR I-4195.

transport consultants, among other things, to have a security lodged with the provincial administration. This requirement was found to be illegal to the extent that it made it 'impossible for account to be taken of obligations to which the person providing the service is already subject in the Member State in which he is established'.[106] The very same requirements were also struck down by the Court for exactly the same reasons in relation to the activities of temporary labour agencies operating in Italy, in *Commission v. Italy, temporary labour agencies.*[107]

Similarly, in Commission v Italy, sanitation services[108] a registration requirement was held to violate Article 49 EC to the extent that it did "not exclude from its scope a provider of services who is established in a Member State other than the Italian Republic and who, under the legislation of its Member State of establishment, already satisfies formal requirements equivalent to those under the Italian Law".[109] Although this judgment predates the two mentioned above, it is more earth-shattering, insofar as it does not concern a mere financial guarantee, but the very authorisation itself delivered by the host State authorities.

In Commission v. The Netherlands, private security firms[110] the Court held Article 49 EC to be breached both by a prior authorisation requirement and by a system of special ID cards for security personnel 'in so far as it [did] not take account of the controls or verifications already carried out in the Member State of origin'.[111] The Court further held that the identity of the individuals concerned could be proven by the valid passport or ID card delivered by their home state authorities.[112]

The above judgments stand, first, for the idea that all controls and checks carried out by the home State should be taken into account by the authorities of the host State, irrespective of whether they refer to purely formal guarantees, such as the deposit of some financial security, or to substantial qualifications, such as the competence and integrity of

---

106 *Ibid.*, para 24.

107 Case C-279/00, Commission v. Italy, Temporary Labour Agencies, [2002] ECR I-1425.

108 Case C-358/98, *Commission v. Italy, Sanitation Services*, [2000] ECR I-1255.

109 *Ibid.*, para 13, emphasis added.

110 Case C-189/03, Commission v. The Netherlands, Private Security Firms, [2004] ECR I-9289.

111 *Ibid.*, para 30.

112 This judgment is just one, albeit the most concise and clear, of a series of infringement cases concerning private security firms and decided by the Court upon quasi-identical facts: Case C-355/98, *Commission v. Belgium, Private Security Firms*, [2000] ECR I-1221; Case C-283/99, *Commission v. Italy*, [2001] ECR I-4363; Case C-165/98, *Mazzoleni*, [2001] ECR I-2189; Case C-171/02 *Commission v. Portugal* [2004] ECR I-5645.

service providers. What is more, this obligation of the host State authorities covers not only checks that have been made by the home State in view of the exercise of the specific service activity, but also of those aimed at different purposes (such as the issuance of the passports in the Dutch case). Second, these judgments stand for the idea that the application of some variety of the home State principle comes as an integral component of the proportionality test of national measures. Hence, although the Court is not in a position to implement a fully fledged home State control whereby the host State authorities would be devoid of any competence over service providers from other Member States, it does nonetheless introduce such a principle through the back door, by way of the strengthened control of the proportionality of national measures.

### *2.3.2. Duty of cooperation between national authorities*

A corollary to the above imperfect home State principle and a technical condition for its application is the duty of Member States' authorities to cooperate with one another. Such cooperation may take two forms.

First, it may require the authorities of the host state to fully take into account and/or make full use of all the information, documents, certification etc. provided by the home state authorities'. The case law discussed above, concerning authorisations, notifications, the deposit of some form of guarantee or the issuance of duplicate (host) identification documents etc. illustrates this.[113] It constitutes a typical application of the principle of mutual recognition.

Second, the duty to cooperate may demand that the authorities of the Member States concerned work actively together, in order to positively promote the pursuance of the Treaty fundamental freedoms. This is a much more delicate path to venture upon and the Court has displayed both caution and firmness. In a first series of cases the Court has built upon the specific cooperation obligations imposed by texts of secondary legislation. In *IKA v Ioannidis*,[114] where the right of a Greek pensioner to claim a refund from his fund for treatment received in Germany under the terms of Regulation 1408/71[115] was at stake. The Court held that the

---

[113] See 2.3.1 above.

[114] C-326/00, *Ioannidis v. IKA*, [2003] ECR I-1703, and for a thorough presentation of this case the comment by Hatzopoulos in CML Rev. (2003), 1251-1268.

[115] Council Regulation (EEC) No 1408/71 of 14 June 1971 on the application of social security schemes to employed persons, to self-employed persons and to members of their families moving within the Community. This Regulation has been modified at least thirty times, the last important modification extending its personal scope to cover nationals of non Member States legally residing within the EU, see Council

authorities involved could not restrict themselves to a mechanic application of their obligations under Regulation 1408/71. Rather, they should '*in accordance with Article 10 EC* [...] *cooperate* in order to ensure that those provisions are applied correctly [...] with a view to facilitating the freedom of movement of those insured persons are fully respected'.[116]

In *Kapper*,[117] a case where the German authorities were contesting the validity of a driving license delivered by the Dutch, the Court found a violation of Directive 92/439/EC[118] and of Articles 39, 43 and 49 EC. Not only did the Court completely rule out the possibility that a license issued by the authorities of one member be invalidated by those of another Member State, but it also recognised the possibility of initiating infringement proceedings against States, the authorities of which fail to cooperate effectively.

A step further was taken in *Danner*,[119] where the Court rejected the Danish governments' argument that the effectiveness of fiscal controls justified that pensions paid to residents by foreign funds did not qualify for a deduction from taxable income. The Court held that even where the secondary legislation in place (Directive 77/799[120]) does not effectively meet the legitimate objectives pursued by the host State's authorities, the latter are required to look into and to accept further evidence provided by the interested party, before imposing a restrictive measure.

Such an obligation may also be imposed upon Member States' authorities even in the absence of any specific text of secondary legislation. In *Oulane* the Court held that the requirement that all Member States' nationals should posses a valid passport or ID card while in another Member State, could not be imposed in an absolute way, if the person concerned were able to provide unequivocal proof of their nationality by other means. This implies that the authorities in question may not rely only on the official documents they are familiar with, but may further be required to adduce evidence, concerning the person's

---

Regulation (EC) 859/2003 of 14 May 2003, OJ L 124/1. It has recently been codified and repealed by Regulation (EC) 883/2004 of 29 April 2004, OJ L 166/1.

116 *Ioannidis v. IKA*, above, para 51, emphasis added.

117 Case C-476/01, *Kapper*, [2004] ECR I-5205.

118 Council Directive 91/439/EEC of 29 July 1991 on driving licenses (OJ 1991 L 237, p. 1), as amended by Council Directive 97/26/EC of 2 June 1997, OJ 1997 L 150, p. 41.

119 This case contains the bolder statement of the duty of cooperation between Member States fiscal authorities, but almost all recent tax cases follow the same logic.

120 Council Directive 77/799/EEC of 19 December 1977 concerning mutual assistance by the competent authorities of the Member States in the field of direct taxation, OJ 1977 L 336, p. 15.

identity, by other means, probably in collaboration with the authorities of the Member State of origin of the person concerned.

Through these cases it may be said that the Court, within the material limits of its capacity as an actor of negative integration, is, in some indirect and imperfect way, trying to foster positive cooperation obligations between Member States' authorities. This does not (and may not) go as far as a proper 'home state control', since the home State authorities maintain the last word on the operation of foreign service providers in their territory. It would be technically impossible and politically undesirable for the Court to substitute the will of the legislature and to impose a fully fledged home State control. What the Court does, however, is that it stresses the cooperation duty between the Member States' authorities, in order to ensure an enhanced application of the principle of mutual recognition.

This last development, together with all the others presented above, substantiated by hundreds of judgments of the ECJ, underpin the desirability some general legislative text in the field of services. Further, the pursuance of the Lisbon Agenda, expressly requires action in this same field. These factors put together explain the initiative of the Commission which eventually led to the adoption of Directive 2006/123/EC on services in the internal market (hereinforth: 'the Services Directive' or 'the Directive').[121]

## 3. A modest but not insignificant regulatory attempt: the services directive 2006/123

### *3.1. Introduction*

The services directive is the text of secondary legislation the most widely and most passionately discussed in the history of the EU. It has been adopted after two years of fierce negotiations between the three poles of the EU legislature, animated by massive demonstrations in Brussels, Strasbourg, Paris and elsewhere and relayed by hundreds of news articles. Further, the negotiations for its adoption have (wrongly) been associated to the failed constitutional Treaty. The text finally adopted marks a neat retreat compared to the (over-)ambitious proposal of the Commission.[122] The Commission intended to regulate with one single horizontal text all services not covered by sector-specific legislation. The way to do that would be through the implementation of the

[121] Directive 2006/123, of the EP and the Council, of 12 December 2006, OJ [2006] L 376/36.

[122] COM (2004) 2 final, of 13 January 2004.

country of origin principle (CoOP), by virtue of which service providers would offer their services in all Member States, according to the rules applicable in their own. Both the above ambitions (universality of the text, CoOP) have 'hit the rock' of the European Parliament and have been partly or wholly abandoned. The fact that the Directive has indeed a modest regulatory content (3.2.) should not mask, nonetheless, that it offers precious new instruments for the governance of the service economy (3.3).

## *3.2. A modest regulatory content – in retreat from the case law?*

From the more-than-a-hundred modifications forced by the European Parliament on the Commission's draft, the single most important one is the abandonment of the country of origin principle (CoOP) in favour of the imprecise 'free provision of services' principle (3.2.1). The important increase of the activities which are excluded from the scope of the Directive is the second most striking feature (2.2.2).

### *3.2.1. Free movement of services v CoOP*

The CoOP has received a lot of, often misplaced, attention. Not only have politicians and journalists used the concept according to their respective agendas, but also legal writers are in pains finding some common ground concerning this principle.

*First*, the role of the CoOP as a rule of conflict of laws is highly controversial: some qualify the CoOP as a brand new rule of conflicts specific to the provision of services;[123] others see it as a mere exception to traditional conflict of law rules, applicable only when these rules end up in seriously obstructing the free movement of services;[124] others, finally, only identify a substantive rule, completely foreign to private international law.[125]

*Second*, the grounding of the CoOP in the Treaty is also disputed: some writers think that it is inherent in Article 49 (together with Article 10) EC;[126] on the opposite side are those who think that the CoOP is not

---

[123] See O. de Schutter and St. Francq, 'La proposition de directive relative aux services dans le marché intérieur: reconnaissance mutuelle, harmonisation et conflits des lois dans l'Europe élargie', (2005) CDE 603-660; p. 640.

[124] See M. Audit, 'Régulation du marché intérieur et libre circulation des lois' (2006) *JTDI p.* 1333-1363.

[125] See for a brief presentation of this idea, with further bibliographic references, M. Wilderspin, 'Que reste-t-il du principe du pays d'origine? Le regard des internationalistes' (6/2007) *Europe* p. 26-28.

[126] See M.-D. Garabiol-Furet, 'La directive Bolkenstein, bouc émissaire d'une Europe incertaine' (2005) *RMUE* p. 295-302, 295; see also P. Pellegrino, 'Directive sur les

to be found into the Treaty, but need to be specifically provided for by some text of secondary legislation,[127] which need be adequately motivated and have limited scope.[128]

A *third* disputed issue is whether the Directive in its current version has completely dropped the CoOP,[129] or whether to the contrary, it has just dissimulated it under less shocking terms.[130]

*Fourth*, and most importantly, the very content of the CoOP is unclear. It is this last uncertainty which explains, to our eyes, all the previous ones. This is why some further developments on the origins and the content of the CoOP follow.

#### 3.2.1.1. The genesis of the CoOP

A point in which all writers do agree is that the CoOP finds its source of inspiration in the case law of the Court in *Van Binsbergen* and *Cassis de Dijon*. In these two judgments, and the following Commission Communication,[131] the idea was clearly put forward, that services or goods which are lawfully provided or marketed in their home country should be free to cross the borders of the EU. Since then, however, much more has happened. For one thing, the Court has recognised to the principle of mutual trust[132] and to that of mutual recognition,[133] the status of a general principles of EC law. Moreover, the EC Institutions have had recourse to the 'new approach', followed by the 'global approach' of legislation, in order to regulate the internal market; in both approaches the home state regulation of the producer/provider occupies a pivotal role. Thirdly, several sector-specific pieces of legislation have put to work variants of the CoOP. However, the version of the CoOP put forward by the Directive was indeed different from all the previous

---

services dans le marché intérieur, Un accouchement dans la douleur' (2007) *RMUE* 14-21, p. 17.

127 See O. de Schutter et St. Francq, above n. 123, p. 606; S. Micossi, 'Fixing the Services Directive' *CEPS Policy Brief* 100/2006, p. 7.

128 B. de Witte, Setting the Scene: How did Services get to Bolkenstein and Why?, EUI, workingpapers Law2007/70, at http://cadmus.iue.it/dspace/bitstream/1814/6929/1/LAW_2007_20.pdf.

129 See M. Wilderspin, above n. 125, Micossi above, the House of Lords, Completing the internal market in Services, Report with Evidence, 6th Report of Session 2005-6, p. 63-74.

130 See P. Pellegrino above n. 126, p. 18; see also C. Kleiner, 'La conception des règles de droit international privé dans la directive services' in (6/2007) *Europe* 48-54.

131 OJ (1980) C 256/2.

132 Ever since Case 25/88 *Bouchara*, [1989] ECR 1105.

133 This has been a more complicated process, for which see V. Hatzopoulos above n. 104 p. 116 *et seq*.

ones. If we try to systematise the above, we can distinguish three generations of the CoOP in the legislative practice of the EC.

The first generation is constituted by the so called 'passport' directives in the field of insurance, banking and financial services. These are based on a clear distinction between, on the one hand, authorisation requirements and, on the other hand, operation conditions.[134] The former are put under the 'home country control', and any authorisation delivered by the home State is a valid 'passport' for entering the market in any other State. The operation conditions, however, remain subject to control of the host State, where the operator has to respect all applicable regulations. Moreover, in order to foster mutual trust on the authorisations thus delivered, the directives proceed to some substantial harmonisation, at two levels. Are harmonised not only the minimal levels of liquidity and of solvability of the undertakings, but also the rules concerning the keeping and publishing of accounts.[135] Therefore, this first generation of the CoOP, based on the home country control, was restricted in two ways: first, it only concerned the access to – not the exercise of – any given activity; second it presupposed substantial harmonisation.

The second generation of CoOP was clearly more ambitious. First and foremost, it was not restricted to the authorisation but also concerned the operation of service providers in other Member States. What is more, it only imposed minimal harmonisation. This second generation of CoOP has been put to work for the first time in the 1997 modification of the 'TV without frontiers' Directive.[136] The 'electronic signature'[137] and the 'e-commerce'[138] Directives have followed suite, followed themselves by the recent Directive on data protection in the field of elec-

134 It is true that in practice such a distinction is not always easy to draw, see e.g. Case C-347/02, *Commission v. France, Insurance*, [2004] ECR I-7557.

135 For a more detailed account of the 'passport' system see E. Lomnicka, 'The Home Country Control Principle in the Financial Services Directives and the Case Law' (2000) *EBLRev*, p. 324-336 and V. Hatzopoulos, above n. 104 p. 413-450.

136 Directive 97/36/EC of the EP and the Council of 30 June 1997 modifying Directive 89/552/CEE on the coordination of certain provisions laid down by Law, Regulation or Administrative Action in Member States concerning the pursuit of television broadcasting activities, 'Directive TV without frontiers', (1997) OJ L 202/60.

137 Directive 1999/93/EC of the EP and the Council of 13 December 1999, on a Community framework for electronic signatures, (2000) OJ L 13/12.

138 Directive 2000/31/EC of the EP and the Council of 8 June 2000, on certain legal aspects of information society services, in particular electronic commerce, in the internal market ('Directive on electronic commerce'), (2000) OJ L 178/1.

tronic communications.[139] All these directives contain an 'internal market' clause whereby 'Member States shall ensure freedom of reception and shall not restrict retransmissions on their territory of television broadcasts from other Member States for reasons which fall within the fields coordinated by this Directive'.[140] An 'internal market clause' is also to be found in the draft Directive on credit agreements for consumers.[141]

Besides the 'internal market clause' all these directives share some important common features: a) they do suppose some prior harmonisation; b) they all contain detailed rules allowing to determine the country of establishment of any given operator, in order to avoid settings which would amount to an abuse of rights; c) their scope is precisely defined and filled with permanent exceptions or temporal derogations and, more important of all, d) they all concern services which are provided at a distance, without the provider physically moving to any other Member State. Therefore, the powers the directives confer to the home state authorities, both to deliver the authorisation and to control the operation of undertakings concerned, come as no surprise.

Compared to the above two generations of CoOP, the one put forward by the draft Directive clearly constituted a third generation, in at least three respects. First and foremost, because it was deemed to govern not only the authorisation and operation conditions of the service activity, but also because it would also determine the applicable law, in case of dispute. Hence the totality of the service provision (authorisation, operation, conflict resolution) was to be covered by it. This difference also justifies the evolution of terminology from 'home country control' mainly used in the field of passport directives to the more far-reaching 'country of origin principle'. Second, the draft Directive had an extremely large scope of application, by no means restricted to services offered at a distance. Third, the level of harmonisation put forward by the draft Directive was so elementary, that one could legitimately question whether the very term of harmonisation is appropriate.[142] These three differences have stood on the way of this third generation of CoOP to flourish.

139 Directive 2002/58/EC of the EP and the Council of 12 July 2002, for data protection in electronic communications (2002) OJ L 201/37; this Directive replaces Directive 97/66/EC.

140 Directive 'TV without frontiers', Art. 2a para. 1.

141 COM (2005) 483 final/2, of 23.11.2005, Art. 21(2).

142 For the harmonisation put forward by the Directive see below 3.3.1.2.

3.2.1.2. Abandonment of the HCC principle

The CoOP put forward by the draft Directive, without being entirely new, constituted a clear departure from previous regulatory methods used for the internal market. This is the reason why its promoters had devised various means to ensure its smooth application (a.). Nevertheless, in view of the real or imaginary dangers it presented for the European social model, the CoOP had to be dropped altogether (b.).

a. How it should function

Three series of provisions, within the draft Directive, should help fine-tune the CoOP's innovative character.

First, there were important exceptions to the CoOP's application, both of a permanent and of a transitional nature (proposal, Articles 17 and 18, respectively), as well as of an individual character for activities related to public order and public health (proposal, Article 19).

Concerning permanent exceptions two remarks should be made. First, most services of general economic interest now enumerated in Article 17(1) were also excluded in the draft. However in the draft were excluded the individual services listed, and not all services of general economic interest as a comprehensive category. Second, and more interestingly, the draft provided for three extremely important exceptions from the CoOP: were excluded all consumer contracts (Article 17(21)), the cases where the parties in any given contract had expressly chosen the applicable rules (Article 17(20)) and the extra-contractual (tort) liability of the service provider in case of accident (Article 17(23)). Therefore, at the horizontal level (i.e. in the relationships between private parties), the CoOP, would only apply to business to business (B2B) relationships and only to the extent that the parties involved had not expressed their will to the contrary. Therefore, all the 'pain and suffering' that the CoOP was supposed to deliver to weak and helpless consumers had nothing to do with the text of the Directive – except for problems arising in sub contracting situations. Third, the CoOP would not apply to posted workers (proposal, Articles 24-25). These are few clarifications which show how much the public debate has been misleading.

Moreover, the draft Directive foresaw minimal harmonisation of several aspects of service provision. Hence, in the Chapter 'quality of services' minimal requirements of information, publicity, etc., were imposed on service providers by their home States. In the same vain, the Chapter 'convergence programme' put forward some soft harmonisation, in the form of Community codes of conduct, while further harmonisation was foreseen in identified activities.

Last but not least, the draft Directive put into place quite elaborate mechanisms for administrative cooperation between national authorities, in order to ensure the effective application of the CoOP.[143]

b. Where it could fail

Despite the above precautions, the CoOP was not risk-free in, at least, three ways.

First, because the CoOPs application requires close cooperation between the authorities of the home and host States. Indeed, since the supervision of the service provider lies with the home State authorities, these have to work closely together with their counterparts in the host State, not only for the exchange of information, but also in order to secure operational cooperation. However, experience shows that such cooperation is not always an easy task, despite the parties 'best intentions'. Hence, cooperation procedures provided for in texts as fundamental as Regulation 1408/71 on the coordination of social security systems, or as specific as Directive 77/799[144] on the cooperation in fiscal matters, still prove to be problematic and call for the Court's interpretative intervention.[145] Therefore, the application of the CoOP could be source of tensions between the Member States' authorities and of inefficiencies detrimental to consumers.

Second, the application of the CoOP as a rule of conflict of laws concerning the provider's liability may also be detrimental to consumers. Traditional conflict of laws rules are conceived to protect the weaker party. To this effect they contain basic rules (such as the application of the law of the country where the service is provided, typically the consumer's state[146] – and the competence of the jurisdictions of this same State).[147] Extensive exceptions further refine these basic rules in order to account for the different factual situations, but (almost) always with the aim of protecting the weak. The CoOP, on the contrary, would be a monolithical rule which would suffer no exceptions other than the ones specifically provided for in the proposal. What is more, it would reverse the traditional weighing of interests: prevalence is given to the service providers who can henceforth, deploy their activities without

---

143 For these see below at 3.3.

144 Directive 77/799/EEC of the Council of 19 December 1977, concerning mutual assistance by the competent authorities of the Member States in the field of direct taxation (1977) OJ L 336/15.

145 See cases *IKA c Ioannidis* and *Danner*, both cited above n. 114 and 28 respectively.

146 Rome Convention of 1980, OJ [1998] 27/34, Art. 4.

147 Regulation (EC) 44/2001 of the Council of 22 December 2000 on jurisdiction and the recognition and enforcement of judgments in civil and commercial matters, (2001) OJ L 12/1, Art. 5(1)b.

bothering to adapt their services and/or methods to the host State legislation. This has considerable economic advantages for providers as they save both on information and on adaptation costs. Further, it may also benefit the economy as a whole.[148] However, this is a 'zero sum operation' whereby the providers' gains are consumers' losses, since the latter will have to defend their interests, in case of dispute, before the jurisdictions and according to the laws of another Member State.[149] Such a transfer of risks is not necessarily inadmissible.[150] However, it corresponds to a purely political choice and may not come about as a mere 'collateral damage' to a technical rule for services in the internal market. This last point hides an extra difficulty: since the CoOP would only apply to services, what would happen to 'mixed' contracts where goods and services are intertwined and how would cross-provision of services be regulated?

Third, the application of the CoOP would lead to regulatory competition between the Member States,[151] and could end up in race to the bottom and social dumping. This risk is now more present than in the past, for at least three reasons.

Firstly, there are the economic reasons. Member States participating in (or getting ready for) the euro have lost command of both their monetary policies and of demand side policies, since spending is contained by the Stability and Growth Pact. Therefore, the only means to face negative economic conjecture is through demand side policies, i.e. increasing production and/or decreasing costs. Cutting down on social protection costs is the easiest way to cut down total cost. If one Member State engages aggressively in such direction other States will have to follow.

---

148 See House of Lords n. 129 above.

149 For this idea of 'passing the bucket' see among many, M. Audit, above n 124, p. 1353 *et seq*., and O. de Schutter and S. Francq, above n. 123, p. 640 *et seq*.

150 See e.g. the British House of Lords, in the report cited above n. 129, which clearly values the development of commercial transactions, in particular by small and medium enterprises, while it passes under silence the negative consequences for consumers.

151 Concerning the issue of regulatory competition see, among many, M. Audit, above n. 124; V. Mayer-Schönberger and A. Somek, 'Introduction: Governing Regulatory Interaction: the Normative Question' (2006) *ELJ* 431-439; P. Zumbansen, 'Spaces and Places: A Systems Theory Approach to Regulatory Competition in European Company Law' (2006) *ELJ* 534-556; and in a more general way, C. Barnard and S. Deakin, 'Market Access and Regulatory Competition' Jean Monnet Working Paper n. 9/2001 available at http://www.jeanmonnetprogram.org/papers/01/012701.html and F. Scharpf, « Introduction: The Problem Solving Capacity of Multi-level Governance » (1997) *JEPP* 520-538.

Secondly, there are the political reasons. In a Union of numerous and highly heterogeneous Member States, sharing few points in common it pays up to cheat on ones' partners, be it for a limited period.[152] Member States are tempted to maintain what they consider to be their 'competitive advantage' for as long as possible, at the cost of ignoring common policies. The derogations negotiated and the violations inflicted to the common rules opening up the utilities markets, offer a good illustration of the above point. The persistence of several states in violating the Stability and Growth pact, offers yet another very strong illustration.

Thirdly, there are the reasons more directly linked to the enlargement of the EU. The recent enlargements have conferred European citizenship to some millions of low-wage and low social protection workers – subject to an optional transitional period of seven years at most. Therefore, rhetoric trickeries like that of the 'polish plumber' menacing local service providers easily hit the bull's eye.

Therefore, the applicable standard remains the Court's imperfect country of origin principle, with all its shortcomings and limitations.[153]

### *3.2.2. Exclusions*

The conciliation procedure has left its traces both on the length and on the clarity of the Directive. The European Parliament's main additions, both at the recital and at the substantive level, all tend to limit the Directive's scope of application. The end result is a text which is quite clear on what it does *NOT* regulate, but quite ambiguous as to what it does regulate. This general negativism which has led some authors to treat the text of 'anti-legislation',[154] impregnates the very structure of the Directive (3.2.2.1). Some exclusions merit special attention (3.2.2.2).

#### 3.2.2.1. Anti-legislation?

The Directive contains long series of exceptions, both to its general scope (a.) and to some of the specific rules it establishes (b.).

a. Exceptions to the scope of the Directive

The very first Article of the Directive which is supposed to describe its 'object' (a single phrase of 28 words in the draft proposal) is a long list of seven paragraphs (423 words) in which we are told of things the

[152] In this sense S. Collignon, in his oral presentation in the CEPS commemorative conference for the 50 years of the Treaty of Rome, 'From Rome to Berlin', Madrid, 19-20 June 2007.

[153] See above 2.3.

[154] Ph. Manin, 'Conclusions' on Directive 2006/123/EC, (6/2007) Europe, p. 29-30, 29.

Directive 'does not deal with', 'does not affect' etc.:[155] liberalisation of services of general economic interest, b) abolition of service monopolies, c) protection of cultural and linguistic diversity, d) penal law, e) labour law, f) fundamental rights.

Article 2, describing the 'scope' of the Directive contains a further list of activities (not entire sectors, like in the previous article) which are excluded from the Directive's scope.[156] These activities range from services of general non economic interest, social and healthcare services to transport and financial services and to gambling and private security activities. There is no apparent logical link underpinning the various excluded activities, other that they were the ones best represented in Brussels[157]...

Article 3 of the Directive further limits its scope of application, this time in a very understandable way. It is foreseen that other sector-specific legislative texts, such as the posted workers Directive,[158] the TV without frontiers Directive[159] the recent professional qualifications Directive[160] or Regulation 1408/71 on the coordination of social security systems,[161] are not affected by the Directive. And the list is not exhaustive.

Only after this prelude of exclusions, non affectations etc., does Article 4 of the Directive give the definitions to be followed in the Directive.

---

155 It is worth noting that in the French version of the text, para. 6 of the said provision introduces a third variation, according to which the Directive 'does not apply' to labour law etc., while the English version sticks to the terms 'does not affect'.

156 Taxation, an entire sector (which should have been moved to Article 1 after its modification by the EP) is also excluded from the scope of the Directive by virtue of Article 2.

157 This view seems to be confirmed if we compare the text finally adopted with the one proposed, which only contained three exceptions.

158 Directive 96/71/EC of the EP and the Council, of 16 December 1996, concerning the posting of workers in the framework of the provision of services (1997) OJ L 18/1.

159 Directive 89/552/EEC of the Council of 3 October 1989, on the coordination of certain provisions laid down by Law, Regulation or Administrative Action in Member States concerning the pursuit of television broadcasting activities (1989) OJ L 298/23.

160 Directive 2005/36/EC of the EP and the Council of 7 September 2005, on the recognition of professional qualifications (2005) OJ L 255/22.

161 Regulation 1408/71/EEC of the Council of 14 June 1971, on the application of social security schemes to employed persons and their families moving within the Community (1971) OJ L 149/2.

b. Exceptions to the free provision of services principle

Article 16 of the Directive was to be the core Directive provision, as it introduced the ambitious CoOP. This has now been replaced by the modest principle of 'freedom to provide services'. This unclear principle has been further limited in scope by the adjunction of three paragraphs to Article 16. Therefore, paragraph 1 poses the principle that "Member States shall respect the right of providers to provide services in a Member State other than that in which they are established". Immediately thereafter in the same paragraph, however, it is stated that the above principle does not rule out restrictive measures which are non-discriminatory, necessary and proportional for the attainment of some objective of public policy, public security, public health or the protection of the environment.[162] If this were not clear enough, paragraph 3 of this same provision reiterates that these same reasons may justify the adoption of restrictive measures by the host State.[163] Therefore, Article 16 of the Directive is nothing more than a codification of the Court's jurisprudence on Article 49 EC.[164]

Article 17 of the Directive has the suggestive title '*Additional* Derogations from the Freedom to Provide Services'. This provision is difficult to understand after the abandonment of the CoOP. Article 17 made sense when it served to exclude from the far-reaching CoOP some activities judged sensible or inappropriate for that type of regulation. Now that Article 16 is restricted to codifying the Court's case law – subject to express exceptions – it is legally unclear what does Article 17 stand for.

Article 18 of the Directive foresees the possibility of 'case-by-case derogations' by measures relating to the safety of services. According to this provision, Member States may adopt restrictive measures following the mutual assistance procedure foreseen in Article 35 of the Directive. Such measures may only be adopted provided that there is no EC harmonisation in the field concerned and that they have some added value in relation to the rules applicable in provider's the home State. This provision also made sense in the original draft of the Directive, but much less now: since Member States are authorised by Article 16 (1st and 3rd paras) to introduce restrictions for the protection of public policy, security, health and the environment, it is difficult to see why

162 It is worth noting that the 'public policy' ground seems much more comprehensive in the English text than in the French where reference is made to '*ordre public*'.

163 It is difficult to understand why the EP insisted on both provisions being inserted to Article 16, since they seem to set the same rule and create confusion.

164 Subject to one eventual and unclear difference concerning exceptions, for which see above 2.2.

they would have recourse to the more restrictive and technical rule of Article 18.

Last but not least, the fact that the Directive expressly provides for exceptions to the free provision of services for the four reasons mentioned above (public policy, order, health and the environment) raises two issues. First, the Directive uses the three Treaty-based grounds for exceptions together with one which is judge-made. This is not only a conceptual shift (already identified several years ago in the Court's case law),[165] but has also substantial implications. According to the Court's case law Treaty-based exceptions may justify both discriminatory and non-discriminatory measures. Article 16 of the Directive, nonetheless, may serve to uphold only non-discriminatory measures. Second, and more importantly, the four reasons listed in Article 16 as justifying restrictions to the free provision of services are different from the more inclusive category of 'overriding reasons relating to the public interest' defined in Article 4(8) of the Directive and used in other parts of it (especially concerning establishment of service providers). Should this mean that within the scope of the Directive, Member States may only invoke these four grounds to justify restrictions of a non-discriminatory nature, while the other judge-made 'overriding reasons' become inapplicable? Such an interpretation could be valid only if we admitted that the Directive fully harmonises the free provision of services – a claim which is certainly not true.[166]

#### 3.2.2.2. Activity-specific exclusions and derogations

##### a. Services of general interest

Following the 2004 White Paper on 'Services of General Interest',[167] the Directive makes clear that this general category may be broken into two: services of general (non-economic) interest, on the one hand and services of general economic interest, on the other.[168]

The former completely evade the application of the Directive, according to Article 2(2)a. This is yet another provision added during the political negotiation leading to the adoption of the Directive, another

---

165 On the relationship between Treaty-based and judge-made exceptions see V. Hatzopoulos, 'Exigences essentielles, impératives ou impérieuses: une théorie, des théories ou pas de théorie du tout?' (1998) RTDEur, p. 191-236.

166 See also Ch. Lemaire, 'La directive, la liberté d'établissement et la libre prestation de services. Confirmations, innovations' (2/2007) *Europe*, p. 15-26, 21.

167 COM (2004) 374 final, du 12 mai 2004.

168 See in an exhaustive manner on this topic, M. Dony, 'Les notions de service d'intérêt général et service d'intérêt économique général' in J.V. Louis & St. Rodriguez, *Les services d'intérêt économique général et l'UE*, (2006) Bruylant, p. 3-38.

senseless provision. Following the terms of Article 50, the Treaty rules only apply to commercial services, offered for remuneration. The Court's case law is fixed on this point.[169] It has been observed above that the court uses imprecise criteria and a very large concept of remuneration in order to ascertain the commercial nature of any given service.[170] One may criticise the Court for its laxist attitude in this respect.[171] However, this does not justify the inclusion in the Directive of a provision stating the obvious.[172]

The added value of the Directive is also unclear in relation to services of general economic interest. Some, such as telecommunications, transport and healthcare are altogether excluded from the Directive's scope (Article 2(2)). Those which do come within the Directives scope are, nonetheless, altogether excluded from the free provision of services provided for in Article 16 (see Article 17(1)).[173] Therefore, the only way in which the Directive may affect the provision of services of general economic interest is through enhanced administrative cooperation and procedural simplification.[174] This end result corresponds to a great extent to the Court's preexisting case law, but for the underlying logic. It is reminded that the Court does respect the Member States' choices for financing services of general economic interest, subject to a lose proportionality control – not in the blanket way suggested by the exclusion of such services from Article 17(1) of the Directive.[175] Here again, the tension between general principles recognised by the ECJ, such as proportionality and non-discrimination and the simplistic solutions adopted by the Directive becomes apparent.

---

169 *Humbel*, above n. 59; Case C-109/92 *Wirth* [1993] ECR I-6447; and more recently, *Freskot*, above n. 27. See also the analysis above 2.1.2.

170 See above 2.1.2.

171 For an overview of the relevant case law see V. Hatzopoulos and U. Do, above n. 84 p. 934-937.

172 B.J. Drijber in 'Les services d'intérêt économique général et la libre prestation des services' in J.V. Louis & St. Rodriguez, *Les services d'intérêt économique général et l'UE*, (2006) Bruylant, p. 65-97, 89 rightly observes that the Court's case law is not always clear on qualifying whether any given service of general interest is economic in nature. Therefore, the clear distinction drawn by the Directive may, in practice, be blurred and services of general non-economic interest may also be affected by the Directive rules, despite their formal exclusion from its scope.

173 This is also a modification wanted by the EP: while the initial version of Art. 17 only excluded from the CoOP an exhaustive list of five services of general economic interest, in the current version all such services are excluded and the list contained in Art. 1 has only indicative value.

174 For which see below 3.3.

175 See above 2.2.3.

b. Healthcare

The way the Court has stretched Article 49 EC in order to include healthcare services has been discussed above. Under these circumstances, the exclusion of healthcare services from the scope of the Directive does not seem to matter much. From a normative point of view, the only added value of the proposed Article 23 of the draft Directive would be to introduce the criterion of overnight stay as a means of distinguishing between outpatient/hospital treatments.

However, because of the peculiar nature of healthcare, its exclusion from the Directive may adversely affect patients rights. First, while administrative cooperation is crucial in this field,[176] national authorities miss the opportunity to closely cooperate within the Directive framework. Second, patients miss all the very precious information which would be made available to them through the single points of contact, the electronic information systems etc. Third, patients cannot benefit from the warranties the Directive offers to service recipients.[177] Fourth, national insurance funds and hospitals will find it easier to ignore previous judgments of the ECJ delivered in other cases, rather than a text of national law transposing the Directive.[178] All the above factors are likely to adversely affect patient mobility. The above explain why the European Parliament, after having insisted for the removal of healthcare from the Directive,[179] in a report of May 10th, 2007 "invites the Commission to submit, to Parliament, a proposal to reintroduce health services into Directive 2006/123/EC, and a proposal to codify European Court of Justice rulings on European patients' rights".[180] The ensuing Resolution, however, only took up the need for codification.[181]

---

176 The Court itself has stressed how important cooperation is in the field of healthcare, see e.g. *IKA v Ioannidis*, above n. 114.

177 For which see below 3.3.1.1.b.

178 See e.g. Case C-444/05 *Stamatelaki* [2007] nyr, which concerned an absolute prohibition of receiving healthcare services in another Member State, clearly contrary to the well-established case law of the Court.

179 For the reasons which motivated the EP's position see one of the reports submitted to it, by R. Baeten, 'The Proposal for a Directive on Services in the Internal Market applied to Healthcare Services' presented at the EP's public audience, November 11, 2004, available at http://www.europarl.europa.eu/hearings/20041111/imco/baeten_en.pdf.

180 Report A6-0173/2007 FINAL, of May 10, 2007, on the impact and consequences of the exclusion of health services from the Directive on services in the internal market, Rapporteur B. Vergnaud, para. 71.

181 Résolution 2006/2275 (INI), of May, 2007.

c. Other excluded activities: playing with legal certainty?

The fact that many economic activities are outside the scope of the Directive raises two series of questions. First, the horizontal and general character of the Directive may appear to be more of a legal fiction, in view of the number and the economic importance of the excluded services: financial services, telecommunications, energy, transport, TV services, health care, gambling and gaming etc. Therefore, the Directive's impact in relaunching the internal market and in promoting the Lisbon objectives, may not be as important as it was thought of by its promoters. Second, in view of the fact that the Directive essentially codifies the Court's case law in the field of services, any exclusion from the scope of the Directive may be source of legal uncertainty. This may be illustrated by reference to two activities which have been recurring before the Court in these recent years.

*Gambling and gaming*

In *Schindler*, *Zenatti*, *Läära* and *Anomar*,[182] the Court has recognised that gambling is a service falling under Article 49 EC, but has shown extreme tolerance towards national restrictions thereto. The Court's 'self-restraint' takes the form of restricted proportionality control of the measures at stake[183] and is explained by the idea that "moral, religious and cultural factors, and the morally and financially harmful consequences for the individual and society associated with gaming and betting, could serve to justify the existence on the part of the national authorities of a margin of appreciation".[184] However, two recent cases concerning the Italian gambling market, mark a clear evolution of the Court's attitude. In *Gambelli* the Court held a concession system which restricted access to the gambling market to violate Article 49. Such a restriction could not be upheld, unless it could be shown to contribute in a 'coherent and systematic'[185] way with the rest of the applicable legislation, to the attainment of the set objectives of general interest (consumer protection, fraud prevention, limitation of spending propensity). This was an issue for the referring jurisdiction to decide. A couple of years

---

182 Case C-275/92, *Schindler*, [1994] ECR I-1039, *Läärä and Others*, [1999] ECR I-6067 and Case C-67/98, *Zenatti*, [1999] ECR I-7289, Case C-6/01, *Anomar*, [2003] ECR I-8621; see for these cases Allen, 'Ladies and Gentlemen, no more bets please', (2000) *LIEI*, p. 201-206.

183 See the comment on *Schindler* by V. Hatzopoulos, (1995) *CMLRev*, p. 841-855 and on *Zenatti* and *Läärä*, by Straetmans in (2000) *CMLRev*, p. 991-1005. In general for the restricted control exercised by the Court in fields touching on public morality, see P. Hetsch, 'Émergence de valeurs morales dans la jurisprudence de la CJCE', (1982) *RTDEur*, p. 511.

184 *Gambelli* above n. 92, para. 63 and *Placanica* above n. 95 para. 47.

185 *Gambelli* para. 67.

later, in *Placanica* the Court really took the situation in its hand. It held that a system of limited concessions could be justified in view of the above-mentioned grounds of general interest. It went on to state, however, that concessions should be given out following a tender procedure, having detailed procedural rules to ensure the protection of the rights which those operators derive by direct effect of Community law.[186] Making a step further the Court even held that "appropriate courses of action could be the revocation and redistribution of the old licences or the award by public tender of an adequate number of new licences".[187] In the same logic, in *Lindman*,[188] the Court had no hesitations in condemning the Finnish taxation scheme, which discriminated among proceedings of luck-games, on the basis of the place the game was organised.[189]

Under these circumstances, the exclusion of gambling from the Directive's scope does not entail freedom of action for Member States.[190] It is true that Member States are not under the cooperation and transparency obligations foreseen by the Directive. They need, however, to comply with the much stricter conditions of the judgment in *Placanica*: if they restrict the number of market participants, they need to put into place a tendering system respectful of the general procurement principles: transparency, non discrimination, proportionality and mutual recognition.[191] Therefore, the judgment in *Placanica*, through its radical content and the timing of its publication clearly constitutes a judicial revision of the unsatisfactory text of the Directive.

*Private security services*

The same may be said in relation to private security services, also excluded from the Directive's scope by Article 2(2)k. In a series of recent judgments[192] the Court has held private security activities to fall

186 *Placanica* para. 63.

187 *Ibid.*

188 Case C-42/02, *Lindman*, [2003] ECR I-13519.

189 This case law should be seen in parallel with the WTO Appellate Body Report in United States – Measures Affecting the Cross-Border Supply of Gambling and Betting Services ('*US-Gambling*'), WT/DS285/AB/R, 7 April 2005, para 373. See also Ortino, "Treaty interpretation and the WTO Appellate Body Report in *US-Gambling*: A critique", (2006) *JIEL*, 117-148.

190 Directive 2006/123, Art. 2(2)h.

191 See, among others, Case C-225/98, *Commission v. France, Nord Pas de Calais*, [2000] ECR I-7445; and in a more explicit way Case C-231/03, *Coname*, [2005] ECR I-7287 and Case C-458/03, *Parking Brixen*, [2005] ECR I-8612.

192 Case C-355/98, *Commission v. Belgium, Private Security Firms*, [2000] ECR I-1221; Case C-283/99, *Commission v. Italy*, [2001] ECR I-4363; Case C-165/98,

under Article 49 EC and not to be exempt by virtue of Article 45, on the exercise of public authority.[193] Hence, the Court has held Article 49 EC to be violated by a) requirements concerning the legal form of security undertakings, b) special qualifications required by their directors, c) the requirement of a permanent presence within the national territory, d) the need for special (identity) documents and even e) the conditions for issuing the authorisation necessary for their operation, if such conditions are already satisfied by the undertaking under the home State regulation.[194]

In this way the Court does more than just 'opening up' the market. It requires national administrations to cooperate closely and to fully embrace the principle of mutual recognition. Therefore, once again, the Court makes it up for the legislator's hesitancy.

#### 3.2.2.3. Posted workers: another false dilemma

The treatment of posted workers under the Directive has been an even deadlier battlefield than the CoOP, where the opponents of the draft Directive won yet another victory over its promoters. Since the judgments of the Court in *Evi c/ Seco*, *Van der Elst* et *Rush Portuguesa*,[195] it is established case law that a service provider may move to another Member State with his personnel. Three principles stem from the above cases: a) the service provider may move to any Member State with his own personnel, irrespectively of their nationality, without having to comply with all the requirements of the host State concerning the entry and working conditions of foreign workers; b) the service provider may, nevertheless, be required to conform himself with the labour law rules applicable in the host State (concerning working time, paid leaves, minimal salaries,[196] health and security regulations, pregnant workers etc. – but not hiring/firing conditions and not social security and complementary pension schemes);[197] c) this notwithstanding,

---

*Mazzoleni*, [2001] ECR I-2189; Case C-171/02 *Commission v. Portugal* [2004] nyr.; Case C-189/03 *Commission v Netherlands* [2004] nyr.

193 *Commission v Italy*, above.

194 The same requirements are to be found in almost all the cases; see in particular *Commission v. Portugal*, *Commission v. The Netherlands* and *Mazzoleni*, all cited above.

195 Joined Cases 62/81 and 63/81, *Seco v. EVI*, [1982] ECR 223; Case C-113/89, *Rush Portuguesa*, [1990] ECR I-1417; Case C-43/93, *Vander Elst*, [1994] ECR I-3803.

196 For the importance of agreements on minimum wages as a means to combat poverty see Funk and Lesch, 'Minimum Wage Regulations in Selected European Countries', (2006) *Intereconomics*, p. 89.

197 S. Micossi in 'Fixing the Services Directive' above n. 127 p. 6 identifies these two fields where the host State rules do not apply. Both exclusions are, however, understandable. Hiring conditions are those applicable in the home State – this could not

the service provider may not be required to comply with all the labour law formalities of the host State in respect of his own workers, unless such formalities substantially add up to the protection of workers. Directive 96/71 takes up and builds upon these through a system of 'cooperation on information' between the competent authorities (Article 4). This system, however, has proven moderately effective[198] and the draft Directive was intended to push further in the direction of free movement.

Contrary to the understanding misleadingly spread by the media, the draft Directive did not apply the CoOP to posted workers. On the contrary, it expressly stated that the CoOP did not affect neither Directive 96/71 nor Regulation 1408/71 on social security. What the Directive did is that in a section named 'posted workers' it contained two Articles: Article 24 intended to strengthen the administrative cooperation between the competent national authorities, while Article 25 was intended to tame national immigration rules in relation to posted workers.[199] The logic underlying both provisions was to transfer some competences from the host to the home authorities, while building up confidence between the two.[200] These have been abandoned and the Directive has been altogether declared inapplicable to posted workers (in at least three points in the text: Articles 1(6), 3(1)b and 17!).

Therefore, posted workers continue to be governed by (the relatively ineffective) Directive 96/71 and by the case law of the Court. If we give a closer look to the Court's case law as it currently stands we shall realise that the situation is equally unsatisfactory for 'nationalistic trade-unionists' and for 'globalised neo-liberals' alike.

In its more recent case law the Court has been more accommodating of economic imperatives and of the desire of service providers to move around wit their own personnel. Therefore, in a first series of judgments

---

be differently. Concerning social security, Article 13 of Regulation 1408/71 already foresees that all activities the duration of which exceeds twelve months are fully subject to the host State rules.

198 Commission Report on the application of Directive 96/71/EC, January 2003 and Communication The application of Directive 96/71/EC in the Member States, COM (2003) 458 final, 25 July 2003.

199 This second provision was directly inspired from the abandoned draft Directive extending the freedom to provide cross-border services to third-country nationals established within the Community, COM (2000) 271 final, 8 May 2000, finally withdrawn by COM (2004) 542 final, 1st October 2004.

200 It would seem exagerated, however, to follow the idea of L. Driguez, 'Le détachement des travailleurs après la directive sur les services', (6/2007) Europe 35-39, p. 36 *in fine* who believes that 'the Commission introduces the CoOP in the administrative modalities for controlling the application of labour law' (translated from the French by the present author).

the Court has applied its own jurisprudence and the principles of Directive 96/71 in an energetic, and yet contained, way. Without putting at stake the principle that the host State legislation should apply, the Court has held contrary to Article 49 EC and/or the Directive the obligation imposed by the host State to a service provider a) to keep all the documents required by the host's State labour legislation,[201] b) to pay social security contributions in the host State on behalf of workers who are already insured in the home State,[202] c) to obtain individual working permits for every posted worker,[203] and d) to have working visas delivered under technical conditions difficult to fulfill.[204]

In a second series of cases, however, the Court has openly questioned the full application of the host State legislation, at three levels.

a) At the administrative level, the Court has held that where the service provider is subject to a prior authorisation requirement such authorisation 'should neither delay nor complicate the exercise of the right of persons established in another Member State to provide their services'[205] Concerning a registration requirement, the Court held that

> The authorisation procedure instituted by the host Member State should neither delay nor complicate the exercise of the right of persons established in another Member State to provide their services on the territory of the first State where examination of the conditions governing access to the activities concerned has been carried out and it has been established that those conditions are satisfied.[206]

The above findings imply that the host State may be required to put into place simpler procedures and formalities compared to the ones concerning their own nationals.

b) Concerning minimal pay, the Court has also shown clear signs of departure from the full and automatic application of the host State legislation. In Mazzoleni[207] the question arose whether the personnel of a French security company occasionally deployed in sites in Belgium should be paid at the higher tariffs applicable in Belgium. The Court held that application of the host country legislation may become, under

201 Joined Cases C-369/96 and 376/96, *Arblade and Leloup*, [1999] ECR I-8453.

202 *Ibid.*

203 Case C-445/03, *Commission v. Luxembourg*, ECR [2004] I-10191, paras 20-21.

204 Case 244/04 *Commission v. Germany* [2006] ECR I-885.

205 Case C-58/98 *Corsten*, [2000] ECR I-7919, para. 47 and Case C-215/01, *Schnitzer*, [2003] ECR I-14847, para 37.

206 *Ibid.*, para 37.

207 *Mazzoleni*, above n. 112.

certain circumstances, neither necessary nor proportional.[208] The necessity test requires the host State authorities to verify whether their national legislation is needed to ensure an 'equivalent' level of remuneration for workers, taking into account fiscal and social charges applicable in the States concerned.[209] Even if the necessity test is satisfied, the application of the host State legislation may still be countered if it entails disproportionate administrative burdens for the service provider or inequalities between its employees (proportionality test).[210] Few months later in Portugaia Construcoes[211] the Court held that the host State's collective agreement on salaries could be applied only if it contributed in a 'significant way' to the employees' social protection.[212] Therefore the sacrosanct principle of the respect of host State minimal pay requirements becomes conditional upon a) significantly adding up to the employees' revenue and b) not demeasurably burdening the employer (!).[213]

c) Broadly the same principles above apply in relation to social security contributions in the host State, following the Court's judgment in Finalarte.[214]

From the above it becomes clear that if a risk of social dumping in relation to posted workers does exist, such risk is unrelated to the (draft) Directive. It is true that in some respects the Directive pushed further than the case law, e.g. by abolishing any authorisation, registration etc. obligation. Closer administrative cooperation, however, foreseen by the Directive, could help ensure the full respect of rules of social protection for workers. The very day of the publication, by the Commission, of the amended draft Directive, whereby the 'posted workers' section had been dropped, the Commission published a COM document together with a report by its services, pursuing broadly the same objectives,[215] through soft law.

In view of all the above, it would seem that the exclusion of 'posted workers' from the Directive is yet another victory of misinformed political will over economic necessities and legal certainty.

---

208 *Ibid.*, para 30, emphasis added.

209 *Ibid.*, para 35.

210 *Ibid.*, para 36.

211 Case C-164/99, *Portugaia Construções*, [2002] ECR I-787.

212 *Ibid.*, para 29.

213 This is a peculiar proportionality test: usually the restrictive measure is appraised as against a less restrictive one, while here the competing interests themselves are being compared.

214 *Finalarte*, above n. 96.

215 COM (2006) 159 final, 4 April 2006 and, of the same date, SEC (2006) 439.

### 3.3. But a significant step forward for the governance of the service economy

Despite all its shortcomings, the Directive does, nevertheless, serve the free provision of services, both on substantive (2.3.1) and on procedural (3.3.2) grounds.

#### 3.3.1. Substantive amelioration

3.3.1.1. Adressing mainstream restrictions

a. Simplified procedures for the establishment of service providers

One of the main inputs of the Directive – and the one least discussed by legal writers – is the extent to which it simplifies the establishment of service providers. Chapter III of the Directive (Articles 9 to 15) constitutes the first piece of legislation of a horizontal nature (i.e. not sector-specific, such as e.g. the TV without frontiers Directive) to align the economic with the legal concept of services, setting aside the unhappy 'duration criterion' contained in Article 50 EC. In this it follows the Court's case law described above in 2.1.3. Hence, it regulates situations which under the traditional establishment/services dichotomy fall in the former, to the extent that they concern service activities. This is why the Directive's legal base is to be found not only in Article 55 EC on services, but also in Article 47 EC on establishment.[216]

Service providers wishing to establish themselves in another Member State, have, in principle, to comply with the host State legislation. This requirement has been tempered, by the Court, through the imposition of the general principles of non-discrimination, necessity, proportionality and mutual recognition. Chapter III of the Directive codifies the relevant case law of the Court in two sections, one concerning authorisation procedures and the other all other measures restricting establishment.

Such codification does offer some clear added value. First, the codification of the case law into the text of a Directive – and its transcription into national law – does away with the casuistic character of the abovementioned principles and brings them closer to both service providers and to Member States' administrations. Second, these principles from *ex post* remedies for service providers transform themselves into *ex ante* obligations for national administrations. Third, the Directive goes beyond mere principles and offers practical details for their application, something the Court may only rarely do. Fourth, Member States' discretionary powers are circumscribed, to the extent that States are subject to

---

[216] See above 2.1.3.

report obligations concerning the restrictions maintained/imposed both to one another and to the Commission (Article 39 of the Directive).

b. Supporting service recipients

The Directive innovates by introducing rules in favour of service recipients. In a short section consisting of three articles the Directive prohibits restrictions imposed by the home State (Article 19), condemns discriminatory measures liable to be adopted by the host State (Article 20) and offers 'assistance to recipients' (Article 21).

More in detail, the recipient's home State may neither impose any authorisation or declaration requirement nor put limits to the financial aid to which the recipient is entitled, just because he/she has opted for receiving a given service in another Member State. Clearly, the principles established in *Kohll, Smits & Peerbooms* and *Vanbraekel* underpin Article 19 of the Directive. Similarly, the Court's judgments in *Trojani, Collins* and *Bidar*,[217] seem to transcend Article 20 which prevents the host State from introducing any discriminatory measure against foreign service recipients. It has to be noted that – unlike Article 16 of the Directive – the above two provisions do not exclude from their scope of application the services of general economic interest. Hence, they may be invoked by nationals of one Member State in order to secure access to services having a social character in other Member States.

The final provision on service recipients aims at making information accessible to recipients and at building up confidence for services offered in other Member States: electronic means of communication, single points of contact, simple guides, etc., all available to the service recipients in their home State.

3.3.1.2. Harmonisation and self-regulation

a. Marginal harmonisation

The fact that the Directive only entails marginal harmonisation is no secret. If, however, direct harmonisation is indeed, very limited, the Directive sets the conditions for indirect and for future harmonisation.

In the initial draft Directive, direct harmonisation was not an aim on its own, rather than a condition indispensable to the application of the CoOP. Now, however, we are left with harmonisation which, despite being narrowly targeted and limited, may nevertheless serve consumers.

---

[217] Case C-456/02 *Trojani* [2004] ECR I-7573; Case C-138/02 *Collins* [2004] ECR I-2703; Case C-209/03 *Bidar* [2005] ECR I-2119; See in general on the 'social sensibility' of the ECJ, V. Hatzopoulos, 'A (more) social Europe: A political crossroad or a legal one-way? Dialogues between Luxembourg and Lisbon' (2005) *CMLREv*, p. 1599-1635.

*Direct (substantial) harmonisation, at the service of service recipients*

Chapter V of the Directive named 'Quality of services' counts six long Articles, and provides for common measures, often of a voluntary nature. These foresee a) the obligation for service providers to offer extensive information both on themselves and on the service offered (inspired to a large extent by Directive 85/577/CE on contracts outside commercial premises and 97/7/CE on distant selling),[218] b) their liability and the need to take up professional guarantees, c) their right to use commercial communications and to set up multidisciplinary activities, subject to exceptions.[219] Voluntary quality policies are encouraged, with emphasis put on certification, evaluation, labels and quality charters. Finally, extra-judicial mechanisms of conflict resolution are to be set up by Member States in order to ease differences between service providers and service recipients. It is true that all these points do not go to the core and only touch the periphery of service provision; it is also true, however, that they focus on one of the main obstacles to the development of trans-border service flows: the lack of information and of confidence. By the same token, they add up to other more specific consumer protection rules.

*Indirect (procedural) harmonisation, at the service of service providers*

Further to the above direct harmonisation, the Directive also pushes forward indirect – but extremely important – procedural harmonisation. Chapter II of the Directive, named 'administrative simplification' harmonises formalities, documents, procedures etc. leading up to the exercise of service activities. Points of single contact will be put into place (Article 6), harmonised forms and documents will be used (Article 5(2)), pre-determined information will be at the disposition of service providers (Article 7) etc. All these provisions end up in some procedural harmonisation, which could be codified in a kind of a vade mecum for the setting up of service activities in any Member State.

*Future harmonisation*

The core content of the Directive is full of measures of negative integration: abolition of unjustified restrictions, discriminations, etc.

---

218 Directive 85/577/EEC of the Council of 20 December 1985, to protect the consumer in respect of contracts negotiated away from business premises, (1985) OJ L 372/31; Directive 97/7/EC of the EP and the Council of 20 May 1997 on the protection of consumers in respect of distance contracts, (1997) OJ L 144/19, as modified by Directives 2002/65/EC and 2005/29/EC.

219 Exceptions necessary to accomodate the case law of the Court in cases such as *Gebhard* and, more importantly, Case C-309/99 *Wouters*, [2002] ECR I-1577.

These, however, also lead to positive integration and *de facto* harmonisation: Member States obliged to give up important packages of their legislation, will have to replace those with measures inspired by the Directive and the Court's case law. Moreover, in some instances the Directive's rules are detailed to such a point that national measures implementing them will necessarily be very similar.

Moreover, the Directive contains a couple of 'rendez-vous (RDV) clauses', whereby the Institutions and Member States are invited to reflect on further harmonisation. There is one sector-specific RDV clause (Article 38) of minute importance (after the European Parliament cut down on the bulk of the activities it would concern). Next to it, there is one general RDV clause, of extreme importance and sophistication, concerning the Directive as a whole (Articles 39-41). This should bear its fruits in 2011 and every three years thereafter.[220]

Finally, the Directive has several 'hooks' whereby further harmonisation measures (of secondary importance) have to (see e.g. Articles 8(3) and 21(4)) or may be (see e.g. Articles 5(2) and 23(4)) adopted by the Commission.

b. Codes of conduct and other self-regulation

The Directive further « harmonises » through the use of European labels, norms etc. (Article 26) and, more importantly, through the promotion of European codes of conduct (Article 37). It is incorrect, technically, to talk of harmonisation through measures of soft law. Such measures have no normative intensity whatsoever and hence are not binding and their normative content is freely determined by the regulatees themselves. However, it has been shown that soft law may be as binding as hard law and that, in certain circumstances, it may even ensure a higher degree of compliance.[221] Self-regulation has also proven quite effective both as a component of the 'new approach' of legislation inaugurated in 1985 and in the regulated network industries. Therefore, the limited harmonisation pursued by the Directive is being completed by soft means.

---

220 This will be further discussed below in 2.3.2.

221 See, among many, F. Snyder, 'Soft law and Institutional practice in the EC', in S. Martin (ed.) *The Construction of Europe, Essays in Honour of Emile Noel* (1994) Kluwer, Dordrecht, p. 197-225, and more recently, D. Trubek, P. Cortell & M. Nance, 'Soft Law, Hard law and European Integration: Toward a Theory of Hybridity', (2/05) Jean Monnet Working Paper, and in a more exhaustive way L. Senden, *Soft Law in EC Law* (2004) Hart, Ofxord/Portland.

### 3.3.2. Procedural improvements

Contrary to the Directive's poor substantive content, its procedural arrangements are both innovative and powerful. The Directive is impregnated with modern methods of governance and embodies a new drafting-style directly issued from the 'Better Lawmaking' Communication[222] and the 'European Governance' White Paper.[223] The Directive's procedural arrangements aim both at securing the attainment of the set objectives (3.3.2.1) and at ensuring its own 'sustainability', through its periodic revision (3.3.2.2).

#### 3.3.2.1. Procedural arrangements for the free provision of services

##### a. Administrative simplification

Administrative simplification is one of the Directive's main objectives. In this respect the techniques followed by the Directive are quite original for a text of hard law – but already well established as means of fostering soft cooperation among States.

For some time now, and quite intensively since the launching of the Lisbon Agenda in 2000, the Commission works on the issue of administrative simplification. Building on the experience acquired by the OECD in this field,[224] the Commission has fostered the exchange of best practices and benchmarking, while it has devised several indicators measuring the performance of national administrations. Up till now, however, all these have remained 'esoteric' to the Commission and have only taken the form of working documents, internal reports and recommendations.[225] Only in 2007 did the Commission launch action programme 'CUT 25' aimed at the reduction of national administrative burden by 25 per cent by the year 2012.[226] In the framework of this action plan the Commission proposed some legislative texts, for the first time in January 2007.

Well before these texts were even proposed by the Commission, the Directive was the first text of a horizontal nature to put forward binding

222 COM 97 (626) final, of 26.11.1997; see also the Commission's webpage on this issue at http://ec.europa.eu/governance/better_regulation/impact_en.htm.

223 COM 2001 (428) final, of 25.7.2001.

224 Several general reports, as well as national reports are available at http://www.oecd.org/topic/0,3373,en_2649_37421_1_1_1_1_37421,00.html.

225 The Commission pursues administrative simplification not only at the Member States level, but also concerning its own legislative acts and proposals, see Commission Communication 'Implementing the Community Lisbon programme: a strategy for the simplification of the regulatory environment' COM (2005) 535 final and the first Report on the application of this strategy, COM (2006) 690 final.

226 COM (2007) 23 final.

rules on administrative simplification. Chapter II of the Directive contains four series of rules.

Article 5 asks Member States to evaluate their requirements concerning access to, and exercise of, service activities. If these prove not to be 'sufficiently simple' Member States have to simplify them. The fact the 'sufficiently' criterion is a very vague one and that the only one to evaluate this is the very Member State concerned, Article 5 should be seen more as a political engagement rather than as a legal norm.

Articles six, seven and eight form a coherent set of rules having the potential to revolutionise the establishment of service providers in other Member States. The 'best practice' of one stop shops is made into a legal obligation. Hence, Member States are to put into place single points of contact, for service providers, with twofold responsibilities. First, these contact points should provide all the information foreseen in Article 7 of the Directive. Second, and more importantly, they should accomplish, on behalf of service providers, all necessary formalities and procedures giving access to the service activity concerned. This is a way around national bureaucracy, bearing its own dynamics for substantial simplification: when one bit of the national administration (the single point of contact) is to cope with the formalities of all the other administrative authorities, a strong incentive is given for the reduction of red tape. The creation of these points of single contact should considerably diminish establishment cost, both in terms of information collection and of setup fixed costs; small and medium enterprises should be the main beneficiaries. The role of points of single contact is all the more important after the abandonment of the CoOP, since service providers need, in principle, to comply with all the host State requirements. However, Member States have no real incentive to offer their best services to providers from other Member States, at considerable cost. Therefore, some monitoring system, either by the Commission or through peer-review, should secure the effective functioning of single points of contact.

The Directive also makes use of the available technology and provides that all the information provided by the single points of contact should also be available by electronic means at a distance and should be regularly updated (Article 7). What is more, all the procedures and formalities necessary for the exercise of any service activity should be made available for online completion (Article 8).

b. Administrative cooperation between Member State authorities

Contrary to section a (above), section b on 'administrative cooperation' has clearly lost in importance from the abandonment of the CoOP, since competence sharing and mutual help between home and host State authorities are now less important. However, one cannot dismiss altogether nine (out of 45) provisions of the Directive. Hence, the creation of one or more 'liaison points' in every Member State, responsible for the exchange of information between national authorities will certainly help the application of the Directive (Article 28). Next to those, a 'European network of Member States' authorities' will run an alert mechanism whenever it 'becomes aware of serious specific acts or circumstances relating to a service activity that could cause serious damage to the health or safety of persons or to the environment'(Article 32). An electronic system for the exchange of information (Article 34(1)) and some rules on the respective competences of the home and host State complete the rules on cooperation.

3.3.2.2. Procedural arrangements for the revision of the Directive

One of the main originalities of the Directive is that it is 'self-sustainable': it provides for its own periodic evaluation and revision. Articles 39 and 41 constitute a startling example of new methods of governance being introduced into more traditional regulatory instruments, such as the Directive at hand.[227] These provisions put into place a system of successive reports which may eventually culminate into legislative proposals put forward by the Commission. More precisely, Member States have to report to the Commission on the use they have made a) of the discretion left to them by the Directive (Articles 9§2, 15§5 et 25§3) and b) of the derogation on the free movement of services, contained in Article 16(3). These reports are circulated to other Member States for peer review. On the basis of the initial reports and the peers' comments on them, the Commission is to present a synthesis report to the European Parliament and the Council. After all these reports have been circulated and subject to evaluation, the Commission shall present in 2011, for the first time, and every three years thereafter, to the Parliament and Council a 'comprehensive report' on the application of the Directive « accompanied, where appropriate, by proposals for amendment of this Directive» (Article 41).

The very fact that this complex system of cross-reporting and circular evaluation is to be found in a Chapter called 'Convergence Programme', rather than in the 'final provisions' of the Directive, talks of the Commission's intentions. Faced with the Parliament's dogged opposition and the public's reprehension for its initial proposal, the Commission has recourse to successive reports and evaluations of an imperfect legal instrument. These, orchestrated by the Commission itself, should create further dynamism, which the Commission should be able steer in the direction it sees fit, in the future. By the same token, the future

[227] For the issue of hybrid formations see above n. 221.

revision of the Directive is being de-politicised and transformed into a technocratic process.

## 4. Conclusion

Out of the numerous questions which emerge from the developments above, one stands out in a most compelling way: in view of the high degree of involvement of the Court in the construction of the internal market for services (briefly presented in part 1), does the 'services directive', as amputated by the European Parliament (briefly presented in part 2), has any reason of being, does it have any added value? The answer to this question is twofold.

For one thing, the Directive will be a source of legal complication and uncertainty. Not so much because it introduces new rules of law, but precisely because it does not. Instead, it meddles in an inconsistent and haphazard way with established principles and accepted rules, while providing for an interminable list of 'exclusions', 'derogations', 'non affectations' etc. Any hope for substantial positive integration went awash with the abandonment of the CoOP. This retreat, imposed as a political necessity, is unsatisfactory both from an economic and from a legal viewpoint. The economies that would accrue to service providers from not having to investigate in, and comply with, the legal systems of other Member States are being lost. At the same time, however, host State authorities are bound by a strong principle of mutual recognition and by compelling cooperation obligations, in unclear terms. In these respects, the adoption of the services directive has added nothing, it may even qualify as a retreat.

On the other, hand, however, there are at least three ways in which the Directive may be valued positively. First, by codifying (as well as it could) the Court's case law, it vested the solutions adopted with democratic legitimacy and silenced voices complaining of judicial activism. Second, the Directive, does contain some rules (of secondary importance, it is true) leading to the simplification of procedures and to some limited harmonisation. Third, the Directive clearly sets the conditions, both procedural and substantial, for the adoption of more far reaching rules, in the future.

# Part III

# The External Dimension of the Internal Market

CHAPTER 7

# The External Dimension of the Internal Market

## An Economic Perspective

Peter HOLMES

*Visiting Professor, College of Europe (Natolin), Professor at the University of Sussex*

## 1. Introduction

This paper[1] will explore the external dimension of the single market from two perspectives. First I will discuss the extent of the challenge faced by the *internal market programme* (IMP) in creating a truly unified trade regime, and second I will discuss what might be termed the internal dimension of the external market.

## 2. The internal market programme

### 2.1. What is 'the internal market'?

The first part of the discussion will highlight the extent to which the elimination of frontier barriers for goods within the common market required important steps to create a genuinely common commercial policy, and the nature of the conflict between liberalism and ideas of 'Fortress Europe' that had to be addressed. The second part will discuss how the internal harmonisation agenda led to an ambitious, but not wholly successful, drive to extend some of the principles of the internal market (IM) to the world economy.

From an economic perspective, the principal way that the European Economic Community (EEC) was characterised in the early years was

[1] I would like to thank Aylin Ege for her very helpful comments. I would also like to thank Javier Lopez Gonzalez.

as a 'Customs Union'. That is to say that the principle model of economic integration that used to analyse the creation of the EEC was 'Customs Union' theory developed in the 1950s by Viner, Meade and Lipsey. This derives from classical international trade theory. The analysis takes a 'country' to be a unit within which barriers to the movement of goods, services and factors of production are non-existent. There are, for example, no internal transport costs. Workers are homogeneous and prices are uniform. These assumptions are taken as so obvious as rarely to be stated explicitly. Each country however has trade barriers against the rest of the world in the form of uniform MFN tariffs, but capital and labour do not move across borders. Then we form a customs union in which goods move as freely internally as within national markets. The customs union theory model does not recognise any barriers other than tariffs (except in some 1960s literature on tax harmonisation).

The message of the model is very clear however, that liberalisation within a market is desirable to the extent that it creates new trade but undesirable to the extent that it diverts trade from the outside towards intra-union trade. The policy implication is that the success of economic integration depends very much on the external policy.

In the early years of the common market many studies suggested that the low level of industrial tariffs meant that trade creation in this area would dominate diversion in agriculture. Thus for economists, the very notion of the 'common market' is defined in terms of its supposedly common face to the outside world, and so in that sense economic integration for economists is seen as just a special case of international trade theory, one which leaves out rather a lot of 'within the border' aspects. Despite, or perhaps because of its generality, therefore, economists were not very well placed to really examine the external implications of the common market in the 1980s because the EEC was already modelled as if it had a free internal market and a common commercial policy.

## *2.2. The internal market plan*

When the internal market proposal emerged in the 1980s, to actually complete the common market, the liberals argued but a major current of opinion was in favour of European Champions and '*reconquête du marché intérieur*'.

The internal market plan was deliberately ambiguous about the external implications. At the time the Member States were still jealous of their residual powers. As for the single market the French were eager to see it as a *reconquête du marché intérieur* while the UK saw the internal market as a liberalising device. No agreement would have been possible had it been explicitly debated beforehand.

The Cockfield White Paper (E.C., 1985) did not make any proposals for external trade policy beyond noting that if barriers to 'trade deflection' were to be applied within the internal market, a mechanism would have to be found that did not rely on the use of intra-EC customs posts and Article 115 of the EC Treaty would have to be implemented differently. But by 1998 when the Cecchini report tried to establish an overall estimate of the effects of the internal market, it was not clear what the external regime would actually be. There was no policy statement that could be referred to, to characterise the external trade regime and an ambiguous text from the Commission was quoted noting merely that there would have to be some common commercial policy.[2]

To some extent the internal market was a response to a perceived external challenge to competitiveness, mostly seen as coming from Japan. There was perhaps a fear that individual states would make their own separate responses that would create further divisions.

## *2.3. What had to be done*

But in 1986 the common market was not even yet a true customs union! Non tariff measures were not unified at the EU[3] level. There was not actually a fully common commercial policy! The most striking examples of this were in cars and textiles. In the case of the textile industry, the Multi-fibre Arrangement (MFA) laid down quotas specific to individual Member States. There was not even a fully common external tariff as East German goods entered the Federal Republic duty-free and any goods travelling further paid duty only at the next border.

In order to prevent trade deflection into more protectionist Member States via less protected ones, a complex set of monitoring devices at internal frontiers was in place. These were sustained by the use of Article 115 of the Rome Treaty which provided for quantitative restrictions on the intra-Community movement of goods originating outside the common market, in circumstances when the Common Commercial policy had not been fully established. This was a rather dramatic, but lawful, derogation from the basic principle of a Common market and a customs union as enshrined in Article 9 of the original Rome Treaty, namely free circulation of goods on Community origin and goods that had paid duty. It seems unlikely that the authors of the Treaty really expected this interim period to last till the 1980s.

---

2 The Cecchini Report was studiedly ambiguous.

3 We use the term 'EU' rather than 'EC' except where the distinction may matter, as in WTO documents.

In the case of cars and certain other industries such as consumer electronics, there was nothing quite as explicit as the Multi-fibre Arrangement (MFA) to justify national quotas, but national measures existed and fragmented the single market. In the case of cars each Member State had a distinctive regime *vis-à-vis* Japan. The UK had a more or less wholly illegal industry to industry Voluntary Export Restraint (VER); France applied administrative measures to restrict imports; Italy had a system of quantitative restrictions it claimed were based on a trade agreement predating the Rome Treaty. The Commission's competition régime tolerated these measures by allowing a block exemption for distribution of cars which allowed manufacturers to segment the European car market. Specious arguments about the value to consumers of specialised servicing arrangements were invoked. Once Japanese investment began, especially in the UK, arguments began to develop about what was a 'European car'. The French government spoke of the need for high percentages of value added to establish European 'origin', even though there was no valid basis to restrict the free movement of components once they entered the EEC and paid their duty. These arguments were not put to rest until the 'consensus' on the car industry of 1991.

The car industry was resolute in trying to preserve the segmentation of the IM and there is evidence that, for the Japanese industry, the ability to price discriminate within Europe was a significant compensation for the continuing restriction of numbers after 1991 (Mattoo & Mavroidis, 1995). Much was made of the issue of the exact meaning of 1991 consensus on Japanese car exports to Europe, and the detailed figures in it, especially as to whether they included the output of EU based plants. However in reality the agreement which was never officially published (Holmes & Smith, 1995), the Japanese government was to determine the export quotas following six monthly discussions with the Commission. The nature of the agreement, the only officially published version of which was a joint press release, illustrates the difficulty of persuading Member States to actually deliver something they had promised only implicitly.

A Commission spokesman in an interview with the author explained that the Commission had been very clever to phase out the national trade barriers in an informal agreement which replaced them with a VER run by the Japanese, because if the EU had put in place a measure that was actually a formal legal instrument of its CCP, it would have been impossible to get rid of it. In fact the EU and Japan had negotiated a special provision in the Article XIX agreement of the Uruguay under which each WTO member was allowed one non-MFA VER until 2000 when car trade would come under the normal rules of the WTO.

Interestingly, the initial fears that the eventual opening of the floodgates would be a disaster for the European motor industry have been totally unfounded. Imports from Japan fell in the 1990s, and the European car industry has bounced back. But it is interesting to speculate on the reasons: free traders will argue that it showed that the protection was unnecessary. Car producers might argue that the 'breathing space was necessary'. Maybe the inward investment that was induced by the import restrictions might conceivably have demonstrated to EU firms that car production was possible in Europe! Without a counterfactual we shall never know.

Hanson (1998) argues that the liberalisation of the car industry was linked to the IMP and can in part be explained by the increasing importance of export as opposed to import competing interests (Hanson, 1998).

The separate national quotas and the ensuing national segmentation for textiles and clothing of Member States probably outlasted the car regime *de facto.* Council Regulation 3030/93 of 1993 after the single market was supposedly complete still left it to Member States to issue import licenses. Moreover it specifically provided for the application of safeguards 'at a regional level' rather than at the level of the whole EU. The preamble included the somewhat paradoxical statement: "Whereas, in certain exceptional circumstances, it may be more appropriate for such quantitative limits to be applied at the regional level rather than at the Community level and it is therefore necessary to lay down efficient procedures for deciding upon appropriate measures which do not disrupt unduly the functioning of the internal market". The final end of the MFA régime did not come until 2005.

The consumer electronics industry had similar barriers, even though in the Pioneer and Grundig-Consten cases, it had, unlike the car industry, been a priority for unification of the common market. Here technical barriers created obstacles to the free circulation of colour TVs in the form of SECAM in France and variants of the PAL system in other states, but their importance has since diminished. The principle device for protecting this industry against tn4id countries soon became anti-dumping duties, which were applied at a Community level and the major firms were all multinationals. This undoubtedly assisted the consolidation of the common external policy but it was far from sufficient.

By 2000 and 2005 the external dimensions of the single market in cars and clothing appeared to be more or less complete, but not without rearguard action by some Member States. It is unlikely that the external market would have been unified without the impetus of the IMP.

It would be difficult to judge the impact of the internal market plan on the horizontal aspects of the EU's anti-dumping regime. A glance at the data indicates that there was a very sharp rise in the number of anti-dumping actions in the 1980s. But can this be attributed to a deliberate plan to undercut the more general liberalising effects of the IMP? It seems unlikely. Anti-dumping was becoming more fashionable throughout the industrial world. It was also rising in the US in the same period (Irwin, 2005).[4]

## *2.4. Regulatory unification and market access*

Economic models were relatively poorly equipped to estimate the impact on external trade of internal regulatory harmonisation. Most economists suppose, however, that regulatory harmonisation is likely to be less trade diverting than tariff policy.

It is very hard to harmonise regulations in a discriminatory manner. In making it easier for EU Member States to access each other's markets third parties are necessarily relieved of the obligation to meet a large number of individual rules. In the case of the car industry the variety of regulations added modest amounts to costs but greatly facilitated price discrimination so mutual recognition of type approval certification was resisted by manufacturers. Even the Japanese whose cars met everyone's standards profited from the barriers to parallel trade through the ability to price discriminate.

It is in fact not yet the case that all regulatory aspects of the internal market have a unified external dimension. Services are much more complex issue. One could write a major essay on the failings of the EU's internal market in services. It is therefore not altogether surprising that the external dimension is also incomplete. The external dimension drove some of the internal debates. There is still a tension between the principles of allowing the 'home' or the 'host' country to regulate third country based enterprises that establish in one EU Member state and then supply services into another. The member sates still retain different rules. The EU's schedules on services under the Uruguay Round which reflected the regulatory differences in the early 1990s are still essentially national, even though the Commission tried to use the Uruguay to coax the Member States into collective offers, and to a limited extent succeeded in some areas such as telecoms (Holmes & Young, 2002). Areas such as higher education were scheduled by the EU but contain a series of national exceptions within the positive list system.

---

4 See Global Anti-dumping database, http://people.brandeis.edu/~cbown/global_ad/.

## 2.5. What was the effect of the IMP on external trade flows?

Unfortunately this question is extremely difficult to answer; we would need to know what the trade policy of the EU would have been in the absence of the IMP but with other things being the same. We then need to know what the consequences of the alternative policies would have been. We can unfortunately have limited confidence in what the models tell us.

We know, however, that the Uruguay Round and the IMP were being carried on simultaneously and the processes fed on each other. For example in estimates of the impact of the Uruguay Round, a major welfare effect for the EU came from removal of national car quotas. This shows up as a trade policy impact but was caused by the decision to unify the car market. On the other hand some elements of the liberalisation of telecommunications, kicked off by the internal market plan were fully completed only as part of the GATS package.

**Figure 7.1. The share of intra-EU imports excluding oil compared to extra-EU imports during the single market process**[5]

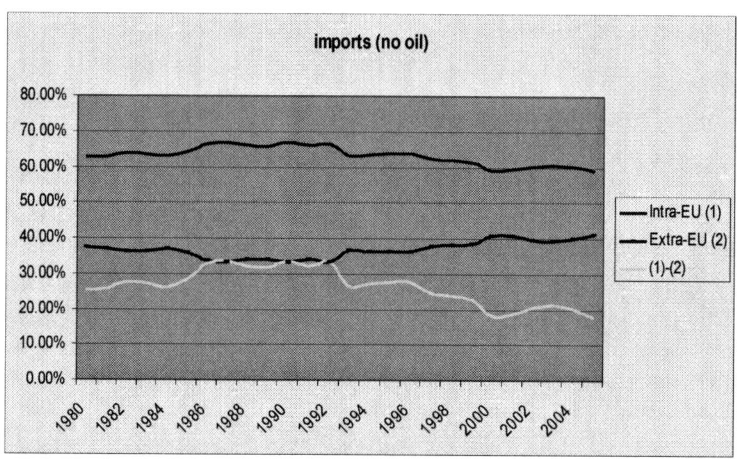


It seems reasonable to attribute tariff reductions to the Uruguay Round alone (Hoeller, Girouard & Collechia, 1998).[6] We do not know for sure how far the nature of the cuts following the Uruguay Round was affected by the IMP, but there are strong grounds for believing that

5 Calculations by J. Lopez-Gonzalez using Comtrade.

6 There is in fact no evidence of any fall in manufacturing tariffs in the data available for 1988-93.

the interaction created a liberalising effect. WTO data on EU average tariffs suggest that Fortress Europe did not appear.[7]

This view has been challenged by Patrick Messerlin (2001), who argues that the combination of contingent protection and non tariff measures meant that between 1990 and 1997 the EU external protection stayed the same, disproving he suggests both the Fortress Europe and liberalism theories, but Messerlin's figures are based on not always clear methodology.

Studies which tried to take account of all the effects come up with a moderately optimistic conclusion – even if as we have noted we really cannot tell what the counterfactual would have been. The raw data do not show any sign of 'Fortress Europe'.

The work of Allen, Gasiorek and Smith (1996) notes that any CGE simulation analysis is likely to predict some trade diversion, because of the way trade models work. However their analysis of the actual *ex post* trade data, both descriptive and econometric suggested that there was not a significant increase in intra-EU trade at the expense of external trade. "This could be interpreted as the IMP having caused external liberalisation, perhaps because of the market access effects of having a single regulatory system, or explicit rules about public procurement. Alternatively, it could be interpreted as the IMP having been accompanied by external liberalisation".

They conclude: "The liberalisation of external trade has been at least as strong as the intra-EU liberalising effects of the IMP. Concerns about 'fortress Europe' effects of the IMP were unnecessary: the IMP has not in itself closed the EU market to third countries, nor has it been accompanied by protectionist measures".

This conclusion was also shared by Stevens and Young (1996) who undertook a more qualitative approach. They concluded that even in textiles and clothing there had been easier access to the internal market. Winters (1992) came to a similar conclusion reviewing a range of studies as did a study for the OECD Secretariat (Hoeller, Girouard & Colecchia, 1998) which concluded, "The empirical evidence provided in the paper points to little evidence for trade diversion due to integration in Europe, while trade is likely to have boosted area-wide income significantly".

The analyses of the Uruguay Round by the World Bank, the OECD and the GATT/WTO secretariat are broadly consistent with this view, but attributing effects to the Round vs the IMP is very hard because

7 See http://www.wto.org/english/tratop_e/tpr_e/tp10_e.htm#The%20Secretariat.

these estimates[8] all suggest that the biggest gains to the EU were from CAP liberalisation assumed to be the effect of the UR (and not to have been due to happen anyway!), and to the impact of the removal of quotas, in particular on textiles and clothing and on cars. The IMP did not in itself eliminate the MFA quotas and there was still a national element after 1993 but the creation of the single market made national measures appear increasingly futile.

The WTO secretariat commented in the first Trade Policy review of the EC in 1995:

> A core element of the internal market process was the elimination of trade restrictions maintained by individual Member States [...] The European Union's Uruguay Round commitments include widespread tariff reductions for manufactures, bringing the average rate down by 38 per cent to 3.7 per cent in 2000.[9]

As we noted most of the studies of the overall effects of the IMP were favourable. A more controversial element has been the tendency of the EU to 'export' its regulatory framework, partly by its very existence, which requires trading partners to adopt EU norms if they are to sell into the EU and partly in the context of trade agreements (Holmes, 2006).

The World Bank has carried out a number of studies that are critical of the EU's alleged tendency to engage in a race to the top in standards.[10] Otsuki, Wilson and Sewadeh (2001) estimated that $670m worth of peanut butter exports would be lost to West Africa under proposals to harmonise the Maximum Reside level (MRL) levels for aflatoxin in peanut butter. By harmonising on the tightest Member State regime the EU risked excluding some producers who could meet the standards of less demanding MS, which, according to the bank, created a negligible risk to health. Mattoo (2001) has argued that even non-discriminatory mandatory standards can have *de facto* discriminatory effects, as they are easier for some suppliers to meet than others.

Chen and Mattoo (2004) argue that EU mutual recognition and harmonisation benefited developed trading partners who were able to profit from the economies of scale, but hurt exports into the EU from developing countries not so able to profit.

However, Jaffee and Henson (2004) have suggested that some of their colleagues at the World Bank may be exaggerating the notion of

---

8 See various chapters in Martin & Winters, 1996.

9 Secretariat summary of 1995 TPR of the EU http://www.wto.org/english/tratop_e/tpr_e/tp10_e.htm#The%20Secretariat.

10 See for example Sun & Pelkmans, 1995.

'standards as barriers'. This is a point we will return to in the final part of the discussion.

The one further area where there is a little evidence available is with respect to foreign direct investment. There was anecdotal evidence that the fears of trade protection would attract more Foreign Direct Investment (FDI) as firms sought to get inside 'Fortress Europe'. Dunning (1997) concluded that there had been a rise in FDI into the EU but that it could be explained by protectionism. Again he notes the driving forces are expected regional demand and the general trend towards globalisation, and that it is hard to imagine the trend of globalisation have been the same without the IMP occurring. Interestingly, there is evidence that an important factor influencing inwards FDI was anti-dumping policy (Belderbos, 1997), though it would take a wider exercise than the present one to discuss whether the IMP actually increased anti-dumping activity as a result of the greater competition within the EU and so greater vulnerability to 'injury'.

Our conclusion on the external impact of the internal market programme has to be that there is little evidence of any adverse impact on third parties in the years of the implementation of the programme. But the evidence is surprisingly tenuous. We don't know what the external trade regime would have been without the IMP and economists are surprisingly ill-equipped to measure the trade effects of regulation. The final estimate of the external impact of the IMP actually requires political rather than economic analysis to generate the anti-monde of EU trade policy without the IMP.

## 3. The internal effects of external trade policy

The apparent success of the internal market programme clearly inspired the Community's external agenda in the years following the completion of the single market.

The push for the Singapore issues and a series of speeches by Pascal Lamy highlighted the view that the WTO should be seen as regulating globalisation rather than merely pushing liberalism to further extremes.

The Uruguay Round already included a number of elements linked to the single market regulatory approach. Both the TBT and the SPS agreements reflected the EU's willingness for a presumption that goods produced to international standards should be acceptable to all WTO Member States. These WTO arrangements, however, left more flexibility for importers to invoke exceptional needs and placed a burden of proof on the complainant.

However, just as the EU was beginning to find political resistance setting in to harmonisation within the EU, the EU itself was finding that the conditions it had agreed to at the WTO were becoming somewhat indigestible. The Beef Hormones and GM cases led the EU to seek a political escape clause from the requirement that food regulations had to be based on scientific evidence not public fears (Lamy, 2004).

The EU has been frustrated by the fact that the WTO lacked the political decision-making capability that the EU itself acquitted with the single market process. There is no body effectively capable of legislating with authority and legitimacy at the WTO except when there is effective unanimity among members. We find ourselves in a situation where the Appellate Body of the WTO is acting as the European Court of Justice (ECJ) did in the years when the Council of Ministers was gridlocked. However, the difference is that when the ECJ threw out a national measure as not compatible with the common market, there was a legislative body, the Council, able to take up the challenge of deciding what the common rules should be (Holmes, 2006, *Ibid.*).

The key dilemma currently facing both the EU and WTO is how to treat public demands for food safety standards that are both strongly sought after by parts of public opinion and also restrictive of trade. The same issues face both the EU and the international system, and the EU's confidence that it had got the matter right in the IMP seems to be eroding. As we noted above, the issue has been raised by the World Bank in the context of the harmonisation of standards for products that are imported on a significant scale. Where there is no single EU mandatory standard, Member States may be able to invoke derogations from the principle of mutual recognition, and so fragment the internal market. It is thought that the Beef Hormone rules were introduced due to the twin pressures of public opinion in some Member States and the desire to avoid fragmentation of the single market if this prevailed. As the World Bank has argued, the choice of a high or low common level of maximum residual levels can have a big effect on third parties. The aflatoxin issue has attracted international attention, but we have also seen complaints about ochratoxin requirements for coffee, amongst others.

An unfortunate parallel has also appeared in services. In the early 1990s the EU was able to tell itself that it was on the way to creating a unified services market. The EU model did indeed work extremely well as a template for the world in telecoms and both internal and external liberalisations sustained each other. But in other areas the resistance to change has been market inside and outside the EU.

The other area where the EU has been pushing the internal market is in its Regional Trade Agreements. There is a clear logic to the strategy of demanding that *candidate* countries adopt the full *acquis* before accession, though there are legitimate questions of timing and priorities. The Commission made it clear that full adoption of the *acquis* was a necessary but not a sufficient condition for market access without being subject to contingent protection. The statement has been made in numerous documents (E.C., 1995):

> Once satisfactory implementation of competition and state aids policies (by the associated countries) has been achieved, together with the application of other parts of Community law linked to the wider market, the Union could decide to reduce progressively the application of commercial defence instruments for industrial products form the countries concerned, since it would have a level of guarantee against unfair competition comparable to that existing inside the internal market.

However the acceptance of the *acquis* is a necessary but not a sufficient condition; only full membership (and the expiry of a transition period) provides guarantees against the use of anti-dumping duties etc., as Turkey has found.

That is not to say that the *acquis* are necessarily a burden. Whilst the replacement of locally appropriate standards by higher cost but inappropriate ones is problematic, the wholesale adoption of a partners' norms where standardisation is weak may well be a way to solve a domestic coordination problem (Evans *et al.*, 2006; Ghoneim, Holmes & Iacovone, 2005).

A recent conference on 'Giving Neighbours a Stake in the EU Internal Market'[11] illustrated the lack of clarity on the Commission's part in these matters, in particular as to whether the neighbours were being invited to adopt the IM norms for the sake of 'upgrading' the domestic economy or for improved market access – in both directions. There is still inadequate evidence about how the different trade offs play out. However there is a clear set of trade offs involved between:

- improving market access for firms in the export sector already able to comply with EU norms;
- giving an incentive to firm at the margin of exporting to 'upgrade';
- raising the quality of output in the domestic market;
- raising costs to firms and consumers;
- risking the disappearance of local firms able to supply to local market demands but not to EU norms;
- risking loss of export sales in other markets.

For neighbourhood partners that aspire to join the EU, there is no alternative but to accept the entire EU *acquis*, but for those that have no desire or chance of joining there is a complex cost-benefit calculation to be done. It is clear that those firms planning to do business with the main export partner must produce to the partner's standards, but how far

[11] http://ec.europa.eu/comm/external_relations/euromed/etn/10mtg_0606/index.htm.

for example should Egypt go in adopting costly EU water quality standards for its irrigation of its domestic farm sector in order to ensure that it exports of new potatoes will secure guaranteed market access to the EU? Everyone in Egypt will benefit from cleaner water but there may be other reforms that bring even greater benefits. EU environmental norms may indeed reflect different social preferences as compared to its neighbours, for example as regards the 'social rate of time preference'.

Moreover the internal market as defined in the IMP was a package deal. It was, as we noted, what was necessary for there to be wholly free movement of goods. How can it be adopted al la carte? An *ad hoc* programme of regulatory harmonisation is another matter.

Very few of the EU's RTAs, other than with Turkey and EEA partners, actually do go beyond modest aspirations for regulatory harmonisation, even on competition law. And even if they do, this does not guarantee market access unless mutual recognition of testing and certification can be adopted, a very big challenge. The new Member States of the EU were obliged to adopt the EU regulatory *acquis* well before the EU agreed to recognise the certificates issued by their test labs affirming conformity. Often costly repeat testing was demanded. Between the EU and Turkey it was not until 2006 that agreement was reached that results of Turkish laboratories would be accepted as proof that Turkish goods did indeed conform to internal market norms, even where Turkey had made these norms compulsory many years before. For ENP partners the risk is that standards and regulations will have to be harmonised but technical inspections will remain at the border. The internal market was difficult enough to create within the RU and the removal of frontier checks for goods from our neighbours will not be easily achieved!

In some cases it might be possible move in the direction of supporting mutual recognition of conformity assessment in specific areas for partner country firms who can meet EU norms rather than insisting on wholesale adoption of EU mandatory norms first. Some of the Economic Partnership Agreement (EPA) negotiating partners are concerned at the prospect of being urged to adopt EU SPS regimes but not to have a guarantee of recognition of their implementation.

The EU has in fact sought to develop mutual recognition of conformity assessment with the US in the absence of any harmonisation, but it has proved very slow to move beyond the framework stage.

Chen and Mattoo's paper is not actually wholly negative for this approach, but it suggests that if there are benefits to the external harmonisation agenda they are likely to accrue mostly to those initially best placed. This has echoes of the thesis of Aghion and Griffith (2005) that intensified competition induces firms near the frontier to innovate, but those far from it to quit.

With the lack progress at the WTO the bilateral aspect of the external internal market is likely to be more significant, but no less controversial.

## 4. Conclusions

It seems likely that the external effects of the internal market have been broadly favourable. This was not a given at the outset; indeed had it been so, there might have been less enthusiasm for the plan. But by eliminating intra-EC barriers to third country goods, the IM left less room for *ad hoc* national measures and consolidated the Community's own external policy-making process. Liberalism was to some extent the default option. Liberalisation was the ethos of the internal market and by creating a greater respect for the rules, it made it harder for protectionist measures to be smuggled in. The Uruguay Round and the IMP almost certainly reinforced each other.

We can say that the internal market has been something of a model for global integration in a number of respects. It has shown the possibility and value of deep regulatory integration and this has been in principle at least an inspiration to other Regional Trade Agreements (RTAs) such as Mercosur. And despite the criticisms of the World Bank, the IMP provides evidence that this kind of deep integration can be market opening. Not even Patrick Messerlin seems to believe that we built 'fortress Europe'.

At the same time the IMP has led the EU to try and emulate its internal achievements on the global level. There have been some successes. But here, however, we have seen the negative side of the template. The EU has been facing the same problems internally in completing its project as it is facing externally in persuading its fellow WTO members. It has also found that the extension of the internal market to non-members is as problematic as it sounds. The European model cannot be easily transplanted to the rest of the world,[12] but the internal market programme can reasonably be said to have been a building block rather than a stumbling block in the process of multilateral liberalisation.

---

12 See Holmes *ibid.* and Erik Jones (2006) "Europe's market liberalisation is a bad model for a global trade agenda", *Journal of European Public Policy*, Vol. 13, No. 6 (September 2006), pp. 943-957.

## References

Aghion, P. & Griffith, R. (2005) *Competition and Growth*, MIT.

Allen, C., Gasiorek, M. & Smith, A. (1996) Trade Creation and Trade Diversion, *Single Market Review*, Subseries IV, Volume 3, European Commission.

Belderbos, R. (1997) *Japanese Electronic Multinationals and Strategic Trade Policies*, Oxford, Oxford University Press.

Chen, M., Xiaoyang and Mattoo, A. (2004) Regionalism in Standards: Good or Bad for Trade?, *World Bank Policy Research Working Paper* 3458, June.

Dunning, J. (1997) The European Internal Market Programme and Inbound Foreign Direct Investment, *JCMS*, *Journal of Common Market Studies* 35 (2), pp. 189-223.

European Commission (1985) Completing the Internal Market, White Paper from the Commission to the European Council, COM (85) 310, Milan, 28-29 June.

European Commission (1995) Preparation of the Associated Countries of Central and Eastern Europe for Integration into the Internal Market of the Union, White Paper from the Commission to the European Council, COM (95) 163 final, 3 May.

Evans, D. *et al.* (2006) Assessing Regional Trade Agreements with Developing Countries: Shallow and Deep Integration, Trade, Productivity and Economic Performance, University of Sussex, Study for DFID, January.

Ghoneim, A., Holmes, P. & Iacovone, L. (2005) TBTs and The EuroMed: An Empirical Analysis, University of Essex, Paper for EU FEMISE programme.

Hanson, B.T. (1998) What Happened to Fortress Europe?, External Trade Policy Liberalisation in the European Union, *International Organisation*, Vol. 52, 1, pp. 55-85.

Hoeller, P., Girouard, N. & Colecchia A. (1998) The European Union's Trade Policies and Their Economic Effects, *OECD Economics Working Paper* 194.

Holmes, P. (2006) Trade and Domestic Policies: The European Mix, *Journal of European Public Policy*, Vol. 13, 6, September, pp. 815-831.

Holmes, P. & Jones, E. (2006) Europe's Market Liberalisation Is A Bad Model for A Global Trade Agenda, *Journal of European Public Policy*, Vol. 13, 6, September, pp. 943-957.

Holmes, P. & Smith, A. (1995) Automobile Industry, in Buigues, P., Jacquemin, A. & Sapir, A. (eds.) *European Policies on Competition, Trade and Industry. Conflict and Complementarities*, Aldershot, Edward Elgar, pp. 125-159.

Holmes, P. & Young, A. (2002) Liberalising and Reregulating Telecommunications in Europe: A Common Framework and Persistent Differences, in Guerrieri, P & Scharrer, H.E. (eds.) *Trade, Investment and Competition Policies in the Global Economy: The Case of the International Telecommunications Regime*, HWWA Studies of the Hamburg Institute of International Economics, Vol. 69, Baden-Baden, Nomos Verlagsgesellschaft.

Holmes, P., Iacovone, L., Kamon-detdacha, R. & Newson, L. (2006) *Capacity-Building to Meet International Standards as Public Goods*, UNIDO. http://www.unido.org/file-storage/download/?file_id=60028

Irwin, A. (2005) The Rise of US Anti-dumping Activity in Historical Perspective, *The World Economy* 28 (5), pp. 651-668, http://people.brandeis.edu/~cbown/global_ad

Jaffee, S. and Henson, S. (2004) *Standards and Agro-Food Exports from Developing Countries: Rebalancing the Debate*, World Bank Policy Research Working Paper No. 3348, June.

Lamy, P. (2004) *The Emergence of Collective Preferences in International Trade: Implications for Regulating Globalisation.*

Martin, W. and Winters, L. (1996) *The Uruguay Round And The Developing Countries*, Cambridge University Press, Cambridge.

Mattoo, A. (2001) Discriminatory Consequences of Non-discriminatory Standards, *Journal of Economic Integration* 16(1), March, pp. 78-10

Mattoo, A. & Mavroidis, P.C. (1995) The EC-Japan Consensus on Cars: Trade and Antitrust Trade-Offs, *The World Economy*, May, pp. 345-365.

Maur, J.C. (2005) Exporting Europe's Trade Policy, *The World Economy*, Volume 28, 11, pp. 1565-1590.

Messerlin, P. (2001) *Measuring the Costs of Protection in Europe: European Commercial Policy in the 2000s*, Institute for International Economics, Washington D.C.

Otsuki, T., Wilson, J. & Sewadeh, M. (2001) Saving Two in A Billion: Quantifying the Trade Effect of European Food Safety Standards on African Exports, *Food Policy*, Vol. 26, issue 5, pp. 495-514.

Stevens, C. & Young, A. (1996) *Single Market Review*, Subseries IV, Vol. 4, European Commission.

Sun, J. & Pelkmans, J. (1995) Regulatory Competition in The Single Market, *Journal of Common Market Studies*, Vol. 33, 1, pp. 67-89.

Winters, A. (1992) The Welfare and Policy Implications of the International Trade Consequences of '1992', *American Economic Review*, Vol. 82, 2, Papers and Proceedings, May, pp. 104-108.

WTO (1995) *Trade Policy Review*, European Community, 2 vols, WTO, Geneva.

CHAPTER 8

# Promoting EU Interest at a Global Level

Roland KLAGES

*Research Fellow at the Institute for German and European Economic Law at the University of Heidelberg*

## 1. Introduction

The internal market has from the outset been conceived, as the title of this paper indicates, primarily as an objective that is to be reached *within* the European Community. Indeed, when the internal market was given its last major legal and political push with the project 1992, starting off with the white paper[1] of the Commission in 1985, external aspects were not in the spotlight.[2] While some attribute this to a lack of awareness on the part of the Commission and the Community as a whole, others subscribe to the view that the Community deliberately sidelined external aspects of the internal market at the time.[3] Be that as it may, the internal dimension of the internal market clearly dominated over the external one.[4]

The internal market is often perceived today as something that has, by and large, been accomplished. It is submitted that this assumption is misleading insofar as it revolves around a static concept of the internal market. The realisation of the internal market should rather be seen, in a

1 Completing the internal market – White Paper of 14 June 1985 of the Commission to the European Council (Milan 28-29 June 1985), COM (85) 310 final.

2 Also, the Cecchini report focused on the interior dimension of the internal market and only considered its exterior dimension marginally, see in detail *Grin*, The Battle of the Single European Market, London 2004, p. 291 *et seq*.

3 For this discussion, see Eeckhout, The External Dimension of the EC Internal Market: A Portrait, (No. 2/1991), 15 World Competition 5 *et seq*.

4 Tietje, E. 25. Außendimension des Binnenmarktes, in Grabitz & Hilf (eds.), *Das Recht der Europäischen Union*, Munich 1999, note 23.

dynamic way, as a moving target. Even if it is possible to identify exactly how policy objectives and legal obligations have been fulfilled, this does not imply that obstacles to the functioning of the internal market may not appear in the future. As technology evolves, so does the creativity of Member States to erect new barriers to trade. Moreover, Member States may want to protect other overriding interests and, as a result, often create a barrier to trade. This can happen even without any protectionist intent.

The Treaty itself only refers to the internal dimension of this market. This makes it difficult to define the external dimension. *Eeckhout* states that the internal market programme not only affects the economies of the Community's Member States, but that it also has a profound impact on international trade and investment on a world scale. It is this impact that he terms the external dimension of the internal market.[5] From a specifically legal perspective, these are the legal problems that arise out of the creation of an internal market for the external relations of the Community.[6] While internal legal relations – that is, relations between Member States and the Community – governing the internal market are spelt out by the Treaty, this is not true for the external dimension.

It will therefore be for this paper to examine this external dimension and to analyse whether a common interest is being promoted at a global scale. I shall first examine the legal framework under Community law. Here, we will first briefly define the internal market, then look at the competences conferred on the Community to give an external dimension to the internal market and finally examine the way in which the Court has contributed to promoting a common interest at a global scale through its jurisprudence on supremacy and direct effect.

## 2. Definition of the internal market

In order to define and delimit the scope of this paper, a definition of the internal market is needed.[7] It is given ground that the concept of an Internal Market is wider than that of a free trade area or a customs union as defined in Article XXIV GATT.

In a nutshell, the Internal Market aims to provide an area in which the free flow of goods, services and factors of production is ensured.[8]

---

5 Eeckhout, The External Dimension of the EC Internal Market: A Portrait, (No. 2/1991), 15 *World Competition* 5.

6 Tietje, E. 25. Außendimension des Binnenmarktes, in Grabitz & Hilf (eds.), *Das Recht der Europäischen Union*, Munich 1999, note 2.

7 See for more detailed presentation Dominik Hanf's contribution to this book.

8 Article 14 (2) and 3 (1) lit. c EC.

Broadly speaking, the Treaty provides two complementary concepts to reach this objective: on the one hand the elimination of trade barriers through the so-called four freedoms,[9] and on the other hand harmonisation or unification of national rules. The former is known as negative integration, the latter as positive integration. History has shown that in many instances when the Community institutions were not active in the domain of the Internal Market, the Court of Justice, taking its role emanating from Article 220 EC[10] seriously, was prepared to step in.[11] It is submitted that the Internal Market has only been able to develop in the way it has because it is firmly anchored in a supranational setting which has been provided partly by the Treaty and partly stems from the jurisprudence of the Court of Justice.[12]

## 3. External economic competences

An external competence enables the Community to enter into international agreements with other subjects of public international law, i.e. states and other international organisations. The Community is a subject of public international law as results from Article 281 EC.[13] There are both explicit and implicit competences. The explicit external compe-

---

[9] Free movement of goods, persons, services and capital.

[10] Article 220 EC reads as follows: The Court of Justice and the Court of First Instance, each within its jurisdiction, shall ensure that in the interpretation and application of this Treaty the law is observed.

[11] The most prominent example is probably the seminal Cassis de Dijon case, in which the Court enshrined the principle of mutual recognition in Article 28 EC (then 30 EEC), thereby minimising the need for positive harmonisation, a process for which at the time unanimity in Council was required, Article 94 EC (then 100 EEC). Cf. Judgment of the Court of 20 February 1979, Case 120/78, *Rewe Zentral v. Bundesmonopolverwaltung für Branntwein*, [1979] ECR 649 – "Cassis de Dijon".

[12] By ruling that certain Treaty provisions fulfilling a distinct set of criteria are capable of having a direct effect on individuals, the Court of Justice has transformed the four freedoms into subjective (economic) rights. Bypassing any political institution, an individual or an undertaking can directly rely on the right conferred through a Treaty provision before a national court. Furthermore, by explicitly declaring that within its field of application Community law takes supremacy over national law, the Court of Justice has contributed immensely to the success of the Internal Market since in case of a conflict its jurisprudence places Internal Market provisions above those of national law. – Please note that in doctrine, a difference is often drawn between the terms of direct applicability and direct effect. While the former merely means that a provision is part of a legal order, the latter deals with the question of conferring subjective rights on in<dividuals. See in more detail e.g. Schmalenbach, in Calliess & Ruffert (eds.), EUV/EGV, 3rd ed., Munich 2007, Art. 300, notes 58 and 65. The Court of Justice uses the terms interchangeably, without drawing a distinction. For the purposes of this paper, we will do likewise.

[13] Article 281 EC: The Community shall have legal personality.

tences of the Community are scattered around the Treaty and do not follow a coherent pattern.[14] The most important ones are the 'common commercial policy'[15] and the competence to enter into association agreements.[16] The implied powers doctrine as developed by the Court of Justice[17] is an implicit external competence.

### 3.1. The 'common commercial policy', Articles 131-134 EC

The most prominent competence is the 'common commercial policy', contained in Title IX of the Treaty, Articles 131-134 EC.[18] This policy is the main instrument with which the Community shapes its interests in the external economic sphere.

According to Article 131 EC, by establishing a customs union between themselves, Member States aim to contribute, in the common interest, to the harmonious development of world trade, the progressive abolition of restrictions on international trade and the lowering of customs barriers. Article 131 EC further stipulates that the common commercial policy shall take into account the favourable effect which the abolition of customs duties between Member States may have on the increase in the competitive strength of undertakings in those States.

It can already be inferred from the wording that the common commercial policy "was originally conceived as little more than an adjunct to the common customs tariff".[19] It was designed to complement the realisation of a customs union (Articles 25 *et seq.* EC).[20] A further

---

14 See Tietje, E. 25. Außendimension des Binnenmarktes, in Grabitz & Hilf (eds.), *Das Recht der Europäischen Union*, Munich 1999, note 30.

15 Articles 131 *et seq*. EC.

16 Article 310 EC. Other external economic competences are to be found in the field of research and technological development (Article 170 (2) EC) and the environment (Article 174 (4) EC). As regards education (Article 149 (3) EC), vocational training (Article 150 (3) EC), culture (Article 151 (3) EC), public health (Article 152 (3) EC) and trans-european networks (Article 155 (3) EC) the Treaty also refers to third countries or international organisations. Here, however, the Community can only take acts of soft law, as results from the text of those provisions.

17 Starting with the ERTA judgment, see Judgment of the Court of 31 March 1971, Case 22/70, *Commission v. Council*, [1971] ECR 263.

18 For a detailed analysis of Articles 131 EC *et seq*. see Bourgeois, in von der Groeben & Schwarze (eds.), *Kommentar zum EU-/EG-Vertrag*, Vol. 3, 6th ed., Baden-Baden 2003.

19 Jacobs, The Completion of the Internal Market v the Incomplete Common Commercial Policy, in Konstandinidis (ed.), The Legal Regulation of the European Community's External Relations after the Completion of the Internal Market, Dartmouth 1996, 3 (4).

20 Tietje, E. 25. Außendimension des Binnenmarktes, in Grabitz & Hilf (eds.), *Das Recht der Europäischen Union*, Munich 1999, note 30.

external dimension to the internal market was not within the conception of this policy.

### *3.1.1. Nature and scope of the 'common commercial policy'*

The Court of Justice has held since 1973 that Article 133 EC constitutes an exclusive competence for the Community.[21] In Opinion 1/75 the Court stated that the common commercial policy "is conceived [...] in the context of the operation of the common market, for the defence of the common interests of the Community, within which the particular interests of the Member States must endeavour to adapt to each other" and that "this conception is incompatible with the freedom to which the Member States could lay claim by invoking a concurrent power, so as to ensure that their own interests were separately satisfied in external relations, at the risk of compromising the effective defence of the common interests of the Community".[22]

Normally, exclusive competence means that only the Community is allowed to act and that Member States cannot take any unilateral measures of their own. An important consequence of the exclusivity of a competence is that the principle of subsidiarity does not apply.[23] This principle applies only to the domain of shared competences between the Community and the Member States. It is not a principle that attributes a competence, but rather one that governs the exercise of a competence.[24] Since Opinion 1/94, however, the Court seems to take a more cautious approach.[25]

But this does not answer the question of what areas are covered by the 'common commercial policy'. It is widely assumed that, contrary to what its wording might imply, the common commercial policy does not constitute a coherent policy for external trade. Indeed, the definition of what constitutes the 'common commercial policy' has been subject to a great deal of controversy that was fuelled by a meandering jurispru-

---

21 Judgment of the Court of 12 July 1973, Case 8/73, *Hauptzollamt Bremerhaven* v. *Massey-Ferguson* [1973] ECR 897, para. 3.

22 Opinion of the Court of 11 November 1975, Opinion 1/75, [1975] ECR 1355 – "OECD-Agreement", p. 1363.

23 Cf. Article 5 (2) EC: In areas which do not fall within its exclusive [emphasis added] competence, the Community shall take action, in accordance with the principle of subsidiarity, only if and in so far as the objectives of the proposed action cannot be sufficiently achieved by the Member States and can therefore, by reason of the scale or effects of the proposed action, be better achieved by the Community.

24 See extensively Calliess in Calliess & Ruffert (eds.), EUV/EGV, 3rd ed., Munich 2007, Article 5 EC, note 20 *et seq*.

25 Opinion of the Court of 15 November 1994, Opinion 1/94, [1994] ECR I-5267 "WTO-Agreement".

dence of the Court of Justice as well as Treaty amendments effected at the treaties of Amsterdam and Nice.

It should be borne in mind that the wording of Article 133 EC reflects the situation as regards international trade law in 1957 with a clear focus on goods. Article 133 (1) EC makes explicit reference only to tariff rates, the conclusion of tariff and trade agreements, the achievement of uniformity in measures of liberalisation, export policy and measures to protect trade such as those to be taken in the event of dumping or subsidies. However, as the term 'particularly' indicates, this enumeration of measures is not comprehensive and further measures are permitted under this article.

Given that these are not explicitly delineated, two conflicting doctrinal views developed regarding an abstract definition of measures available to the Community on the basis of Article 133 EC. The finalist theory[26] sees the aim of a measure to be taken as the determining criterion. According to this theory, an act of law falls under Article 133 EC if it is intended to influence the volume or the flow of trade. The instrumentalist theory,[27] on the other hand, looks at the nature of the instrument that is being applied. Here, an act of law falls under Article 133 EC when it constitutes an instrument to regulate international trade.

The Court of Justice, being faced with concrete cases or precise questions under the Article 300 (6) EC procedure where it delivers opinions, has not had to follow either of those theories. Instead, it has chosen a case-by-case pragmatic approach and over time defined the scope of Article 133 EC.

In Opinion 1/78, the Court stated that the common commercial policy should be interpreted widely. It reasoned that "a restrictive interpretation of the concept of common commercial policy would risk causing disturbances in intra-Community trade by reason of the disparities which would then exist in certain areas of economic relations with non-member countries".[28]

But since Opinion 1/94 it has become clear that the field of application of Article 133 EC is not without limits. The Court was asked whether Article 133 EC covered all areas under the WTO agreement, i.e. trade in goods,[29] services[30] and intellectual property issues.[31] It came

---

26 Cf. Bourgeois, in von der Groeben & Schwarze (eds.), *Kommentar zum EU-/EG-Vertrag, Vol. 3*, 6th ed., Baden-Baden 2003, Article 133 note 3.

27 *Op. cit.*

28 Opinion of the Court of 4 October 1979, Opinion 1/78, [1979] ECR 2871 – "International Agreement on Natural Rubber", para 45.

29 GATT 1994 (General Agreement on Tariffs and Trade).

30 GATS (General Agreement on Trade in Services).

to the conclusion that trade in goods fell under the exclusive competence of Article 133 EC, whereas this was only partly the case for services and intellectual property issues. As a result, the WTO agreement had to be signed as a mixed agreement, with the Member States as contracting parties alongside the Community and the other parties to the WTO. This Opinion has been subject to extensive criticism in doctrine[32] where it was stressed that the Opinion was a restrictive step back from earlier case law. Others, however, welcome the decision and subscribe to the view that too extensive an interpretation of Article 133 EC would render the internal repartition of competences within the EC Treaty superfluous and would therefore create an imbalance between the internal and external competences.[33] It is beyond the scope of this paper to go over this discussion in more detail. Practice has followed the Court's jurisprudence, and the Member States, as masters of the Treaties, have reacted by perpetuating[34] this jurisprudence through amending Article 133 EC in the Treaties of Amsterdam and Nice. With the law as it now stands, Article 133 EC covers acts that regulate trade in goods with third parties as well as measures that have as their aim the channelling of trade flows in goods, besides some aspects of services and intellectual property. Thus article 133 EC does not confer upon the Community a competence to regulate direct investments, competition policy[35] and establishment and the free movement of persons in general.

On the basis of Article 133 EC and other legal bases, the Community is empowered to pursue what is termed an autonomous and a conventional common commercial policy.

*Autonomous common commercial policy* denotes those measures that the Community takes on its own in order mainly to govern access to its markets. The autonomous common commercial policy comprises rules on imports, the common customs tariff, the general system of preferences, antidumping and anti-subsidy measures as well as the new trade policy instrument.[36] The autonomous common commercial policy uses

---

31 TRIPS (Trade-Related Aspects of Intellectual Property Rights).

32 See only Bourgeois, The EC in the WTO and Advisory Opinion 1/94: an Echternach procession, (1995) 32 CMLRev., 763-787; Pescatore, Opinion 1/94 on "conclusion" of the WTO Agreement: is there an escape from a programmed disaster?, (1999) 36 *CMLRev.*, 387-405.

33 Hahn, in Calliess & Ruffert (eds.), *EUV/EGV*, 3rd ed., Munich 2007, Article 133 EC, note 37.

34 *Ibid.*, note 44.

35 *Ibid.*, notes 48 *et seq.*

36 For an extensive examination of these, see Bourgeois, in von der Groeben & Schwarze (eds.), *Kommentar zum EU-/EG-Vertrag, Vol. 3*, 6th ed., Baden-Baden 2003, Article 133 EC, notes 42 *et seq.*

the common legal instruments of Article 249 EC: regulations, directives and decisions.

The *conventional common commercial policy*, on the other hand, is made up of the various agreements that the Community has entered into under public international law. The other parties are other subjects of public international law, i.e. states or international organisations. The conventional commercial policy can take a bilateral or a multilateral form.

The most important agreement is a multilateral one: the WTO agreement. The WTO agreement is the umbrella for 26 agreements and 22 common declarations.

### *3.2. Association agreements*

Association agreements are concluded by the Community on the basis of Article 310 EC.[37] Their objective is wider than that of agreements entered into solely on the basis of Article 133 EC.

As a result of the structure of the Treaty just described, the external dimension of the internal market has always been subject to bigger political influence than the internal dimension for the simple reason that political decisions for the internal side of the internal market were already taken in 1957 with the Treaty of Rome. The fundamental freedoms are the legal expression of the political decision to strike down barriers to intra-Community trade. Through the fact that they enjoy direct effect in all Member States, courts and national administrations need only implement this. The role of the political institutions of the Community (Commission, Parliament and Council) was therefore confined to positive harmonisation.

## 4. A differentiated system of bilateral and multilateral treaties

With respect to the treaties that the Community has entered into, a differentiated pattern emerges. The range of these treaties varies considerably in terms of scope and legal density. There is also considerable variety in the objectives that the Community pursues through these treaties.

In the framework of this paper, only an overview can be given. We will, however, try to classify these treaties with respect to their rele-

[37] For an exhaustive analysis of association agreements see Hanf & Dengler, Accords d'association, in Louis & Dony (eds.), *Commentaire Mégret, Le droit de la CE et de l'Union européenne, Volume XII (Relations extérieures)*, 2nd ed., Brussels 2005 (available online at www.coleurop.be/template.asp?pagename=lawpapers).

vance for the internal market. Whereas the paper on the political aspects of the external dimension of the internal market has focused on policies (i.e. coverage of internal market issues), polity (i.e. the degree of institutionalisation) and politics (i.e. the procedural dimension), this paper shall look at the aspects developed by the Court of Justice, outlined above. It will be analysed in what way the supranational concepts of direct effect and supremacy can also be found in the various forms of these international agreements.

### *4.1. Supremacy*

International agreements concluded by the Community with third states or international organisations are also supreme over national law. In relation to other Community law, in the hierarchy of norms they rank between primary law and secondary law. This constitutes a constant jurisprudence of the Court of Justice and has a normative basis in Article 300 (7) EC, according to which international agreements concluded by the Community are binding on the institutions of the Community and on Member States. The implications of this are twofold: on the one hand the Community itself[38] has to respect them in other acts of secondary law, so as to avoid becoming liable on an international level towards third parties.[39] On the other hand, Member States have to respect obligations of these agreements, just as they have to respect obligations of other acts of Community law. From the perspective of the Member States, therefore, international agreements fully constitute Community law. This also goes for so-called mixed agreements, i.e. agreements which, for reasons of competence, have been concluded between the Community, its Member States and third parties.

### *4.2. Direct effect*

The question of whether certain provisions in international agreements are capable of conferring direct effect on individuals has also been subject to a substantial amount of case law of the Court of Justice.

In order to determine whether a provision has direct effect, the Court proceeds in the way it has ever since *Van Gend en Loos*,[40] i.e. it has to

---

[38] This already results out of the general principle of contract law *pacta sunt servanda* that also applies in public international law and is enshrined in Article 26 of the Vienna Convention of the Law of Treaties.

[39] The procedural consequence of this is also that an action for annulment can be brought against the institutions pursuant to Article 230 (1) EC, see to this effect e.g. Judgment of the Court of 23 November 1999, Case C-149/96, *Portugal v. Council*, [1999] ECR I-8395.

[40] Judgment of the Court of 4 July 1963, Case 24/62, *Van Gend en Loos v. Nederlandse Administratie der Belastingen*, [1963] ECR 1.

be clear and precise, unconditional and be capable of conferring rights upon the individual. In addition, the Court examines in the case of international agreements explicitly whether the spirit, general scheme and terms of the agreement[41] are in favour of a direct effect.

As a rule, international agreements are directly applicable in the Community legal order. This was stated by the Court of Justice in the seminal *Haegeman*-Case[42] where it was said that provisions of international agreements form an integral part of the Community legal order. But in the case of the GATT/WTO, the Court has taken a different approach. For the original GATT 1947, the Court found that there was no direct applicability due to the 'great flexibility' of its provisions.[43] In relation to the WTO Agreement, the Court continues to stress that having regard to their nature and structure, "the WTO agreements are not in principle among the rules in the light of which the Court is to review the legality of measures adopted by the Community institutions".[44]

The reasoning applied by the Court, however, has altered: the WTO agreement accords considerable importance to negotiation between the parties[45] which leaves some leeway to the political institutions of the Community. In addition, some parties to the agreement have explicitly ruled out a direct effect in their national legal order. This leads the Court to conclude that "the lack of reciprocity in that regard on the part of the Community's trading partners, in relation to the WTO agreements which are based on reciprocal and mutually advantageous arrangements [...] may lead to disuniform application of WTO rules".[46] To accept that the role of ensuring that those rules comply with Community law devolves directly on the Community judicature would deprive the legislative or executive organs of the Community of the scope for manoeuvre

---

41 Judgment of the Court of 12 December 1972, Joined Cases 21-24/72, International Fruit Company NV and Others v. Produktschap voor Groenten en Fruit, [1972] ECR 1219, para 20. When the Court considers the direct effect of EC-Treaty provisions, such a test need not be done anymore, as in Van Gend en Loos the Court has looked at length at the spirit, general scheme and terms of the E(E)C-Treaty, without explicitly saying so.

42 Judgment of the Court of 30 April 1974, Case 181/73, *Haegeman v. Belgium*, [1974] ECR 449.

43 Judgment of the Court of 12 December 1972, Joined Cases 21-24/72, *International Fruit Company NV and Others* v. *Produktschap voor Groenten en Fruit*, [1972] ECR 1219, para 21.

44 Judgment of the Court of 23 November 1999, Case C-149/96, *Portugal* v. *Council*, [1999] ECR I-8395, para 47.

45 *Ibid*., para 36.

46 *Ibid*., para 45.

enjoyed by their counterparts in the Community's trading partners.[47] The Court even extends this jurisprudence to decisions of the WTO Dispute Settlement Body (DSB). Here, one could argue that there is no more room for negotiations and that a decision of the DSB is sufficiently clear, precise and unconditional. However, the Court, in the *van Parys* case, argues that according to the WTO Understanding on rules and procedures governing the settlement of disputes (DSU), if the Member concerned fails to enforce those recommendations and decisions within a reasonable period, if so requested, and within a reasonable period of time, it is to enter into negotiations with any party having invoked the dispute settlement procedures with a view to agreeing compensation. If then no satisfactory compensation has been agreed within 20 days after the expiry of the reasonable period, the complainant may request authorisation from the DSB to suspend, in respect of that member, the application of concessions or other obligations under the WTO agreements.[48] The Court recalls that, furthermore, Article 22(8) DSU provides that the dispute remains on the agenda of the DSB, pursuant to Article 21(6) DSU, until it is resolved, that is until the measure found to be inconsistent has been 'removed' or the parties reach a 'mutually satisfactory solution'.[49] Where there is no agreement as to the compatibility of the measures taken to comply with the DSB's recommendations and decisions, Article 21(5) DSU provides that the dispute shall be decided 'through recourse to these dispute settlement procedures', including an attempt by the parties to reach a negotiated solution.[50] The Court therefore concludes that under those circumstances, to require courts to refrain from applying rules of domestic law which are inconsistent with the WTO agreements would have the consequence of depriving the legislative or executive organs of the contracting parties of the possibility afforded by Article 22 of that memorandum of reaching a negotiated settlement, even on a temporary basis.[51]

As an aside, Advocate General *Tizzano* came to a different conclusion in this case. He stressed that a DSB decision would limit to the parties' freedom to seek alternative negotiated solutions as they still

---

47 *Ibid.*, para 46.

48 Judgment of the Court of 1 March 2005, Case C-377/02, *van Parys NV* v. *Belgisch Interventie- en Restitutiebureau*, [2005] ECR I-1465, para 45.

49 *Ibid.*, para 46.

50 *Ibid.*, para 47.

51 *Ibid.*, para 48.

have to find a solution in the framework of the WTO rules and consequently of the DSB decision.[52]

The Court only makes an apparent exception with respect to rules of the WTO when Community rules explicitly refer to precise provisions[53] of the agreement or when the Community intended to implement a particular obligation assumed in the context of the WTO.[54]

The jurisprudence of the Court has been severely criticised in doctrine,[55] but has also met some approval.[56] Again, the debate is too lengthy to be dealt with in this paper in detail. But it is worth noting at this point that the position of Court results in a strengthening of the Community institutions *vis-à-vis* the political institutions of the other contracting parties. Granting direct effect to provisions always means taking power away from political institutions and handing it over to judicial ones. With respect to the internal dimension of the Community and the internal dimension of the internal market this can be conducive to reaching the aims of the Treaty. Member States' judges as well as lower administration are given power at the expense of their higher executive and legislature. The point can very well be made that those institutions may be better suited to promote the common interest at an internal scale. It is doubtful that the common interest is also being promoted at a global scale through the decision to grant direct effect to provisions of WTO law, as this would indeed reduce the margin of manoeuvre for the political institutions. However, such reasoning only applies if one is of the opinion that the common interest is best promoted through political institutions. In any event, the Court has opted not to privatise the pursuit of a common interest, as it has for the internal dimension of the internal market.

---

52 Opinion of Mr Advocate General *Tizzano* delivered on 18 November 2004, Case C-377/02, *van Parys NV* v. *Belgisch Interventie- en Restitutiebureau*, [2005] ECR I-1465, para 57.

53 Judgment of the Court of 22 June 1989, Case 70/87, *Fediol* v. *Commission*, [1989] ECR 1781, para 22.

54 Judgment of the Court of 7 May 1991, Case C-69/89, *Nakajima* v. *Council*, [1991] ECR I-2069, para 19.

55 See only Berrod, La Cour de justice refuse l'invocabilité des accords OMC: essai de régulation de la mondialisation, (2000) 36 *Revue trimestrielle de droit européen*, 419-450; Hilf & Schorkopf, WTO und EG: Rechtskonflikte vor den EuGH? Anm. zum Urt. des EuGH v. 23.11.1999 – Rs. C-149/96, (2000) 35 *Europarecht*, 74-91.

56 Bogdandy, Rechtsgleichheit, Rechtssicherheit und Subsidiarität im transnationalen Wirtschaftsrecht: zur unmittelbaren Anwendbarkeit von Art. 81 III EG und des WTO-Rechts, (2001) 12 *Europäische Zeitschrift für Wirtschaftsrecht*, 357-365; Tridimas, The WTO and OECD opinions, in Dashwood & Hillion, *The general law of EC external relations*, London 2000, 48-60.

In relation to other international agreements, the Court has been less reluctant to grant direct effect to provisions. With respect to the external dimension of the internal market, when the Court examines the spirit, general scheme and terms of an agreement, the crucial question is to what extent the coverage of internal market issues was intended by the contracting parties. Here, the Court tends to take an extensive approach. It follows its classical jurisprudence developed in *Haegeman*,[57] *Kupferberg*[58] and *Demirel*.[59] Direct effect has been granted to many provisions in the association agreement with Turkey.[60]

More recently, however, the Court has extended the jurisprudence on direct effect of internal market provisions to agreements that appear to be of a more political nature, as the following examples are intended to illustrate.

In *El Yassini*[61] the Court held that an article relating to the free movement of persons of a Cooperation Agreement between the EEC and Morocco from 1976 had direct effect. Similarly, the Court continues this jurisprudence for the Euro-Mediterranean Agreements that were entered into by the Community through the so-called 'Barcelona process'. Recently, in *Gattoussi*[62] the Court held that an Article of the Euro-Mediterranean Agreement with Tunisia is directly effective. According to that Article[63] the treatment accorded by each Member State to workers of Tunisian nationality employed in its territory shall be free from discrimination based on nationality as regards working conditions, remuneration and dismissal, relative to its own nationals. In the latter case, although a Joint Declaration to the Agreement specified that this Article may not be invoked to obtain renewal of a residence permit, the Court found that "[...] that provision may have effects on the right of a Tunisian national to remain in the territory of a Member State in the

57 Judgment of the Court of 30 April 1974, Case 181/73, *Haegeman* v. *Belgium*, [1974] ECR 449.

58 Judgment of the Court of 26 October 1982, Case 104/81, Hauptzollamt Mainz v. Kupferberg, [1982] ECR 3641.

59 Judgment of the Court of 30 September 1987, Case 12/86, Demirel v. Stadt Schwäbisch Gmünd, [1987] ECR 3719.

60 See extensively Hanf & Dengler, Accords d'association, in Louis & Dony (eds.), Commentaire Mégret, Le droit de la CE et de l'Union européenne, Volume XII (Relations extérieures), 2nd ed., Brussels 2005, (available online at http://www.coleurop.be/ template.asp?pagename=lawpapers), 22 *et seq*.

61 Judgment of the Court of 2 March 1999, Case C-416/96, El-Yassini v. Secretary of State for the Home Department, [1999] ECR I-1209.

62 Judgment of the Court of 14 December 2006, Case C-97/05, Mohamed Gattoussi v. Stadt Rüsselsheim, [2006] ECR I-11917.

63 Article 64 of the Agreement which is to be found in Chapter I ("Workers") of Title VI ("Cooperation in Social and Cultural Matters").

case where a person has been duly permitted by that Member State to work there for a period extending beyond the period of validity of his permission to remain".[64]

In *Simutenkov*, the Court found that an Article of the Partnership and Association Agreement between the Community, its Member States and Russia which precludes Member States from discriminating, on grounds of nationality, against Russian workers *vis-à-vis* that State's own nationals, so far as their conditions of employment, remuneration and dismissal are concerned, had direct effect.[65]

## 5. Conclusion

The originally inward-looking concept of the internal market has over time opened its gates towards the outside. However, determining and shaping the external dimension has proved a lot more difficult than for the internal dimension.

The Community competences are scattered around the Treaty and do not follow a coherent pattern. More weight is vested in the political institutions of the Community. The internal market coverage of external agreements varies according to the aims pursued by each agreement, as the paper on the political aspects of the external dimension of the internal market of this volume has shown.

Nevertheless, the Court of Justice has contributed to the functioning of international agreements by applying tests comparable to those commonly known. As has been developed, the WTO agreements in all their facets remain an exception to this, but here it can be argued that the promotion of the common interest externally is best vested in the Community institutions.

The new Reform Treaty will not change the current situation. It can therefore be expected that, like the internal dimension, the external dimension of the internal market remains a moving target.

---

64 See para 43 of the Judgment.

65 Judgment of the Court of 12 April 2005, Case C-265/03, *Simutenkov* v. *Ministerio de Educación y Cultura and Real Federación Española de Fútbol*, [2005] ECR I-2579, para 29.

CHAPTER 9

# The Internal Market's External Dimension

## Political Aspects

Sieglinde GSTÖHL

*Professor, College of Europe (Bruges),*
*EU International Relations and Diplomacy Studies*

## 1. Increasing externalisation of the internal market

Over the past two decades, the European Union's (EU) attitude towards the external dimension of its internal market has changed considerably: from an almost exclusive focus on internal aspects of market completion in the mid-1980s to a proactive stance on the international promotion of its internal market norms in recent years. One may even speak of an 'externalisation' of the internal market, especially to the Union's near abroad, or of a Europeanisation[1] of non-member countries.

Whereas the concepts of free trade areas and customs unions have been in use for a very long time (see e.g. Article 24 GATT), the notion of an internal or common market has largely remained unspecified in international economic law (and in political science). Since the Single European Act, Article 14(2) of the Treaty establishing the European Community defines the internal market as "an area without internal frontiers in which the free movement of goods, services, persons and capital is ensured". The creation of such a market involves both national liberalisation removing discrimination (negative integration) and (re-) regulation at the European level: "a common market attains the free movement of products, services and factors of production accompanied

---

[1] Europeanisation most commonly refers to the domestic impact of the EU on its Member States, but is increasingly used with regard to third countries as well (see Schimmelfennig 2007).

by the necessary positive integration for the common market to function properly" (Pelkmans, 2006: 8).[2]

The 1985 White Paper did not directly address the external dimension of the internal market.[3] The Community's general attitude was inward looking as European governments and business had to be convinced that the ambitious '1992 programme' could be realised.[4] It was the Community's main trading partners, especially the United States and the EFTA countries, that placed the external dimension on the political agenda by voicing concerns over the effects that the completion of the internal market would have on them.[5] In an attempt to dispel their fears, the Hannover European Council in June 1988 declared that "the internal market should not close in on itself" but "be open to third countries" in conformity with GATT provisions and "seek to preserve the balance of advantages accorded, while respecting the unity and the identity of the internal market" (European Council, 1988: 165). In October 1988, the European Commission (1988: 1-2) set out the principles that '1992' would be of benefit to Member States and third countries alike, that it would not mean protectionism, that the Community would meet its international obligations, and that it would help strengthen the multilateral system on a reciprocal basis. With a view to the Uruguay Round, the Commission concluded that "the Community will seek a greater liberalisation of international trade: the 1992 Europe will not be a fortress Europe but a partnership Europe" (*ibid.*: 1).

On the one hand, the '1992 programme' shifted the internal market regime to the Community's external borders, for instance by abolishing the remaining national quantitative restrictions on third-country im-

---

2 From a legal point of view, the concept of the internal market is often described as being narrower than that of a common market even though this distinction is not always clearly held up even by the European Court of Justice. In particular, the internal market is said not to embrace "a completed external trade policy, a system of undistorted competition within the common market, and the harmonisation or co-ordination of legislation for reasons other than the elimination of barriers between national markets" (Gormley, 2002: 518).

3 It only states that "the commercial identity of the Community must be consolidated so that our trading partners will not be given the benefit of a wider market without themselves making similar concessions" and suggests the abolition of residual national or regional import quotas (European Commission, 1985: 8, 11).

4 The Commission deliberately chose to neglect the internal market's external dimension in order to avoid opening a 'Pandora's box'. I thank Jacques Bourgeois for this specification.

5 For an analysis of the internal market's external dimension at the time, see Eeckhout (1991).

ports.[6] On the other hand, the EU began exporting the regime beyond its borders (e.g. by prohibiting new quantitative restrictions or measures having equivalent effect on imports in trade agreements). Together with the end of the Cold War that gave rise to a spread of market economies and neoliberal policies, the completion of the internal market triggered a series of preferential EU agreements with third countries as well as efforts of regionalisation in other areas of the world (Sapir, 2000). The EU negotiated the European Economic Area (EEA) with the EFTA countries, the Euro-Mediterranean Partnership with the Southern Mediterranean countries, Europe Agreements with the Central and Eastern European countries, Partnership and Cooperation Agreements (PCAs) with the republics of the Commonwealth of Independent States, a customs union agreement with Turkey and bilateral free trade agreements with non-European emerging markets.

Today, the EU fully acknowledges the external dimension of the internal market. The Commission stresses that globalisation "increasingly blurs the distinction between the internal and external markets" and that the challenge was "to respond to the dynamism and change that flows directly from Europe's engagement with the world economy" (European Commission, 2007b: 4). The internal market "will never be 'finalised' or 'complete'" because it is constantly adapting to new realities and because gaps remain, rules are not always fully implemented and enforced, and new types of barriers emerge as markets evolve (*ibid.*: 3). Moreover, for the internal market to function properly, the EU must ensure that its principles are adequately reflected in international relations. Together with the Member States, the Commission promotes internal market norms in enlargements, when negotiating international agreements, in regulatory dialogues with third countries and in the international fora dealing with internal market policies such as the World Trade Organisation (WTO), the World Intellectual Property Organisation (WIPO) or the Basel Committee on Banking Supervision.

This chapter examines the political dimensions of the European Union's attempts to externalise its internal market. How and to what extent does the EU make efforts to Europeanise non-members? I will show that the policies, polity and politics of third countries' involvement with the internal market, that is the coverage, degree of institutionalisation and of alignment with the *acquis*, vary considerably. The export of internal market norms is most extensive in the EU's neighbourhood. On the

---

[6] In some cases, however, the creation of a Community regime was at odds with the external dimension of the internal market. For instance, the Commission's endeavour in the Lomé IV negotiations to preserve the ACP countries' interests led to a prolonged dispute over European banana imports (McMahon, 1993).

whole, it can be argued that the broader, the more institutionalised and *acquis*-based the relationship between the Union and a third country, the more likely it constitutes a deep, tight and dynamic form of cooperation. Such a cooperation, which covers many behind-the-border issues, closely follows the evolution of the *acquis* and largely mirrors EU institutions, may raise legitimacy concerns in the partner country.[7] Conversely, the narrower, thc lcss institutionalised and *acquis*-based the relationship, the more likely it constitutes a shallow, loose and static form of cooperation that should not provoke many worries about its legitimacy.

The EU's motivations to externalise its internal market norms are manifold: to prepare European countries for accession, to promote goals of foreign and security or development policy, to pursue own commercial interests (e.g. opening new markets, neutralising trade diversion effects of competing free trade agreements or building strategic links with emerging markets), to further regional integration and region-to-region agreements or to shape the international regulatory framework for trade and investment. In the Commission's words, the internal market "needs to position itself, by fostering the development of quality rules and standards which shape global norms, to allow European citizens and businesses to take advantage of the opportunities of globalisation" (European Commission, 2007b: 4). Externalisation thus serves to promote broadly defined EU interests on a regional or global scale.[8]

The next section sets out the analytical framework, while the subsequent two sections examine the current state of externalisation in the neighbourhood and on a global level. The conclusions discuss some implications of the findings.

## 2. Three political dimensions of externalising the internal market

In order to analyse the political aspects of the internal market's external dimension, this chapter draws on all three political dimensions: structure (polity), contents (policy) and procedures (politics).[9] Polity

---

7 Franck (1988: 706) defines legitimacy as that quality of a rule "which derives from a perception on the part of those to whom it is addressed that it has come into being in accordance with right process".

8 It should be kept in mind that there are also internal market norms which the EU is less keen to export such as the free movement of workers or agricultural trade concessions.

9 These three dimensions are often used in the Europeanisation literature in order to analyse the domestic impact of European integration on states: a 'misfit' between European and domestic policies, processes and institutions may create adaptational pressures (see Börzel and Risse, 2003).

relates to the institutional set-up that the EU has established with a third country; the policies may, for instance, cover trade in goods and services, labour migration or foreign direct investment; and politics embraces processes of decision-making or implementation such as the diffusion mechanisms for the EU's internal market norms. The three dimensions are clearly interdependent.

**Table 9.1. Forms of internal market externalisation: polity and policies**

| | | **Polity** – degree of institutionalisation | | |
|---|---|---|---|---|
| | | *low* | *medium* | *high* |
| **Policies** – coverage of internal market issues | *low* | regulatory dialogues, global standard setting | Partnership and Cooperation Agreements | Energy Community Treaty |
| | *medium* | free trade agreements | EuroMed Association Agreements, Stabilisation and Association Agreements, ENP Action Plans | EC-Turkey customs union |
| | *high* | EU-Swiss bilateral agreements | Accession Partnerships | European Economic Area |

Table 9.1 combines policies (the internal market issues covered) and polity (the degree of institutionalisation) and provides prominent examples in each cell of the matrix. In general, the broader the coverage, the more likely the cooperation constitutes deep integration (measures applied behind the borders) rather than just shallow integration (measures applied at the borders). And the more institutionalised the relationship, the tighter the form of cooperation in terms of emulating the EU's institutional setup. The EEA, the Accession Partnerships that prepare candidates for EU membership and Switzerland's many bilateral agreements with the EU provide the most far-reaching coverage of internal market policies. In terms of institutionalisation, the EEA offers the closest internal market association, followed by the EC-Turkey customs union and the sectoral Energy Community Treaty with the Western Balkan countries. The still rather young European Neighbourhood Policy (ENP) builds on the existing PCAs and the Euro-Mediterranean Association Agreements (EMAAs) and adds country-specific 'stakes' in

the internal market with the aid of ENP Action Plans.[10] Among the less institutionalised forms of cooperation are the bilateral (or bi-regional) free trade agreements that the EU has concluded with non-European countries like Mexico, Chile and South Africa or is negotiating with Mercosur, the Gulf Cooperation Council, South Korea, India and ASEAN. The loosest forms of cooperation are regulatory dialogues or other EU attempts to act as a global standard setter by exporting its internal market norms to third countries or international fora.

**Table 9.2: forms of internal market externalisation: politics**

| | | | |
|---|---|---|---|
| **Politics** – degree of internal market alignment | *high* | adoption of the *acquis* | accession process<br>internal market association<br>customs union agreement<br>'quasi-supranational' sectoral agreement |
| | *medium* | 'reciprocal liberalisa-tion' | free trade agreement<br>mutual recognition agreement<br>recognition of equivalence |
| | *low* | 'standard setting' | regulatory dialogue<br>international standardisation<br>international harmonisation<br>export of 'regional model' |

A third dimension is added by politics, which comprises the processes, tools and mechanisms of internal market externalisation. The larger the extent to which this is based on the *acquis*, the more likely a dynamic approach that allows for the *acquis*' evolution, granting the EU a powerful position. Table 9.2 distinguishes three types of processes according to the degree of alignment with the internal market: taking on the *acquis*, reciprocal liberalisation and standard setting.[11] First, with an

[10] This classification is dynamic. Turkey, for instance, is moving down towards broader issue coverage (and an Accession Partnership), as do the political ENP Action Plans compared to the legal agreements on which they are based.

[11] For comparison, Schmidt (2007) distinguishes three approaches to integration within the internal market: national treatment, mutual recognition and harmonisation. The simplest method is national treatment, whereby states open their markets to foreign goods and services, provided that these comply with the host country's rules. It has largely been constrained to legitimate exceptions from the market freedoms, when Member States cannot be obliged to accept mutual recognition and do not agree on (minimum) harmonisation. Moreover, this principle of non-discrimination is a basic feature of the WTO. Harmonisation based on the Community method constitutes a 'vertical transfer of sovereignty' for the EU Member States and mutual recognition a 'horizontal transfer of sovereignty', breaking up the "previous unity of territory, legitimation and the setting of rules" (*ibid.*, 672).

adoption of the *acquis*, the partner country unilaterally adapts to internal market norms. This is the case for accession negotiations, internal market associations (e.g. EEA) or customs union agreements (e.g. Andorra, San Marino, Turkey). The Stabilisation and Association Agreements (SAAs) with the Western Balkan countries also involve alignment with the *acquis* in many areas, as do a few sectoral agreements such as the Energy Community Treaty or the EU-Swiss agreements on civil aviation and on the Schengen/Dublin association.

The second process is 'reciprocal liberalisation' in terms of a mutual undertaking among notionally equal partners. Free trade agreements between the EU and third countries may 'reproduce' trade liberalisation provisions contained in the EC Treaty. Technical barriers to trade can also be reduced by the mechanisms of harmonisation (replacing national rules by a common rule), equivalence (keeping different national rules but recognising foreign rules with the same regulatory objective as equivalent to one's own) or mutual recognition (general principle establishing that if a product or a service can be sold lawfully in one jurisdiction, it can also be sold freely in the other participating jurisdiction without having to comply with additional requirements).[12]

Third, the process of 'standard setting' in a broad sense generally leaves the EU in a weaker position as it tries to influence its partners' policy. A case in point are regulatory dialogues (e.g. with the US or Japan) that serve to make each other's regulatory and market surveillance systems more understandable and compatible, but also efforts at international standardisation (elaborating and using international standards for regulation) or international harmonisation (drawing up new rules). The European standardisation organisations[13] cooperate closely with the EU (and the EFTA states), *inter alia*, in order "to provide

12 Mutual recognition agreements (MRAs) apply this general principle to specific instances by laying down the conditions under which the EU and the third country concerned accept test reports, certificates and marks of conformity issued by the conformity assessment bodies of the other party, in conformity with the latter's legislation.

13 The internal market's 'new approach' twenty years ago limited the regulatory function of the EU institutions to specifying 'essential requirements' that products or services must meet in terms of health, safety, environmental or consumer protection and delegated the task of developing detailed standards to private European standardisation organisations such as CEN (Comité européen de normalisation), CENELEC (Comité européen de normalisation électrotechnique) or ETSI (European Telecommunications Standards Institute). Drawing on the input of interested parties, these bodies prepare voluntary standards at the request of industry or the European Commission. Compliance with 'harmonised standards' (that is, standards adopted by CEN, CENELEC or ETSI, following a Commission mandate) provides presumption of conformity to the corresponding 'essential requirements' of EC directives and consequently free movement in the internal market.

candidate countries and neighbouring countries with a major tool for the facilitation of adaptation of their economies to the Community market" and to encourage the use of European standards "as an instrument of economic and technological integration within and outside the European market" (European Union, 2003: 9-10). They also work closely with the international standardisation bodies (such as the International Standardisation Organisation, the International Electrotechnical Commission or the International Telecommunication Union). European standards are often identical to world standards. Furthermore, the Union since the mid-1990s shows a "propensity to 'export' actively to partner countries its model of regional integration" as a complement to its own relations with a region (Maur, 2005: 1567).

The typology in Table 9.2 is of a dynamic nature, and mixtures of politics processes are possible. Through the ENP, for instance, the PCAs and EMAAs are moving upwards towards a partly high degree of alignment with internal market rules. There are also certain correlations between these forms of politics and the other two political dimensions, policies and polity: the EEA, the EC-Turkey customs union and the Energy Community – but also the Accession Partnerships – demand a high degree of alignment (or adoption of the *acquis*), whereas the free trade agreements, the EMAAs and the SAAs require a medium degree and the PCAs or regulatory dialogues merely a low or no degree of alignment. In general, cooperation on the global level is located in the categories of low or medium alignment processes, but relations on the regional level show a medium to high adaptation.

To varying degrees, the different mechanisms of norm diffusion rely on legal obligations, incentives (attempting to induce the partners to embark on certain policies out of material self-interest) or on persuasion (aiming at a change of the partners' preferences through discourse). In other words, third countries may adopt internal market rules either because they have to, because they want to obtain the rewards that come with the 'policy import' (respectively avoid the costs of non-compliance), or because they view these EU norms as appropriate and legitimate. Deliberation and persuasion are particularly important when the *acquis* as such needs to be implemented, but mutual recognition also requires a high degree of trust on both sides. 'Selling' the regional integration model abroad is likely to involve intense discourse as well. Finally, the export of internal market norms tends to be stronger in the EU's immediate vicinity. "Through the EEA and increasingly through the European neighbourhood policy the rules and standards of the single market stretch beyond the borders of the EU" (European Commission, 2007b: 5).

## 3. The neighbours' stake in the internal market

Most of the EU's neighbouring countries are taking over the *acquis communautaire* either in its entirety through accession negotiations or partly through an internal market association, a customs union or sectoral agreements.

The *enlargement* process is the most evident example of an externalisation of the internal market. Candidate countries must align their regulatory systems with the EU in order to be able to fully participate in the internal market, and they need to develop the necessary administrative capacity to implement the *acquis*.[14] Such an obligation is "difficult to reconcile with the sovereignty requirements", considering that the candidates do not participate in the drafting of the *acquis* "until the eventual future membership has taken place" (Albi, 2001: 201). The EU is currently negotiating accession with Croatia and Turkey. Macedonia has obtained candidate status but not yet opened negotiations. Since the mid-1990s the EU uses a 'pre-accession strategy' to prepare candidates for membership. This strategy usually consists of bilateral agreements with the candidate countries (e.g. Europe Agreements), Accession Partnerships, opening of Community programmes and agencies, pre-accession assistance and political dialogue (Maresceau, 2003). Accession Partnerships determine the short-term priorities and medium-term objectives on the basis of the 'Copenhagen criteria' and the specific needs on which financial assistance should be targeted. The candidate country draws up a national programme for the adoption of the *acquis*, which sets out a timetable for putting the partnership into effect. A regular evaluation of the candidates' progress is carried out by the Commission. The accession process clearly aims at full integration into the policies and polity of the EU. As Grabbe (2001: 1014) points out, studies of Europeanisation have mainly focused on EU Member States, "yet the EU exerts similar pressures on the applicant countries".

Stopping short of EU membership at the time of its conclusion in 1992, the *European Economic Area* covers the free movement of goods, services, capital and persons, competition rules as well as horizontal policies (e.g. environment, social policies, consumer protection, statistics and company law) and flanking policies (e.g. cooperation in research and development or education). The principle of mutual recogni-

14 The approximation of law under the Europe Agreements covered about 80,000 pages of *acquis*, including the Treaties, secondary legislation, case law, soft law and international agreements, as well as some policies which have not been adopted by all the Member States (e.g. Schengen, monetary union). The Accession Partnerships even added areas beyond EU competences such as judicial reform, prison conditions, social security or civil service reform.

tion has been extended to goods originating in the EEA; and the national standards bodies of the EFTA states are members of CEN and CENELEC. The EEA constitutes an extended free trade area which is best described as a dynamic internal market association between the Community and the countries of the European Free Trade Association, with the exception of Switzerland. It excludes the EU's external relations,[15] the common agricultural, fisheries and transport policies,[16] budget contributions and regional policy,[17] taxation as well as economic and monetary policy.

The Commission retains the exclusive right to initiative, whereas the EFTA countries have the right to raise a matter of concern at the EEA level at any time (*droit d'évocation*). EFTA experts are consulted by the Commission in the preparatory stage of new measures. The main discussions take place within the EEA Joint Committee in the so-called decision-shaping phase after the Commission transmitted its proposals to the EU Council and to the EFTA states (Reymond 1993). The EEA Joint Committee decides by consensus as closely as possible in time to the adoption of the same rules by the EU Council in order to allow for a simultaneous application. On average, the EEA EFTA states incorporate some 300 EU acts into their legal systems each year (Vahl and Grolimund, 2006: 87). In case of an opt-out, the EFTA countries, which need to 'speak with one voice', face the threat of a suspension of related parts of the Agreement. In addition, the EEA Council meets at ministerial level twice a year to give political impetus, and an EEA Joint Parliamentary Committee and an EEA Joint Consultative Committee for the economic and social partners act as advisory bodies. On the EFTA side, surveillance and enforcement is carried out by the EFTA Surveillance Authority and the EFTA Court. The principles of primacy and direct effect of EEA law apply. In order to secure a uniform interpretation of EEA rules, the EEA Joint Committee reviews the development of the case law of the European Court of Justice and the EFTA Court.

The EEA combines a comprehensive internal market 'policy integration' with a limited participation in terms of 'polity' despite a complex two-pillar system. EEA legislation mirrors any relevant new *acquis*, but

---

[15] Nevertheless, EFTA follows a policy of 'shadowing' the EU in concluding trade agreements, and Norway and Iceland are closely associated with the EU on foreign, security and defence policies and with the Schengen and Dublin agreements. The latter are also being extended to Switzerland and Liechtenstein.

[16] The sensitive issues of Alpine transit and Nordic fisheries, like trade in agricultural products, were dealt with separately in bilateral agreements with the EFTA states concerned.

[17] However, the EFTA countries had to establish financial mechanisms to contribute to the reduction of social and economic disparities in the EU.

EFTA lacks a real right of co-decision.[18] As a result, Switzerland opted out of the EEA through a negative referendum in 1992, which also lead to a 'freezing' of its EU membership bid, and most other EFTA states joined the EU in 1995. The 'EEA EFTA pillar' was reduced to Norway (whose referendum on EU membership failed), Iceland and Liechtenstein. The EEA has most likely set the maximum limits of how the EU deals with third countries' requests to participate in its decision-making procedures.

Instead, *Switzerland* pursued a bilateral approach to integration, building mainly on its 1972 free trade agreement with the European Communities. In two package deals it concluded in 1999 and 2004 sixteen new sectoral agreements with the EU.[19] Most of the agreements of these 'bilaterals I and II' are based on the notion of equivalence of laws between the two parties (Felder, 2001 and 2006).[20] In contrast to the EEA Agreement, the *Cassis de Dijon* principle is not included in the bilateral agreement on technical barriers to trade. In general, the Commission consults with Swiss experts in the fields where Swiss legislation is recognised as equivalent, and in a few EU committees Switzerland has observer status. Typically, the Joint Committees set up by individual bilateral agreements may make technical changes to the annexes of the agreement but not add new obligations. However, there are three 'partial integration' agreements where Switzerland accepts the *acquis*: in the area of air transport (where the European Commission and the European Court of Justice have competences in surveillance and arbitration in specified areas) and in the Schengen and Dublin association agreements, where new *acquis* requires approval from the Swiss legislature (but in case of a refusal, the agreement could be terminated). These associations foresee an adaptation to new *acquis* in the future, and Swiss representatives participate without a vote in the Commission's comitology and informal expert groups and, with regard to Schengen, also in the relevant committees and working groups of the Council (Cornu, 2006). Hence, at least in these sectors, Switzerland participates in the EU's decision-shaping process.

---

18 The idea of mutual recognition of equivalent legislation and of joint decisionmaking institutions had early on in the EEA negotiations been abandoned. EFTA's hope to be able to have a say on future EEA rules by 'buying the past' (i.e. taking over the existing *acquis*) was equally frustrated (Gstöhl, 1994).

19 Free movement of persons, technical barriers to trade, public procurement, civil aviation, overland transport, agriculture, research, Schengen/Dublin association, taxation of savings, fight against fraud, processed agricultural products, environment, statistics, media, education, and pensions.

20 This was facilitated by the fact that since 1988 any new Swiss legislation has systematically been compared to, and if possible made compatible with, the relevant EU law.

Overall, the scope of the EU-Swiss bilateral agreements falls short of the EEA with respect to both policies and polity. Switzerland's access to the internal market is more limited, perhaps most notably exemplified by the absence of an agreement on services.[21] The EU linked Swiss wishes of cooperation to its own preferences (e.g. taxation of savings, fraud, financial contribution[22]) and introduced a 'guillotine clause' in the 'bilaterals I' that was to ensure that Switzerland would ratify all agreements, in particular with a view to the controversial free movement of persons. Since this bilateral sectoral approach lacks an overarching framework agreement, "there is less institutionalised political dialogue between the EU and Switzerland than between the EU and most other third countries" (Vahl and Grolimund, 2006: 112). Opportunities for further bilateral rapprochement seem almost exhausted as it would increasingly touch on politically sensitive sectors, and the Swiss lack of influence would further cumulate.[23] Moreover, the Union had early on made clear that it would offer less than in the EEA.

Pursuant to their 1963 association agreement, the European Community and Turkey in 1996 established a customs union, and three years later, Turkey became a candidate country. The *EC-Turkey customs union* covers industrial goods and processed agricultural products, but not (yet) agriculture, services or public procurement.[24] Turkey had to adopt the common external tariff and align to the *acquis* in essential internal market areas, notably technical barriers to trade, competition policies and protection of intellectual property rights. The agreement makes use of the pan-European system of (diagonal) cumulation of origin, the technical standards of the European standardisation bodies are also valid in Turkey, and the principle of mutual recognition has been extended to Turkish goods. Moreover, Turkey has to bring its trade policy into line with the common commercial policy and, for instance, negotiate agreements with many third countries.[25]

---

21 Negotiations on a bilateral agreement on services were suspended in 2003 because the two sides could not agree on the sectors to be included.

22 The European Commission argued that "the EU-Swiss bilateral agreements overall gave Switzerland access to roughly two-thirds of the internal market" and therefore it should make a financial contribution of two-thirds in per capita terms of the EEA Financial Mechanism (Vahl and Grolimund, 2006: 78).

23 New negotiations are underway with regard to the electricity market and Eurojust.

24 In fact, the association agreement had foreseen to include agriculture in the customs union but this was not pursued further; Turkey first needs to align to the Common Agricultural Policy. Moreover, the provisions of the Additional Protocol on the free movement of workers, services and capital were not implemented, and the EU's financial aid commitments had not been met, mainly due to objections by Greece.

25 In this respect, the customs union agreement goes further than the Swiss 'bilaterals' or the EEA.

The Commission informally consults Turkish experts when drafting new relevant *acquis*, and further consultations may take place in the customs union's Joint Committee. Turkey then adopts the necessary national legislation. To some extent, the customs union's consultation mechanism has been taken from the EEA, but "the flaws in the EEA provisions have been compounded by the failure to adjust them to reflect Turkey's involvement in the EC's trade policy" (Peers, 1996: 423). Even though the EU and Turkey should act in tandem, Turkey cannot affect the (re)negotiation of trade agreements and is excluded from consultations on trade policy measures. In case of a dispute, the Association Council tries to find a solution or may unanimously decide to submit the dispute to the European Court of Justice or an arbitration tribunal (Kabaalioglu, 1997). In view of the supposedly temporary nature of the customs union, Turkey accepted to apply Community policies and legislation without taking part in the EU's decision-making process. The final goal of the association agreement was not the establishment of a customs union "but the completion of a real common market, thereby removing all barriers to factor movements between Turkey and the EC", including the possibility of a Turkish membership (*ibid.*: 158). In October 2005, the European Union opened accession negotiations with Turkey.

Processes of Europeanisation can be found well beyond (potential) EU Member States. "Evidence of what may be termed 'external Europeanisation' – the extension of EU rules (laws, institutions, and practices) beyond Member State borders and the adoption of EU rules by non-member countries – can be found globally, but the phenomenon is most pronounced in the European peripheries" (Magen 2006: 386). In the framework of the multilateral *Euro-Mediterranean Partnership*, of which Turkey is a member, the EU has negotiated bilateral association agreements with additional nine Mediterranean countries which in most cases replaced older cooperation agreements from the 1970s (Philippart, 2003).[26] The so-called Barcelona Process among other things envisages the establishment of a Euro-Mediterranean free trade area for industrial goods by 2010. In 2006 additional negotiations on liberalising services, trade in agricultural and fisheries products and on the right of establishment have been launched, and the pan-European cumulation system is extended to the region.[27] The Association Agreements emphasise the necessity to cooperate on standards and envisage mutual recognition agreements as soon as the conditions for them are met.

26 Agreements are in force with Algeria, Egypt, Israel, Jordan, Lebanon, Morocco, the Palestinian Authority and Tunisia. The agreement with Syria has been initialled.

27 The Pan-EuroMed Protocol allows to diagonally cumulate processing in the region in order to obtain preferential treatment.

In contrast to the Mediterranean neighbours, the EU's bilateral *Partnership and Cooperation Agreements* with the transition countries to the East grant no preferential treatment for trade. The parties basically apply most-favoured nation status to one another with respect to tariffs on industrial goods. The PCAs feature mutual trade liberalisation and political dialogue, supervised by the Cooperation Council whose decisions have no binding effects.[28] The EU distinguishes between 'European' and 'Asian' partner countries: the PCAs with Russia, Ukraine and Moldova envisage a free trade agreement as soon as circumstances permit, while those with the South Caucasian and Central Asian countries embrace no such perspective (Hillion, 1998).[29] Each Partnership and Cooperation Agreement is concluded for ten years, and the EU-Russia PCA was the first one to expire at the end of 2007.[30] Russia and the participants of the European Neighbourhood Policy may, after accession to the WTO, expect to negotiate enhanced 'deep and comprehensive free trade agreements' with the EU (Hillion, 2007). Negotiations with Ukraine have been launched in March 2007.

Both the EMAAs and the PCAs serve as legal basis for the *European Neighbourhood Policy* that the Union developed in the run-up to its 2004 enlargement. After Russia's opt-out in favour of an individual Strategic Partnership and the extension of the ENP to the three South Caucasian republics, the policy embraces sixteen EU neighbours to the South and East.[31] The ENP does not offer an accession perspective but a deeper political relationship and economic integration based on a mutual commitment to common values (such as democracy, human rights, rule of law, good governance and market economy principles). Tailor-made bilateral Action Plans define the political and economic reform priorities for the next three to five years. With regard to internal market policies, they include measures to improve the respective regulatory systems on issues such as intellectual property rights, services, public procurement, free movement of capital, the right of establishment and company law. The European Commission (2007b: 9) unmistakably states that the EU should "extend aspects of single market policy through the neighbourhood policy", and that it intends "to push for a

---

28 In contrast to an Association Council, it cannot oblige the parties to act or settle disputes. New obligations would require the conclusion of a further agreement.

29 The PCA with Belarus was signed in 1995 but, due to the country's non-democratic regime, not ratified.

30 A PCA will be prolonged, however, if both parties do not request otherwise.

31 The eligible participants are Algeria, Armenia, Azerbaijan, Belarus, Egypt, Georgia, Israel, Jordan, Lebanon, Libya, Moldova, Morocco, the Palestinian Authority, Syria, Tunisia and Ukraine.

high level of convergence of rules and standards, in line with the EU approach" (European Commission, 2007d: 10).

The Action Plans encourage ENP countries to use EU standards, join European standardisation bodies and improve the exchange of information on regulations. They work with both incentives and discourse-based instruments and resemble the Accession Partnerships (Gstöhl, 2008). The incentives comprise, for instance, financial aid, preferential market access, technical assistance, interconnected infrastructure, but also suspension clauses in the agreements (e.g. deferral of aid or withdrawal of trade preferences in case of human rights abuse). What the promised 'stake in the internal market' means has yet to be clearly defined, but is at least "understood to refer to a substantial reduction of (tariff and non-tariff) barriers across many dimensions of the internal market" (Dodini and Fantini, 2006: 511). The Union has in particular left open the perspectives of free trade in agricultural products and of free movement of labour. Improved market access is now considered to "stand at the heart of the intensified ENP" (Council of the European Union, 2007: 7). "It should in particular focus on partners' comparative advantages and thus feature elements of asymmetry in their favour as appropriate. In return, partners must continue opening their economic systems and selectively adopt relevant parts of the EU *acquis*" (*ibid.*). The deliberative instruments are generally based on arguing and frequent interaction on multiple levels. They include 'joint ownership' of the process with a shared setting of reform priorities and monitoring of their implementation, policy dialogues as well as other interactive tools for the approximation of national economic legislation to the *acquis* such as the twinning of legal experts and targeted expert assistance (e.g. TAIEX). In addition, the EU issues regular reports that would allow it to 'name and shame' foot-draggers and to create a certain peer pressure among the ENP countries. Besides the principle of conditionality (withholding 'carrots' and applying certain 'sticks' if crucial conditions are not fulfilled), the principle of differentiation states that the level of common values will affect the degree to which the ambitions are shared. That is to say, the EU does not intend to uniformly deal with the ENP countries as a group, but to take individual progress into account.

In sum, the ENP carries the potential to cover many internal market policies, with several politics tools being partly borrowed from the accession process. Regarding polity, it is based on the institutions provided by the bilateral agreements. Its future shape is still open, but a participation in the EU's decision-making process is not foreseen – the ENP idea is to rely on "sharing everything but institutions" (Prodi, 2002: 6).

The countries of South Eastern Europe, in the context of the *Stabilisation and Association Process* (SAP) launched in 1999, are also increasingly aligning themselves to the EU *acquis*. Based on strong political conditionality, the SAP offers trade liberalisation, financial assistance and new contractual relations in the form of Stabilisation and Association Agreements, an extensive part of which relate to internal market issues (Pippan, 2004). It may be considered a 'pre-pre-accession strategy' since the European Council in 2000 officially recognised the Western Balkan countries' vocation as 'potential candidates' for EU membership. In the same year, the EU has granted autonomous trade preferences to these countries with duty-free and quota-free access to the internal market for almost all goods, including agricultural products (except for wine, certain fisheries products, sugar, baby beef and textiles). The SAAs will gradually replace these measures by asymmetrical reciprocal obligations and a free trade area for industrial goods. The EU plans to extend the pan-European cumulation system to the Western Balkans (and in a second step their inclusion in the Pan-EuroMed system). Some provisions on the movement of workers, establishment, services and capital as well as a commitment to legal approximation in particular with regard to competition, public procurement and intellectual property rights are enshrined in the SAAs. To date such agreements are in force for Croatia and Macedonia. The SAAs with Albania and Montenegro are awaiting ratification and those with Serbia and Bosnia Herzegovina have been initialled.

The key decision-making bodies are the Stabilisation and Association Councils but the process is rather one of unilateral alignment by the 'potential candidates'. In fact, the SAAs resemble the former Europe Agreements, and the European Partnerships, which identify short- and medium-term priorities for reforms, are modelled after the Accession Partnerships (Phinnemore 2003). The countries are expected to draw up national plans for the implementation of the partnerships which will be monitored by the EU. The SAP countries also benefit from pre-accession assistance, twinning, TAIEX and the opening of Community programmes. In addition, the SAAs entail a commitment to engage in regional cooperation with the other SAP countries. The Western Balkan states (and Moldova) thus have concluded a network of bilateral free trade agreements which in late 2006 was transformed into a single regional trade arrangement, the Central European Free Trade Agreement (CEFTA), that benefits from technical assistance through the CARDS programme.

The SAP also aims at the gradual re-integration of the region into the European infrastructure networks (e.g. transport, energy, border management). The most successful project in this regard is the Treaty establishing the *Energy Community*, which entered into force in July 2006 and creates a single regulatory energy space. It extends the EU's internal market for electricity and gas to the region of South Eastern Europe (Walendy, 2004). Albania, Bosnia Herzegovina, Croatia, Kosovo/UNMIK, Macedonia, Montenegro and Serbia agreed to adopt the relevant *acquis* on energy, environment, renewables and competition. Moldova, Norway, Turkey and Ukraine are observers and have applied to join. In view of the EU's emerging external energy policy, the Commission and the High Representative for the Common Foreign and Security Policy even suggest "to extend the EU's internal market, through expansion of the Energy Community Treaty to include relevant EEA and ENP countries" (Council of the European Union, 2006: 4). The Energy Community's institutions consist of the Ministerial Council, the Permanent High-Level Group, the Regulatory Board, the Fora (composed of representatives of industry, regulators and consumers and chaired by a EU representative) and the Secretariat in Vienna, which assists the European Commission. It thus constitutes a sectoral but highly institutionalised policy area of internal market externalisation. Even though the Energy Community has no supranational competences, the Union has successfully 'reproduced' itself. "The Energy Community Treaty is consciously modelled on the European Steel and Coal Community that was the genesis for the European Union" (European Commission, 2005b: 1).

An externalisation of the internal market beyond its neighbourhood is evidently more difficult and less important for the European Union. Nevertheless, the EU increasingly attempts to export its norms to more distant third countries and to international bodies as well.

## 4. Promoting internal market norms on a global level

Foreign exporters need to ensure that their products comply with the EU's requirements in order to be able to sell them on the internal market. On the one hand, regulations, standards and conformity assessment procedures may serve legitimate objectives such as protection of safety and health, the environment or consumers and the promotion of quality. On the other hand, they have a potential to impede trade.[32] Compared to the EU's near abroad, the degree of internal market alignment (politics),

[32] Even among the EU Member States the internal market for goods is still not fully completed. National rules may still constitute important barriers due to the weak application and enforcement of the Treaty rules, and many EU rules are still inconsistent or burdensome. The Commission has therefore recently taken different initiatives which will, *inter alia*, place the burden of proof on the national authorities denying market access, streamline and facilitate the various conformity assessment procedures and strengthen market surveillance activities (European Commission, 2007a).

the fields of cooperation (policies) and the degree of institutionalisation (polity) are much more limited on the global level.

To improve their market access, third countries may negotiate bilateral agreements with the EU, as many neighbouring countries have done. In the 1990s, the EU has also concluded agreements with more distant trading partners. For example, the *free trade agreements* with Mexico, Chile and South Africa provide reciprocal but asymmetric liberalisation of trade in goods and services, public procurement, competition, intellectual property rights, investment and dispute settlement (Woolcock, 2007: 5-9). In addition, the EU has already for a few years been negotiating bi-regional association agreements with MERCOSUR and the Gulf Cooperation Council covering similar issues. In 2007 new negotiations have been launched with South Korea, India and ASEAN. According to the European Commission (2007d: 10), such free trade agreements with non-neighbouring countries should also involve regulatory "convergence towards EU or international standards at least in selected priority areas".

Other forms of 'reciprocal liberalisation' are agreements to avoid unnecessary duplication of certification by accepting each other's conformity assessments (mutual recognition) or agreements recognising the equivalence of foreign rules with the same regulatory objective. Nicolaïdis and Egan (2001) argue that the success of European regulatory cooperation has had negative 'spillover effects' on outsiders such as the United States, leading to a demand for inter-regional cooperation and international standardisation. For foreign partners, the precondition for entry into the internal market became either to seek EU-based certification on an *ad hoc* basis or to negotiate *mutual recognition agreements*. The EU thereby benefited from a 'first mover advantage' by exporting core elements of its model (*ibid.*). Bilateral MRAs covering various industrial sectors are currently in place with Australia, Canada, Israel, Japan, New Zealand, Switzerland and the USA. *Recognition of equivalence* is more complex and little used for technical barriers to trade. However, in the area of sanitary and phyosanitary measures, where health protection normally is the core objective, the EU has, for instance, concluded a few veterinary equivalency agreements (Canada, Chile, New Zealand, Switzerland, USA).

A lower degree of internal market alignment includes efforts in favour of regulatory convergence. In recent years, the European Commission has developed *regulatory dialogues* with key partners such as the United States, Japan, China, India and Russia. These dialogues serve to enhance the compatibility of policies, mainly in the field of financial services and capital markets, intellectual property rights and public procurement.[33] Since in highly interdependent markets differing regulatory systems can create obstacles to trade and investment, "it is essential that the internal market legal framework is adequately attuned to the global economic framework in general and to key marketplaces in particular, and vice-versa" (European Commission, 2005a: 3). Most dialogues start with a process of confidence building and information sharing on domestic regulation before they engage in closer cooperation. Regulatory dialogues are only successful if they receive sufficient political attention and commitment. A further condition is that "dialogues mainly take place between the regulatory experts themselves, in a non-confrontational climate of expertise and understanding" and that they are kept flexible and informal (*ibid.*: 6).

Moreover, the EU aims at *global standard setting* by promoting "the adoption overseas of standards and regulatory approaches based on, or compatible with, international and European practices" (European Commission 2001: 8). Harmonisation requires adaptation, either through bringing one party's rules into alignment with another's or through the development of new international rules, in order to create compatibility and interoperability of products. The European Commission (2007b: 9) recently called for more responsiveness to the global context and to "promote greater global regulatory convergence – including where appropriate the adoption of European standards – internationally through international organisations and bilateral agreements". The internal market "gives the EU the potential to shape global norms and to ensure that fair rules are applied to worldwide trade and investment", and it serves as "the launch pad of an ambitious global agenda" (*ibid.*: 7). In the years to come, the European Commission (2007c: 7) observes the emergence of a "new international approach focusing on regulatory cooperation, convergence of standards and equivalence of rules [...] with the EU being looked upon as the global standard-setter in many areas such as product safety, food safety, environmental protection, public procurement, financial regulation and accounting". EU competition policy has a global reach, the GSM standard is used worldwide, and new rules in areas such as $CO_2$ emissions trading, aviation safety and chemicals "are gradually being adopted across the world" (*ibid.*). This development has, *inter alia*, been driven by the sheer size and regulatory sophistication of the Union's home market and by the fact that the EU wields up to 27 votes in international bodies (Buck 2007). Compared with other jurisdictions, the EU's rules tend to be stricter. Companies that produce their goods to European standards can therefore

33 Regulatory work is, of course, also done within multilateral organisations (e.g. WTO, WIPO) or international agreements.

assume that their products can also be marketed elsewhere (European Commission 2007d: 6). Moreover, the EU has gathered much experience on how to deal with different regulatory traditions, and the EU framework is available in many different languages (*ibid.*).

Finally, a special form of 'standard setting' is the *promotion of regional integration* in other areas of the world, with the EU as a sponsor but not a partner in the new grouping. In the 1990s, the EU first sought to persuade neighbouring countries to pursue regional integration among themselves. Examples include the Visegrad countries, the Baltic Free Trade Area and CEFTA. This policy has recently been extended to non-European partner countries as well, for instance the customs union of the Gulf Cooperation Council, the Agadir Agreement in the Mediterranean region or the negotiation of Economic Partnership Agreements with regional groupings of the ACP countries (Maur, 2005). In view of the successful completion of the internal market, the EU has thereby increasingly emphasised its own example as a model to follow. This strategy complements the EU's bilateral trade and association agreements, which to varying degrees export EU trade rules, for example its product classification, the pan-European rules of origin, trade facilitation measures (e.g. Single Administrative Document), EU standards (e.g. technical barriers to trade, sanitary and phytosanitary measures) and regulations (e.g. competition policy, intellectual property rights).

The final section discusses some implications of the internal market's external dimension, in particular with regard to the legitimacy of "expanding the 'regulatory space' of the EU beyond its borders" (European Commission, 2007d: 9). Third countries' compliance is at least partly secured by the perception of these rules as being legitimate.

## 5. Conclusions: some political implications

The European Commission (2007d: 5) has recently observed that

> through the enlargement process and the European Neighbourhood Policy, the Community rulebook is gradually being adopted across large parts of the European continent. Beyond this, the EU is emerging as a global rule maker, with the single market framework and the wider EU economic and social model increasingly serving as a reference point in third countries as well as in global and regional fora.

In view of the fact that "the extraterritorial projection of EU rules and their impact on third country systems remains under-theorised" (Magen, 2006: 387), this chapter has taken a first step and examined how and to what extent the Union attempts to externalise its internal market by outlining the policies, polity and politics of its external economic relations. The three political dimensions vary considerably, leading to different depths and dynamics of a 'Europeanisation beyond Europe'. A shallow, static and loose form of cooperation does not provoke many worries about its implications for legitimacy. Yet, the broader the coverage of internal market issues, the higher the degree of institutionalisation and the closer the alignment with the *acquis*, the more likely is a deep, dynamic and tight relationship with the EU that may raise concerns about the appropriateness of rules. "Immediate EU neighbours such as Switzerland and Norway as well as countries in eastern Europe, the Balkans and North Africa are committed to keeping their regulatory regimes as close as possible to the EU approach to ease trade" (Buck, 2007). They are affected by internal market decisions but not represented in their making. This poses a problem in particular for the more dynamic relationships which require an almost 'automatic' alignment with the evolving *acquis*, thus leaving little room for parliamentary control.

The EEA offers the EFTA countries at least a say in the decision-shaping phase of new legislation as well as own surveillance and enforcement mechanisms and – if they wanted to – the possibility to join the EU. For Switzerland, three of its many bilateral agreements are directly based on an adoption of the *acquis*, but the cumulative effect of all treaties might nonetheless raise sovereignty concerns. Kux and Sverdrup (2002: 264) conclude with regard to both Switzerland and the EEA member Norway that "the process they are involved in remains formally intergovernmental, but the effects they experience are supranational". Turkey has not much influence in Brussels either, even with regard to economic and trade issues. "The Customs Union is thus undemocratic insofar as Turkey had to cede important parts of its national sovereignty without being represented in the EU's political decision-making mechanism and without having any influence on the multinational decision-making process" (Karakas, 2006: 325). The EU decision makers cannot be held accountable by third-country nationals; they can only vote their own national representatives out of office.

Both the ENP and the SAP rely closely on the enlargement model which the EU developed for Central and Eastern Europe. Whereas this strong path dependency can arguably be justified with reference to the 'potential candidate' status of the Western Balkans, it is more striking in the ENP context. "EU demands for pre-accession legal and institutional alignment – however onerous, one-sided, and asymmetrical they may be – are legitimised by the prospect of full inclusion and the promise of future equality of participation" (Magen, 2006: 422). This membership perspective is absent in the European Neighbourhood Policy. The pressure for future EU enlargement might therefore increase, the more successful the ENP – or the less attractive the EEA for the EFTA countries – becomes. On the other hand, increasing Europeanisation, in particular if based on political conditionality and lacking a membership perspective, may lead to more Euroskepticism in third countries. In addition, one might expect more lobbying efforts from public and private actors in Brussels, especially from the candidate and ENP countries.

It is also questionable whether the EU can effectively become a global power without addressing certain problems of consistency between internal and external objectives and of coherence between different external policies "such as championing multilateralism while blanketing the planet with bilateral trade agreements, or promoting the cause of economic development while protecting European agriculture" (Meunier and Nicolaïdis, 2006: 907). The Union also uses access to its internal market as a bargaining chip to obtain domestic changes in its trading partners. "Since the EU is itself a system of market liberalisation, its external efforts are about replication more than domination" but this does not mean "that the former does not include elements of the latter" (*ibid.*: 912).

On the global level, the diffusion of internal market norms is more limited than in the EU's neighbourhood. The three political dimensions may serve as indicators for the degree of Europeanisation. Even if the Union has deficiencies in input legitimacy (government by the people), it may in some policy areas deliver output legitimacy (government by the people) through effective problem solving (Scharpf, 1999). Menon and Weatherill (2002) argue that the EU institutions may also contribute to input legitimacy compared to nation-states by taking into account interests (e.g. consumers, foreign exporters) that are often affected by decisions but excluded or underrepresented on the national level. With regard to the external dimension of the internal market, the input legitimacy is obviously very low given the non-members' lack of influence in the EU decision-making process, but to a certain extent "the realisation of a more efficient market for Europe offers itself as a factor of output legitimation that can be taken as a justification for an apparent absence of orthodox input legitimacy" (*ibid.*: 120). The question then is under what conditions economic (and political) gains, in particular in areas which surpass the governments' problem-solving capacity, may justify an alignment with the *acquis* – and whether a membership perspective is on hand. In the long term, output legitimacy will not be sufficient to balance a deficit of input legitimacy.

## References

Albi, A. (2001) Europe Agreements in the Light of Sovereignty and Legitimacy: The Case of Estonia, in Kellermann, Alfred E., de Zwaan, Jaap W. and

Czuczai, J. (eds.) *EU Enlargement: The Constitutional Impact at EU and National Level*, The Hague, T.M.C. Asser Press, pp. 195-214.

Börzel, T. A. and Risse, T. (2003). Conceptualizing the Domestic Impact of Europe, in Featherstone, K. and Radaelli, C. M. (eds.) *The Politics of Europeanisation*, Oxford, Oxford University Press, pp. 57-80.

Buck, Tobias (2007). Standard Bearer: How the European Union Exports its Laws, *Financial Times*, 10 July 2007.

Cornu, A. (2006) Les aspects institutionnels des Accords d'association de la Suisse à Schengen et à Dublin, in Kaddous, C. & Jametti Greiner, M. (eds.) *Accord bilatéraux II Suisse-UE et autres accords récents*, Bruxelles, Bruylant, pp. 207-244.

Council of the European Union (2007) Strengthening the European Neighbourhood Policy – Presidency Progress Report, Brussels, 10874/07, 17 June 2007.

Council of the European Union (2006) An External Policy to Serve Europe's Energy Interests, Joint Paper by the Commission and the Secretary General/High Representative Javier Solana for the European Council, Brussels, S160/06, June.

Dodini, M. & Fantini, M. (2006) The EU Neighbourhood Policy: Implications for Economic Growth and Stability, *Journal of Common Market Studies*, 44(3), pp. 507-532.

Eeckhout, P. (1991) The External Dimension of the EC Internal Market: A Portrait, *World Competition*, 15(2), pp. 5-23.

European Commission (2007a) Communication from the Commission to the European Parliament, the Council and the European Economic and Social Committee, The Internal Market for Goods: A Cornerstone of Europe's Competitiveness, Brussels, COM(2007) 35 final, 14 February 2007.

European Commission (2007b) Communication from the Commission to the Council, the European Parliament, the European Economic and Social Committee and the Committee of the Regions 'A Single Market for Citizens', Interim report to the 2007 Spring European Council, Brussels, COM(2007) 60 final, 20 February 2007.

European Commission (2007c) Communication from the Commission to the European Parliament, the Council, the European Economic and Social Committee and the Committee of the Regions, A Single Market for 21st Century Europe, Brussels, COM(2007)724 final, 20 February 2007.

European Commission (2007d) Commission Staff Working Document, 'The External Dimension of the Single Market Review', Accompanying Document to the Communication from the Commission to the European Parliament, the Council, the European Economic and Social Committee and the Committee of the Regions A Single Market for 21st Century Europe, COM(2007)724 final, Brussels, SEC(2007) 1519, 20 February 2007.

European Commission (2005a) International Regulatory Dialogues Concerning the Policies of DG Internal Market and Services, *DG Internal Market and Services Working Document*, DG MARKT/20 May 2005.

European Commission (2005b). The EU and South East Europe Sign a Historic Treaty to Boost Energy Integration, Press Release, IP/05/1346, Brussels, 25 October 2005.

European Commission (2001) Commission Staff Working Paper, 'Implementing Policy for External Trade in the Fields of Standards and Conformity Assessment: a Toolbox of Instruments', Brussels, SEC(2001) 1570, 28 september 2001.

European Commission (1988) Europe 1992: Europe World Partner, Information Memo P-117, Brussels, Spokesman's Service of the European Commission.

European Commission (1985) Completing the Internal Market: White Paper from the Commission to the European Council (Milan, 28-29 June 1985), Brussels, COM(1985) 310 final, 14 June 1985.

European Council (1988) Conclusions of the Presidency of the Hanover European Council, 27-28 June 1988, *Bulletin of the European Communities*, No. 6/1988, pp. 164-167.

European Union (2003) General Guidelines for the Cooperation between CEN, CENELC and ETSI and the European Commission and the European Free Trade Association, 28 March 2003, *Official Journal of the European Union*, C91, 16 April 2003, pp. 7-11.

Felder, D. (2006) Cadre institutionnel et dispositions générales des Accords bilatéraux II (sauf Schengen/Dublin), in Kaddous, Christine and Jametti Greiner, Monique (eds.) *Accord bilatéraux II Suisse-UE et autres accords récents*, Bruxelles, Bruylant, pp. 93-117.

Felder, D. (2001) Appréciation juridique et politique du cadre institutionnel et des dispositions générales des accords sectoriels, in Felder, D. & Kaddous, Ch. (eds.) *Accord bilatéraux Suisse-UE (Commentaires)*, Bruxelles, Bruylant, pp. 117-148.

Franck, T. M. (1988) Legitimacy in the International System, *American Journal of International Law*, 82(4), pp. 705-759.

Gormley, L. W. (2002) Competition and Free Movement: Is the Internal Market the Same as a Common Market?, *European Business Law Review*, 13(6), pp. 517-522.

Grabbe, H. (2001) How Does Europeanisation Affect CEE Governance? Conditionality, Diffusion and Diversity, *Journal of European Public Policy*, 8(6), pp. 1013-1031.

Gstöhl, S. (2008) Blurring Economic Boundaries? Trade and Aid in the EU's Near Abroad, in, Mahncke, Dieter and Gstöhl, Sieglinde (eds.) *Europe's Near Abroad: Promises and Prospects of the EU's Neighbourhood Policy*. Brussels, P.I.E. Peter Lang, pp. 133-159.

Gstöhl, S. (1994) EFTA and the European Economic Area or the Politics of Frustration, *Cooperation and Conflict*, 29(4), pp. 333-366.

Hillion, C. (2007) Mapping-Out the New Contractual Relations between the European Union and Its Neighbours: Learning from the EU-Ukraine 'Enhanced Agreement', *European Foreign Affairs Review*, 12(2), pp. 169-182.

Hillion, C. (1998) Partnership and Cooperation Agreements between the EU and the New Independent States of the ex-Soviet Union, *European Foreign Affairs Review*, 3(3), pp. 399-420.

Kabaalioglu, H.A. (1997) The Turkish Model of Association: Customs Union before Accession, in Demaret, P., Bellis, J. & García Jiménez, G. (eds.) *Regionalism and Multilateralism after the Uruguay Round: Convergence, Divergence and Interaction*, Brussels, European Interuniversity Press, pp. 115-160.

Karakas, C. (2006) Gradual Integration: An Attractive Alternative Integration Process for Turkey and the EU, *European Foreign Affairs Review*, 11(3), pp. 311-331.

Kux, S. & Sverdrup, U. (2000) Fuzzy Borders and Adaptive Outsiders: Norway, Switzerland and the EU, *Journal of European Integration*, 22(3), pp. 237-270.

Magen, A. (2006) The Shadow of Enlargement: Can the European Neighbourhood Policy Achieve Compliance?, *Columbia Journal of European Law*, 12(2), pp. 383-427.

Maresceau, M. (2003) Pre-Accession, in Cremona, M. (ed.) *The Enlargement of the European Union*, Oxford, Oxford University Press, pp. 9-42.

Maur, J. (2005) Exporting Europe's Trade Policy, *World Economy*, 28(11), pp. 1565-1590.

McMahon, J. (1993) Fortress Europe: The External Dimension of the Internal Market? *The Northern Ireland Legal Quarterly*, 44(2), pp. 130-148.

Menon, A. & Weatherill, S. (2002) Legitimacy, Accountability, and Delegation in the European Union, in Arnull, A. and Wincott, D. (eds.), *Accountability and Legitimacy in the European Union*, Oxford, Oxford University Press, pp. 113-131.

Meunier, S. & Nicolaïdis, K. (2006) The European Union as a Conflicted Trade Power, *Journal of European Public Policy*, 13(6), pp. 906-925.

Nicolaïdis, K. & Egan, M. (2001) Transnational Market Governance and Regional Policy Externality: Why Recognise Foreign Standards?, *Journal of European Public Policy*, 8(3), pp. 454-473.

Peers, S. (1996) Living in Sin: Legal Integration under the EC-Turkey Customs Union, *European Journal of International Law*, 7(3), pp. 411-430.

Pelkmans, J. (2006) *European Integration: Methods and Economic Analysis*, Harlow, Pearson Education, 3rd edition.

Philippart, E. (2003) The Euro-Mediterranean Partnership: A Critical Evaluation of an Ambitious Scheme, *European Foreign Affairs Review*, 8(2), pp. 201-220.

Phinnemore, D. (2003) Stabilisation and Association Agreements: Europe Agreements for the Western Balkans?, *European Foreign Affairs Review*, 8(1), pp. 77-103.

Pippan, C. (2004) The Rocky Road to Europe, The EU's Stabilisation and Association Process for the Western Balkans and the Principle of Conditionality, *European Foreign Affairs Review*, 9(2), pp. 219-245.

Prodi, R. (2002) A Wider Europe – A Proximity Policy as the Key to Stability, Speech/02/619, Brussels, Sixth ECSA-World Conference, 5-6.12.2002.

Reymond, C. (1993) Institutions, Decision-Making Procedure and Settlement of Disputes in the European Economic Area, *Common Market Law Review*, 30(3), pp. 449-480.

Sapir, A. (2000) EC Regionalism at the Turn of the Millennium: Toward a New Paradigm?, *The World Economy*, 23(9), 1135-1148.

Scharpf, F. W. (1999) *Governing in Europe: Effective and Democratic?* Oxford, Oxford University Press.

Schimmelfennig, Frank (2007) Europeanization beyond Europe. *Living Reviews in European Governance*, 2(1), www.livingreviews.org/lreg-2007-1 (18 November 2007).

Schmidt, S. (2007) Mutual Recognition as a New Mode of Governance, *Journal of European Public Policy*, 14(5), pp. 667-681.

Vahl, M. & Grolimund, N. (2006) *Integration without Membership: Switzerland's Bilateral Agreements with the European Union*, Brussels, Centre for European Policy Studies.

Walendy, J. A. (2004) Stabilität durchs Netz? Die Energiegemeinschaft Südosteuropa, *Osteuropa*, 54(9-10), pp. 263-277.

Woolcock, S. (2007) European Union Policy towards Free Trade Agreements, *ECIPE Working Paper*, 3, Brussels, European Centre for International Political Economy.

# PART IV

# THE EU AND OTHER INTERNAL MARKETS

CHAPTER 10

# The Emergence of the US Internal Market[1]

Michelle EGAN

*Professor at the School of International Service, American University, Washington, DC*

## 1. Introduction

The focus of this paper is nineteenth century American market consolidation. But the discussion begins with the present where EU countries have orchestrated a major economic transformation over the past two decades that has fostered a single market and single currency. Early analysts of market integration in Europe focused on the coordination of liberalisation initiatives and the need to ensure credible commitments through incentives and investments to promote trade, currency convertability, and managed production (Eichengreen, 2007; Brusse, Diebold, 1959). The substantive benefits of market integration were believed to generate substantial economies of scale and welfare effects. With the rapid expansion of the early post war years, West European states achieved such growth through capital formation, the reallocation of labor and resources, and the efficient use of factors of production (Eichengreen, 2007). Critical to the overall success of the post war economy was the price mechanism and acceptance of private property rights. One manifestation of this resurgence of post war integration was the rise of so called intra-industry trade (Grubel and Lloyd, 1975). Unlike international trade in the nineteenth century, an increasing share of global trade was taking place between countries with similar resource endowments, trading similar types of goods – mainly manufactured products among industrial countries. Another important factor was the set of coordinated market institutions that fostered the post war consen-

[1] I want to thank participants in Bruges, especially Jacques Pelkmans and Dominik Hanf for prior comments.

sus by allowing social actors to coordinate their actions through both formal means embodied in law and through more informal norms and structures. The core model of economic development proved remarkably successful.

Subsequent massive economic crises brought about political demands and pressures to change the rules. Recessionary impulses pushed states into monetarism, as Keynesian demand management, was abandoned, and together with fiscal policies designed to stabilise or lower deficits, governments shifted towards market incentives. To overcome anticipated resistance to the implementation of market reforms, the European Union relaunched its efforts to complete the single market, and adopted schemes to compensate losers in order to overcome opposition to trade liberalisation measures. Scholars have developed numerous kinds of explanations that privilege institutional, ideational, international or coalitional factors to explain the resurgence of market-oriented reforms. This literature has not generated a consensus around the factors that led to the resurgence of market integration, and has offered a number of explanations including information technology and financial market developments (Sandholtz, 1992), societal interest group mobilisation (e.g. Frieden, 1991; Cowles, 1995; Sandholtz and Zysman, 1989; Frieden and Rogoswki, 1996) policy diffusion (e.g. Majone, 1997; Moran, 1991) and the interaction of domestic political and economic factors (Moravscik, 1991; 1993; Milner, 1999). Each offers different views about thc transmission mcchanism that spurs an integrated economy, with emphasis placed on the macroeconomic and external conditions, the preference of interest groups, and the cognitive and intellectual frameworks, being critical elements in explaining the resurgence of market integration in Europe (see McNamara, 1998).

As market integration has deepened, attention has shifted to making the single market deliver – and this has focused on capacities of different governance mechanisms to improve the functioning of the single market through an expansion of impact assessment and monitoring mechanisms (Radaelli, 2005). Yet trade liberalisation often has simultaneous and contradictory effects, and the implementation of reform proposals further complicates the context of interest calculations. European integration has involved substantial reforms in the areas of trade, regulation, exchange rates, macroeconomic stabilisation across different markets. As such, market integration has changed many economic parameters, and has also generated uncertainty, so that its political salience has declined and resistance sharpens over further efforts to promote further market liberalisation and openness of the economy (Ch. 2 in this volume). As Europe deals with the simultaneity of democratic transition and market capitalism, the advent and extension of the single market, and the internationalisation of market forces, critics have drawn attention to the trade-offs and tensions promoting growth and efficiency, and the necessity of dealing with the equity and distributional impacts (Scharpf, 1999; Joerges).[2] Consequently, attention has gradually shifted towards how to generate support to sustain market reforms in adverse circumstances without jeopardising democratic governance. This critique argues that the economy has to be reembedded and political control over the economy established (Polanyi, 1957).

Given the multiplicity of arguments and analyses that have been put forth with regard to the single market, the persistence of doubts over the efficacy of market reforms and the compatibility of political and economic liberalisation, this chapter seeks to examine *how the United States dealt with many of the same challenges facing the European polity.* How did the United States create a single market? What efforts did the US make to deal with uneven economic development, different vulnerabilities, and wide disparities in income and employment? How did the US tackle the political backlash against further economic integration?

My contention is that the historical case of market integration in the United States provides a striking analogy to contemporary Europe. The purpose of this paper is to study the historical process of market development in the United States to make sense of contemporary market transformations in Europe. While attention focused on constitutional development in the early US, as enshrined in the Philadelphia convention and the constitution it produced, much less attention has been paid to the influence of American capitalism and economic development upon constitutional jurisprudence, federalism, separation of powers, equal protection and preferred economic freedoms (Gillman 1999; Scheiber, 1975). The need to manage an industrialising society affected many of the decisions agreed upon in Philadelphia. While one of the central concerns of the constitutional convention was the security and structure of a new form of government, the framers were also concerned with the development and working character of market institutions. The early course of American public policy reflected the central position of the market, and its importance for sustained growth and social harmony (Hurst, 1982). As Hurst points out, "throughout the nineteenth and twentieth century, no organisation was more critical in organising social relations than the market" (Hurst, 1977).

The challenges of managing production, distribution and social conflict that followed from the shift from local markets to national and

---

2 European scholars see an asymmetry in the fact that Community competences mostly encompass market and economic matters and very few, or modes, social ones.

international markets required crucial policy choices by governmental institutions. The operation of the market was not left unfettered. The market needed protection not only against private transactions that threatened the fair operation of market processes but also against the abuse of public power with regard to resource allocation, monopolies and protectionism. The processes at work in transforming the American economy were tied to state building, and the consolidation of markets was linked to democratic participation and the large social movements of the age. How the American polity constructed and maintained a single market presents analytical challenges at least as difficult and rewarding as any other problem or issue in this period (Bensel, 2000).

By drawing on the experience of market consolidation in the United States, this politically contested process has much in common with the European experience, and may illustrate some of the same political and institutional dynamics driving the consolidation of the single market in Europe. Given the recent wave of interest in the nineteenth century as an example of early globalisation in which there was unprecedented integration of capital, labor and commodity markets, the historical precedents have a direct bearing on contemporary market integration (Rourke and Williamson, 1999).[3] The European parallel to the US is not surprising since early advocates often referred to the economic success of the United States as evidence of the advantages of a large integrated economy (Dell, 1959; Spaak, 1955; Scitovsky, 1958). There is, in both cases, a strong relationship between economic and political developments, as the single market and its ancillary policies require political support and legitimacy on the one hand, and institutional capabilities and effectiveness on the other. And arguably what has evolved is not simply about rationalisation and efficiency but also about forging new ideas about sovereignty, administration and ultimately about how to govern markets (Garson, 2001; McNamara, 2001; Scharpf, 1999; Weingast, 1995).

The chapter is structured as follows. Part two begins with a comparison of the American and European case. Part three then highlights how the process of state building and market building are interlinked. Attention is given to the organisational and institutional innovations in markets and the remaking of states in order to constitute, preserve and maintain market capitalism. Part four then provides a capsule history of market integration and corresponding political and social developments

---

3 While the historical antecedent to contemporary integration is an important starting point, the differences and similarities between the nineteenth-century and the process underway at present need careful attention. For a detailed discussion see Egan, forthcoming.

in US. The final section of the paper identifies and analyses the essential elements necessary to foster an integrated economy, so we can suggest to apply the analytic lessons for the development of sustained, widely supported global market integration, as well as to market integration in other regions. As regional economic integration efforts continue to evolve, they will face the same kinds of dilemmas that the US and EU have faced in integrating their markets. Among the most crucial dealt will be resolving conflicts and interests among different constituencies affected by the changing terms of trade.

## 2. Comparison of America and Europe

As a multi-level polity, the EU has been compared to a wide variety of federal and confederal polities (Brizinski, 1999; McKay, 1999).[4] While there is growing recognition among scholars who study territorial politics and institutional design of the European polity of the need to make comparisons, the focus has primarily been on federalism to examine the allocation of power between constituent units (Sbragia, 1992; Goldstein, 1997; Scharpf, 1987; Menon and Schain, 2006; Keleman, 2004). The comparison has centered on governance in divided power systems. Scholars have been interested in the intersection of constitutionalism, federalism and democracy (Stein, 2001; Stein, 1981; Nicolaidis and Howse, 2001; Fabbrini, 2004; Moravscik, 2002) to assess the legitimacy of the European polity, and also the dynamics of territorial politics, building on the work of Tiebout, to examine the impact of interjurisdictional competition in federal systems on the provision of public goods (Tiebout, 1956; Hooghe and Marks, 2003).

Any comparative discussion cannot ignore the differences between the EU and US as political systems.[5] While some elements of the EU

4 Early scholars of integration sought to understand the dynamics of integration in terms of state and community formation drawing on examples from multinational empires, states and international organisations (Caporaso, 1996; Deutsch, 1953). Highlighting the importance of transactions or communications in promoting a sense of community from which shared customs, identities, values, and norms would merge due to cooperation, this approach focused on the conditions necessary for the development of a political community (Deutsch, 1953).

5 Though using a spatial and temporal dimension may raise some methodological concerns, the justification of this approach is based on variation in analysis which can be obtained through observations of the same unit (markets) at different points in the temporal sequence (nineteenth and twentieth centuries) (Bartolini, Year p. 135). If as is often argued, institutional analysis is inherently historical, then examining the consolidation of markets into larger economic entities means tracing outcomes over time, and recognizing that the development of common markets is a study of patterns of commonalities along causally relevant dimensions may shed light on the condi-

may seem similar to the US system of federalism, the US is a sovereign state and the EU an unusually strong international organisation with well-defined supranational institutions that has been variously described as a confederal or quasi-federal system (see Sbragia, 1992; Sbragia, 2004). And yet when we think about the US and EU experiences, the former is tied to state-building which implies the internal consolidation of power (see McNamara, 2003), whereas the latter is tied to post-national democracy with a different pattern and organisation of power and institutions.[6] Once we think about them as political systems characterised by compromises and bargains based on deeply rooted territorial cleavages, we begin to understand the critical importance of their efforts to balance their goals of a centralised economic order while preserving regional and local diversity (Sbragia, 2004).

While there are important differences in the political, economic and social histories of the American and European experience, it is possible to provide some general comparisons that allow us to compare their respective experiences at market consolidation. First, the United States and European Union disperse power widely (Sbragia, 2006: 5) so that intergovernmental cooperation ensures that decisions are implemented through the collective exercise of public authority (Elazar, 1975; Sbragia, 2006). While states remain strong in the European context, the United States has seen a decline of territorial politics beginning in the late nineteenth century.[7] Although both polities sought formal state equality that allows equal representation for constituent units, going to extraordinary lengths to address the concerns of small states, "Community politics and national politics are intertwined rather than insulated from one another [...]" Consequently, "the privileged status employed by member governments in the Community's political system has no analogue in the US System" (Sbragia, 1992: 5).

However for much of the nineteenth century, the US was a fragmented and ever enlarging political system, loosely connected by the experience of colonialism, and divided over questions of sovereignty

tions or prerequisites for market integration in other polities (Marks, 2001; Skocpol and Pierson, 1999).

6 The EU has been variously described as a regional state (Schmidt, 2004), consociational state (Boodgaard and Markus, 2002), regulatory state (Majone) post-modern state (Caporaso, 1996) and federal state (Sbragia, 1992).

7 That said, different states can play a role in setting the domestic agenda in specific areas such as the California effect in car emissions or Wisconsin on income tax for example. Also territorial politics matters much more in the West than in other regions where the federal government owns much of the land and plays a much more intrusive role in state politics and regulatory affairs. American federalism could thus be described as asymmetrical.

and the constitutional powers of the federal government. Yet the American Constitution and Treaty of Rome provide the legal framework for the creation of a single market. These documents set out the formal provisions that have become the basis for their efforts to integrate diverse economies into an economic entity that is neither homogenous nor completely free of restrictions to interstate commerce. In both cases, the founding documents contain a mixture of express provisions and restrictions, and thus constitute efforts to promote both negative integration, in terms of the removal of discriminatory barriers between economies, and positive integration, in terms of agreement on common economic policies for the future (Tinbergen, 1954). In fact, the Framers of the Constitution envisioned the allocation of services and goods in the American economy to be private decisions, and the Commerce Clause, Due Process Clause and other articles were evidence of that commitment (Hovencamp, 1992). The negotiations indicate that the private market was considered the essential institution in the social order, and while the Constitution also has non-discriminatory provisions, including the provisions with regard to ports and vessels, there are certain prohibitions on states regarding activities that affect the functioning of markets (see Hurst, 1982).

On the surface, the most striking difference between the US and EU appears to be the level of economic development. The early United States was an agrarian economy, engaged in both modernisation and industrialisation, while the EU, though recovering from World War II, was industrialised with a modern economy and all its properties. Yet similarities exist in the two cases. Both had a significant agricultural base with regional specialisation being a significant feature of both economies. As the rapid expansion and integration of the American economy took place, the shift from a localised subsistence economy to a nationally integrated market economy also encouraged government activity in shaping the development of the market. The economic roles of the federal and state governments were significant in responding to market pressures. Concern about the polarisation effects of integration, potentially impeding the laggard regions and creating a division of production between labor intensive and capital intensive economies is a feature common to both (Hirschmann, 1957). In the United States, economic cleavages extended beyond the North-South cleavages to secessionist movements in the mid-West region and Western expansion states (Bensel, 1990). Slavery was tied into this ideological cleavage that included trade and other partisan issues. Political strife over the pace of industrialisation intensified existing conflicts between labor and capital, which had different characteristics in different regions. The inevitable tension between localism and concentration and between promotion and protectionism meant that the response to the changing economic conditions emerged from an aggregate of different ideologies, interests and institutions that was sometimes at cross-purposes (Keller, 1997: 5).

Therefore, one of the most notable features of the two founding documents is the emphasis placed on the social impact of economic development. In the US, efforts to serve communal values or societal interests in the area of eminent domain and police powers were also designed to promote the public good in a society undergoing rapid social and economic change (Scheiber, 1988: 141; Scheiber, 1984). Developmental policies are an underlying characteristic of both the US and Europe. Public authorities at federal or supranational levels in each has been continuously involved in aiding industries and sectors, believing this to be the key for promoting economic development and winning political legitimacy for the new regime (Eisinger, 1988). Though they may have taken different forms, concerns about addressing socio-economic adjustment and modernisation has been an important element in shaping the development of market integration.

Market correcting measures undertaken in the US and EU are, however, distinguished by their respective budgetary authority. Several important provisions bolster the financial authority of the US federal government in a way that is missing in the European Treaty. The possibility of the federal state raising new revenues is expressly granted in the Constitution, with the power of taxation vested in Congress. The Treaty of Rome provides for no such taxing authority. The EU is distinctive in that it originally lacked an autonomous source of revenue (Laffan, 1997). The lack of budgetary resources highlights an important feature of how the EU has fostered market integration, namely that regulation is the main instrument of public power in the Union. While the EU is severely constrained in the fiscal area, since it cannot impose direct taxation, run deficits or issue public debt, its limited extractive power has much in common with the United States in the antebellum era. The tax impact of federal activity was minimal, and "local political units follow(ed.) independent fiscal policies with few interstate fiscal mechanisms to promote redistribution or encourage political solidarity across the union" (McNamara, 2001; Scheiber, 1975). The American Constitution makes clear that the power to levy and spend taxes is retained at each level of government. While the development of new revenue raising possibilities on the part of the federal state increased dramatically due to the pressures of waging war and the expenditures entailed during the Civil War, the same imperatives have not been present in the European Union.[8] However, as the single market is considered a key reason for the drive towards a single currency, and Treaty revisions have restructured the public expenditures of Member States to meet the criteria for economic and monetary union, there may be considerable pressures to make further Treaty changes and expand the fiscal capacity of the European Union (McNamara, 2001; Sbragia, 2001; Eichengreen, 1990).

In terms of political structure, the effort to balance territorial interests and divide policy responsibilities between constituent states and the national has been highly uneasy and often sharply contested in the US. The accretion of authoritative competencies at the national level is now well-established in the US, with the most significant domestic activities of the national government settled. Federal actions were largely related to tariff policies, land management, and banking and monetary policies. None of these policies required substantial administrative or fiscal resources, and hence the overall impact of tax policy and revenue collection was minimal. Like the federal experience in the nineteenth century, the EU institutions are not in a position to use fiscal transfers as a means of influencing Member States and their constituent units.

The contrast between the political foundations of the US and EU is nowhere more apparent than in the development of democratic institutions and electoral practices. In the United States, democratic institutions and electoral practices were far from perfect in the nineteenth century with widespread violence, fraud and disenfranchisement. But the growth and integration of the American economy was tied to the impact of popular opinion, political parties and electoral outcomes. Conflicting demands by the electorate over elements of industrialisation, including the monetary system, tariff protection and gold standard indicate that economic development and market integration were tied to electoral success and the coalition building efforts of the major political parties (Bensel, 2001). The democratic deficit rooted in the institutional framework of the European Union is based, in part, on the fact that the constitutional principles that apply to nation-states are not evident at the European level. The weakness of direct representation (initially) meant that representational legitimacy was subordinate to that of territorial state based representation (Marks, 1997).

---

8 Not until the Sixteenth Amendment passed in 1916 did the emphasis on intergovernmental transfers emerge in its modern form with the use of taxing and spending powers to advance national policies. The Sixteenth Amendment provides that the Congress shall have power to lay and collect taxes on incomes, from whatever source derived, without apportionment among the several states, and without regard to any census or enumeration.

The US and EU have expanded their geographic borders through annexation and accession, respectively. In the United States, territories must apply for statehood as the federal government cannot unilaterally create a state. The process of territorial expansion is also related to the issue of security and stability in both Europe and the US. Though the expansion of investment and markets is often a key factor driving states to seek greater association or membership, there are also defensive or strategic motives at the heart of the enlargement process (see Riker, 1964). Early American movement westward was concerned with the search for markets and profitable investment outlets for labor, capital and entrepreneurship, and the drive to secure borders (Fowke, 1956). Public land policy and railroad development were the twin factors responsible for the subsequent enlargement and incorporation of the West into the national economy. Similarly, developmental imperatives also guide European enlargement. This began in the case of Southern enlargement, where the promotion of market economies and democratic institutions were key goals after the collapse of authoritarian regimes. Unlike the US, where the prospect of secession held out much deeper prospects of disunion, the European Union has not faced such threats of withdrawal to destabilise the Community. Enlargement has become more dynamic and ambitious, with trade liberalisation and market access assuming an important place in this process. The economic leadership of the EU has acted as a magnet for applicant states, anticipating economic growth and trade creation, extending the boundaries both physically and economically as the US absorbed Western frontiers in the nineteenth century (Kindleberger, 2000).

Finally, the creation of a national economic system is a central and often controversial issue in American history. Westward expansion, the Civil War, the Interstate Commerce Commission and the Federal Reserve System raised and answered crucial questions for intergovernmental relations. Judicial rulings also fostered capital formation and market development through granting of exemptions and privileges to corporations, specifying the rights and obligations of contracts, and the vesting of property rights, which established certain economic priorities and promoted specific types of economic development (McCurdy, 1978; Freyer 1979; Hurst, 1982). These developments have many parallels with the more recent establishment of the European single market. In both cases, establishing one market, one currency, and a more unified banking and financial system transformed largely autonomous or sovereign constituent units into a more unified economic entity. Both required sustained political and legal intervention to construct an integrated market free of restrictions for trade and commerce. Neither effort can be judged completely successful, with lingering restrictions on commercial transactions.[9]

## 3. State building and market making

Scholars of comparative economic and political development have focused on the role and effectiveness of both political and market institutions, examining the sources of economic growth and integration in the historic and institutional experience of specific states (see Dobson and Weiss, 1988; Taft, Morris and Adelman, 1988; North, 1981). While scholarship on European state formation is based on categorising state formation as a fusion of power and unitary territorial organisation, only very recently have analysts attempted to link the research on state building to processes of market integration in the EU context. Drawing implicitly on the work of Rokkan, scholars have sought to compare the processes of integration with state-building and state formation (Bartolini, 2004; Marks, 1997; cf Caporaso, 1996). There are certainly differences in structural features as well as development paths between European integration and European state building, as the logic of European integration is considered very different from state-building in terms of resource extraction, democratic representation and coercive authority (Tilly, 1992; Laffan, 1992). As taxing, spending and borrowing privileges remain overwhelmingly at the national level in Europe, European integration revolves around the purported efficiency gains of market consolidation. However, state-building in the United States provides important parallels with the European Union as market integration promoted state-building in a variety of ways that enhanced property rights, revenue extraction and regulatory needs of an industrialising economy. Such expansion of political authority and rule-making, and the strong connection between political development and market construction illustrate how the process of state building and market building are interlinked in both polities. Thus, "the creation of a market system, accompanied by the establishment of legal institutions and an administrative bureaucracy, centralises authority over time as a newly deepened polity is constructed in tandem with the newly enlarged market" (McNamara, 2003: 10). The American state is and has been consistently stronger, larger, more durable, more interventionist and more redistributive than often described. The most critical aspect of marketisation is the assertion of state power. Though economic reform left a number of allocative functions to the private sector, at the same time, state action and public economic policy in nineteenth-century antebellum America

9 In the case of the US in areas of insurance, professions and agricultural standards, and trucking regulations.

resulted in major state social regulations (Novak, 1996). The powerful role of the state in policing the institution of slavery, Indian removal, and westward expansion; the role of the federal government in promoting and regulating national commerce is indicative of significant regulatory capacity. Along the way, the organisational configuration of the state was shaped by war and security imperatives (Tilly, 1975; 1990) as the United States sought to achieve economies of scale in the provision of protection through a modern administrative system for defence and expanded the federal tax system into many avenues that were dismantled after the Civil War. In the Reconstruction era, the central state focused on creating a national economy based on the removal of regional and local trade barriers, the integration of capital markets, and the construction of a physical and financial infrastructure that was nothing less than an effort to 'make a state' (Foner, 1988: 364). Many centralised, federal services were created, expanding administrative capacities, in response to internal economic developments. Such coordination, justified by the existence of market failure and thus based on the internal logic of economics and the ideology of efficiency, generated specialised single purpose administrative agencies designed to insulate administrative politics from the pressures of party politics and factionalism.

American market integration took place in tandem with the modern state, a contentious process over authority, competencies and governance. The market consolidation efforts involved among other things, a stricter definition and enforcement of property rights, effort to revamp revenue collection procedures through hardening of budgetary constraints and enacting state debt limits, and the centralisation of economic policy-making. The state form emerging sought to expand trade, reduce transaction costs, and in broadening the economic reform process to include military purchasing, postal operations, land management and currency consolidation, there resulted in unprecedented changes in the country's political and institutional configurations. As we shall see relationship between state and market building in US (and EU) provided the framework for contestation over the distribution of gains, where claims and counterclaims were made through the legal institutions and administrative bureaucracy. As industrialism proceeded in the United States, different groups turned to courts to further their objectives. In this conceptualisation, studying the American experience historically as a contentious political process of polity building and market formation can help us understand the dynamics of market consolidation today. The next section looks at the causal factors promoting the single market, and the conditions under which segmented markets were integrated and extended.

## 4. American market building

The spread of the market economy and interregional flows of goods, services and productive factors in the United States (see North, 1961; Sbragia, 1992) is a considerable achievement. In the early period, foreign commerce was the predominant interest, and internal commerce was initially limited to the Atlantic and Gulf Coasts (Schmidt, 1939). Subsequent trade expansion and the development of a more diversified manufacturing sector generated a rise of interregional trade. Yet internal commerce was affected by cyclical disturbances, although fluctuations were less extreme than that experienced by foreign commerce (Taylor, 1962: 175). A number of scholars from a diverse spectrum of theoretical perspectives have sought to explain the dynamics of market consolidation in ways that seem similar to the European experience. North stresses the importance of external trade and the growth of foreign demand as crucial for economic development (North, 1961). Frankel suggests that the development of manufacturing production was tied to embargoes and war in Europe, which enabled American infant industries to develop and later seek protection from foreign competition (Frankel, 1982).

Challenging those who discerned a liberal tradition and ideology as driving American economic development, Scheiber and Goodrich have drawn attention to the active government presence in shaping the process, pattern and pace of American economic development (Scheiber, 1975; Goodrich, 1961: Hartz, 1961). The advent of public investment, first through canals and railroads, and then subsequent development of telegraph and postal operations, merged markets that had been national and regional. Technological advances in transportation, both waterways and rail, further promoted the expansion and integration of the US economy (Taylor, 1962). According to this view, the consolidation of national markets in the nineteenth century, in terms of capital formation, industrial consolidation, technological change and trade flows is the product of a large conscious resource allocation by governments. By contrast, business historians have tended to focus on the unregulated nature of the US market, arguing instead that the rise of modern business enterprises from the late nineteenth century onwards were little affected by public policy and capital markets, but rather were driven by the logic of economic development (Chandler, 1962: 376ff). According to Chandler, the national market came about under pressure from technological innovations which enabled the modern business enterprise to emerge to provide large-scale mass production and distribution. Vertical integration, facilitated by refinements in best-practice corporate governance made regions increasingly inter-dependent, as did the rationalisation of national finance and insurance. In his view, the growing volume of economic activities required new institutional forms that were more efficient than market coordination. Such large business enterprises have been the products of and prime movers in the industrialisation and market expansion of the United States (Chandler, 1978; 1969). Such structural changes in American manufacturing and the growth of transportation networks certainly lowered the costs of production and facilitated the growth of internal trade flows as large scale businesses tapped into larger and larger segments of the domestic market (Rourke and Williamson, *op. cit.*: 4). Internal labor mobility also played a key factor as inter-regional differences in wages, benefits, working conditions, and unionisation,[10] integrated labor markets nationally as well.

By contrast, legal historians such as Hurst and McCurdy point to judicial governance with the (initially reluctant and often challenged) federal court playing an increasingly important role in determining the scope of state legislation, and often preempting state policy through judicial doctrines that supported federal intervention (Scheiber, 1975: 100). Because states and municipalities issued statutes and ordinances affecting internal trade within their own borders, these increasingly posed important restraints on cross-border trade in goods and services (Zimmerman, 1996; Abel, 1940). There would inevitably be conflict regarding trade between the reserved powers of states and the federal level as markets outgrew local limits.[11] Legislatures, courts, and administrative agencies generated substantial regulation of the American economy in areas of health, morals, labor, education, immigration, transportation, energy, and public utilities (Novak, 1996; Keller, 1977). All of the regulatory responses began at the state and local levels, but were quickly superseded by federal government counterparts. The transaction costs of different state regulations, different administrative systems, and other regulatory impediments hindered the operation of a large integrated market. And for state governments, the resulting regulatory competition meant that they fell short in their efforts to protect welfare since they continued to develop discrete sets of regulatory and competition policies in what was progressively becoming an integrated market in which it was more difficult to enforce local or state compliance.

Furthermore, interstate rivalry meant that state legislatures confronted pressures for an immediate response to out-of-state competition, and often provided special assistance or subsidies to specific interest groups within their own localities. The fate of many state and local enactments hinged on judicial action during the nineteenth century, as

---

10 See Commons *et al.* (1936) for the argument American product market integration fomented labor market integration.

11 Welton versus Missouri in 1876.

judicial rulings on the commerce clause played a key role in the political construction of the national market (see also Bensel). Before the last quarter of the nineteenth century though, appellate courts regularly upheld such statutes. The Supreme Court, armed with an enlarged jurisdiction and three new constitutional amendments in the aftermath of the Civil War, had the opportunity to forge new doctrines and boundaries between the public and private sectors (McCurdy, 1975: 971). The result was a noticeable tendency for big business to seek federal legislation in order to avoid the problems of adjusting to multiple state laws (see Lindsay PSQ).[12] Such tariff walls which hampered large scale production generated challenges from integrated corporations, as they faced constraints in distributing and marketing across local and state borders. Subsequently the national court system created laws that reduced the uncertainty of interstate business by more clearly specifying the rights and obligations of parties to contracts, particularly regarding the negotiability of bills of credit as well (Freyer, 1979). The Court strongly asserted its right of judicial review with regard to discriminatory taxation, and promoted the dormant power clause, upholding congressional statues, at the expense of states, and continuing to strike down harmful state actions, through using the fourteenth amendments due process provisions (McCurdy, 1975; see Passenger cases).[13] The limitations of the powers of states and municipalities, through the tight rein held on public finances and their restriction to the barest necessities of health, safety and education meant that states were subject to scrutiny under a substantive interpretation of the due process clause that complemented the judicial doctrine of dual sovereignty (McCurdy, 1975). Moreover, the rapidly integrating national market made it essential to reorganise the chaotic monetary system of thousands of currencies and the courts upheld the view that federal currency regulation was linked to successful commerce across state borders, and therefore appropriate (Hurst, 1973, 72).

Yet, market integration generated substantial social mobilisation and protest. Social historians have focused on the role of progressive politics to address economic inequalities, social inequities, and manage social change. The process of market adjustment generated both protest and populist movements, supplemented by urban and intellectual support

---

12 As examples, states often attempted to pass laws that required licensing or taxing of merchants that were known as commercial travelers, drummers or peddlers to protect local interests. States often curbed non-resident insurance company efforts to foreclose on farm mortgages. Many others tried to establish criteria for foreign corporations, this often required incorporation in the state which would subject them to the regulations of that state.

13 Passenger Cases (Smith v. Turner), 48 US (7 How.) 282 (1849).

often directed towards the banking and currency system, and the wage and agricultural pricing system. Although different segments of the economy fared differently in terms of distributive politics and welfare gains, the increased turmoil that accompanied industrial change in US generated continued social unrest. However, those adversely affected by growing inequality of wealth and rural-urban dislocation, reflected at least some of the idiosyncrasy of their environment, and a set of values that sought to preserve diversity by embedding the market system through series of social changes, constraints on business power, and political reforms against rampant corruption and cronyism. However, the welfare state in terms of labor protection, unionisation and bargaining was initially contested, and viewed as contrary to the American common market, and so the ensuing welfare safety nets often came after the single market had been consolidated.

In an effort to depict the political history of economic development over a long period of change and upheaval, this paper emphasises the interaction between market development and political change, in terms of the relationship between public authority and private rights, as well as the distribution of power and authority between different governmental units, and their mediation by the rule of law. A study of economic consolidation, through an analysis of the construction of a national economy in the nineteenth century, is one that involves contentious struggles over issues of governance and authority, and has much in common with contemporary European efforts at market integration. If market integration was a shared ideal, its shape and attributes were not always the source of consensus. Market consolidation in US was partly a collective effort to resolve different interests and preferences, which were often in conflict, but also an effort to enhance institutional capacity in order to make markets work effectively and to reconcile different ideas about the constitutive nature of markets.

## 5. Tentative lessons: stocktaking on wider issues of market integration

To understand the transformation created by the integration of their respective markets in the nineteenth and twentieth century, this concluding section addresses the dynamics of market consolidation on either side of the Atlantic, with some ideas about what may be relevant in terms of the economic successes of the EU and US for broader efforts elsewhere. Successful market integration in the past has proceeded only given certain social and political supports, and so the paper concludes with some general lessons about the necessary underpinnings for market integration in other regional markets. While many studies of globalisation have suggested that we are moving towards greater levels of economic integration, they have paid much less attention to recognising that market integration is part of a larger project of institutional development. In other parts of the world, economic integration is proceeding but political integration is either not desired or so limited that many debates about sovereignty, territoriality and governance have not yet been addressed (Sbragia, 2004). The political processes that evolve – or not – in support of the single market certainly play an equally important role in the economic successes of the European Union and United States. The lessons drawn from these two experiences can highlight – from a political economy perspective – whether there are common elements of regulatory and political evolution that seem to be necessary to legitimise single market momentum that can be usefully transferred to other attempts at deeper regional integration.

### *5.1. Political mobilisation and representation*

The coupling of market restructuring has been and should be tied to political reform. Political, economic and social pressures have generated institution-building efforts aimed at bolstering norms of democratic governance and instilling greater transparency, accountability and citizen input into the policymaking process. The political economy of support building constitutes a crucial dimension of successful market consolidation. In the process of market building, expanding democratic mechanisms may have a contradictory logic as market integration implies a concentration of authority whereas democracy implies devolution and decentralisation of the polity. Yet economic integration and political reform are interrelated as expanding the geographic scope of the market, increased market entry and contestability, rationalisation of finance, and increased regional interdependence, all promoted regulatory and political reform.

Just like the pressures of globalisation and Europeanisation, the social consensus on the capacity of open markets to generate socially acceptable outcomes had, by the last third of the nineteenth century broken down, largely in the face of the emergent concentrations of power. One could observe a similar development – to current situation in Europe – in the United States in the post civil war period largely as a response to the forces of industrialisation that generated the dramatic upheavals and protest over the distribution of resources and terms and conditions under which market forces operated. In the United States, there were varied political proposals to make the political system more responsive to the transformations brought by industrialism. Many of these such as the direct election of senators, civil service reform, citizen initiatives, referendums, and recalls all emerged at this time as instruments of this new democracy. Generating political support for market integration is essential but it also raises issues about minority populations within state structures who may generally have their own law (e.g. Indian reservations).

## 5.2. Distributional preferences and welfare gains

Despite indicators of the overall positive effects on economic growth due to increased economic interdependence, there needs to be a strategy in place to deal with market failures. If we look at other regional trade blocs, social issues have been left off the agenda, thereby raising potential concerns about immigration, employment and social welfare (see Zamora, 2006; Pastor, 2001). The distributional effect that generates winners and losers in local economies creates a need to have a more coordinated approach to mitigate social demands and foster improved social welfare. While economic regionalism privileges trade and competition, the distributional stakes and outcomes are key factors in explaining the continued commitment to economic policy coordination in the US. The need to assure an acceptable distribution among states and classes led the United States to consider the social impact of its economic development (Polanyi, 1957). The promotion of a national market in the United States generated substantial protest and conflict about wealth and market position, in large part because of the pattern of uneven development and differential economic benefits (Sklar, 1988; Fryer, 1994). Substantial political opposition came from those threatened by increased market competition, with farmers voicing populist demands about bankers and railroads, state politicians resisting federal control and declining industries seeking protectionism through tariffs and other controls. For integration to thus succeed, "differing claims had to be either supported or deferred" (Bensel, 1990: 3).

Economic integration created pressures to modify market outcomes to correct market failures and carry out various forms of redistribution. In the US and EU, this has resulted in flanking measures, in order to mitigate the effects of increased competition, and respond to demands for regulation beyond the confines of the economic sphere to include important areas of social and environmental regulation (Novak, 1996). Arguably, the ensuing growth in social safety nets in the American progressive era in the late nineteenth and early twentieth century provide important legitimising effects for market integration. However, the welfare state in terms of labor protection, unionisation and bargaining was initially struck down by the courts and viewed as contrary to the American common market, whereas the post war settlement between labor and capital was a crucial factor in generating support for European market integration (Sbragia 2004). In addition, greater labor mobility in the US fostered income convergence, and provided substantial economic opportunities whereas restrictions on labor mobility have hindered market development in Europe. Though they have taken different forms, concerns about addressing socio-economic adjustment and modernisation has been an important element in shaping the development of market integration. In this respect, the relationship between economic rights and social rights needs to be considered since viable and sustainable integration is likely to be more successful if economic growth is fairly distributed (Maduro, 1999; Jones, 2003). Of crucial importance for other regional trade blocs is dealing with 'development gaps'. Without distributive strategies in place, other integrating efforts cannot address the failures and externalities of an integrating market.

### *5.3. Creation of enforcement and compliance capacity*

The process of market consolidation requires well-developed mechanisms to respond and support the growth of the single market and its ancillary policies. The need to create and sustain markets, that is, of nurturing individual economic choice and of creating a supportive environment for enterprise requires competent public administration and governance since they provide an environment of known, stable, and enforceable rules (North, 1961). Thus, the elements of functioning markets are dependent on the characteristics of the state which means that we need to pay attention to state capacity as government is responsible for overall economic management and performance (Bruszt, 2002). Other regional trade blocs should create strong institutions to implement and monitor activities.

The expansion of American political and economic authority domestically is a crucial factor in understanding market consolidation. The transformation of American liberalism and public policy between the end of the Civil War and the end of the New Deal enhanced jurisdictional authority at state and federal level across a range of policy areas. While a centralised, administrative, regulatory, welfare state was created in the US, there was a corresponding increase in intergovernmental collaboration and sharing of functions, as implementation and enforcement was often decentralised (Scheiber, 1975). Such regulatory expansion also meant the growth of regulatory agencies, and the corresponding delegation to non-majoritarian institutions has subsequently been criticised as undermining the legitimacy of majoritarian political arrangements (Lowi, 1979; Majone, 1996). Yet the process of building markets can foster fundamentally different approaches to compliance as polities can use both formal legal measures as well as voluntary, market driven measures to enforce compliance (Glenn, 2007; Heritier, 2002). The effect has been to transform the role of the state, and the ensuing government practices to stabilise and regulate markets, while at the same time implementing and searching for new innovative mechanisms to manage and steer the economy (e.g. soft law, capable of adoption by either states or parties, mutual recognition). Addressing such concerns about enforcement and implementation practices has become increasingly salient on the European agenda as evident by the effort to assess the efficiency and effectiveness of the single market (Egan, 2001). For other regional trade blocs, the need for an acceptable set of credible institutions to promote compliance with the terms of any free trade agreement is crucial, given that the reorganisation of economic activity into regional trade agreements brings to the fore differences in rules and regulations.

## *5.4. The role of law and central judicial jurisdiction*

The economic functions of law and its corresponding impact on the structure and operation of the market are an integral part in shaping government strategies. In the US and EU, legal scholars have focused attention on the relationship between law and the functional requirements of a market economy (Cappelletti *et al.*, 1986; Stein and Sandalow, 1982; Hurst, 1977). Market consolidation is viewed as a product of a legal and constitutional framework that provides for a stable and enforceable structure of laws that give market participants specific rights and opportunities. It has been up to courts in many instances to shed their passivity, to the point of assuming a quasi-legislative role. Law shapes the boundaries between public and private authority, and between governments. Judicial governance has been instrumental in constraining both state and market actions as well as providing for the public use of legal authority to design new instruments and policies to govern markets (Novak, 2000).

Yet the interaction between courts, governments and markets is instructive in showing how the legal system responded to competing values and objectives, as the functional role of law shifted in response to the changing administrative, regulatory and welfare demands incurred by market integration (See Egan, Forthcoming). Legal scholars have acknowledged the varying tension that accompanies legal decisions in determining the boundaries between state and federal authority. As different factor and product markets integrated, courts face pressures to deal with market failures, as well as issues of resource allocation and redistribution that emerge from the growing complexity of economic transactions. This generated significant pressures on the legal system to respond to salient demands, and often tackle conflicting goals and values in determining the distribution of political authority and economic resources. Many used courts to assist in fashioning change or to respond to changing economic circumstances. It is not enough then to focus on law in removing impediments to trade and thus creating the conditions for market integration, as law functions as both a facilitating institution and as a restraint on the market (cite). Judicial decisions have played a key role in defining and redefining concepts like the market itself, and in doing so have played a key role in the US and EU in balancing the freedom of the market against the need for coercion and control in terms of regulation, administration and enforcement. This should persuade others of the need to create a court in which trade and development practices can be deliberated and adjudicated.

### *5.5. Market supporting regulations*

Successful integration requires a stable, effective and sustainable market system based on rules and reciprocity. Markets need regulatory support and such efforts may introduce competition, by maintaining market entry for new competitors or participants in areas where there are often concentrations of power in the form of oligopolies or monopolies. Market integration must also address the externalities stemming from an integrating market including currency crises, development gaps, environmental degradation, and infrastructural impediments which created challenges. The American experience is instructive here as well. State led economic development was discarded in favor of independent regulatory agencies. As administrative agencies arose, they became new and important instruments of action. So did the role of associational or professional organisations who found that as organised groups they could wield more power and also shape market entry requirements. Thus, governments at different levels wrested with the problems that emerged from the rapid expansion of market transactions such as the concentration of private economic power, and the dilemmas of uneven development. The effect was to try and stabilise and regulate markets, while at the same time implementing and searching for new innovative mechanisms that were alternative to the traditional system of governance.

### *5.6. Membership and accession provisions*

The history of the European Union and United States is one of persistent geographical expansion. Both polities have established criteria and formalised procedures for membership. Much attention in Europe is given to the transformative power of European integration through conditionality requirements under the Copenhagen criteria. However, the United States also established the terms and conditions under which the newly settled land became part of the American system under the Northwest Ordinances, and stipulated that the state must be accepted on the basis of equality with existing state (ie territorial representation and sectional balance) (Atack *et al.*, 2000: 291). Though the expansion of investment and markets is often a key factor, driving states to seek greater association or membership, there were also defensive or strategic motives at the heart of the enlargement process (Riker, 1964). The enlargement in Europe, premised on economic growth and trade creation, extending the boundaries both physically and economically, is similar to the US absorption of the Western frontiers in the nineteenth century. Geopolitical stabilisation through the maintenance of safe borders has also been a crucial factor of their respective territories (see Wallace, 2001). Thus it is possible to consider – as the European and American experience suggests – that security fears might serve as a catalyst for deeper integration, and that other blocs might consider new structures or strategies such as association or enlargement to assure mutual security which would overcome the tension between security and trade considerations.

## 6. Conclusion

By thinking about the European experience in broader comparative perspective, we can move beyond the dominant paradigm that has taken European integration to be 'exceptional'. The United States – as well as the European Union – can provide guidance on market integration measures. The American experience suggests that national market building can be much like regional market building. In essence, institutional, political and economic forces guide and influence the process of market consolidation. Such market developments promote the participation of societal actors, both in promoting and resisting changes in market organisation, restructure and institutionalise public authority at different levels, and reallocate authority and governance. The contemporary challenges that the European Union faces have been further heightened by the perception that they are unique when in fact the imperatives of market building in the United States have also continuously faced challenges, about how to deal with the dilemmas of democratic legitimacy, economic governance, security, and enlargement for example (cf. Menon, 2006; Katznelson, 2002).

However the American experience of the nineteenth century has some important parallels for contemporary political developments. The late nineteenth century was a period of unprecedented globalisation. Massive emigration and substantial wage convergence, vast capital flows and integrated capital markets, and plummeting transport costs that facilitated trade. Open economy forces were critical in explaining patterns of relative growth in nineteenth century (O'Rourke & Williamson, 2001). In addition, the history of American political economy is also tied to American political-legal development and the growth of state capacity. As a result, market consolidation illustrates the heterogeneous and layered character of institutions and governance arrangements. From large mass production corporations, that shifted from loose combinations to consolidated companies, to associational practices that used benchmarking and innovation, American industrial development was characterised by distinctive varieties of capitalism (Berk and Schneiberg, 2005). Yet as new modes of production and consumption and new issues in public affairs continually clashed with the more familiar and traditional, and the local and the communal, there were predictable effort to seek market stabilisation, rent-seeking cartels, redistribution and protectionism. While American political development involved the challenge of building institutions, such as tax agencies, customs services and antitrust agencies, the process of market building also involved emergent patterns of civic engagement and mobilisation (Witt, 2002; Skocpol, 2000). The crucial institutional transformations of the regulatory state, were of a highly partisan character, as efforts to regulate a burgeoning industrial economy shifted the American polity from one of diversely organised states into a consolidated state and market.

The American 'regulatory state' meant that federal rules and regulations governed and affected the national banking system, public land disposal, rivers and harbors projects, land grants for higher education for agriculture, subsidies and land grants to transcontinental railroads, soldiers and widows pensions, protective tariffs, and laws providing for and regulating the creation and supply of money.[14] New initiatives for extending the federal government engagement in regulating the economy came as a response to a growing power that had emerged in the market on the part of capitalist enterprises, usually in form of trusts, oligopolies or monopolies, first in railroads and then in some manufacturing industries. Changing market circumstances meant changes in governance, and the broad based acquisition of regulatory powers, was designed to provide social accountability, maintain the public interest and the general welfare, provide protection and social security for business and other interests, and essentially satisfy diverse constituencies. To me, it seems that contemporary European integration seems to be facing similar issues of how to deal with diverse broad based demands to respond to changing market circumstances.

Yet for some, the United States market building process is widely seen as legitimate as it is based on a constitutional republic where

---

[14] While Majone is associated with the regulatory state in Europe, there is a similar literature in the US with work by Morton Keller, Martin Sklar, Richard Bensel and Stephen Skronewek and others which I have drawn upon.

different sectors of society accepted the system of public authority in place that was settled after internal political strife and civil war (Fabbrini, 2004). By contrast the EU is considered more contested, as it has no such constitution, and the 'commercial republic' that has evolved lacks the democratic legitimacy that characterises the American polity (Fabbrini, 2004; 2003; Siedentopf; Moravscik, 2002). Acceptance of European integration was in part based on the purported gains from market efficiency which can be sustained up to a point based on the so-called permissive consensus. The breakdown of this process had led many to express concerns about the 'democratic deficit'. Yet time and again in American history, market consolidation took place against a diverse set of legal and economic priorities, party divisions, populism, ideological pressure, and specific issues that proved difficult to resolve. The current backlash against integration in Europe and concerns about the changes wrought by increased competition, globalisation, and integration seem remarkably similar to the nineteenth century. Nonetheless, scholars in the EU have increasingly analysed problems of legitimacy predominantly in terms of institutions at the expense of emergent patterns of citizen behaviour and organisation.

Arguably, deeper market integration cannot be understood independently of the legal, institutional and political realities that both create and constrain it. As regional trade blocs continue to proliferate, the analytic lessons learned from the US experience can be valuable as it focuses attention on state regulatory capacity and effective public administration to make markets work; the credible rule of law; and the importance of social policies to make market integration politically viable. Bringing together different models of market integration can provide valuable insights on the condition that are conducive to deeper integration and can contribute to economic growth, and also on the cautionary lessons that past experiences can provide. The American experience with integration has much to teach contemporary policy-makers, as accounts of how governance has changed in response to the dilemmas of modernisation and whether governments have the capacity to temper market competition has implications for the success and stability of greater international integration.

## References

Abel, A.S. (1940) Commerce Regulation before *Gibbons v Ogden*: Trade and Traffic Part II, *Brooklyn Law Review*, pp. 38-77.

Abseek Brusse, W. (1997) *Tariffs, Trade and European Integration, 1947-1957*, Macmillan.

Atack *et al.* (2000) Northern Agriculture and the Westward Movement, in Engerman and Gallman (eds.), *Cambridge Economic History of the United States* (vol. 2), Cambridge, Cambridge University Press, pp. 285-328.

Bartolini, S. (2004) Old and New Peripheries in the Processes of European Territorial Integration in Ansell, C. & Di Palma, G. (eds.) *Restructuring Territoriality*, Cambridge, Cambridge University Press, 4.

Bartolini, S. (1993) On Time and Comparative Research, *Journal of Theoretical Politics* 5, pp. 131-167.

Bensel, R. (1984) *Sectionalism and American Political Development, 1880-1980*, Madison, University of Wisconsin Press.

Bensel, R. *The Political Economy of American Industrialisation, 1877-1900*, Cambridge, Cambridge University Press, 2000.

Berk, G. & Schneiberg, M. (2005) Varieties in Capitalism, Varieties of Association: Collaborative Learning in American Industry, 1900-1925, *Politics and Society* 33 (1), pp. 46-87.

Bogaards (M) & Markus, M.L. (2002) Crepaz Consociational Interpretations of the European Union, *European Union Politics* 3 (3), pp. 357-381.

Brzinski, J., Thomas, B., Lancaster, D. & Tuschhoff, C. (1999) *Federalism and Compounded Representation: Key Concepts and* Project Overview, Publius, Winter, 29, pp. 1-18.

Bruszt, L. (2002) Market Making as State Making – Constitutions and Economic Development in Postcommunist Eastern Europe, *Constitutional Political Economy*, 2002/1, vol. 15, pp. 53-72.

Capelletti, M. *et al.* (1986) *Integration Through Law: Europe and the American Federal Experience-A General Introduction*, Berlin De Gruyter.

Caporaso, J. (1996) The European Union and Forms of State: Westphalian, Regulatory or Post-Modern?, *Journal of Common Market Studies* 34, pp. 29-52.

Chandler, A. (1962) *Strategy & Structure: Chapters in the History of the Industrial* Enterprise, Cambridge, MIT Press.

Chandler, A. (1969), (1969) The Structure of American Industry, *BHR* 1969 v.43 pp 255-298, reprinted in *The Essential Alfred Chandler* pp 247-92.

Chandler, A. (1978) *The Visible Hand: Managerial Revolution in American Business*, Cambridge, Mass., Cambridge University Press.

Commons, J. C *et al.* (1936) *History of Labor in the United States* (vols. 1-4), New York, Macmillan.

Cowles, M. G. (1995) Setting the Agenda for a New Europe: The ERT and EC 1992, *Journal of Common Market Studies* 33, pp. 501-526.

Diebold, W. (1959) The Shuman Plan: A Study in Economic Cooperation 1950-1959, in New York, Praeger (1995) *States and Economic Development: A Comparative Historical Analysis.*

Dell, Edmund S. (1959) Economic Integration and the American Example, *The Economic Journal*, Vol. 69, No. 273, pp. 39-54.

Deutsch, K. (1953) *Nationalism and Social Communication: An Inquiry into the Foundations of Nationality*, Boston, MIT Press.

Dobson, J. & Weiss, L. (1995) *States and Economic Development: A Comparative Historical Analysis*, Cambridge, Polity Press.

Egan, M. (forthcoming), *Single Markets: Economic Integration in Europe and the US*. Oxford University Press.

Egan, M. (2001) *Constructing a European Market*, Oxford, Oxford University Press.

Eichengreen, B. (2007) *The European Economy since 1945: Coordinated Capitalism and Beyond*, Princeton, Princeton University Press.

Eichengreen, B., Obstfeld, M. & Spaventa, L. (1992) One Money for Europe? Lessons from the US Currency Union, *Economic Policy*, Vol. 5, 10, Europe, April, pp. 117-187.

Eisinger, P. (1988) *The Rise of the Entrepreneurial State: State and Local Economic Development Policy in the United States*, Madison, Wisconsin Press.

Elazar, D (1987) *Exploring Federalism*, Tuscaloosa, University of Alabama Press.

Fabbrini, S. (2003) A Single Western State Model? Differential Development and Constrained Convergence of Public Authority Organisation in Europe and America, *Comparative Political Studies* 36(6), pp. 653-678.

Fabbrini, S. (2004) The European Union in American Perspective: The Transformation of Territorial Sovereignty in Europe and the United States, in Ansell, C.K. & Di Palma, G. (eds.) *Restructuring Territoriality*, Cambridge, Cambridge University Press, pp. 163-187.

Foner, E. (1988) *Reconstruction: America's Unfinished Revolution, 1863-1877*, New York, NY, Harper Collins.

Fowke, V.C. (1956) National Policy and Western Development in North America, *Journal of Economic History* 16, pp. 461-79.

Frankel, J. (1982) The 1807-1809 Embargo Against Great Britain, *Journal of Economic History* 42 (2), pp. 291-308.

Freyer, T. (1994) *Producers versus Capitalists: Constitutional Conflict in Antebellum America*, Charlottesville, VA, University of Virginia Press.

Frieden, J. & Rogowski, R. (1996) The Impact of the International Economy on National Policies: An Analytical Overview, in Keohane, R. & Milner, H. (eds.), *Internationalisation and Domestic Politics*, New York, Cambridge University Press, pp. 25-47.

Frieden, J., Inverted Interests (1991) The Politics of National Economic Policies in a World of Global Finance, *International Organisation* 45(4), pp. 425-451.

Fryer, T. (1976) Negotiable Instruments and the Federal Courts in Antebellum American Business, *Business History Review* 50 (4) (1976), pp. 435-455.

Garson, R. (2001) Counting Money: The US Dollar and American Nationhood, 1781-1820, *Journal of American Studies* 35, pp. 21-46.

Gillman, H. (1999) Reconnecting the Modern Supreme Court to the Historical Evolution of American Capitalism, in Gillman, H. & Clayton, C., Lawrence (eds.), *The Supreme Court in American Politics, New Institutionalist Interpretations*, University of Kansas University Press.

Glenn Patrick (2007) The Idea of a North American Legal System, paper presented at the American University College of Law, February.

Goodrich, C. (1960) *Government Promotion of American Canals and Railroads 1800-1890*, New York, Columbia University Press.

Goldstein, L. (1997) State Resistance to Authority in Federal Unions: The Early USA (1790-1860) and the European Community (1958-1994), *Studies in American Political Development* 11, pp. 149-189.

Grubel, H. G. & Lloyd, P.J. (1975) *Intra-Industry Trade: The Theory and Measurement of International Trade in Differentiated Products*, London, Macmillan.

Hartz, L. (1955) *The Liberal Tradition in America: An Interpretation of American Political Thought since the Revolution*, New York, Harcourt, Brace.

Hendrikson, D. C. (2006) Of Power and Providence, *Policy Review* 135, pp. 223-42.

Héritier, A. (2002) New Modes of Governance in Europe: Policy Making without Legislating? Working paper, *IHS Political Science Series* 81.

Hooghe, L. & Marks, G. (2003) Unraveling the Central State, but How? Types of Multi-level Governance, *American Political Science Review 97*, pp. 233-243.

Hirschman, A. (1970) *Exit, Voice and Loyalty*, Cambridge, Cambridge University Press.

Hovencamp, H. (1991) Capitalism, in Blank, K (ed.) *American Companion to the Supreme Court*, Oxford, Oxford University Press.

Hurst, J. W. (1971) *A Legal History of Money in the United States 1774-1970*, Lincoln, NE, University of Nebraska Press.

Hurst, J.W. (1977) *Law and Social Order in the United States*, Ithaca, NY, Cornell University Press.

Jones, E. (2003) Idiosyncrasy and Integration: Suggestions from Comparative Political Economy, *Journal of European Public Policy* 10(1), pp. 141-159.

Kelemen, R. D. (2004) *The Rules of Federalism: Institutions and Regulatory Politics in the EU and Beyond*, Cambridge, MA, Harvard University Press.

Katznelson, I. (2002) Flexible Capacity: The Military and Early American Statebuilding, in Katznelson & Shefter M. (eds.) *Shaped by War and Trade: International Influences on American Political Development*, Princeton University Press.

Keller, M. (1977) *Affairs of State: Public Life in the Late Nineteenth Century*, Cambridge, MA, Harvard University Press.

Kindleberger C.P. (2000) *Comparative Political Economy*, MIT Press, January.

Laffan, B. (1977) *The Finances of the European Union*. Basingstoke, Macmillan Press Ltd.

Lindsay, S.M. (1910) Reciprocal Legislation, *Political Science Quarterly* 25 (1), pp. 435-457.

Lowi, T. (1979) *The End of Liberalism: The Second Republic of the United States*, W.W Norton.

Maduro, M. Poiares (1999) Striking the Elusive Balance between Economic Freedom and Social Rights in the EU, in Alston, P., Cassese, A., Lalumière, C., Leuprecht, P. (eds.) *An EU Human Rights Agenda for the New Millennium*, Oxford, Hart Publishing, pp. 449-472.

Majone, G. (1997) From the Positive to the Regulatory State: Causes and Consequences of Changes in the Mode of Governance, *Journal of Public Policy*, 17 (2), pp. 139-167.

Marks, G. (1997) A Third Lens: Comparing European Integration and State Building, in Klausen J. & Tilly L.A. (eds.), *European Integration in Social and Historical Perspective: 1850 to the Present*, New York, Rowan & Littlefield, pp. 23-50.

McCurdy, Ch. (1978) Can Law and the Marketing Structure of the Large Corporation, 1875-1890, *Journal of Economic History* 3, pp. 631-649.

McKay, D. (1999) *Federalism and European Union: A Political Economy Perspective*, Oxford, Oxford University Press.

McNamara, K. (1998) *The Currency of Ideas*, Ithaca, NY, Cornell University Press.

McNamara, K. (2002) State Building, the Territorialisation of Money, and the Creation of the American Single Currency, in Henning, R., Andrews, D. & Pauly, L. (eds.) *Governing the World's* Money, Ithaca, NY, Cornell University Press.

McNamara, K. (2003) Does Money Make the State? Political Development, the Greenback, and the Euro, unpublished paper Georgetown University, 2003.

Menon, A. & Schain M. (2006) *Comparative Federalism: The European Union and the United States in Comparative Perspective*, Oxford, Oxford University Press.

Milner, H. (1999) The Political Economy of International Trade, *Annual Review of Politics* 2, pp. 91-114.

Moravscik, A. (2002) In Defence of the Democratic Deficit: Reassessing Legitimacy in the European Union, *Journal of Common Market Studies* ($40^{th}$ Anniversary Edition) 40(4), pp. 603-624.

Moravscik, A. (1993) Preferences and Power in the European Community: A Liberal Intergovernmentalist Approach, *Journal of Common Market Studies* 31, pp. 473-524.

Moravsick, A. (1991) Negotiating the Single European Act: National Interests and Conventional Statecraft in the European Community *International Organisation* 45, pp. 19-56.

Moran, M. (1991) *The Politics of the Financial Services Revolution: The USA, UK, and Japan.* New York, St. Martin's Press.

Nicolaidis, K. & Howse, R. (eds.) (2001) *The Federal Vision: Legitimacy and Levels of Governance in the United States and the European Union*, Oxford, Oxford University Press.

North, D. (1961) *The Economic Growth of the United States from 1790 to 1860*, Englewood Cliffs, NJ, Prentice Hall.

North, D. (1981) *Structure and Change in Economic History*, New York, NY, W.W. Norton and Company.

Novak, W. (2000) Law, Capitalism, and the Liberal State: The Historical Sociology of James Willard Hurst, *Law and History Review* 18, pp. 97-145.

Novak, W. (1996) *The People's Welfare: Law and Regulation in Nineteenth-Century America*, Chapel Hill, NC, University of North Carolina PRess.

Novak, W. (2006) The Not-So-Strange Birth of the Modern American State, *Law and History Review* 24, pp. 193-198.

O'Rourke, K. & Williamson, J. (1999) *Globalisation and History: The Evolution of a Nineteenth-Century Atlantic* Economy, Cambridge, MA, MIT Press.

Pastor, R. (2001) Towards a North American Community, Washington D.C., Institute for International Economics.

Polanyi, K. (1957) *The Great Transformation*, Boston, Basic Books.

Radaelli, C. (2005) Diffusion Without Convergence: How Political Context Shapes the Adoption of Regulatory Impact Assessment, *Journal of European Public Policy* 12(5), pp. 924-943.

Riker, W. (1964) *Federalism: Origins, Operation, Significance*. Boston, Little, Brown.

Sandalow, T. and Stein, E. (eds.) (1982) *Courts and Free Markets: Perspectives from the United States and Europe*, Oxford, Clarendon Press.

Sandholtz, W. & Zysman, J. (1991) Recasting the European Bargain, *World Politics* 42, 1, pp. 95-128.

Sandholtz, W. (1992) *High-Tech Europe: The Politics of International Cooperation*, Berkeley, University of California Press.

Sbragia, A. (1991) Thinking About the European Future: The Uses of Comparison, in Sbragia A. (ed.) *Europolitics: Institutions and Policymaking in the European Community*, Washington, D.C., Brookings.

Sbragia, A. (2004) The Future of Federalism in the European Union, Paper presented at the 2004 Biennial Conference of the European Community Studies Association of Canada, Montreal, Canada, 2004.

Sbragia, A. (2006) The United States and the European Union: Comparing Two Sui Generis Systems, in Menon, A. & Schain, M. (eds.) *Comparative Federalism: The European Union and the United States in Comparative Perspective*, Oxford, Oxford University Press.

Scitovsky, T. (1958) *Economic Theory and Western European Integration*, New York, Routledge.

Scharpf, F. (1988) The Joint-Decision Trap: Lessons from German Federalism and European Integration, *Public Administration*, 66, pp. 239-278.

Scharpf, F. (1999) *Governing Europe*, Oxford, Oxford University Press.

Scheiber, H. (1975) Federalism and the American Economic Order, 1789-1910, *Law and Society Review* 10, pp. 58-118.

Scheiber, H. (1980) Federalism and Legal Process: Historical and Contemporary Analysis of the American System, *Law and Society Review* 14 (3), pp. 663-722.

Scheiber, H. (1981) Regulation, Property Rights, and Definition of 'The Market': Law and the American Economy, *Journal of Economic History* 61, pp. 103-109.

Schmidt, L. (1939) Internal Commerce and the Development of National Economy Before 1860, *Journal of Political Economy* 47(6), pp. 798-822.

Schmidt, V. (2004) The European Union: Democratic Legitimacy in a Regional State?, *Journal of Common Market Studies* 42(5), pp. 975-997.

Siedentopf, L. (2000) *Democracy in Europe*, Columbia University Press, New York.

Sklar, M. (1988) *The Corporate Reconstruction of American Capitalism 1890-1916*, Cambridge, Cambridge University Press.

Skocpol, T. *et al.* (2000) A Nation of Organisers: The Institutional Origins of Civic Volunteerism, *American Political Science Review* 93(4), 2.

Skowronek, S. (1982) *Building an American State: The Expansion of National Administrative Capacities, 1877-1920*, Cambridge, Cambridge University Press.

Spaak, P.H. (1956) Rapport des chefs de délégation aux Ministres des Affaires étrangères April 21.

Stein, E. (1981) Lawyers, Judges and the Making of a Transnational Constitution, *American Journal of International Law* 25, pp. 1-27.

Stein, E. (2001) *Thoughts From a Bridge: A Retrospective of New Writings on Europe and American Federalism*, Ann Arbor, MI, University of Michigan Press.

Taft, M., Adelman C. & I. (1988) *Comparative Patterns of Economic Development, 1850-1914*, Baltimore, Johns Hopkins University Press.

Taylor, G. (1962) *The Transportation Revolution 1815-1860*, New York, Harper & Row.

Tiebout, C. (1956) A Pure Theory of Local Expenditures, *The Journal of Political Economy* 64(5), pp. 416-424.

Tilly, C. (1992) *Coercion, Capital and European States: A.D. 990-1992 (Studies in Social Discontinuity)*, Malden, MA, Blackwell Press.

Tinbergen, J. (1954) *International Economic Integration*, Amsterdam, Elsevier.

Wallace, W. (2000) *Governance, in Policy Making in the European Union*, (eds.) Wallace W. & H., London, Oxford University Press.

Weingast, B. (1995) The Economic Role of Political Institutions: Market-Preserving Federalism and Economic Development, *International Political Science Review* 11, pp. 1-31.

Witt, J. F. (2002) *The Accidental Republic*, Cambridge, MA, Harvard University Press.

Zamora, S. (2007) Is the Adoption of a Social Charter for NAFTA a Necessary Step in North American Integration? Comparing the NAFTA and EU Experiences, Paper presented at the Conference on Legal Harmonisation in NAFTA, American University, February.

Zimmerman, W (1996) *Interstate Relations: The Neglected Dimension of Federalism*, Westport, CT, Praeger, ND.

CHAPTER 11

# Canada's Internal Markets

## Legal, Economic and Political Aspects

François VAILLANCOURT[1]

*Professor at the Economics Department, Université de Montréal*

## 1. Introduction

The purpose of this paper is to present the legal, economic and political aspects of internal markets in Canada with respect to goods and services, financial capital and labour. This wide mandate given to us by the conference organisers reflects the country study aspect of this paper. The paper is divided in three main parts, with each part divided into three sections one for each of the three markets listed above. The paper begins with a description of the institutional and legal framework. We then turn to an examination of the economic importance of the internal markets and of the impediments to the relevant flows. We then discuss recent changes or attempts at changes pointing out the role of politics. We caution the reader that while interesting comparisons may be made between the EU and Canada, key differences remain. In particular, Canada is country with a central government that accounts for about 40 per cent of direct public spending and thus about 15 per cent of GDP and that also has important regulatory competences while spending by the EU only accounts for about 1 per cent of EU GDP.

[1] We thank Roman Staranczak from Industry Canada for both useful documents and insights, as well as extremely useful comments on a first draft of this paper. We also thank Jacques Pelkmans our discussant and other participants in the April 2007 conference for their useful comments on the conference draft of the paper and the editors for their comments on the revised draft.

## 2. The institutional and legal framework.

We begin this part of the paper by a brief presentation of the constitutional framework before turning to internal markets for respectively goods and services, capital and labour. Canada was created in 1867 by the union of three British colonies: Nova Scotia, New Brunswick, and Canada. It is now composed of ten provinces and three (northern) territories. While there is some debate on this point among historians, it seems fair to state that the drafters of the Canadian Constitution (the British North America Act or BNA Act)[2] intended to create a strong central government. The new Government of Canada was, for example, given sole possession of the key revenue source at that time, customs duties, and made responsible for economic development related activities, while the new provinces were left to handle such local matters as education, health and social services which were not very important governmental spending items in the nineteenth century. To further reinforce central power, the federal government was also permitted, in certain circumstances, to disallow provincial legislation and to declare certain 'local works' of national interest.

The constitution contains a list of exclusive federal powers, a list of exclusive provincial powers, and a list of concurrent powers (agriculture and immigration with federal paramountcy, and since 1951 pensions with provincial paramountcy). Federal powers include defence, foreign affairs, money and banking, transportation, and communications. In particular, the federal government is responsible for regulating air, rail and sea transportation, telecommunications and broadcasting and interprovincial pipelines. It also operates the postal service. Provincial powers include education (subject to linguistic/religious safeguards for minorities), health, municipal and local affairs, police, and so on. Provinces regulate road transportation. With respect to the mobility of goods and implicitly capital, the following articles of the original constitution are particularly relevant:

- Article 121(BNA): "All Articles of the Growth, Produce, or Manufacture of any one of the Provinces shall, from and after the Union, be admitted free into each of the other Provinces";
- Article 91(BNA) which sets out the powers of the federal parliament" (2) The Regulation of Trade and Commerce; (14) Currency and Coinage; (15) Banking, Incorporation of Banks, and the Issue of Paper Money; (16) Savings Banks".
- Article 92(BNA) which sets out the powers of provincial legislatures particularly "(13) Property and Civil Rights in the Province and (16)

[2] Also referred to as the Constitution Act 1867.

Generally all Matters of a merely local or private Nature in the Province".

No constitutional article of direct relevance to labour mobility was identified. However, the interpretation of 92 (13 and 16) as giving the right to the provinces to set the occupational credentials does give them a key and even paramount role to play in this area.

## *2.1. Goods and services*

With respect to the internal market for goods, one should note that section 121 applies only to goods, not to services. It is seen as a general principle prohibiting the maintenance of tariff and non-tariff barriers between the provinces, whether such barriers are raised by parliament or the provincial legislatures (Bernier *et al.*, 1986: 45). It, along with Article 122 that pertains to external tariffs, can be seen as ensuring that in Canada a classic customs union is established with no internal border taxes and a single external tariff (Silzer and Krasnick, 1986: 156). However, Bernier *et al.* note with some surprise but without being able to put forward a convincing rationale that the courts have mainly referred to section 91(2) when addressing issues of inter-provincial trade barriers. Vegh (1997) reviews the jurisprudence in this area which dates back to a Privy Council decision of 1882 known as the Parsons case. He writes that

> The flow of inter-provincial trade [...] is within Parliament's jurisdiction over the regulation of trade and commerce pursuant to section 91(2) [...] However, pursuant to sections 92(13) and 92(16) provincial legislatures may pass laws respecting local trade (p. 356) the problem with which the courts have wrestled has been to arrive at a method of reconciling the federal interest in national trade regulation with the provincial interests in regulating local trade (Vegh, 1997: 367).
>
> He argues that The Court has taken two contradictory approaches to this issue. The first has been to restrict provincial jurisdictions to transactions which are entirely completed within the province so as to prevent any interference with inter-provincial trade. The second has been to hold that the effect of provincial regulation on interprovincial trade is constitutionally irrelevant (p. 362).

Thus reconciling federal and provincial powers to regulate trade, the courts have found that intra-provincial trade is within provincial jurisdiction while inter-provincial trade is subject to federal regulation. For example, certain meat products can be sold within a province provided they meet that province's health and safety standards. However, to be sold in another province or outside the country, federal standards apply. One of the results of the various judicial interpretations of the regulatory powers with respect to inter-provincial trade is that in 1980 the federal government released a white paper on Securing the Canadian Economic Union in the Constitution (Bernier *et al.*, 1986: 47). This is the first step in a series of changes put forward and discussed in the last part of this paper. It culminated in an 'Agreement on Internal Trade' (AIT) that was signed by the provinces and territories (then two) in 1994 for implementation on July 1, 1995.[3] It was preceded by the Atlantic Provinces procurement agreement in 1992.[4] It can be summarised as follows.[5]

### *2.1.1. Guiding principles*

There are six general rules in the AIT to prevent new trade barriers and reduce existing barriers. They are: no discrimination between Canadian persons, goods, services and investments, right of entry and exit across provincial or territorial boundaries, no government obstacles to trade, minimum impact of non-trade objectives on inter-provincial trade, reconciling standards and regulations across Canada and transparent information. These guiding principles apply to the sectoral chapters listed below to the extent that they are specifically referenced in them. Moreover, the AIT only applies to the 11 sectoral areas in the agreement. Important sectors (e.g. financial services) are excluded from its scope. The eleven sectors are procurement[6] (local price preferences and other practices hindering non-resident suppliers), investment (local residency requirements and corporate registration requirements), labour mobility (residency requirements and reconciling differences in occupational standards), consumer standards, agricultural and food products (supply management systems and grade standard), alcoholic beverages[7] product listing and pricing), natural resources processing (prohibiting new barriers to processing of resource product), energy, communications, transportation (harmonising safety standards and weights and dimension rules) and environmental protection.

This list is misleading both in terms of what is really committed to and what is actually done. For example, the agriculture chapter only covers a handful of issues (e.g. margarine colouring, fluid milk distribution) and even then unsuccessfully for some (margarine colouring again).

---

3 The text of the agreement is found at http://strategis.ic.gc.ca/epic/site/ait-aci.nsf/en/h_il00034e.html.

4 For information on this agreement: http://www.bids.ca/termscond/agmte.htm.

5 http://www.ait-aci.ca/index_en/ait.htm.

6 In brackets, we present when relevant a subset of issues mentioned in the agreement.

7 Liquor control boards are provincially owned public monopolies that retail liquor and wine (some brands also sold in stores in Québec) in all provinces except Alberta where it is present at the wholesale level.These bodies were created as part of the prohibition activities that occurred in North America in the early part of the twentieth century.

And comparing commitment versus action, although governments said they would examine supply management as it relates to internal trade issues, nothing has happened and supply management remains untouched (even in TILMA discussed later).

Another example is the natural resources processing chapter. If a company has an existing mine, then a province cannot ask that its output be processed within the province. However, most of the issues here relate to getting a license to open a mine. As this is a provincial responsibility, the province may ask a company for further processing within its territory as a condition of granting the license. It also applies to the right to cut trees on Crown lands. Discussions on this chapter have foundered on the existence of local preferences related to offshore oil and gas developments. Newfoundland has insisted that these preferences which are embedded in the offshore oil and gas acts of Canada as well as mirror legislation in Newfoundland be maintained.[8] Others, primarily led by Alberta, insist that they should be open for review on a periodic basis.

The main aim of the energy chapter is to give a province the right to transmit electricity through another to a third market, either in Canada or the United States. Thus, for example, should Newfoundland develop a hydroelectric project in Labrador, it would have the right to transmit electricity through Quebec to the US and pay only the 'costs' of transmission. The economic rent would accrue to Newfoundland and not be subject to bilateral negotiations with Quebec.[9] Quebec has supported the completion of a chapter because it would help the province to secure 'wheeling' rights to the US markets for its own electricity exports. US regulatory authorities insist on provinces showing open markets.

Finally, with telecommunications meanwhile completely under federal jurisdiction, that chapter is now redundant. There was a period of time during which Saskatchewan exercised regulatory control in this area but that is over.

### *2.2. Capital*

Turning to capital markets, as shown above, the Canadian constitution explicitly assigns banking to the federal government (91-15 and 91-16). Thus banks have federal charters and are supervised by federal

8 For a recent example of this, see the August 200 Newfoundland Hebron oil filed agreement at http://www.releases.gov.nl.ca/releases/2007/exec/0822n02.htm.

9 A previous agreement between Newfoundland and Québec that requires power from Churchill falls to be sold to Hydro Québec and then resold by it rather than wheeled through Québec is strongly resented in Newfoundland. See http://www.releases.gov.nl.ca/releases/1996/exec/1119n06.htm.

agencies. Other financial institutions such as trusts and insurance companies, however, can have either a federal or provincial charter and may thus choose to be supervised by one or the other level of government. Still other financial institutions, such as credit unions and brokerage firms (stockbrokers), are subject to provincial supervision as are stock exchanges.[10] Provincial powers in the area of financial institutions flow implicitly from their constitutional powers over property and civil rights (92-13) and all matters of a merely local or private nature (92-16). There is not much case law in this area. The key policy issue has been the existence of thirteen Securities and Exchanges Commissions and thus the lack of a national regulator. We discuss in the fourth part of this paper the ongoing debate. Here we show that it is apparently not the constitutional arrangements that explain the exercise of provincial powers and the absence of a national/federal regulator. Legal opinions[11] were sought from three Canadian law firms by a federal advisory panel (Wise Persons' Committee; discussed in section 4) on the constitutional validity of federal and provincial legislation implementing the Canadian Securities Commission ('CSC') model proposed by the Wise Persons' Committee. More specifically, the questions posed were:[12]

1. Does Parliament have constitutional authority to enact the Act?
2. Do the provinces have constitutional authority to enact legislation: (i) incorporating the Act by reference; (ii) delegating administrative powers to the CSC; and (iii) dissolving their existing securities regulators?
3. If one or more provinces decide not to enact such legislation, and if the federal government concludes that this would jeopardise the successful operation of the scheme in other parts of the country, would Parliament have the constitutional authority to include an express paramountcy clause in the Act?

All three firms were in agreement that the federal government could implement a national securities commission. One will note that this power is said to derive from 91(2).

In all three opinions, great weight is given to the fact that the proposed scheme appears to meet the test laid out in a Supreme Court decision (General Motors of Canada Ltd. v. City National Leasing,

---

10 In the mid-1980s, banks were first allowed to own brokerage firms and within a few years most large stockbrokers were owned by banks. An accord (the Hockin-Kwinter accord, after the names of the ministers who signed it) was reached in 1987 between the federal and Ontario governments that these brokerage firms would be subsidiaries of banks regulated by the provinces. See http://www.irpp.org/po/archive/sep05/hartt.pdf for a discussion of the accord.

11 See Constitutional Opinions at http://www.wise-averties.ca/report_en.html.

12 As summarised in the Ogilvy, Renault opinion. http://www.wise-averties.ca/reports/html/1A_opinion_E/index.html.

[1989] 1 S.C.R. 641) which states:[13] "The true balance between property and civil rights and the regulation of trade and commerce must lie somewhere between an all pervasive interpretation of s. 91(2) and an interpretation that renders the general trade and commerce power to all intents vapid and meaningless".

### *2.3. Labour*

As part of constitutional changes discussed in section 4 of the paper, Article 6, of relevance to the mobility of individuals, was introduced in the Constitution Act, 1982.

It states that there is a right "(i) to move to and take up residence in any province"; and "(ii) to pursue the gaining of a livelihood in any province". These rights are then qualified by allowing for laws providing for requirements of specific qualifications and for reasonable residency requirements for the receipt of publicly provided social services and by permitting laws and programmes for the amelioration in a province of conditions of individuals in that province who are socially or economically disadvantaged if the rate of employment in that province is below the rate of employment in Canada.

One must be aware that the effective meaning of these provisions is very limited. They cannot be used to address the problems individuals face in having their occupational qualifications recognised in another province. One must also note that the AIT has a section on labour mobility. Lee and Trebilcock (1987) and De Mestral and Winter (2001) examined the issue of internal mobility in Canada. One can summarise them by stating that prior to this amendment to the Constitution, various obstacles to inter-provincial mobility were in place, with the most famous one being perhaps the restriction imposed by Québec on access to construction jobs by non-residents. Since this clause has been introduced, the most flagrant abuses have been set aside but as discussed below barriers remain due to the acceptability of general requirements to practice in a given profession.

## 3. Economic aspects

In this third part of the paper, we turn to the economic aspects of internal barriers to trade. For each case, we attempt to quantify the phenomenon studied and then examine the impact of barriers to trade.

---

13 http://www.wise-averties.ca/reports/html/1C_opinion_E/1C_opinion_E_complete.html.

### *3.1. Goods and services*

Table 11.1 below presents evidence on the importance of internal trade within Canada. Examining it, one notes that:

- international exports are more important than inter-provincial exports in all three years for Canada as whole;
- inter-provincial exports are declining through time while international exports have increased. In 2001, they are twice as large as inter-provincial exports;
- while in 1984, several provinces had a share of inter-provincial exports larger than that of international exports, in 2001, this is only true for PEI.

**Table 11.1: Importance of inter-provincial and international trade, Canada, 1984, 1990 and 2001**

| | Inter-provincial Exports / GDP | | | International Exports / GDP | | |
|---|---|---|---|---|---|---|
| | 1984 | 1990 | 2001 | 1984 | 1990 | 2001 |
| NFLD | 10.35 | 10.67 | 8.97 | 28.71 | 29.19 | 26.30 |
| PEI | 30.93 | 27.77 | 23.68 | 14.63 | 13.23 | 22.02 |
| NS | 22.66 | 20.31 | 17.21 | 17.66 | 15.66 | 19.44 |
| NB | 28.71 | 27.46 | 25.85 | 30.69 | 26.91 | 29.18 |
| QUÉ | 22.94 | 21.72 | 16.57 | 21.39 | 19.41 | 30.01 |
| ONT | 23.15 | 20.71 | 15.97 | 33.03 | 27.19 | 41.41 |
| MAN | 29.23 | 27.47 | 25.70 | 19.33 | 18.07 | 26.08 |
| SASK | 24.03 | 22.86 | 21.16 | 38.03 | 25.81 | 34.25 |
| ALTA | 36.69 | 26.38 | 15.92 | 23.03 | 23.36 | 23.77 |
| BC | 13.79 | 13.81 | 11.64 | 28.29 | 24.76 | 25.83 |
| Total | 24.02 | 21.02 | 16.18 | 27.49 | 24.05 | 34.77 |

Source: Bird and Vaillancourt (2007).

That said, inter-provincial exports account for 180 billion $(Can) in 2001, a not unsubstantial amount. If we examine the composition of inter-provincial trade[14] that year, we find the following:

- 43 per cent of trade is in services, 57 per cent in goods;
- 25 per cent of trade of goods is in petroleum products, refined or not; and chemical products;
- 20 per cent of trade of goods is in agricultural goods and food products;

[14] Calculations by the author using data for 2001 from CANSIM: Table 386-0002 Interprovincial and international trade flows at producer prices.

- Other broad categories account each for less than 10 per cent of trade in goods.

How much of these exports are subject to inter-provincial trade barriers? The simple answer is that we do not know since there is no agreement on what an inter-provincial barrier is. Schwanen (2000) puts forward a typology of trade barriers to list potential barriers; this could be used to identify goods and services subject to barriers to trade but has not been done recently. Whalley reports an inventory of barriers from the 1980s (2007: 10) and notes that it has not been updated.

Notwithstanding the lack of quantitative evidence on internal trade barriers, there are various opinions on their importance. Whalley (2007: 3) summarises the issue as follows; the limited literature that exists suggests two polar positions. Illustrative of the position that severe effects are at stake is a recent COMPASS (2004) poll of business leaders which reports opinions that inter-provincial barriers to trade are as damaging as Canada-US trade barriers. More specifically, barriers to labour mobility cause the most harm and barriers to trade the least. Illustrative of the opposite position that the issue is a tempest in a teacup are Whalley (1983), Trela and Whalley (1986), Whalley (1996) and Boadway (1996). Their argument is that the coverage of barriers is extremely small.

Grady and MacMillan (2007a: 2) concur:

> Academic studies have, by and large, concluded that internal trade barriers have a minimal effect on overall GDP...the IMF also regard(s) Canada's internal market as functioning relatively free from impediments...The small number of cases brought (to the) dispute settlement system lends support to the notion that trade in goods, service and capital within Canada is relatively unencumbered.

Another interpretation is that it is not worth the time and expense required to launch a dispute, especially when there's no guarantee that a government will implement a panel's recommendation.

Grady and MacMillan (2007a: 4) summarise the results of existing studies on the impact of trade barriers. They find:

- Whalley (1983) finds an impact of 0.2 per cent of GDP;
- Rutley (1991) states that 10 to 15 per cent of GDP faces barriers to competition; the cost of these barriers is about 0.5 per cent of GDP;
- Copeland (1998) argues that Rutley overestimates costs and that the answer is 0.05 to 0.1 per cent of GDP.

So at one end of the spectrum, one finds the estimate by Copeland and at the other the estimate by Rutley for the Canadian Manufacturers' Association (CMA). This high estimate was criticised because it included distributional costs as well as inefficiency costs. That governments choose to pay more for their goods and services owing to local preference policies is simply a re-distribution of income and should not be counted as an efficiency costs. The only loss to the economy is the inefficiency, resulting for example from the loss of economies of scale.

Grady and MacMillan (2007a: 5) note that two of the important barriers noted by Whalley and Trela (1986), those with respect to provincial procurement policies and those with respect to alcoholic beverages are much less important now than twenty or so years ago due respectively to the AIT and to GATT challenges. The Conference Board (2006) notes that "little research has been done on non tariff barriers to competition". One key issue raised by Porter (1991) in a study of Canada is that these barriers may have a dynamic impact in that they prevent smaller firms from reaching a size such that they can compete internationally. This is probably true for firms outside Ontario, particularly those in Atlantic Canada where provinces are small markets. This is not taken into account in any of these estimates. In their opinion, the remaining key issues are:

- public procurement barriers which are still identified in various surveys of businesses as important. One important issue is procurement for services as opposed to goods;
- agricultural barriers with the most famous being the margarine colouring issue and with the grading of potatoes and the wrapping of butter (foil or paper) also mentioned. Here one should note that federal legislation prevents inter-provincial shipment of meat products from provincially inspected plants; only those from federally inspected plants can thus be shipped.
- general regulatory barriers such as those on trucking weights and length, etc.

One issue is: what is a trade barrier? The Canadian Chamber of Commerce (2004) notes that its "*Internal Trade Questionnaire* demonstrated that the most common barriers to trade were overlapping of regulations between jurisdictions, multiple licensing requirements, and local preferences in awarding government contracts"(p. 3). However, the first two items are not barriers to trade but costs of operating in multiple jurisdictions. Indeed, if one looks at the specific examples noted in that study, several businesses show little respect for the constitutional division of powers (lack of national regulation of food, national teacher certification, national training standards, national recycling regulations and national tax regulations are all cited as trade barriers to be removed). Or as Copeland (1998) puts it "Much of the debate is not really about inter-provincial trade, but rather about how decentralised the policy regime should be in Canada and how much flexibility governments should have to intervene in markets" (p. 4). Finally, it is worth noting the point that the response to so called trade barriers varies by size of business: "Small firms of less than 50 employees were more likely not to proceed [...] large companies (500+) were more likely to work with the government to resolve the barrier" (p. 5); hence there is an issue of differentiated impact by size implicit in trade barriers that has not been well studied.

Another approach is to note that the AIT is aimed at "overcoming discrimination against out-of-province trade – that is at so called negative integration – but also at committing parties to achieving a greater degree of harmonisation among standards and regulations that are not intended to discriminate – that is, at so called positive discrimination" (Lenihan, 1995: 103). The goal is to find in a federal country a "way of striking a balance between the pan-Canadian goal of economic integration and legitimate provincial concerns about protecting diversity" (Lenihan, 1995: 117).

Given the above, one can see why Bird and Vaillancourt (2007) argue that both the importance and impact of the IAT are debatable. Few goods and services were subject to inter-provincial trade barriers before its signature. The only notable changes since its signature have been the use of open tendering with no *place of business* clause by provincial governments in 1995, extended to the important MSH (Municipal/Academic/Schools/Hospitals) sector, in 1999. Little has changed in the areas of public enterprise procurement, energy trade, processing of natural resources or transportation. Schwanen (2000) sums up by saying that "some of the oldest of inter-provincial barriers have so far survived the AIT very well" (p. 52). A small illustration of how things work in Canada may help explain the perhaps surprising lack of concern about such obviously inefficient provincial policies. Since 1997, the provinces have been attempting to reach agreement on a uniform rule with respect to the coloring of margarine. Québec, which has a relatively large dairy industry (Bird and Vaillancourt, 2005) requires margarine not to be colored to look like butter. Other provinces do not. Thus, margarine producers in Canada must produce at least two shades of yellow margarine Various AIT panels have been struck on this issue but as of September 1st 2007, margarine coloring requirements remain in force in Québec.[15] Indeed, a 1999 Québec court decision upholding the right of that province to impose margarine coloring rules different from the rest

[15] For details of the various steps taken between 1997 and 2007, see Proceedings of the Standing Senate Committee on Banking, Trade and Commerce, Issue 15.

of Canada[16] states that the AIT is a political and not a legal agreement. This decision was upheld by the Quebec court of Appeals and finally by the Supreme Court of Canada in 2006.

It is not surprising to see that Schwanen (2000), while praising the dispute settlement mechanisms of the AIT, and, in particular, its accessibility by individuals and firms and the Code of Conduct on Incentive writes that "a new impetus is needed if the Agreement is to better realise its objectives" (p. 54). One issue is who should provide this impetus: the federal government using its exclusive trade and commerce constitutional powers, the provincial governments or both. If this is not done, the AIT may be replaced by other agreements. This will be raised again in part 4.

### *3.2. Capital markets*

The importance of shares (the securities that would be regulated by a national securities commission) increased as a share of total assets held by Canadians from 6.1 per cent in 1991 to 9.3 per cent in 2005 and from 10.2 per cent to 14 per cent of financial assets over the same period.[17]

In that last year, they account for 1,296,502,000,000 $(Can) of assets. By size of stock market capitalisation, Canada's stock market is ranked 6$^{th}$ in the G-7, according to data for 2000 (Boissonneault, 2003). A significant number of Canadian firms raise equity capital outside of Canada, although Canada accounts for only a small share of international equity issues. Inter-listing of Canadian firms shares in the USA is increasing. From 1980 to 1998, the number of inter-listed firms increased from 82 to 244, and the volume of trading of these shares in the USA increased from 23 per cent in 1991 to 31 per cent in 1995 (Beaulieu and Bellemare, 2000) Indeed, 50 of the 60 biggest companies listed on the TSX (= Toronto Stock Exchange) are interlisted on a US exchange.

We know little about the regional dimension of capital markets in Canada. With respect to market capitalisation of shares, evidence indicates that:

- Ontario accounts for 53 per cent of the market capitalisation of the Toronto stock exchanges, followed by Alberta with 19 per cent, Quebec with 17 per cent and British Columbia with 5 per cent (Puri, 2003);

---

16 Québec dairy farmers are an important political force. This coloring rule requires margarine sold in Québec to be colored so as to make it look different from butter.

17 CANSIM Table 378-0004 National balance sheet accounts, by sectors, annual.

- in specific sectors, one finds clusters that match the industrial structure of the provinces. Hence Ontario accounts for 76 per cent of the financial services sector and Alberta 56 per cent of the oil and gas sector. In the forest sector, Quebec with 60 per cent and British Columbia with 26 per cent dominate.

The overall result explains the *de facto* national role of the Ontario Securities Commission. It seems reasonable to argue as Puri (2003) did that "in considering optimal securities regulatory structure, it is important to determine whether distinctive local and regional capital markets exist [...]. If so, they should be taken into account in the long-standing debate on reform of the securities regulatory framework in Canada".

Her study analyses whether distinct local markets exist in Canada by (i) examining issuer data; (ii) discussing investor location. With respect to issuers, she finds evidence of the existence of: LICR (*Local* Infrastructure for Capital Raising) for some industries in some provinces. She then notes that

> The location of an industry's LICR does not provide any indication of the location of its investors. The province in which an issuer's head office is located, which is the basis for determining LICR, does not indicate where the majority of its investors reside. While Professors Cumming, Kaul and Mehrotra (2003a) find that most private equity investors reside in the same province as the entrepreneurs in whose companies they invest, their findings cannot be generalised for all stages of financing and investors because of the distinct nature of the venture capital and private equity market.

Her conclusion is that:

> Overall, the analysis in this study finds that the majority of local regulatory responses are not the product of local and regional distinctiveness. As a result, the main conclusion to be drawn from the study is that existing local and regional differences can be accommodated under different regulatory models without appreciable differences in regulatory outcomes.

Her findings are in agreement with the evidence on the co-movements of stock indices provided by Cumming, Kaul and Mehrotra (2003a):

> They compute the correlations between returns and volume for the ASE and the VSE and the TSX, and then for the TSX Venture Exchange and the TSX and find that the correlations and, therefore, the extent of equity market integration have fluctuated through time. However, integration was at impressive levels as long as five years ago. The large correlations suggest that the TSX Venture Exchange and the TSX have been relatively well-integrated for some time, and that market participants on the TSX and TSX Venture Exchange are homogenous.

This leads to the observation that the correlation between the ASE and the VSE increased in the year following the formation of the TSX Venture Exchange, suggesting that a unified regulatory structure promotes integration, although these effects got weaker over longer intervals. It also leads to the proposal of a regulatory model based on trading volume or price levels (or, by extension, firm size) that would remain the same across provincial boundaries.

### 3.3. Labour mobility

There is no data as such on labor mobility in Canada; rather we have data on mobility of individuals, be they or not in the labor force. Vachon and Vaillancourt (1999) examined individual mobility over the 1971-1996 period. Figure 11.1 summarises the flows for Canada for the 1971-2005 that period. It shows that the decline in inter-provincial migration observed in the 1971-1996 period (Vachon and Vaillancourt, 1999) has ended and the rate has stabilised at about 0.9 per cent of the population per year or about 300 000 individuals per year in 2005.

**Figure 11.1. Internal migration rate, Canada, 1971-2005 (per cent of population)**

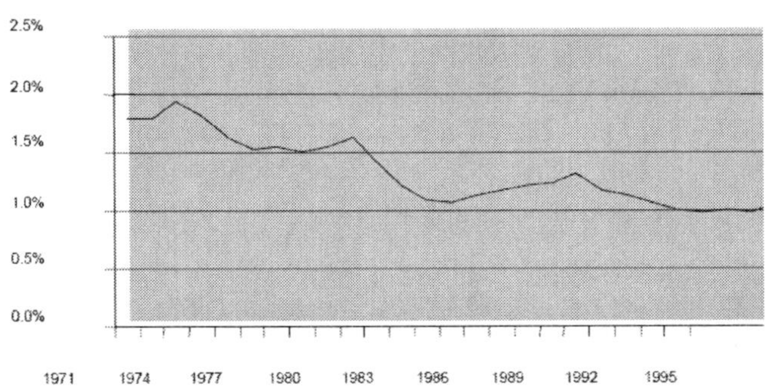


Gomez and Gunderson (2007) summarise the literature on inter-provincial mobility as follows:

- mobility occurs from the low wage, high unemployment provinces to the higher wage, low unemployment provinces;
- mobility is negatively affected by the distance and other costs of the move;
- mobility is lower for older persons, the less educated, and married persons;
- mobility into and out of Quebec is lower than most provinces, reflecting the language and cultural differences. Quebec francophones are the least mobile. One should note that 62 per cent of

Quebec francophones, as defined by mother tongue, do not speak English according to the 2001 Census;[18]

- transfers to individuals from the federal government such as Employment Insurance discourage mobility but the evidence is not conclusive;
- the evidence on the effect of migration induced by resource rents is mixed;
- Quebec, Saskatchewan, Manitoba and Newfoundland are the main provinces of out-migration, and British Columbia, Ontario and Alberta are the main destination provinces or recipients of in-migration (Cousineau & Vaillancourt, 2000: 150), with Alberta being the main recipient province in recent years;
- inter-provincial migration has declined consistently from 1.94 per cent of the population in 1970 to 1.12 per cent in 1995 (Cousineau & Vaillancourt, 2000: 149). Although the precise reasons for that decline have not been sorted out, contributing factors could include:
  - aging of the population with fewer older persons moving;
  - increased proportion of two-earner families which complicates moving;
  - decrease in family size which can facilitate moving but which also means the numbers reflect fewer movers;
  - increased international immigration which may be a substitute for inter-provincial mobility;
  - increased government transfers and regional development policies
  - reduced income differentials across the provinces.

What per cent of Canada's labour force faces barriers to mobility? Grady and Macmillan (2007b: 5) report that 11.1 per cent of the labour force belongs to the 39 occupations regulated in Ontario, whose list is similar to that of other provinces. The top ten ones are listed in Table 11.2. It is interesting to note how the top five occupations account for 2/3[rds] of the total of regulated employment. The 11[th] one, dental assistant, represents only 1.4 per cent of this employment. Grady and Macmillan (2007b: 26) note that there are no studies that have examined as such the impact of regulatory barriers on inter-provincial mobility. Gomez and Gunderson (2007) report that there is some American evidence that occupational licensing reduces inter-state labour mobility. Using a cost-benefit framework, they argue however that inter-provincial barriers to mobility affect "a minuscule number of workers and with a potential wage increase only being a fraction of the overall wage, it should not be surprising that any credible estimates of the

---

18 Statistics Canada (2001) Langue Maternelle Détaillée Quebec, No. 97F0007XCB 2001009 in catalogue.

economic cost of barriers to labour mobility are likely to be minuscule" (p. 28).

**Table 11.2: Occupation (by decreasing order of share of regulated occupations)**

| | % of regulated employment | Cumulative% of regulated employment |
|---|---|---|
| Teachers (primary and secondary) | 23.9 | 23.9 |
| Nurses | 13.4 | 37.3 |
| Engineers | 10.4 | 47.7 |
| Accountants (CMA, CGA, CA) | 9.9 | 57.6 |
| Engineering technicians | 9.2 | 66.7 |
| Physicians | 3.8 | 70.5 |
| Lawyers | 3.7 | 74.2 |
| Real estate agents | 2.9 | 77.1 |
| Practical nurses | 2.7 | 79.8 |
| Social workers | 2.7 | 82.5 |

Source: Grady & MacMillan (2007) Table 1, p. 7.

One should note, however, that this perspective neglects two points. First tradespersons (plumbers, etc.) are not included in this estimate of impaired mobility. If one includes trades, then the percentage of Canadian workers who might face mobility impairment is closer to 20 per cent.[19] Why? Because while the AIT says that tradespersons with the Red Seal certificate can work in their occupation across Canada, most do not have this certificate. They only have a provincial certificate as required when they first began to work in a specific province; it is not valid in another province. Second, the inability of a professional to provide a service to a client in another jurisdiction, even though he or she does not move, is not taken into account.[20]

The AIT contains provisions with respect to a framework agreement on labour mobility. These are based in part on mutual recognition of qualification. One requirement in this respect was for various professional associations to agree on a Mutual Recognition Agreement (MRA) in 2001. This appears to have been done in all cases, fifty or so.[21] An example of this for surveyors shows that provincial associations do make a reasonable attempt to harmonise requirements but do not uni-

19 Roman Staranczack, personal communication, 2 April, 2007.

20 For example, a company may wish to use its own engineer located in its headquarters to provide advice on matters in another province.

21 http://www.ait-aci.ca/index_en/progress.htm.

formise[22] them (CCLS, 2002). A survey of relevant regulatory bodies was conducted by provincial governments in 2004. It shows that:

- 65 per cent of applicants during the October 1st 2003 – September 30th 2004 period had their credentials recognised under an MRA;
- 8 per cent of regulators reported that residency was still a requirement to obtain registration with a professional body, a violation of the AIT;
- 18 per cent of regulators still need to change their regulation in late 2004 to comply with the AIT or their MRA.

Depending on the perspective one takes, this is good or too little progress. The date for full compliance with the MRA requirements has now been set as April 2009 by the Council of the Federation.[23]

Also, as of January 2007 (Grady and Macmillan, 2007: 11, table 2), out of 50 occupations, sixteen occupations have MRA signed by all provinces, thirty by most (one or two missing) and four (community urban planner; hunting guides; podiatrists/chiropodists; social workers) by none of the provinces. Some see this as progress while others argue that the MRA are little more than transparency agreements. Prior to the AIT, an individual had to check with the appropriate regulatory body in the province he or she was considering moving to. That regulatory body would often decide on a case-by-case basis whether and/or to what extent that individual was qualified. To the extent that individuals now know what the requirements are in different provinces, that is progress. However, it does not give you the automatic right to work in your occupation across the country.

Grady and Macmillan (2007: 13) indicate that there have been only twenty-two disputes under Chapter 7 or roughly two per year since the AIT was signed; "this is not a very large number of disputes" (p. 13) they note. But perhaps individuals do not access the dispute resolution process to settle labour mobility issues because it's too cumbersome with no guarantee of any panel recommendation being accepted. The most interesting ones are by respectively the Certified General Accountants (CGAs) of Manitoba against Ontario and the CGAs of New Brunswick against Québec. In both cases, the AIT was used to widen access to the task of auditing public companies, a task reserved for Chartered Accountants (CAs) in both provinces.[24] In 2001, Ontario was found in

22 A total of 392 bodies out of 425 contacted, responded, Forum of Labour Market Ministers, 2005.

23 www.councilofthefederation.ca/pdfs/Competitiveness_Trade_Aug8_EN.pdf.

24 http://www.ait-aci.ca/index_en/dispute.htm.

breach of the agreement and by 2005 had modified its regulations but CGAs still cannot do public accounting in Ontario.

In the case of Québec, the complaint was only lodged in 2004 and Québec found in breach in 2005; in 2007, it is studying how to respond. What is interesting is that the issue was not the right of practice by CGAs in one province but the right of CGAs to do the same work in one province as in another.

The most important irritant in the area of inter-provincial labour mobility both in terms of numbers and notoriety was access to construction work in Québec by Ontario firms and thus workers. At the root of the issue is the divergence in the regulatory approaches between the two provinces. In Quebec, it is much more difficult to enter into the construction business, either as a contractor or a construction worker than in Ontario or in other provinces. For example, tradespersons have to be qualified by Quebec authorities before they can be hired. This means, among other requirements, belonging to a trade union, passing a written exam, and proving they have worked a certain minimum number of hours in a year. This applies to both Québec and non Québec residents. Consequently, Quebec claims that its provisions do not discriminate against workers or contractors from Ontario.

Gomez and Gunderson summarise this dispute as follows:

> This had been a long-standing and contentious issue between Ontario and Quebec with Quebec shutting out Ontario construction workers saying that they do not meet Quebec training standards. In the late 1990s, this led to their being six times as many Quebec construction workers in Ontario than Ontario workers in Quebec. The culminating incident was the Quebec government excluding Ontario contractors from bidding on the Hull casino. Ontario argued that such restrictions were designed to limit competition from out-of-province firms, and instituted the Fairness is a Two-Way Street Act in 1999 which resulted in hundreds of Quebec workers being dismissed from Ontario construction projects. As well, informal pressures were used such as the assigning of more inspectors in Ontario […] Also, the Ontario government encouraged municipalities, school boards and hospitals to voluntarily not accept bids from Quebec contractors. This reminds us that informal pressures can be as important as formal rules and regulations (p. 10).

Interestingly, this issue was not resolved by using the AIT. Ontario did not use the AIT to resolve its dispute with Quebec simply because there is no way to enforce a panel recommendation.[25] It was the use of retaliation by Ontario against Québec practices through the Fairness is a

[25] In 2002, Quebec initially launched a dispute against Ontario's legislation under the AIT; it was withdrawn in 2006.

Two-Way Street Act[26] as well as the establishment of administrative practices that mirrored those in Quebec. Such practices were lifted in 2006 following the signing of the Agreement on Labour Mobility and Recognition of Qualifications, Skills and Work Experience in the Construction Industry (2006) between the Government of Ontario and the Government of Québec.[27] The recently signed Quebec-Ontario construction agreement did nothing to change the regulatory regime in Quebec. Basically, it allowed contractors who have work in Quebec to bring in their qualified workers under certain conditions.

Provincial policies can also significantly affect labour mobility. For example, since provinces are responsible for post-secondary education, they can levy differential tuition fees on out-of-province students. Québec is the only province to do so at present. Also Québec requires all professionals not schooled in French to pass a French language test before they can be licensed to practice in Québec (Office québécois de la langue française, Art. 35).

Finally Gomez and Gunderson (2007: 16) report on provincial policies to retain skilled labour:

> New Brunswick instituted a plan that rebates 50 per cent of the tuition cost paid for any university or college to a global maximum of $10,000 and an annual maximum of $2000 per year, with claims being allowed for up to 20 years after graduation. The education does not have to be acquired in New Brunswick but the beneficiaries have to pay taxes in New Brunswick, the rationale being to attract higher educated youths from other provinces as well as retaining New Brunswick grads. Manitoba has a policy of rebating tuition for Manitoba graduates who stay in the province for five years after graduation and Saskatchewan offers a one-year post-secondary tax credit for graduates who stay in the province.

## 4. The politics

We first present some background events and subsequently turn to each market. The first attempt to revise substantially the constitutional/legal framework pertaining to internal markets in Canada occurs in 1981 during the negotiations to renew the Constitution. This constitutional round resulted from the election of the Parti Québécois in Québec in November 1976, the holding of a referendum on sovereignty in May 1980 (which was lost by the secessionists 60-40) and the promise made during the referendum campaign for a renewed federalism by the federal

---

26 http://www.labor.gov.on.ca/english/news/2002/02-08b.html.

27 http://www.labour.gov.on.ca/english/news/2006/06-oqclm.html; http://www.labour.gov.on.ca/english/about/ontque/oqlma_toc.html.

Prime Minister. Shortly after the referendum, a First Ministers' conference – the mechanism used to consult the provinces in all attempts to repatriate the constitution – ended in failure in September 1980. Prime Minister Trudeau soon announced, however, that the federal government would nonetheless proceed unilaterally with repatriation, as well as with the introduction of a Charter of Rights and Freedoms and a constitutional amending formula. All provinces except Ontario and New Brunswick initially objected to the federal proposals. Manitoba, Québec and Newfoundland asked their courts of appeal whether provincial consent was a constitutional requirement for a request to the British Parliament to change the Constitution in the ways contemplated by the federal government. The courts in Manitoba and Québec said provincial consent was not a requirement; Newfoundland's court took the opposite view. Finally, in September 1981, the Supreme Court ruled that while the federal government's request to the British Parliament did not legally require provincial consent, unilateral action went against Canada's constitutional conventions. Ottawa, said the Court, should obtain a 'substantial degree' of provincial consent. The federal government respected the Court's decision and returned to negotiations in November 1981. Nine provinces came to an agreement with the federal government; this was seen as representing a 'substantial degree' of provincial consent. One province did not agree: Québec. Despite this lack of agreement, the federal government proceeded. On April 17, 1982, in a ceremony in Ottawa, Queen Elizabeth II officially proclaimed the 1982 Constitution Act.

In the 1984 federal electoral campaign, the leader of the federal Conservatives promised that, if elected, he would reach an honorable constitutional agreement with Québec. He was elected, and constitutional discussions between First Ministers were renewed in 1985. After extensive discussion, in April 1987 the First Ministers drafted the so-called 'Meech Lake Accord'. In order to be adopted the Meech Lake Accord had to be ratified by Parliament and by the legislatures of all the provinces. Once the resolution was supported by one legislature, the other legislatures had three years to ratify it. Québec's National Assembly was the first to pass the resolution of approval on June 23, 1987. Ratification by the remaining nine provincial legislatures therefore had to occur before June 23, 1990. This was not done by two provinces.

The failure of the Accord was interpreted by many Quebeckers as an outright rejection of their aspirations and hopes by English Canada. The immediate result was a sharp rise in the support for sovereignty reported in polls, reaching a high of 60 per cent at one point. The political picture nationally was also altered by the rejection of Meech Lake. From the failure of Meech in June 1990 to the spring of 1992, yet another series of extensive public consultations as well as negotiations between First Ministers were held. The end product of this process was the Charlottetown Accord.

In October 1992, for the first time in Canadian history, a national referendum was held to decide whether Canada's constitution should be modified. The Charlottetown Accord was rejected by 54 per cent of those who voted. It is in this context that the next sections must be read.

### *4.1. Goods and services*

In the 1980-1981 constitutional negotiations, a revised article 121 was put forward by the federal government. The main clause (out of four) read:

> (1) Neither Canada nor a province shall by law or practice discriminate in a manner that unduly impedes the operation of the Canadian economic union, directly or indirectly, on the basis of the province or territory of residence or former residence of a person, on the basis of the province or territory of origin or destinations of goods, service or capital or on the basis of the province or territory into which or from which goods, services or capital are imported or exported.

Article 6 of the 1982 Constitution Act presented in section 2.3 of this paper is the only part of this economic union clause that was actually adopted, as part of the Charter of Rights and freedoms that covers individuals.

In 1991, a new section 121 was proposed by the federal government along with a section 91A (Trebilcock and Behboodi, 1995: 27-29). However, the negotiation process led to a watering down of the proposed section 121 which was already quite weak such that economic interests denounced it. In the end, the Charlottetown accord did not include it either but was accompanied by a political accord to refer to the First minister conference the study of how to strengthen the Canadian common market. This work in 1993-1994 led to the AIT. Thus the failure of the Meech Lake and Charlottetown accords heightened interest in an agreement on internal trade at a time just before upcoming 1994 provincial election in Québec when Canada could not be seen to have failed another time.[28]

Doern and MacDonald (1999) have prepared an excellent study of the negotiations of the AIT. Some of the key points they make in concluding are that:

---

[28] The AIT was seen as strengthening the federalist side in the 1994 provincial election in Québec.

- AIT is the result of a macro multi-policy field approach with the trade policy field ascendant at the time (fresh from the approval of CUFTA in 1989 and NAFTA in 1993) and the regional policy and federal-provincial policy fields on the defensive. Indeed, in the mind of the chair of the Macdonald commission who recommended free trade with the USA in 1986, this would be a backdoor way to achieve free trade *within* Canada;
- "The core of the internal-trade agreement was the battle over general rules versus exceptions and legitimate objectives. In short, it centered on two competing visions among the participating governments: those who saw it primarily as a trade agreement and those who tended to see it more as an agreement on governance in a federation (Doern and MacDonald, 1999: 155)";
- Discussions differed from issue to issue with procurement issues being more political while labour mobility was more of a work in progress approach. One common feature was the relative lack of involvement of interest groups, except for the business community;
- The dispute resolution mechanisms reflect the fact that this is a political, non-constitutional, court-avoiding agreement. It is weak and slow.

Ten years after the AIT came into force, an interesting development has been the signing by Alberta and British Columbia in 2006 of the B.C.-Alberta Trade, Investment, and Labour Mobility Agreement known as TILMA. It had been preceded in 2003 by the Alberta-B.C Protocol of Cooperation.[29] Why was this agreement signed in 2006 and not before? The answer is that Alberta, a province with a tradition of conservative market oriented provincial governments, has traditionally supported open markets and was frustrated at the failure to make greater progress under the AIT. The presence since 1989 in British Columbia of a government more favorable to free markets than in the past meant that they could negotiate a bilateral agreement with that neighbouring province. As a result, their agreement is different from the AIT. TILMA is comprehensive, with the few exceptions clearly listed. It adopts the principle of mutual recognition. It has an effective dispute settlement mechanism with the possibility of a monetary penalty of up to 5 million dollars. Signed in April 2006, it commences on April 1, 2007, with a transition period to April 2009 before it comes into full effect.[30] The agreement creates a more open, competitive economy where goods, services and investments move freely between the two provinces with in

[29] http://www.iir.gov.ab.ca/trade_policy/documents/TILMA_FactSheet-Oct06.pdf.

[30] http://www.gov.ab.ca/acn/200609/204517FC0FB89-E642-178B-BCE2F24E8F2CA-50D.html.

particular: occupational certifications of workers and businesses registration in one province automatically recognised in the other; coverage of all sectors and harmonisation of standards; access to government contracts; and creating a clear, comprehensive and enforceable dispute avoidance and dispute resolution mechanism.

TILMA is criticised by some as constraining the possible interventions of governments in various markets (Gould, 2007). But it can be seen as a challenge to the rest of Canada by two provinces that account for almost 30 per cent of its GDP[31] to get serious about internal trade. And indeed in their 2007 August meeting, Canadian premiers resolved to develop an effective enforcement mechanism for the AIT.[32] Saskatchewan, after examining the issue[33] chose not to join TILMA but rather to strengthen the AIT.[34]

Finally we note that the Senate Committee on Banking, Trade and Commerce has been conducting hearings since June 2006 on the issue of inter-provincial barriers to trade. An examination of the proceedings as of September 1st 2007 shows that the *usual suspects* appeared and held to their usual positions. Two points to note are the interest of the committee in TILMA and its relevance or not for other provinces and their struggle to figure out how quantitatively important trade barriers are.[35]

### *4.2. Capital markets*

The first in-depth discussion of a national securities commission for Canada appears to have been in the 1966 report of the Royal Commission on Banking and Finance (Porter Commission). This report noted there was wide interest among brokers, dealers and corporation lawyers in more uniform legislation across Canada. Even where the legislation was similar, the discretionary powers allowed the different provincial commissions, could result in important differences in administrative practices.

Consequently, the Commission suggested that the federal government should encourage the development of uniform standards of secu-

31 http://cansim2.statcan.ca/cgi-in/cnsmcgi.pgm?Lang=E&SP_Action=Result&SP_ID=3012 &SP_TYP=5&SP_Sort=1.

32 http://www.councilofthefederation.ca/pdfs/Competitiveness_Trade_Aug8_EN.pdf.

33 http://www.gr.gov.sk.ca/Default.aspx?DN=2ba2b9b9-817e-43f9-bfc3-ce42c19c74e3.

34 http://www.gov.sk.ca/news?newsId=ebd5e9bd-7b8e-46ca-9e3a-e738abef91a7.

35 http://www.parl.gc.ca/common/Committee_SenProceed.asp?Language=E&Parl=39&Ses=1&comm_id=3.

rity legislation in Canada, noting that a federal agency would establish uniform standards.

In 1967, the Ontario Securities and Exchange Commission put forward a proposal for a Canadian Securities Commission (CANSEC)[36] but nothing happened. Banwell (1969: 21-22) noted that 'there is a necessity for national administration and regulation, and such a scheme appears most readily attainable though co-operation between the governments'. In 1973, a study was commissioned (Anisman and Hogg, 1979): it proposed setting up a federal commission with primacy in interprovincial and international securities matters. Again, nothing was done.

The issue was again raised in a study for the Royal Commission on the Economic Union and Development Prospects for Canada (the MacDonald Commission) by Courchene (1986). Courchene argued that "one prerequisite for achieving market efficiency is to ensure that the market is truly national in scope" (p. 154) even if, "because of the dominance of the TSE [Toronto Stock Exchange] and the OSC [Ontario Securities Commission], securities legislation tended to be more national in scope than would be expected from a decentralised regulatory process" (p. 156). Nonetheless, in the end the possibility of national securities regulation was not even mentioned in the main body of the MacDonald Report.

In 1991, the issue was mentioned in the federal throne speech (a statement of policy intent by the government for the next parliamentary session). Opposition was soon heard from the Western provinces and from the Investment Dealers Association of Canada (IDA). Tse (1994, p. 428), noted that Ontario and all western provinces "have gone to the extent of enacting uniform securities legislation and a further group of Uniform Act Policies". In contrast to Banwell (1969), however, who thought that what was needed was essentially more inter-provincial cooperation, Tse (1994) went on to argue that the existence of such legislation actually proves the need for a federal body because, despite the cooperative efforts of the provinces, significant gaps remained in the regulatory structure. Nonetheless, Tse (1994: 430) concluded that on constitutional grounds there remained a clear need for "some provincial securities regulation. To the extent that securities are property and fall within the enumerated head of property and civil rights in the province, the general rule must be that securities are more properly a provincial concern."

Building on a 1993 Atlantic Premiers meeting which raised the issue, work on a possible Memorandum of Understanding (MOU) was

[36] http://www.crawfordpanel.ca/BackgroundPaperB.pdf.

carried out in 1994. This lay the foundation for the February 1996 federal throne speech to state explicitly that "the government is prepared to work with interested provinces towards the development of a Canadian Securities Commission." Mention of this proposal in the throne speech elicited a mixed reaction from the provinces. The Ontario Securities Commission supported it, the Québec Securities Commission opposed it, and the Alberta and BC commissions had reservations. To some extent, this proposal seems to have reflected the explicit support for this idea that had been expressed a few months earlier by two of the most prominent industry groups – the IDA, which had changed its position since 1991, and the Canadian Bankers Association (CBA). Again, nothing was done.

In early 2002, the issue arose anew when a review of the Ontario Securities Act "recommend(ed.) that the provinces, territories and federal government work towards the creation of a single securities regulator with responsibility for the capital markets across Canada" (Ontario Securities Commission, 2002). Submissions to the committee preparing this review had emphasised the importance of regulatory costs and the need for a single voice for Canada on the international scene.[37] Repeating their earlier roles, the TSE argued for a single national regulator, while Québec's SEC again said no.

The federal minister of Finance government gave new life to this idea by creating a Wise Person's Committee. In December 2003, it recommended that the federal government enacts a new Canadian Securities Act that would provide a comprehensive scheme of capital markets regulation for Canada. The Act would be administered by a single Canadian Securities Commission consisting of nine Commissioners (two from each of Ontario and Quebec, one from each of British Columbia and Alberta, two from the remaining provinces and territories and one at large. The Commission's head office would be located in the National Capital Region while strong, functionally empowered regional offices would be set up in Vancouver, Calgary, Winnipeg, Toronto, Montreal and Halifax.

These recommendations were justified mainly by arguing that the structure of the capital market in Canada is a national one, not a provincial one and that Canada is the exception in the world amongst industrialised countries in not having a national SEC, making the interface with the international regulatory environment more difficult. Reactions to

[37] Estimates from the British Financial Service Agencies show SEC costs for 2000 of $493 million for Canada, $497 million for the UK, and $235 million for Australia, with employees numbering 3,780 in Canada, 2,765 in the UK, and 2,113 in Australia (Ontario Securities Commission, 2002).

these recommendations were similar to those observed in the past: the Ontario Securities Commission[38] endorsed them while other provinces and in particular Alberta, British Columbia and Quebec, regrouped under the label 'Provincial-Territorial Securities Initiative' did not, putting forward in September 2004:

- A 'passport system' for securities regulation, resulting in a single window of access to capital markets in participating provinces and territories, to be established by August 2005;
- Highly harmonised, streamlined and simplified securities laws to be implemented by the end of 2006.

Progress has been made since this agreement was signed. By the end of 2007, all legislative amendments are expected to have been made in the signatory provinces.

The latest substantive contribution to this saga is the Crawford panel report published in 2006. It was created by the Ontario government. It argues that the passport system can be seen at best as a first step in harmonisation leading to a single regulator. It argues that:

> Under the Panel's proposed framework for a Canadian Securities Commission, a single Canadian securities act and rules would apply and be interpreted consistently across all participating jurisdictions. This would reduce compliance costs for issuers, create certainty for capital market participants, assure investors that Canada is an attractive and safe place in which to invest capital, and ensure that enforcement investigations and proceedings are conducted efficiently and predictably.

In view of the extensive rationalisation of Canadian stock that has taken place in the last ten years, the lack of resolution of this issue is hard to understand. The Vancouver and Alberta exchanges, where junior stocks were traded, merged into the Canadian Venture Exchange (CDNX) (the smaller Winnipeg exchange joined CDNX in March 2000). The TSE thus became the sole Canadian exchange for senior stocks, giving up derivative trading to the Montréal stock exchange in exchange for its delisting of these stocks. A small market for junior stocks was also kept in Montréal. In 2001 these junior stocks were moved to the CDNX, which was then taken over in the fall of 2001 by the TSE. Regulation may not have been rationalised (let alone nationalised) but securities trading, it seems, has moved a long way in this direction. Hence this *cri du coeur* by Purdy Crawford: "After 40 years of discussion and study, market participants that we consulted hope that our political leaders will finally find a way to agree that a single regulator can ensure more efficient and competitive capital markets for the

---

38 http://www.osc.gov.on.ca/Media/Speeches/sp_20040420_db-ciri.jsp.

benefit of all Canadians" (Crawford Panel, 2006). This appeal was heard in Ottawa; the March 2007 federal budget states:

> In rapidly evolving, intensely competitive global capital markets, Canada simply cannot afford 13 securities acts and securities regulators. Currently, Canada is the only jurisdiction not represented by a national regulator in the International Organisation of Securities Commissions. In order to remain competitive and fully engaged internationally, Canada must act now and move towards a common securities regulator. (Department of Finance, 2007)

Given the numerous past statements of intentions, whether this will be done is another matter. One argument raised in September 2007 in favor of this change is that fragmented and thus weak and inefficient securities law enforcement creates a Canadian discount (or at least contributes to it), thus increasing the cost of capital in Canada and thus reducing potential output.[39]

Finally, one should note that a number of provinces offer special tax incentives to residents who purchase financial instruments (shares, etc.) from issuers who are active or will invest in their province of residence, following the pattern initially set by the Québec Stock Savings Plan introduced in 1979 and the first Labour Sponsored Venture Capital Fund (Fonds de Solidarité) created in 1983 (Vaillancourt, 1997). For example, various Labour Sponsored Venture Capital Funds (LSVCF), which grant personal income tax credits for investments by individuals in funds that will invest within the borders of their provinces to help save/create employment, emerged, with as usual, Québec leading the way. Such funds are clearly a new source of fragmentation of the Canadian capital market (Vaillancourt, 1997) – the last thing needed, it might be argued, in the face of the increasing integration of that market within the American market. Nonetheless, there seems to be no evidence that variability across provinces in access to financial instruments such as rights offerings (Mohindra, 2002) matters in any measurable way, and such measures have not given rise to any serious policy debate.

The current structure of the LSVCF market makes it difficult for individual investors to diversify their portfolio regionally or by type of investment in a tax effective way. It also puts the small firms of a province with a monopoly fund in a weaker bargaining position than they would in a multi-fund province. Finally, the supply of venture capital may not be optimally distributed across regions, sectors and firms due to tax-induced distortions.

---

[39] See Chase, 2007. This article summarises the findings of Coffee, 2007.

## *4.3. Labour mobility*

Chapter 7 of the AIT was prepared by the Forum of Labour Market Ministers at the request of the Council of Ministers on Internal Trade. Provinces had different views on what approach to take, depending on both ideology and mobility patterns. The federal government was particularly keen on harmonised national standards for qualifications following the Canadian Labour Force Development Board lead. But facing strong provincial opposition and with education a provincial responsibility, the federal government opted for the MRA approach, referred to by Doern and MacDonald as the driver's licence approach (1999: 107).

In 1999, as part of the Social Union Framework Agreement, signed by all provinces except Québec, labour mobility was given a new impulsion.[40] Section 2 of the agreement states that:

> Governments will ensure that no new barriers to mobility are created in new social policy initiatives.
>
> Governments will eliminate, within three years, any residency-based policies or practices which constrain access to post-secondary education, training, health and social services and social assistance unless they can be demonstrated to be reasonable and consistent with the principles of the Social Union Framework.
>
> Accordingly, sector Ministers will submit annual reports to the Ministerial Council identifying residency-based barriers to access and providing action plans to eliminate them.
>
> Governments are also committed to ensure, by July 1, 2001, full compliance with the mobility provisions of the Agreement on Internal Trade by all entities subject to those provisions, including the requirements for mutual recognition of occupational qualifications and for eliminating residency requirements for access to employment opportunities (Canadian Federal/Provincial/Territorial Ministerial Council on Social Policy Renewal, 2001).

In a 2003 review, the Canadian Federal/Provincial/Territorial Ministerial Council on Social Policy Renewal finds that good progress that has been made on promoting the mobility of Canadians within the country.

One must note here that the picture painted in that report is somewhat at odds with the situation described above. This can be explained by the official nature of these documents. In particular, the Mutual Recognition Agreements may not be as efficient in ensuring labour mobility as they may appear to be In 2006 and 2007 (see above), the Council of the Federation (2004, 2006) has committed itself to improve

40 http://www.hrsdc.gc.ca/en/hip/hrp/corporate/labourmobility/labourmobility.shtml.

labour mobility in Canada.This would probably not be necessary if reality agreed with the above statements.

## 5. Conclusion

From the review of the evidence presented above, one can conclude that:

- *mobility of labour* has been enhanced in Canada since 1982 and more so since 2001 with a combination of Charter rights, political agreements and mutual recognition agreements with the later two playing a more significant role. Overall, impediments to labour mobility appear to be relatively unimportant but one should note the outstanding issue of inter-provincial provision of employee and professional services;
- *free trade in goods* and to a lesser extent services exists in Canada with governments acting as purchasers being historically the principal culprit in implementing restrictive trade practices. Markets have become more integrated since 1995 and overall restrictions have little impact except for some food products;
- *mobility of capital* is high in Canada due in part to the existence of large nation-wide banks but the existing SEC structure is inefficient and increases the cost of raising capital for firms and/or reduces the access of investors to financial instruments.

One interesting question is: why was it possible to carry out some reforms in the case of labour and goods and services markets while there has been little success in the case of capital markets? The answer we believe is a combination of pre existing institutions and legal instruments:

- in the case of *labour*, there were not many restrictions or government policies preventing labour mobility in place and the legal instrument, was in part a constitutional one. That said, the most important barrier could only be undone by political bargaining;
- in the case of *goods and services*, procurement policies of governments and their public enterprises are an explicit policy tool that they were reluctant to abandon while the legal instrument was a combination of court judgments that had little impact and thus spawned the AIT having some impact;
- in the case of *capital markets*, there are well established semi autonomous provincial bodies which are self funded or even a source of revenues while the federal government is treading on uncertain constitutional grounds. Perhaps a solution similar to that used in the case of social security with both a Canada Pension Plan (outside Quebec)

and a Quebec Pension Plan, with two SEC, both autonomous but *de facto* harmonised could be considered.[41] Provinces outside Quebec could be brought onside with a solution similar to the one used when implementing the Harmonised sales tax[42] where lost revenues resulting from the replacement of a provincial sales tax at a higher rate by a combined federal and provincial VAT (8 per cent) were made over a four year period up by a special federal transfer.

The reader will have noted the role that Québec and the federalist / sovereignist issue plays in these matters. Interestingly, the AIT has been supported by successive Quebec governments whether sovereignists or federalists. For the sovereignist Parti Québécois, the AIT is just another international agreement and proves that the province can negotiate with Canada. For the federalists, the AIT is a way of strengthening the economic union. Presumably, the autonomist provincial party in Québec, the ADQ, will also support the AIT as an example of how to negotiate with Canada. But none of these parties favors abolishing the Québec SEC.

## References

Anisman, P. & Hogg, W. (1979), Constitutional Aspects of Federal Securities Legislation, in *Proposals for a Securities Market Law for Canada*, Background Papers, Vol. 3, pp. 135-200, Minister of Supply and Services, Ottawa.

Banwell, Peter T. (1969) Proposals for a National Securities Commission, *Queen's Intramural Law Journal* 1(3).

Beaulieu, M. & Bellemare, G. (2000) Canadian Stock market and North American Integration, *Isuma* 1(1).

Bernier, Y., Roy, N., Pentland, C. & Soberman, D. (1986) The Concept of Economic Union in International and Constitutional Law, in *Perspectives on the Canadian Economic Union* (Mark Krasnick, ed.), University of Toronto Press, Toronto, pp. 35-154.

Bird, M. & Vaillancourt, F. (2005) The Interregional Incidence of Public Budgets in Federations: Measurement Issues, Evidence from Canada and Policy Relevance, in: *Spatial Aspects of Federative Systems* (G Farber and N Otter, eds) Research Institute for Public Administration, Speyer, Germany, pp. 73-111.

Bird, M. & Vaillancourt, F. (2007) Reconciling Diversity with Equality: The Role of Intergovernmetal Fiscal Arrangements in Maintaining an Effective

[41] Evidence on investor behaviour supports this dichotomy (Cumming, Kaul & Mehrotra, 2003b).

[42] http://www.cra-arc.gc.ca/tax/business/topics/gst/menu-e.html.

State in Canada, in Bird, R. & Ebel, R. (eds.) *Fiscal Fragmentation in Decentralised Countries*, Edward Elgar, Northampton, pp. 49-88.

Boadway, R. (1996) Comment on Whalley in Howitt, P. (ed.) *The Implications of Knowledge Based Growth for Micro Economic Policies*, University of Calgary Press, Calgary, pp. 178-186.

Boissonneault, G. (2003) The Relationship between Financial Markets and Economic Growth: Implications for Canada, Research study prepared for the Wise Persons'Committee, Vancouver, October. http://www.wise-averties.ca/reports/WPC_2.pdf

Canadian Chamber of Commerce (2004) Obstacles to Free Trade in Canada: A Study on Internal Trade Barriers. http://www.chamber.ca/cmslib/general/InternalTrade041108.pdf

CCLS., Canadian Council of Land Surveyors (2002) An Agreement Regarding The Mutual Recognition of Registered/Licensed Surveyors in the Jurisdictions of Canada, The United States of America, and The United Mexican States, NAFTA Mutual Recognition Document, version 7. http://www.ccls-cag.ca/files/NAFTA%20Mutual%20Recog%20Eng.pdf

Canadian Federal/Provincial/Territorial Ministerial Council on Social Policy Renewal (2001), *Report* to the Ministerial Council on Social Policy Renewal, Sufa Mobility Commitments.http://www.socialunion.gc.ca/sufa-mob_e.htm

Canadian Federal/Provincial/Territorial Ministerial Council on Social Policy Renewal (2003), Three-year Review Report of the Social Union Framework Agreement (SUFA), June.

Chase, St. (2007) Lack of Single Watchdog Costs Billions, Ottawa Told, Globe and Mail, 17 September, p. B1.

Conference Board of Canada (2006) Death by a Thousand Paper Cuts. http://www.conferenceboard.ca/documents.asp?rnext=1653

Council of the Federation (2004) Second Progress Report on Internal Trade Workplan, Fredericton, August.

Council of the Federation (2006) Third Progress Report on Internal Trade Workplan, Quebec City – June 2005, January.

Cousineau, J. and Vaillancourt, F. (2001) Regional Disparities, Mobility and Labour Markets in Canada, in Riddell, W.C. & St. Hilaire, F. (eds.) *Adapting Public Policy to a Labour Market in Transition*, Institute for Research on Public Policy, Montéral, pp. 143-174

Copeland, Br. (1998) Interprovincial Barriers to Trade: An updated review of the Evidence, Vancouver, mimeo, 39 pages.

Courchene, J. (1986) *Economic Management and the Division of Powers*, University of Toronto Press for Royal Commission on the Economic Union and Development Prospects for Canada (McDonald Commission), Toronto.

Crawford, P. (2006) *Blueprint for a Canadian Securities Commission*, Crawford Panel On A Single Canadian Securities Regulator http://www. crawfordpanel.ca/Crawford_Panel_final_paper.pdf; http://www.crawfordpanel.ca/news2006.html

Cumming, D., Kaul, A. & Mehrotra, C. (2003a) Fragmentation and the Canadian Stock Markets, Research Study Prepared for the Wise Persons' Committee, Vancouver, October.

Cumming, D., Kaul, A. & Mehrotra, C. (2003b) Provincial Preferences in Private Equity, Research Study Prepared for the Wise Persons' Committee, Vancouver, September. http://www.wise-averties.ca/reports/html/3E_provincial/index.html

De Mestral, A. & Winter, J. (2001) Mobility Rights in the European Union and Canada, *McGill Law Journal* 46, pp. 979-1009.

Department of Finance Canada (2007) *Creating a Canadian Advantage in Global Capital Markets, Aspire to a Stronger, Better Canada, Canada's New Government*, Budget 2007, March. http://www.budget.gc.ca/2007/themes/bkcmae.html#return_1

Doern, B. & MacDonald, M. (1999) *Free-Trade Federalism: Negotiating the Canadian Agreement on Internal Trade*, University of Toronto Press, Toronto, pp. xiv &186.

Forum of Labour Market Ministers (2005) Report Of Survey Results: Inter-Provincial Labour Mobility in Canada 2004/*05*, May. http://www.ait-aci.ca/en/reports/01_10_2006/NATIONAL%20REPORT%20-%20APPROVED%20VERSION%20MAY%2018-2005.pdf

Gould, E. (2007) Asking for Ttrouble. The Trade, Investment and Labour Mobility Agreement, Canadian Centre for Policy Alternatives, BC Office, February.

Gomez, R. & Gunderson, M. (2007) Barriers to the Inter-Provincial Mobility of Labour Industry Canada and HRSDC, Toronto, mimeo, 25 p., prepared for the 'Internal Trade: Opportunities and Challenges' roundtable, March 30, 2007, Ottawa.

Governments of Alberta & British Columbia (2006) Alberta-British Columbia Trade, Investment and Labour Mobility Agreement (TILMA) http://www.iir.gov.ab.ca/trade_policy/TILMA_Agreement.asp

Governments of Alberta & British Columbia (2003), Alberta-British Columbia Trade, Investment and Labour Mobility, Protocol of Cooperation.

Grady, P. & MacMillan, K. (2007a) Inter-provincial Barriers to Internal trade in Goods, Services and Flows of Capital: Policy, Knowledge Gaps and Research Issues mimeo, 22 p., prepared for the 'Internal Trade: Opportunities and Challenges' roundtable, March 30, 2007, Ottawa. http://global-economics.ca/report_internal_trade.pdf

Grady, P. & MacMillan, K. (2007b) Inter-provincial Barriers to Labour Mobility in Canada: Policy, Knowledge Gaps and Research Issues mimeo, Industry Canada and HRSDC, Ottawa, 35 pages prepared for the 'Internal Trade: Opportunities and Challenges' roundtable, March, 2007, Ottawa. http://global-economics.ca/report.labour_mobility.pdf

Lee, T. & Trebilcock, M.J (1987) Economic Mobility and Constitutional Reform, *University of Toronto Law Journal*, n° 37, pp. 268-317.

Lenihan, D. When a legitimate Objective Hits an Unnecessary Obstacle in Getting There, An Assessment of the Agreement on Internal Trade, Trebilcock, M. & Schwanen, D. (eds.), C.D. Howe Institute, Toronto, pp. 98-118.

Mohindra, N. (2002) Securities Market Regulations in Canada, Fraser Institute Critical Issues Bulletin, Vancouver. http://www.fraserinstitute.org/COMMERCE.WEB/product_files/market.pdf

Office Québecois de la langue française, Charte de la langue française, article 35. http://www.olf.gouv.qc.ca/charte/charte/clflgparap.html

Ontario Securities Commission (2002) LLP Five Year review Committee Draft Report Reviewing the Securities Act.

Porter, M. & Monitor Company (1991) Canada at the Crossroads, Business Council on National Issues. http://www.ceocouncil.ca/publications/pdf/test_9a8e02f7232dc8e32bd05f0bef872edb/OCT_1991_ENG_Canada_at_the_Crossroads.pdf

Porter Commission (1964) Report of the Royal Commission on Banking and Finance, Ottawa.

Puri P. (2003) Local and Regional Interests in the Debate on Optimal Securities Regulatory Structure, Research Study Prepared for the Wise Persons Committee on Security Regulation, Canada, October. http://www.wise-averties.ca/reports/html/4E_puri/index.html

Rutley, Todd (1991) Canada 1993 – A plan for the Creation of a Single Economic Market in Canada, mimeo, CMA, Toronto.

Senate Committee on Banking, Trade and Commerce Canadian Senate (2007), Proceedings, Evidence, Issue 15. http://www.parl.gc.ca/39/1/parlbus/commbus/senate/Com-e/bank-e/15ev-e.htm?Language=E&Parl=39&Ses=1&comm_id=3

Sharpe A. & Ershov D. (2007) The Impact of Interprovincial Migration on Aggregate Output and Labour Productivity in Canada, 1987-2006, Center for the Study of Living Standards Research-report, 2.

Silzer, N. & Krasnick, M. (1986) The Free Flow of Goods in the Canadian Economic Union, in Krasnick, M. (ed.) *Perspectives on the Canadian Economic Union*, University of Toronto Press, Toronto, pp. 155-187.

Schawnen, D. (1992) Open Exchange: Freeing the Trade of Goods and Services within the Canadian Economic Union, in Brown, D., Lazar, F. & Schwanen, D. (eds.) *Free to Move: Strengthening the Canadian Economic Union*, CD Howe Institute, Toronto, pp. 1-37.

Trebilcock, M. & Schwanen, D. (1995) *Getting There: An Assessment of the Agreement on Internal Trade*, C.D. Howe Institute, Toronto.

Tse, D. (1994) Establishing a Federal Securities Commission, *Saskatchewan Law Review* 58 (1).

Trebilcock, M. & Behboodi, R. (1995) The Canadian Agreement on Internal Trade: Retrospect and Prospects, in Trebilcock, M. & Schwanen, D. (eds.)

*Getting There An Assessment of the Agreement on Internal Trade*, C.D. Howe Institute, Toronto, pp. 20-89.

Vaillancourt, F. (1997) Labour Sponsored Venture Capital Funds in Canada: Institutional Aspects Tax Expenditures and Employment Creation, in Halpern, P. (ed.) *Financing Growth in Canada*, University of Calgary Press (Industry Canada), Calgary, pp. 571-592.

Vaillancourt, F. & Vachon, M. (1999) Interprovincial Mobility in Canada, 1961-1996: Importance and Destination, in Lazar, H. & McIntosh, T. (eds.) *Canada: The State of the Federation 1998/99 (How Canadians Connect)*, McGill-Queen's University Press, Montréal, pp. 101-122.

Vegh, G. (1997) The Characterisation of Barriers to Interprovincial Trade under the Canadian Constitution, *Osgoode Hall Law Journal*, 3492, pp. 355-410.

Whalley, J. (1983) The Impact of Federal Policies on Interprovincial Activity in Prichard, R., Trebilcock, M., Courchene, J. & Whalley J. (eds.) *Federalism and the Economic Union*, University of Toronto Press, Toronto, pp 201-242.

Whalley, J. (1996) Interprovincial Barriers to Trade and ndogenous Growth Considerations, in Howitt, P. (ed.) *The Implications of Knowledge Based Growth for Macro Economic Policies*, University of Calgary Press, Calgary, pp. 163-177.

Whalley, J. & Trela, I. (1986), Regional Aspects of Confederation, Vol. 68, Research Papers for the Royal Commission on the Economic Union and Development Prospects for Canada, University of Toronto Press.

Whalley J. (2007) Interprovincial Trade Barriers towards Goods and Services in Canada, mimeo, Industry Canada, London (Ontario), 38 p.

Wise Person's Committee on Canadian Securities Regulation (2003), Report on Canadian Securities Regulation for the Federal Ministry of Finance, Ottawa, December. http://www.wise-averties.ca/reports/html/E_Final/index.html http://www.fin.gc.ca/news02/02-094e.html

## College of Europe Studies

Europe is in a constant state of flux. European politics, economics, law and indeed European societies are changing rapidly. The European Union itself is in a continuous situation of adaptation. New challenges and new requirements arise continually, both internally and externally. The College of Europe Studies series exists to publish research on these issues done at the College of Europe, both at its Bruges and its Warsaw campus. Focused on the European Union and the European integration process, this research may be specialised in the areas of political science, law or economics, but much of it is of an interdisciplinary nature. The objective is to promote understanding of the issues concerned and to make a contribution to ongoing discussions.

*Series Editors*
Professors D. Hanf, D. Mahncke, I. Govaere and J. Pelkmans
for the College of Europe (Bruges and Warsaw)

## Series Titles

No. 9 – Jacques PELKMANS, Dominik HANF & Michele CHANG (eds.), *The EU Internal Market in Comparative Perspective Economic. Political and Legal Analysis*, 2008, 314 p., ISBN 978-90-5201-424-1

No. 8 – Inge GOVAERE & Hanns ULLRICH (eds.), *Intellectual Property, Market Power and the Public Interest*, 2008, 315 p., ISBN 978-90-5201-422-7

No. 7 – András INOTAI, *The European Union and Southeastern Europe. Troubled Waters Ahead?*, 2007, 414 p., ISBN 978-90-5201-071-7

No. 6 – Inge GOVAERE & Hanns ULLRICH (eds.), *Intellectual Property, Public Policy and International Trade*, 2007, 234 p., ISBN 978-90-5201-064-9

No. 5 – Dominik HANF & Rodolphe MUÑOZ (dir.), *La libre circulation des personnes. États des lieux et perspectives*, 2007, 329 p., ISBN 978-90-5201-061-8

No. 4 – Dieter MAHNCKE & Sieglinde GSTÖHL (eds.), *Europe's Near Abroad. Promises and Prospects of the EU's Neighbourhood Policy*, 2008, 318 p., ISBN 978-90-5201-047-2

No. 3 – Dieter MAHNCKE & Jörg MONAR (eds.), *International Terrorism. A European Response to a Global Threat?*, 2006, 191 p., ISBN 978-90-5201-046-5

No. 2 – Paul DEMARET, Inge GOVAERE & Dominik HANF (eds.), *European Legal Dynamics – Revised and updated edition of* 30 Years of European Legal Studies at the College of Europe / *Dynamiques juridiques européennes – Édition revue et mise à jour de* 30 ans d'études juridiques européennes au Collège d'Europe, 2007, 571 p., ISBN 978-90-5201-067-0

No. 1 – Dieter MAHNCKE, Alicia AMBOS & Christopher REYNOLDS (eds.), *European Foreign Policy. From Rhetoric to Reality?*, 2004, 2nd printing/ 2e tirage 2006, 381 p., ISBN 978-90-5201-247-6